STAGE LIGHTING DESIGN IN BRITAIN

THE EMERGENCE OF THE LIGHTING DESIGNER, 1881-1950

Nigel Morgan

ENTERTAINMENT TECHNOLOGY PRESS

Historical Series

To the pioneers of British theatre lighting design

STAGE LIGHTING DESIGN IN BRITAIN

THE EMERGENCE OF THE LIGHTING DESIGNER, 1881-1950

Nigel Morgan

Entertainment Technology Press

Stage Lighting Design in Britain
The Emergence of the Lighting Designer, 1881-1950

© Nigel Morgan

First edition Published May 2005 by
Entertainment Technology Press Ltd
The Studio, High Green, Great Shelford, Cambridge CB2 5EG
Internet: www.etnow.com

ISBN 1 904031 34 X

A title within the
Entertainment Technology Press Historical Series
Series editor: John Offord

CONTENTS

ACKNOWLEDGEMENTS

I wish to thank the following people, without whose generous and kind assistance this project would have been diminished:

Joe Aveline	David Ayliff
Clive Barker	Richard Berry
Christopher Burgess	Dr. Robert Cannon
Martin Carr	Richard Cave
Rajan Chetsingh	John Collis
John Copley	Douglas Cornellissen
Joy and Graeme Cruickshank	Christopher Denys
Kitty Fitzgerald	Roger Fox
Hildegaard Fryda	Helmut Grosser
Denis Groutage	Mike Gutterage
Michael Hall	John G. Holton
Roger Howells	David Ikeda
Nesta Jones	Geoff Joyce
Brian Legge	Veronica Lewis MBE
Bill McGee	Stan Miller
Eddie Ruffell	Molly Steele
Peter Streuli	Pat Walker
Mrs. R. Walter	Paul Weston

and above all my wife Janet for all her patience and support.

Whilst every attempt has been made to source and credit all illustrations, in some cases this has not been possible. However, when the information becomes available, it will be included in future editions of this book.

INTRODUCTION

Background

Light has always been a key component of theatrical performance. In a modern blacked-out auditorium, the stage is lit by artificial light that not only serves as an illuminant for the actor and scenery but also creates atmosphere and heightens dramatic tension to fuse the performer and their circumstances with the text, scenario or other source material to make performance.

Yet controlled lighting is not a recent addition to theatre-making. In early times, when daylight lit the stage, even this was considered to give a value beyond that of simple illumination. The ancient Greeks aligned some amphitheatres to the rising or setting sun, to afford the impact of low angle, mellow light that gave further meaning to their drama. Artificial light sources too played their part in early theatre, for instance in medieval street theatre, where light, either by naked flame or pyrotechnic, was commonly used in a symbolic way, usually to indicate God or the devil. By Shakespeare's time, lighting took on the role of indicating times of day, with a candle held by an actor to indicate night. When theatre moved indoors in the 1600s, lighting was charged with a new responsibility, to illuminate the stage. No longer was it confined to the domain of tricks and effects. When it became apparent that indoor lighting could never echo the qualities of the sun, and that any artificial light source gave significance to what was presented, the notion of light as a controlling agent of drama was born, and the potential to manipulate meaning became apparent. The quest to make lights contribute creatively to the staging of plays and to put forward a rationale for their use began. Lighting design was in its infancy.

Yet the first requirement of these primitive early lights was raw illumination. The actor must be seen: any added meaning was a bonus. It would be a long time before this could adequately be achieved. However, as sources slowly got brighter, atmosphere and effect became more distinctly articulated in thought, technique and application. The potential influence light might have on drama became apparent and was exploited.

Stage lighting achieved sufficient brightness to supersede the function of mere illumination by the early to mid nineteenth century, when the first bright light source, the limelight, was used on stage. Lighting now took on a more profoundly important role in influencing *how* we see the stage. The introduction of incandescent electric light in 1881 heralded brighter stages; thereafter lighting was in the hands of man's ingenuity, and at the service of his imagination.

Indeed the role of lighting as accepted in theatre today became established well before modern technology allowed the medium to be manipulated to such a degree that it would be considered to be 'designed'. The digitally controlled, high-technology contemporary lighting rig regularly seen on the West End or rock concert stage in fact offers nothing beyond what had been demonstrated or discussed in pre-electric days. It is the reliance on lighting that has changed in the twentieth century, within the context of the theatre stage growing in technical complexity and artistic ambition. It was this growth that prompted the emergence of the specialist position of lighting designer.

In today's theatre, good lighting is inseparable from direction, performance and scenic design as a storytelling device. The lighting designer is now firmly established in the creative team, on the playbill and in the public's awareness, being employed to light all performance events from the most complex musical, opera or play to the simple platform concert, from the largest to the smallest venues.

Although it could be argued that either the Greek theatre architects or the medieval stage managers were the first lighting designers, it is not really appropriate to call them so (in the modern meaning of the word, where a designer works over a range of styles and consistently finds fresh ways to interpret ideas). Creating local 'effects' or a 'stock' ambience could hardly warrant the use of such a grand title. As lighting became more complex in the nineteenth and early twentieth centuries, setting the lights became an increasingly important part of the job of the producer, scene designer, chief gasman / electrician or stage manager. Specific techniques and general theatre know-how increased in complexity, and this was mirrored in the ambition of each of these areas of theatre practice. A time came in the early to mid twentieth century when multi-tasked individuals could no longer meet the growing demands of lighting in an increasingly complex production environment and a specialist was required to do so. Public acknowledgement soon followed.

Since then the profession of lighting design has gone from strength to strength, with now over fifty years of 'lighting design' credits in this country. There is a professional association, the Association of Lighting Designers (ALD),[1] and

---

[1] The Association of Lighting Designers (ALD) was formed in 1982, arising out of the Society for British Theatre Lighting Design (SBTLD) which had been founded in 1961 (with the word 'Lighting' dropped in 1975).

the subject can now be studied to degree level in this country.[2] There is a significant body of published information to promote knowledge and research.

The job of a lighting designer today requires many diverse skills and understandings, the principles of which remain rooted in tradition. Usually engaged on a show-by-show basis (rather than being contracted to a venue or company for a continuous period of time), most professionals are able to sustain full time employment because of the quantity of work available and the perceived need for their services. For many years lighting design had been poorly paid in relation to directing and stage design, yet the last ten years have seen far greater opportunity for good earnings. Lighting is now associated with and has been increasingly pivotal to the success of many high profile projects.

The Book

In this book I attempt to ascertain the main course of events and the controlling factors that determined the emergence of the lighting designer in Britain, starting with the introduction of incandescent electric light to the stage, and ending at the time of the first wave of lighting design around 1950. The book explores the practitioners, equipment, installations, techniques and procedures that led to lighting design being clearly established as an essential component of performance, and it charts the role of lighting in shaping performance styles and traces the growing influence of lighting on the development of the visual aesthetic of theatre. The book also considers important influences from other countries and their impact on British lighting.

It has been written for professional colleagues by a practising lighting designer, to further our understanding of our professional past. Therefore technical language, techniques discussed and protocols employed may be for the practitioner alone to understand. Experience as a practitioner has informed my objectivity when pursuing the evidence.

Defining the Field of Exploration

I believe that four key questions must be answered in order to gain an understanding of what lighting design is, and how we can recognise when it is being practised. These questions are:

---

[2] Rose Bruford College, London has offered a three year Bachelor of Arts with Honours degree in Lighting Design from 1996, validated by the University of Manchester.

- What constitutes a 'lighting design'?
- What skills and attributes does a 'lighting designer' need in order to achieve this?
- What is an appropriate technical platform for the work?
- What is appropriate human interaction to frame the work?

Let me examine each in more detail.

(1) What constitutes a lighting design? Has this changed over time? What are the characteristics that separate ordinary, functional lighting from artistically supportive work that is considered to be *design*?

To illustrate the objectives of lighting design, I have chosen complementary statements by two of Britain's (and indeed the world's) leading modern lighting practitioner – writers. Richard Pilbrow wrote in *Stage Lighting* of 1970 that the properties of light "intensity; colour; distribution; and movement" combine within the objectives of stage lighting which are to offer: selective visibility; revelation of form; composition in space and time; and mood.[3] He said: "these four objectives are equally valid no matter what style of production may be embarked upon". Francis Reid, in *The Stage Lighting Handbook* of 1976, consolidated Pilbrow's ideas, stating that: "stage lighting is a fluid, selective, atmospheric, dimensional illumination appropriate to the style of a particular production".[4] These definitions highlight the need for sophisticated, precise, controllable equipment, deployed in a flexible environment by an individual who understands the contribution that lighting can make to support performance.

I believe that there is sufficient evidence to suggest that these definitions could have been written much earlier in time, and if so the objectives of stage lighting design were known well before they were acknowledged to have been achieved.

(2) What attributes, skills and knowledge should a lighting designer possess to do the job? Pilbrow goes on to state that three key personal qualities are needed: "first and foremost, imagination, the ability to conceive visions"; secondly, the ability to turn ideas into practice; and, finally, dedication and professionalism.

To extend this thinking, and in order to establish key aspects of the knowledge and sensitivities required in the modern lighting designer, in 1998 the ALD published a paper that detailed the criteria a course of study in lighting design

---

[3] Pilbrow, R. *Stage Lighting,* London: Studio Vista, 1970, p16+

[4] Reid, F. *The Stage Lighting Handbook,* London: Pitman, 1976, p9

should address in its content.[5] This paper serves as an independent, authoritative benchmark of the fields of skill and knowledge a lighting designer must possess.

The paper states that the contemporary lighting designer should study and practise the arts and understandings of theatre performance and design, the technologies of light control, and the skills to manage a range of theatre people, time and resources. This breaks down into five categories:

- Cultural reference
- Creative thought and practice
- Lighting technique
- Lighting technology
- Professional skills

The full ALD document is recorded as Appendix i.

My own experience confirms that an individual without any one of these five key aspects of knowledge present would be unlikely to become a successful designer.

Could any aspect recommended for study in 1998 not have been possible to achieve in 1950? There is only one that is solely relevant to the modern world – proficiency in the use of Computer Aided Design (CAD). This has become important, but before computerisation manual drafting was the norm. Planning on paper has always been a part of design: CAD merely automates this process. It has added nothing to advance the art of lighting, but remains invaluable as a time-saving and trouble-shooting device.

I believe the ALD paper could have been published much earlier in time, and therefore with the omission of CAD is relevant to apply to practitioners from all eras.

(3) The technical platform. Lighting design is considered a craft art, and only flourishes when appropriate tooling and support framework are in place. As the painter works with brushes, paint and canvasses, in a bright, evenly lit studio, so too the lighting designer is bound by the availability of appropriate technology and the suitability of the designated environment in which to work.

The lighting designer relies on high quality technologies. The quotation from Reid stresses the importance of the lighting instruments, which must be sufficiently precise to offer a controllable intensity, colour, beam size, shape, and pattern, and be capable of precisely illuminating a particular point on stage from a chosen position, either alone or in combination with others. They must

[5] *Focus,* Nov 98, p14.

be controlled by a system capable of smoothly or otherwise changing the lighting pictures, with a capacity to form an endlessly flowing collage of imagery.

Although there is much evidence to suggest that many early practitioners had limited success in controlling light, it will be shown that only since the mid 1930s have lanterns and control equipment been manufactured to a sufficiently precise standard to meet the above specification. This book will establish the important developments in technology that led to the establishment of a platform of equipment from which 'design' could regularly be achieved.

(4) The presence of a supportive production team. Theatre production today usually works in a highly co-operative interactive inter-personal manner, a mode of working that is led, or 'chaired', by one individual – the director. This has not always been so: prior to World War One a more dictatorial style of leadership prevailed, that of the man usually called the actor-manager or producer. This is not to say that lighting was overlooked, and there were many who placed great importance on creating atmospheric lighting. But a move to collaborative working occurred mainly as the technologies of the stage became too complex for one person to fully command. This began with the producer sharing ideas and responsibilities with the stage designer, and then the stage manager and chief electrician, from which process eventually emerged the lighting designer.

This loosening of control required a new technique of communication to be employed. As the producer and stage designer became more adept at commanding the stage manager to light the stage, so too the stage manager and electricians grew in confidence in finding practical solutions. Thus the creative team emerged, with certain stage managers and electricians graduating to become 'lighting specialists'. As trust in their work developed, coupled with their own ability to predict appropriate lighting and to debate in the forum of production, so the lighting designer was born.

With three practitioners now at the helm – the director, stage designer and lighting designer – the use of visual imagination came into greater play. The creative team proved to function best when the director and stage designer recognised the specialist understanding of a lighting designer, who could go beyond technical facility and organisation and become an artistic collaborator and adviser.

This collaborative pattern was first seen in theatres where artistic standards were highly prized, and where time could be scheduled for experiment in the plotting and rehearsal of lighting. Only then did lighting become an integrated component of theatrical performance, working in harmony with the text, direction and acting. Collaboration allowed the individual to use specialist skills within a common framework of understanding.

Lighting design faced one more difficulty. Sharing ideas and goals was key to successful collaboration, but, due to the ethereal nature of light, it proved particularly hard for the lighting designer to do this. The stage designer built models and sketched costumes to show ideas, and the director developed performance in the rehearsal room. Both had a process of accountability and an opportunity to demonstrate their credibility early in the production process. For both, if ideas failed, there was time for correction. The lighting designer did not have a similar opportunity, as their work was dependent on the setting being built and the actor rehearsed to performance conditions before lighting could commence.

Those that progressed to design status found ways to overcome this problem by sharing ideas within the creative team without the aids their collaborators had. For some this meant working with lit scale models – for others it meant exercising verbal persuasiveness or even making capital of their reputation and strength of personality.

Summarising the Ideal Conditions for Lighting Design

The following summary indicates the ideal conditions for lighting design to be successfully achieved:

The individual engaged to light must:
- be aware of the objectives of lighting performance.
- have a range of appropriate cultural references and sensitivities.
- show insight in creative thought, expression and practice.
- command lighting techniques.
- understand lighting technology.
- possess appropriate professional skills to interact creatively, logically and speedily with those around.
- master a methodology that allows lighting to be conceived, planned and envisaged and discussed before production.

The venue in which they work must:
- attract practitioners with a commitment to high artistic values and an ethos of collaborative working.
- contain an appropriate and flexible technical facility.

- allow sufficient time and access for the process of lighting.

From this it is clear that the range of venues where lighting design would be likely to emerge is narrow:

- major London and regional 'classical' playhouse theatres, such as the Old Vic and the Memorial Theatre Stratford.
- major opera houses, such as the Royal Opera House Covent Garden.
- selected West End commercial theatres, such as His Majesty's (and usually only when the licensee had a particular interest in lighting).
- 'Art' and 'Fringe' venues, such as The Gate Covent Garden

Lighting design was less likely to emerge in mainstream commercial theatre, where equipment, time and experiment were normally in minimal supply. With this form of theatre dominating British practice throughout the twentieth century, there were few practitioners working in this sector who made a significant contribution to the art of lighting.

Structure of the Book

To establish the emergence of the lighting designer in Britain, this book will follow four lines of enquiry. Each will form a chapter, and aim to:

- establish the growing understanding of the role of stage lighting in theatre by verifying the potential of pre-1881 practice.
- chart the development of resources.
- indicate the principle influences from home and abroad.
- ascertain when, where and by whom the objectives of lighting design were first achieved and credited in Britain, and record and discuss the standard of work 1881-1950.

This enquiry will then be drawn together in *Conclusions*. The work is supported by a portfolio of photographs, referenced into the text as appropriate.

Appendices give further insight into issues that surround and inform the main argument. These include:

- the ALD Education Policy.
- reviews of the facilities in selected key venues.
- the role of lighting companies in promoting stage lighting.
- the education of the lighting designer.
- the work of Frederick Bentham.
- Colour Music.

The book is completed by a Bibliography.

Sources of Material

For this work most information comes from books and journals. Unfortunately authoritative material published before the twentieth century is scarce, but fortunately this situation changed after World War One.[6] It focuses on material published before 1950, as this could have formed a part of the practitioners' education. Books published after this date are reviewed selectively for their potential to contribute to this work. Trade Journals became influential from the 1930s and, after separating commercial self interest from objective reporting, contain much useful information. Specialist theatre collections, such as the holdings of the Theatre Museum, individual theatres and ABTT provide valuable additional material, particularly for show reviews. Much material has been gleaned from press reviews for the key practitioners' work, and this is used as the main vehicle for establishing their credentials.

Unfortunately there are few alive today who can give a first hand account of the pioneering days of lighting design. Contact has been made with as many as possible with helpful links to the past, and some valuable material from interviews and correspondence is included. Therefore the main method to establish the credentials of practitioners has been the use of press reviews, and I am in debt to those who recorded the use of light in their writings.

Few photographs remain of productions from the period under stage lighting conditions, and it is hard to authenticate those that exist. Even today there is still a tendency to set lighting at full for a photo-call. With poorer quality film and a lower light level on stage in the early twentieth century, it is not easy to be sure the photos that do exist are accurate. Processing too can distort contrast and light levels. However, there are sufficient pictures of interest to support the argument of a developing aesthetic in lighting, and these are included as appropriate.

Conventions in the Text

All theatres are located in London and all dates are from the twentieth century – unless otherwise indicated.

---

[6] At the launch of the Association of British Theatre Technicians (ABTT) in 1961, Norman Marshall stated (looking back to the time of the Festival Theatre Cambridge around 1930) "one of the weaknesses of the theatrical profession in this country is that producers and designers and theatre architects are apt to be extraordinarily ignorant of what was going on in the theatre *just before their own time*... Theatre historians think little of the immediate past..." *Sightline* 20/1, Sum 1986, p19.

1 A RATIONALE AND AESTHETIC FOR LIGHTING THE STAGE EMERGES

This chapter establishes the language of lighting that developed in the period in which theatre was lit by the naked flame. It is interesting to note that while practitioners struggled to achieve sufficient brightness from their sources during this period, an aesthetic and theatrical use for light soon became apparent.

Lighting by Candle and Oil

When theatre moved indoors in the sixteenth century, performance became hindered by the need to provide artificial illumination. The earliest forms of artificial indoor illumination, the candle and the oil wick lamp, gave off so little brightness that basic visibility of the actor and the stage was problematic. The quest for visibility, rather than decisions based on any creative or interpretative understanding of performance, was the determining factor for the next 300 years. Such was the feeble power of these sources that they had to be used *en masse*, and located in positions as close to the actors as possible. Their low power, coupled with smoky emissions, meant that actors became confined to working near the light sources. These were most easy to place in a row downstage or on the forestage and became known as footlights, and were supplemented by overhead chandeliers and lights in wing positions.

Early indoor theatres had windows set into the sides, rear and roof of both the stage and auditorium to allow natural light in. Performances were held during daylight hours, as artificial lighting alone was simply not bright enough to light the stage. The architecture of these buildings has been researched to suggest that there would have been enough daylight to act until 3pm on an overcast winter's day, the darkest daytime of the year, in London.[1]

Yet even the earliest practitioners could see the creative potential of light, and made the best possible use of it. As soon as light was used to illuminate performance, it was manipulated to develop dramatic meaning. In the process, these first practitioners established a visual language that was to remain largely unchanged, still framing our expectation of the conventions of performance today.

---

[1] Graves, R. Lecture on lighting plays in London during Shakespeare's time, at the Globe Theatre, March 2001.

Light had been used as a symbolic device in pre-sixteenth century outdoor theatre. In early liturgical plays, light was used to symbolise God and the elements.[2] Paintings from this period closely linked light with the powers of both God and the devil, and so it was a natural extension to apply a similar treatment to the performance of sacred drama.

Most early developments in stage lighting occurred in Italy, slowly spreading to other parts of Europe including Britain. A range of designers, architects and writers commented on stage lighting conditions. The first documentation that discussed indoor stage lighting was by the theatre architect and painter **Sebastiano Serlio** (1475-1554). In his *Architectura Volume 2* 1545, translated into English in 1611, he mentioned the use of candles and glass bowls called *bozze* containing coloured waters to colour the light,[3] and reflectors made from barbers' basins to focus beams and increase intensity. He detailed three types of stage light: general stage light, decorative light inserted into the stage scenery, and mobile light.[4]

His writings identified the source of modern lighting. He detailed the optical system of a lantern and the colouring of the light beam. The glass vessels he used may well have also acted as a lens, to concentrate the light, or focus, on a prescribed point on stage. His writings on the differing types of light suggest that lights were distributed in a considered manner to create an overall brightness for the action, that lights were pointed at specific locations on the stage to highlight fixed positions such as scenery, and that sources could be moved to create the illusion of a sun or moon.

A little later the dramatist **Leone di Somi** (1527-1592), responsible for theatre entertainment at Mantua, wrote a dialogue about drama between three noblemen that expanded on the role of lighting. He commented that everything on stage should "heighten the joy of living, give bliss, intoxicate the senses, but

---

[2] Filippo Brunelleschi (1377-1446), the famous Florentine architect, was credited with creating a lighting effect for the S. Felice church in Florence where "on high was a heaven full of living and moving figures, and a quantity of lights which flashed in and out" (Nagler, A. *A source book in theatrical history* Dover 1952 p41, citing Vite G. Vasari (sixteenth C.)). Hell's Inferno was created by fire and smoke and, from 1500 onwards, stage directions referring to lighting can be found: "paint Raphael's face red"; "let there be a big sun behind Jesus; "brightly polished basin reflecting sunlight or torches" (Bergmann, G. *Lighting in the theatre*, Stockholm: Almqvist and Wiksell, 1979, p42). A Passion Play at Valanciennes in 1547 used fiery devils, fire sprouting dragons and a fiery mouth of hell. Angels had fireworks for a "magnificent light" (Fuchs, T. *Stage Lighting*, London: Allen & Unwin, 1929, p34).

[3] The colours were made by: red wine for red; white wine for amber; aqua vita, vernis and sulphuric acid for blue. (Fuchs, Stage Lighting, p35)

[4] Bergmann, *Lighting in the Theatre,* p58/9.

also a flight of imagination beyond reality". He made some key observations about how light behaved, and proposed the lighting cue, a change in lighting conditions that could be used to punctuate performance and enhance the tension of a dramatic moment. He also suggested dimming light, the controlled raising or lowering of light levels that forms a fundamental part of today's theatre experience. He experimented with intensity levels, playing tragedies brightly until a moment of incident, and then he rapidly dimmed the stage to heighten the dramatic effect. This 'discovery' was staggeringly perceptive, and when this was first implemented it must have had a profound effect on the audience, as man would never have seen light behave like this before. He noted that it was not good to see the light sources: any light shining directly into the eye having the effect of closing the iris, and thus giving the impression that the overall light level was darker than it actually was. Dimming the auditorium also helped maintain focus on the stage area and trick the eye into believing that the stage was brighter than the darkened peripheral areas.[5]

Each successive era produced developments in technique. **Bernardo Buontalenti** (1536-1608), a scenic designer who worked for the Medici family from 1547 onwards, organised firework displays and was the first to be credited with the use of footlights, which were probably the most efficient way to illuminate the actor, being close enough to the actor to be effective and also easy to shield and conceal from the audience. Although footlights cast a rather unnatural shadow, this would have been a small price to pay for otherwise good illumination, and would have given lighting another theatrical 'signature'. He was also noted for use of concealed sources of light behind scenery that would have allowed upstage areas to be illuminated, although probably this would have been for the lighting of scenic elements rather than the actor.[6]

In *Della poesia rappresentativa e del modo di rappresentare le favole sceniche* 1598, **Angelo Ingegneri** (1550-1613) stressed the importance of lighting. He too favoured concealing light sources and dimming the auditorium, and addressed lighting faces by using sources placed on a hidden bridge behind the proscenium to find a more favourable angle and counterbalance the shadows caused by the footlights.[7] This was the first known use of lighting from above and in front of the actors' face, which would have created a much more natural light.

---

[5] Nagler, *A Source Book in Theatrical History*, New York: Dover, 1952, pp 63 & 102.
[6] Bergmann, *Lighting in the Theatre*, p71.
[7] Bergmann, *Lighting in the Theatre*, p66.

These early experiments with light remain at the heart of today's visual language.

Nicola Sabattini (1574-1654), craftsman and architect, in *Practica fabricar scene e machine ne' teatri* (1637/8), a reference book of theatre architecture and design, described what must have been a typical lighting installation of the period. He noted that house lights were concentrated near the stage and remained lit during the performance – thus having a dual purpose – but also that the auditorium might be dim. On stage there were footlights, proscenium lights behind scenery and side lights – all of which were concealed. Lights were placed symmetrically, and were thus used to aid a sense of perspective rather than highlight one aspect of the stage area.

He also was aware of the characteristic effect that lighting from certain positions had on actors and scenery. He was the first to note that front light flattened and created a two-dimensional effect, backlight cast shadows, and side light was best for modelling. He also made some significant technical contributions. He developed a simple dimmer system by lowering cylinders on wires over lights, which, with the wires tracking back to a central control point, allowed co-ordinated fading of the whole lighting rig. The lighting control system was born: this established the first centralised lighting control point, and the first simple fade-up and -down lighting cues could be integrated with performance.[8]

Josef Furtenbach (1591-1667), architect and author, in his *Architectura Civilis* of 1628 described masked footlights, to shield the light from the audience, and vertical rows of lamps just behind each wing, and a large number of *bozze* concealed behind scenery on stage. In *Mannhafter Kunstspiegel* (1663), he noted that light concealed from the audience in front and rear stage pits and behind borders "gives glorious effect". Although these lighting principles had already been established, he noted that lights could be rotated away from the stage for another form of dimming. Clearly the notion of the dimmable light was proving irresistible. He also detailed windows in the wings to allow daylight in, as performances were still generally held in the afternoon.[9]

In Britain **Inigo Jones** (1573-1652)[10] experimented with reflectors placed behind light sources to improve intensity.[11] He was a pioneer in the use of

---

[8] Bergmann, *Lighting in the Theatre*, p80.

[9] Fuchs, *Stage Lighting*, p36.

[10] An artist, architect and stage designer, he visited Italy in 1600 and 1613 and designed costumes and scenery for the Court Masques 1605-1640.

translucencies – flats covered with material that let light through, in conjunction with many coloured lights that he called 'jewel glasses'.[12]

From the evidence so far presented we can deduce how the stage must have looked. It is interesting to note how many of the modern day techniques and lighting positions had been established. Thus at the end of the sixteenth century lights were placed at the footlight position as the primary source of actor lighting; and over-stage chandeliers, overhead lighting behind the proscenium and wing lights created a stage ambience and illuminated scenery. Simple reflectors might be used to improve focus and intensity, and primitive colouring was possible. Dimming had been experimented with, although it is unlikely it was used except for a general fade-in or -out, due to the complexities of co-ordinating such an activity. Any lighting beyond basic illumination would be for special effects only, such as the use of fire to symbolise hell, fireworks to conjure the wrath of God, and candle crowns for angels.

The auditorium was usually, but not always, lit during performance, with chandeliers or wall lights as the most common positions.[13] A dark auditorium did not stay in fashion for long, and this set back advances in lighting technique on stage. It was not recognised that dimming the auditorium would focus the audience's attention on the performance, and that by creating a contrast in lighting levels between a dark auditorium and a lit stage, the stage would appear brighter. It was not until the late nineteenth century that this practice was widely adopted, signalling the start of the performance.[14]

Despite many lighting principles being firmly established, the naked light source was simply not bright enough for purposes beyond basic illumination. Although there had been many successful attempts to increase the power of the naked flame, the stage remained a large space to light and increases in

---

[11] Fuchs, *Stage Lighting*, p36.

[12] Hartnoll, P. *Oxford Companion to the Theatre*, 3rd Edition, Oxford: OUP, 1983.

[13] There was mixed opinion on this, and also there must have been a safety issue involved in darkening the auditorium. An interesting example of how this was overcome – and also to act as a signal to the audience that the play was about to start - was at the San Giovanni Opera House in Venice, which opened in 1678. Here, it was normal practice to winch the auditorium chandelier into the roof just before the performance starts, returning it at an interval or the end to be a more effective house light (Nagler, *A source book in theatrical history*, p272 citing Goldoni *Memories* 1814) .

[14] Nineteenth century travellers noted a surprising amount of light in British auditoria when those in France, Germany and especially Italy were regularly darkened (*Theatre History Studies* Vol. VIII 1998, Victor Emeljanow Observation on nineteenth century lighting, p110, citing *The Dramatic Argus*, Dublin II, viii 1825).

light intensity, although significant in themselves, remained modest in terms of what was really needed. Little changed for the next two hundred years.

Despite this, a greater awareness of how light might be used on stage developed in the eighteenth century. As scenery became more realistic, it was recognised that lighting could help the audience respond to the scenic environment. There was a growing awareness of how light was used in paintings, as a device to emphasise focus, create depth, and generate atmosphere.[15] This gives clear evidence of the development of a more advanced visual aesthetic, copying techniques of the great artists in the lighting of scenery, and suggesting breaking away from the traditional symmetrical approach to lighting the stage evenly without emphasis. The quest for an uneven distribution of light gained momentum, with light sources placed to highlight scenery rather than flood it evenly as before.[16]

However, the overarching quest for brightness left no clear solution to the

---

[15] **Count Francesco Algarotti** (1712-64), the foremost Italian art critic of his day, in *Essai sur l'opera* of 1755 wrote: "Another thing which is also very important to observe and which would be a great mistake to neglect, is the lighting of sceneries. One does not know at all how to distribute it evenly and economically. The elements are always poorly illuminated and always with insensitive shades, which do not make them stand out. Still, if they learnt the art of distributing light, if it were to be concentrated *en masse* on some parts of the stage, excluding others, wouldn't it then transpose to the stage the power and vivacity of the *clair obscure* that Rembrandt succeeded in putting into his paintings? It might even be possible to convey to the sceneries that delightful interplay of light and shade that you find in Giorgione's and Titian's paintings?" (Bergmann, *Lighting in the Theatre*, p178). In 1762 the Count wrote in a similar vein: "What wonderful things might not be produced by the light when not dispensed in they equal manner, and by degrees, as is now the custom. Were it to be played off with a masterly artifice, distributing it in a strong mass on some parts of the stage, and by depriving others as it were at the same time, it is hardly credible what effects might not be produced thereby; for instance a chiaroscuro, for strength and vivacity not inferior to that so much admired in the prints of Rembrandt." (*Tabs* 33/3, Aut 75, p18).

[16] The ballet master **J.G. Noverre** (1727-1810) in an essay *Lettres sur la danse* of 1760 wrote: "It is not the great number of lamps, used at haphazard or applied symmetrically that gives good light on the stage. The difficult thing is to be able to distribute the light unevenly so as to set off the parts that need strong light, to tone down where necessary and to put wholly in shadow where no light is needed. In the same way as the painter provides shades and degradations in his pictures for the sake of perspective, the person setting the light should consult him, so that the same shades and degradations can be seen in the lighting. There is nothing so ugly as a scenery painted in the same hue and without shades. *Lointain* and perspective are lacking there. In the same way: if the different parts of the painting which, together, form the whole, are illuminated with the same intensity, there will be no united effect, no contrasts, and the painting will be without effect". To achieve these new lighting techniques, Noverre wrote in 1781 of the need to model lighting on painting by abolishing footlights, and employing greater use of overhead and side light (Bergmann, *Lighting in the Theatre*, p180). It is interesting that Noverre stated that the lighting person should refer to the artist for guidance on how the scene should be lit. This either suggests that lighting people of the time were technicians rather than artists, or is it an early example of the scenic artists (cont...)

problem of finding lighting positions by which this distribution of light could be achieved.

The artificial up-lighting effect of the footlights came under attack.[17] **Pierre Patte** (1723-1814), a French architect, suggested in his book *Essay sur l'Architecture Théâtrale* 1782 that lights should be mounted on the box fronts, to provide a more natural face light angle by correcting the shadows caused by footlights. This was the beginning of front-of-house lighting positions.[18]

In Britain, most lighting developments in the eighteenth century happened under the actor **David Garrick** (1717-1779) at the Theatre Royal, Drury Lane. On his return from European travels in 1765 he removed the forestage chandeliers, added reflectors to the auditorium lights to concentrate light on the stage, and also deployed lights behind the proscenium.[19] Bergmann quotes a journal from the period: "The public were agreeably surprised on the opening of Drury Lane Theatre, to see the stage illuminated with a strong and clear light, and the rings removed that used to supply it".[20] From 1773-1781 Garrick employed the scene painter **Philip de Loutherbourg** (1740-1812), who was

---

exerting their power and creating a hierarchical position? Similar sentiments were being expressed in other parts of Europe. In 1771 Giambatista Pasquali published in Rome a book entitled *Del Teatro in Venezia,* quoted in translation: "If instead of illuminating the entire stage equally, the lights were concentrated on one part in such a way as to leave the other darker, one could then be able to admire in the theatre that same force and vivacity of light and shade that one sees in the paintings of Titian and Giorgione. And, first of all, let us abolish that triple and quadruple series of lights which encircle the proscenium arch. What a barbarous invention it is! And those ugly gutters, full of light, placed at the foot of the stage and seen by all the spectators! What an outlandish idea! What monstrous unnaturalness to light from below! Worse still to confound these lights from below with those from above which are behind the scene! There is no longer any effect of light and no distribution, but merely a battle between them all, producing only an ugly confusion in everything." (Fuerst, W. and Hume, S. *Twentieth Century Stage Decoration,* London: Knopf, 1928, p3).

[17] Commenting on the need for a better angle of front light than that provided by the footlight, Bentham in *Tabs* quoted Percy Fitzgerald from *The Theatre*, 1/10/1878: "Footlights…are really the rudest and coarsest of devices…There may be hopes that the electric light may work a change, and I would suggest to its patron…whether he could… find some way of directing this light on the stage, say, from the panels of the private boxes…" (*Tabs* 22/1, Mar 64, p117).

[18] However, when during the nineteenth century there was a trend in auditorium design for the forestage to disappear, with the downstage edge now aligned to the proscenium arch, the need for front lighting became less important (as the proscenium bridge provided this). The most important limitation lighting had still to conquer was its inability to light the centre of the stage brightly, as this position tended to be furthest from any light source. Thus the point on the stage that was dramatically very strong appeared weak because of the lighting. An actor at the edge of the stage would be much brighter. This situation remained so until a brighter light source was found that could be projected into the centre of the stage.

[19] *Tabs* 4/1, Sep. 46, p5.

[20] Bergmann, *Lighting in the theatre*, p216, citing *Universal Museum* Sept 1765.

successful at creating illusions such as fire, volcano, sunlight, moonlight and cloud effects and brought a touch of realism into the artificial scenic effects of the time. He employed coloured light to achieve these effects, and used light within an integrated approach to stage design and choice of scenic fabrics and textures. Examples of their innovative approaches were the use of silk colour changers, fitted to wing lights for *A Christmas Tale* in 1773, and flying out the auditorium chandelier to darken the auditorium and indicate the start of the performance. Together, they were instrumental in changing acting style to a more natural method, a change afforded by the better quality of stage illumination.[21]

The late eighteenth century saw a succession of breakthroughs in the quest for brighter lights. The most notable was the development of the Argand lamp in France. Launched in 1784, the design of the lamp forced air over the flame, increasing brightness to the equivalent of 9-12 wax candles and without the equivalent amount of smoke. Although expense initially restricted their use, these lamps were deployed at the Comedie Francais in 1784 and the Paris Opera in 1785, and first came to Britain at the Theatre Royal Drury Lane in 1790. As well as being brighter, the better the quality the oil, the whiter the light. At last the centre of the stage could be adequately lit. Not only did this allow acting to develop away from the forestage, but darker colours could also be used for costumes and scenery.[22]

Lighting by Gas

The next major breakthrough was the introduction of gas in the early 1800s. The gas jet had many advantages over the candle or oil lamp. It was a brighter, whiter light that gave better visibility and better colour rendering of scenery and costume. It was said to be twelve times brighter than oil light and flicker-free, until the occasional surge in supply made flames leap and cause panic in the audience.[23] It was cheaper than the Argand lamp, with fuel a quarter the

---

[21] However, Garrick's stage lighting was not universally popular. In 1772 the artist Gainsborough had written to him concerned at some of his more garish effects: "when the streets are paved with Brilliants and the skies are made of Rainbows, I suppose you will still be satisfied with red, blue and yellow... Maintain all your light but spare the poor abused colours till the eye rests and recovers" *(Tabs* 4/2, Dec. 46, p25).

[22] By the end of the eighteenth century, stage lighting was considered bright enough for evening performances, and the admission of daylight was no longer pre-requisite in theatre architecture (Osborne, J. *The Meiningen Court Theatre,* Cambridge: C.U.P., 1988, p37).

cost. Gas light had a softness that was highly praised, although like the candle still partially deficient in the blue element of the spectrum.

Another major advantage was that the supply to the whole stage could be easily controlled from a centralised position by a control system called the 'gas table' or 'gas plate'. This was the first proper lighting control, if the early attempt to centralise control of lowering sleeves over candles is discounted. No longer would the lighting operator's role be to light the candles before performance and keep wicks trimmed during the show, but now the whole stage could be dimmed to blackout. Moreover, lighting did not now have to be either 'on' or 'off'. Intermediate levels of intensity could be set by partially opening the stopcocks, and therefore intensity could be set to suit the mood of the moment, adjusted in real time with the performance, tracking the highs and lows of emotion and meeting the needs of matching temporal conditions such as sunlight and moonlight.[24] Pipes feeding different sections of the stage lighting, such as footlights, stage left wing and overhead batten, meant they could each be controlled by their own regulator, affording changes to lighting composition locally in addition to whole stage dimming by the master regulator. Intensity could be further graded by some lighting positions being fitted with larger burners than others and fed by broader pipes for a greater flow of gas. Thus light sources with different brightness factors had been introduced.

Cueing was now needed to co-ordinate operations of lighting control and scenery movement, coupled with operating plots and the beginnings of lighting terminology that is still used today, such as "footlights at half"; "fade to blackout over five seconds".

Gaslight had a major effect on performance, as its brightness released the hitherto gloomy upstage to become an acting area. There was also greater potential for effects. Gas supplies could be localised on the set and portable light sources, fed by leather gas bags independent of the main supply, were used. Scenery and make-up became more realistic as there was less need to compensate for poor illumination. But perhaps the most fundamental change was in acting: more light heralded a move to a more naturalistic manner.

As gas production advanced, a range of base materials were considered to

[23] Richard Wills *The joys of gas lighting* / TDT/ ABTT News, 10/1984 & Ernest Woodrow, *Inland Architect* 10/1890.

[24] Giovanni Aldini, an Italian visiting Britain in 1820, noted that there could be an emotional value in the more subtle variations of intensities, suggested fitting calibration scales to gas taps so "dawn, sunset, lightning and storm could easily be achieved consecutively" (*Tabs* 7/3, Dec. 49, p18).

find the fuel that would produce the brightest, cleanest light.[25] Increased power meant that coloured silks could be placed in front of jets to colour the light, and automated colour changers – forerunners of today's 'colour scrollers' – were commonly fitted to overhead battens to provide a facility for a range of atmospheres or moods. The downside to gas was that it created a very hot and obnoxious stage and auditorium environment. Although gas was said to be a little cooler than candles, forestage temperatures were still known to reach 30°C,[26] the fly tower 40°C and the upper circle 35°C; and the fumes were poisonous.[27]

Gas lighting was demonstrated at the Lyceum Theatre in 1804, and was noted as being a very "brilliant and fanciful light".[28] It was first used regularly at the Opera House, Covent Garden from 1815, where a central chandelier was installed out of sightlines "equal to 300 Argand lamps".[29] Front of house lighting began to develop as lamps with reflectors were mounted on the front of boxes to counteract the unpleasant shadows caused by the footlights. The Lyceum became the first gas lit stage in August 1817, when the press noted the lighting to be "as mild as it is splendid – white, regular and pervading".[30] When gas was first used at Drury Lane in September 1817, *The Times* commented on its control: "the advantage anticipated from these lights consists mainly in the facility with which they can be instantly arranged so as to produce more or less of illumination."[31] By 1850 almost every major theatre was lit by gas.

Gaslight technology made steady advances, such as the invention of the

---

[25] Oil gas produced twice as much light as coal gas (*Tabs* 7/3, Dec. 49, p18).

[26] Bergmann, *Lighting in the Theatre*, p263.

[27] Richard Wills said in 1872 that "theatre goers always suffered from headaches the next day.. an accepted part of such a night's entertainment" (Richard Wills *The joys of gas lighting* / TDT/ ABTT News, 10/1984 & *New York Times* 19/5/1872). He said that actors faired little better ".. terrible ordeal.. throat parched up.. by the oppressive heat and vapours" (Richard Wills *The joys of gas lighting* / TDT/ ABTT News, 10/1984 & *American Architect* 10/1887). As stage lighting became more adventurous, so fire became a major hazard: 385 theatres burned down between 1801 and 1877. An article of the time said "..gas was allowed to flare in its customary manner behind the scenes, in the flies and, in short, wherever it had the greatest chance of working mischief!" *(ABTT News*, 1/1988 + *The Telegraphic Journal and Electrical Review* 6/1/1888).

[28] *Tabs* 13/3, Dec. 55, p26.

[29] This was before gas was first used as a source of illumination to light the streets of London, which was in 1816 (Inwood, S. *A History of London*, London: Macmillan, 1998, p460).

[30] Bergmann, *Lighting in the Theatre*, p256, citing *The Examiner*, 7/9/1817.

[31] *Tabs* 13/3, Dec. 55, p27. The newspaper went on to describe the lighting rig as having "on the sides of the stage... 12 perpendicular lines of lamps, each containing 18, and before the proscenium a row of 80."

brighter Welsbach gas mantle in 1866,[32] whereby the gas jet heated a mantle to incandescence. The mantle developed further, when in 1890 a gauze impregnated with thorium oxide improved the whiteness as well as the intensity of the light. However its impact on the stage was short-lived, as this development coincided with the arrival of electricity.

The Lime and Arc Lights

An even more important technological breakthrough was the discovery of limelight in 1826.[33] This brilliant white compact light source with a slightly green tinge was soon adopted by the theatre, and with the addition of a reflector and lens for more precise beam control the first practical spotlight was created.[34]

The small point of intense light, although requiring constant attention from a gas jet to keep illumination steady, was well suited to the task. The lime was the first really bright light on stage since daylight had been excluded. It was first used on stage in 1837 at Covent Garden by **William Macready** (1793-1873) for a diorama and moonlight effect painted by **Clarkson Stansfield** (1793-1867). Its first recorded use as a followspot was also at Covent Garden in the same year. Initially it was placed on stage, but 1846 saw the first followspot positioned front of house.[35] **Charles Kean** (1811-68) introduced the first focused lime for his production of *King Henry VIII* at the Princess's Theatre in 1855.

The hard shadow, high contrast lighting of the lime must have made an extraordinary impact on stage, as until then all lighting sources would have

---

[32] *Tabs* 27/1, Mar. 69, p 25.

[33] The British engineer and surveyor **Capt. Thomas Drummond** (1797-1840) heated a block of compressed quicklime with a lit oxygen-hydrogen gas jet. The block of lime heated to incandescence. This gave out a blindingly white light "softer and, above all, warmer in tone than electric light" (Bergmann, *Lighting in the theatre*, p273, citing M.J. Moynet *L'envers du théatre*, Paris 1873).

[34] Lenses had been common since the 12th century, being used for spectacles and for astronomical purposes (Burnie, D. *Light*, London: Dorling Kindersley Ltd., 1992, p15). However it was not until the early nineteenth century that the lens was used to focus light intensity. Early uses were in industry, such as lace making, to focus a dim candle light source onto detailed work to improve light levels. An oil burning lamp fitted with a bulls eye lens was manufactured at the same time, and the coming of light signals for the railways helped develop cheap mass produced plano convex lenses. By the 1880's the lime was being constructed to allow a variety of lenses to be fitted, to afford a variety of beam angles and beam focus as well as variations in intensity (Nagler, *A source book in theatrical history*, p189, citing B. Stoker *Irving and Stage Lighting, nineteenth century and after*, 1911).

[35] *Lighting and Sound International*, June 92, p34.

given a soft, warm, gentle, glowing effect to the stage picture. Such was its intensity that it proved hard to integrate into the stage picture, and thus it was initially used to represent sunlight or moonlight as an effect light when coloured, or, most commonly, as a followspot. The notion of the star performer always being lit in their own dedicated pool of bright light was attractive to all actor-managers of the time, and a new motif was added to the language of theatre lighting. The limelight made a relatively compact spotlight and could be mounted on a swivel stand and fitted with guide handles. It was ideal for the role of following. But because a person was needed to keep the light output steady by adjusting the gas jets, its stage positioning was restricted, usually to the wings or perch positions[36] or a front of house gallery where easy access could be maintained (see illustration below).

The lime was never universally accepted because it was so difficult to control

*Limes on fly floor, The Illustrated Sporting and Dramatic News, 1876.
Courtesy Illustrated London News picture library.*

---

[36] On the growing importance of side-light positions, Bentham said that traditionally the lime (or later the arc) was used from the wings as a followspot position to pick out the artist without hitting the scenery in a wing and cloth setting (*Tabs* 8/3, Dec. 50, p26).

with any degree of sensitivity, and it made little impact in America where it was often criticised for being too strong and garish. It was expensive to run, and was often cut from a production after press notices had been posted. However, the lime opened the way for a greater use of colour as it had the power to project deeper hues than before, and colour changers were often fitted to the lantern to increase their versatility.

The introduction of the limelight allowed the 'gauze dissolve' to develop as a design tool and scene change device. Deployed from the wings, the lime was sufficiently powerful to make a subject behind a gauze visible to the audience, developing the notion of scenic transformation. This was first seen in the 1850s.[37]

The slide projector, called 'Magic Lantern', had developed by the mid nineteenth century following the manufacture of high quality lenses, with lime as the light source. This technology was deployed in the theatre from the 1860s, and this heralded the first stage use of scenic projection, with both front and back projection used. Clouds or other atmospheric effects were painted onto rotating discs and projected, enhancing realism on stage. Practical problems with projection were also noted – such as seeing the light source through the cloth when back projecting and the need for low light levels of ambient light on stage to allow projections to 'read'. However, this method of creating scenery and effects was cheap and added a new dimension to stage design.

Experiments with light made by electricity took place in the mid nineteenth century and soon this was tested in theatres. The first electric lantern was the arc, with a blue/white, flickering, powerful, non-dimmable beam. It became a rival to the lime. It was first used on stage in Paris in 1849, for a sunrise in Meyerbeer's opera *Le Prophète*. Another example of its innovative stage use was in creating a rainbow effect (by lighting through a prism) for the opera *Moïse* in 1860.[38] It offered little more artistic potential than the lime, as it still required the attentions of an operator to constantly adjust the carbons. It was

---

[37] An article by Alex Shanks noted the first known use of a hidden staging element made to "appear" by judicious crossfading on stage (*Tabs* 15/1, Apr. 57, p4). A notable example of its use was in a production of *The Ring* at Covent Garden in the mid 1850's, when one whole act was played behind a gauze, coupled with projections of stylised painted effects. Another gauze dissolve worthy of note was in Kean's *Henry VIII* at the Princess's Theatre in the 1855. Shanks recorded that "one sensational effect was the apparition of a flight of angels to the dying Queen in *Henry VIII*, apparently suspended in a diagonal shaft of white light from a lime in the flies, and seen through what had appeared to be a solid backing of tapestry". Gauze reveals became a common sight on stage after this.

[38] Bergmann, *Lighting in the Theatre*, p278.

used as a fixed spot, a followspot and a projector, carrying accessories similar to the lime. Its major advantage was that the light had a slightly blue 'daylight' quality, which was more useful than the green-tinged lime. Its power and low cost were such that it remained in regular use as a light source for a followspot until the 1980s.

How the Stage was Lit, in the Period Leading up to the Introduction of Electricity

These then were the principal technological developments prior to the introduction of electric incandescent light to the stage in 1881. The following two extracts summarise typical gas lighting rigs found in theatres just before the introduction of electricity and consolidate the techniques in use at the time. The first is from an article printed in 1867 that detailed the installation found in the larger theatre, reprinted in *Tabs* in 1968. The article commenced with a description of the prompt corner and lighting control:

> "An interesting point on the stage is the prompt corner, from which the prompter has command of all the lights of the house, and bells to warn every man of his duty at the proper moment. He has a large brass plate, in which a number of handles are fixed, with an index to each, marking the high, low etc. of the lights; and as each system of lights has a separate main pipe from the prompt corner, each can be managed independently ...."

The article went on to describe a typical lighting installation, first detailing front of house lighting positions:

> "The house, or auditorium department, is generally lighted by means of a large lustre or sun-light in the centre of the ceiling, and much of the effect of the building depends on how this is managed. There are also smaller lights round one tier of the boxes at least. The proscenium is lighted by a large lustre on each side, and by the footlights, which run along the whole of the front of the stage. These are sometimes provided with glasses of different colours, called mediums, which are used for throwing a red, green, or white light on the stage, as may be required."

Lighting on stage comprised the following:

> "The stage is lighted by rows of gas-burners up each side and across the top at every entrance. The side-lights are called *gas-wings* or *ladders*; and the top ones, *gas-battens*. Each of these has a main from the prompt corner. They can be pushed in and out, or up and down, like scenery. There is also provision at each entrance for fixing flexible hose and temporary lights, so

as to produce a bright effect wherever required. The mediums for producing coloured light in this case are blinds of coloured cloth. Another means of producing brilliant effects of light is the lime-light, by which, together with lenses of coloured glass, bright lights of any colour can be thrown on the stage or scenery when required."[39]

The second article published in 1879, reprinted in *Tabs* in 1970, gave guidelines on how to light the smaller stage, which still often had to rely on naked flame for illumination. There are no references to limelight or the arc, which only featured in major houses, and this paints a picture that would have been common to the typical theatre-goer:

"To light the stage well is an important point. All light should be thrown upon the actors from the front of the stage, or at the front sides of the scene, so that there should be no shadows cast on their faces, as would be the case if the light came from behind or above them. Footlights are necessary; small oil lamps with glass shades over them answer well; or, failing these, wax candles, if put close together, will suffice. There must be a wire put at a little distance from the footlights, and interposed between them and the stage, or the chances of the dresses catching fire are great. An actress must not have to think of the risk of fire to her dress every time she moves.

A table at each side of the stage, with a good moderator lamp on it, makes a pleasant light. There ought also to be a bracket or two on each side of the stage, with lamps on them. The more the stage can be lighted from the front the better, so that the different expressions of the face may be well seen. The room for the audience ought to be darkened at the time of the performance, to enhance the effect of light on the stage; but as it is dismal to come into a dimly lighted room, it is well to have the lights managed as to make it possible to remove some of them when the curtain is drawn up.... In lighting the stage it is well to avoid gas, for it is a trying light, and a hot one, and the stage ought to be kept as cool as possible.

It frequently happens in plays of all kinds that the stage is supposed to grow darker or lighter, either suddenly or by degrees. Most of our readers have probably observed how, when the stage of a real theatre is dark, the appearance of one small candle creates a sudden blaze of light, which is of course produced by the prompter's turning up the stage lights, or, if things are badly managed, before the candle makes its appearance. If gas footlights are employed in private theatricals, there is of course no difficulty in

---

[39] Legge, B. "Stage Lighting in the Nineteenth Century": *Tabs*, Sep. 68, p17, citing *Chambers Encyclopaedia* 1867.

producing either a sudden or gradual increase or decrease of light. But if the candles or oil lamps are used, it will be well to have some little way - say six inches - between them and the actors, a board running the whole length of the footlights and working on a hinge, so that it can either lie flat on the ground, or an arrangement of pulleys be moved about by the prompter so as to partially or wholly cover the footlights on the stage side. For moonlight effects tinted glass in a wooden board can be substituted for the board." [40]

Tabs recalled, in an article in 1977, the qualities of gas lighting in the 1880s at the Drury Lane theatre in the *Illuminating Engineer* of May 1919:

"In those days at the Drury Lane such a thing as a hard shadow was unknown, partly by the great number of gas burners in the battens and footlights, and partly by the low power of the gas limes and the great distance they were from the object to be illuminated." [41]

Another example of stage lighting from this period can be deduced from the *Gas and Lime Plot* (see illustration opposite) for a production of *Lights o' London* by George Sims, staged at the Princess's Theatre London in September 1881, one month before electricity came to the London stage. The plot, reproduced in *Tabs*, listed a series of unnumbered light states, scheduled by Act and Scene. Some cues were triggered by the script, others presumably by instruction from the Stage Manager. Most cues involved full stage colour changes: some integrated limes, with colours, into the overall picture; some involved either checking or building overall intensity. Occasionally practical fittings were illuminated, but without any compensation from the rest of the rig. [42]

A further example of a lighting plot is that by Forbes Robertson for the 1897 production of *Hamlet* at the Lyric Theatre. [43] He recorded a full prop/costume/ setting plot for all the season's productions, and in a level of detail that must have made revivals easy. The 'Electrics/gas/limes plot' included a list of cues, by scene, with each section of stage, e.g. footlights or battens, given an intensity (¼, ½, ¾, or full), with colour. Occasionally there was a cue during a scene, but this is not common. Fade times were given as, for example "gradually" or "very, very gradually". No mention was made of timings in seconds:

[40] Legge, B. *Tabs* 28/1, Mar. 70, p62, citing *Amateur Theatricals* by Walter Herries Pollock and Lady Pollack, 1879.

[41] *Tabs* 35/2, Sum. 77, p9.

[42] *Tabs* 20/1, Spr. 62, p18.

[43] Theatre Museum Archives. This plot is typical of many held in the archive.

```
Hamlet          Lyric Theatre 1897
                Electric / Gas / Limes plot


Act 1
Sc 1     FLOAT       Blue full up
         BATTENS     No 2 Blue half up
         LENGTHS     2 Blue lengths behind castle piece OPS
                     1 Blue length behind castle piece PS
Sc 2     FLOAT       White ¾ up
         BATTENS     White 4 & 5 up
         LENGTHS     1 to light sea backcloth
                     1 to light small battlement row
         etc
```

The lime plot was similar to a modern followspot plot, and including cue position in the script, intensity, colour, beam width, pick up point, and movement instructions. Some plot sheets called for blackout between scenes.

By 1880 lighting had the potential to be a sophisticated, controllable medium, and stage lighting effects were commonplace on the Victorian stage. Command of the effect was still the province of the stage director or producer, but a body of gasmen were emerging with skills in creating these effects night after night. As technology was developing, coupled with considered insight into the effect lighting had on the stage picture, actor and meaning, so started to emerge the style of lighting that we see today. Brighter lighting liberated the stage space, and in turn acting and scenic design style, prompting new performance styles in the late nineteenth and early twentieth centuries, with lighting an integral component of performance.

Summary
By the time electricity was introduced to the stage, many lighting techniques and conventions had become firmly established in theatrical language. A light, or group of lights, would be placed in any convenient place where it would either light the actor's face and body, or light scenery; it could be faded in or out alone or in combination with others; it could be set at a level of intensity relative to lights from other parts of the stage and in response to the dramatic

moment and context; lights could be coloured, and colour conventions such as blue for night, blue-green for moonlight, and pink and yellow for sunlight were well established. Colours could also be changed during the course of the play, either crossfading 'live', or while moving via blackout. Light could localise an actor and follow him/her around the stage.

While gas lighting created a soft ambience without significant shades of contrast, the lime and arc allowed keylight to be introduced, either to motivate a scene by representing sun or moonlight (or any light that cast a strong shadow), or placing the principal actor in their own bright light, and 'following' them around the stage until their exit. Lighting had become sufficiently complex for shows to have begun to adopt a 'cue sheet' to co-ordinate lighting, so that lighting could be both planned in advance and executed in the same way every performance.

Yet lighting in this era had only the crudest resemblance to today's stage expectations.[44] There was little sense of visual aesthetic, with effects produced in a formulaic manner, rather than conceived to meet the particular requirements of the show. Indeed, the arrival of gas appears to have brushed aside the movement of those who saw the potential of a more refined approach, based on the model of the fine artist, that had gained momentum in the latter days of candle light. When considering whether Francis Reid's definition, cited in the introduction ("stage lighting is a fluid, selective, atmospheric, dimensional illumination appropriate to the style of a particular production"), could have been applied to lighting from this era, probably it could except in relation to the aspect concerning *style*. Other than in colour variation, most lighting from this era would have almost certainly looked very similar. Gas practitioners reverted to the even, symmetrical wash of light, perhaps now restrained by more complex pipework installation that, while gaining in the potential for greater brightness and controllability, lacked the flexibility and freedom of the single candle placement. The lighting designer would not emerge until lighting rigs could offer the technical flexibility for stylistic variation suggested by the use of the lime, as was later mastered by Henry Irving.

The medium of gas, complemented by the lime, did have the potential for creating high aesthetic values, and perhaps should have gained more champions that it did. No sooner than it became established, however, it was superseded

---

[44] A review of lighting at Buxton Opera House written in the mid 1930s draws attention to how simple lighting was: "in those leisurely days of gas the lighting plots were of delightful simplicity and control was bereft of the intricacies (of today)" (*Tabs* 2/1, also *Sightline* 13/2, Aut. 79, p91).

by electricity. The attraction of the new medium was immediately apparent. It had the artistic potential of gas, but without the heat, fumes and risk of fire. Good reasons alone for running with the new technology.

2 THE TECHNICAL PLATFORM

This chapter examines the important technical developments that gave a platform for the emergence of lighting design, and examines when equipment was of sufficient minimum quality to allow design to be achieved on a regular basis.

The chapter commences with a review of the technical platform afforded by first electric stages, and then divides into three chronological periods: 1881-1914; 1918-1935; and 1935-1950. At the end of each of these periods, the typical lighting equipment and techniques in use at that time are considered in a summing-up.

Material has been selected to clarify the potential of the rig for design. To establish the importance of technical developments in prompting lighting design, the quotation by Francis Reid, cited in the Introduction, provides a useful framework:

> "Stage lighting is a fluid, selective, atmospheric, dimensional illumination appropriate to the style of a particular production".

An analysis of the capacity of equipment available to achieve design according to Reid is summarised at the end of the chapter.

The First Electric Stages

Joseph W. Swan invented the electric incandescent carbon filament lamp in 1879, first used in the theatre two years later.[1] Although some perceived immediate aesthetic advantages, particularly that the whiter light gave better colour rendition of the scenery and costumes, most gains for the next twenty to thirty years came in health and safety. Fewer theatres burned down, actors and audiences were no longer overcome by obnoxious gases and ambient temperatures fell to a reasonable level.[2,3]

---

[1] At a demonstration in Newcastle in 1880, he said: "electric light by incandescence is just as simple as arc lighting is difficult. All that is required is a material which is not a very good conductor of electricity, highly infusible, and which can be formed into a wire or lamina, and is neither combustible in air, or if combustible, does not undergo change in a vacuum" (*Tabs* 26/3, Sep. 68, p17, from *Engineering* 29/10/1880).

The first electrical installations attempted to replicate gas. The position of the electric lights simply replaced the existing gas burners. Battens and footlights, supported by bunch-lights and hanging lengths from the wings remained the standard installation. Limes and arcs continued to provide key lighting and effects. Due to the scarcity of electric equipment and power supply, many theatres continued to install gas, with pipes running alongside electric cables for many years.[4]

Electricity was first used at the Savoy Theatre, installed for its opening on 6th October 1881, although the installation was not completed until December 1881.[5] Richard D'Oyly Carte, its founder, lit the whole of the theatre with 1,200 electric lamps. The lamps, powered by steam generators parked adjacent to the theatre, were located in the same place as gas jets would be found: footlights, border lights and wing lights. Carte also equipped the theatre with gas as a backup.

At first only the auditorium was lit by electricity as a test for the system, and this was recorded as giving "a soft, soothing light, clearer and far more grateful than gas…"[6] It was noted that difficulty in regulating the speed of the generators caused intensity changes and that the extra 'whiteness' of the new light sources needed to be toned down to simulate gas.[7]

The first performance with the entire theatre lit by electricity was the matinee of *Patience* on 28th December 1881. *The Times* noted the significance of the occasion:

"an interesting experiment was made at a performance of *Patience* yesterday

---

[2] Richard D'Oyly Carte said: "the greatest drawbacks to the enjoyment of the theatrical performances are, undoubtedly, the foul air and heat which pervades all theatres. As everyone knows, each gas-burner consumes as much oxygen as many people, and causes great heat besides. The incandescent lamps consume no oxygen, and cause no perceptible heat." (Rees, T. *Theatre Lighting in the Age of Gas*, London: STR, 1978, p169, from a prospectus for The Savoy Theatre).

[3] The grid, normally the hottest part of the theatre, was measured at 68°F at the Savoy, whereas at the gas-lit Sadler's Wells it was 88°F, the Comedy 100°F and the Alhambra 105°F.

[4] Poor insulation often meant gas pipes were "live" (Charles La Trobe 1879-1967, Stage Director, Haymarket Theatre, *Tabs* 11/2, Sep. 53, p10).

[5] Electric lighting was used in only a few public buildings in London. The Savoy, built to stage the works of Gilbert and Sullivan, was intended to be at the forefront of modern innovation, and was one of the first examples of the electric lighting of a high profile public space.

[6] Rees, *Theatre Lighting in the Age of Gas*, p170.

[7] "Occasional sudden changes from light to darkness showed that the machinery was not yet under perfect control, but it is hoped that the defect will be remedied in a few days. It will also be desirable to change the white globes for others of a yellow tinge" (*The Times*, 1/10/ 1881, p8).

afternoon, when the stage for the first time was lit up by electric light, which has been used in the auditorium ever since the opening of the Savoy theatre. The success of the new mode of illumination was complete, and its importance for the development of scenic art can scarcely be overrated. The light was perfectly steady throughout the performance, and the effect was pictorially superior to gas, the colours of the dresses – an important element in the 'aesthetic' opera – appearing as true and as distinct as by daylight. The Swan incandescent lamps were used, the aid of gaslight being entirely dispensed with. The ordinary electric apparatus has the great drawback for stage representations that the flames (sic) cannot be lowered or increased at will, there being no medium between full light and total darkness. This difficulty has been successfully overcome by interpolating in the circuit ... what in technical language is called a 'resistance'. This 'resistance' consists of open spiral coils of iron wire..." [8]

Engineering magazine reported that 824 lamps were used to light the stage, arranged in the manner of a gas rig. [9] Carte had installed six dimmers, operated from the fly gallery. Fades were not smooth, as the lights were dimmed in six

---

[8] *The Times*, 29/12/1881, p4.

[9] "6 rows of 100 lamps each above the stage

1	"	"	60	"	"	"	" "
4	"	"	14	"	"	fixed upright	
2	"	"	18	"	"	" "	
5	"	"	10	"	"	ground lights	
2	"	"	11	"	"	" "	

The Auditorium is lighted (sic) by 114 lamps attached in groups of three within a ground or opaloid shade, by which arrangement a most soft and pleasant light is produced.

Pilots lights in the engine room ...in the same circuit ... indicate when the lights are turned up or down. Any series of lights can in an instant be turned up to full power or gradually lowered to a dull red heat as easily as if they were gas lamps, by the simple turning of a small handle. These are arranged side by side in a little room on the left of the stage. Each handle is a six way switch which, by throwing into its corresponding magnet circuit greater or lesser resistance (increasing or decreasing it in six stages), the strength of the current passing through the lamps is lessened or increased by as many grades.

In an artistic and scenic point of view nothing could be more completely successful than the present lighting of the Savoy Theatre; the illumination is brilliant without being dazzling, and while being slightly whiter than gas, the accusation of 'ghastliness', so often urged against the light of the electric arc, can in no way be applied. In addition to this the light is absolutely steady, and thanks to the enterprise of M. D'Oyly Carte, it is now possible for the first time in the history of the modern theatre to sit for a whole evening and enjoy a dramatic performance in a cool and pure atmosphere" (*Engineering*, Vol. XXXIII No. 844, 3/3/1882, pp. 204-5). The number of lamps on stage meant that the stage was as bright as a modern stage lit with an approximate equivalent of 3kW of light (Cue 13, Sept 1981).

steps by switching into circuits of greater or lesser resistance. Houselights were left on to allow the audience to follow the libretto. Practical lights, fed from storage cells, could also be carried by actors and dancers, free from connection to the supply: "Self-lighting fairies, with electricity stored somewhere about the small of their backs, constitute the last thing in Savoy innovations. They are dazzling… certainly constitute a picturesque feature in the rich tableau of colour and light with which the new fairy-opera very brilliantly and appropriately concludes".[10] However, not all agreed: "The effect… is too dazzling to be pleasant, and in a dark scene obscures the face".[11] Despite this criticism, 'electric scenes' proved tremendously popular and were used by many theatres. The Savoy had set a pattern for installations that other theatres followed.[12]

Geoffrey Snelson, an employee from 1890-96, detailed much of the lighting installation at The Savoy. By his tenure a more permanent power supply had been installed as well as other developments from the original lighting rig:

> "The electric supply originally was generated under the hotel with cables running to the switch room at the corner of the stage. The supply was generally quite stable, although sometimes it dropped before recovering. There was only one failure in seven years that I was there, although the gas supply was always lit before a show to check the system as a backup. Battens and footlights were arranged the same as today, with lamps at about every 6", fixed to timber battens. Dipping was used to colour lamps. The carbon-filament lamps were equivalent to a modern 25 watt lamp or less and never produced a white light. Lengths were also used behind the wing flats. Early lamps were attached to their feed wires by bare wires protruding from the lamp and a spring to keep a tension. They were prone to dropping off, hitting the stage with a loud "plop", followed by the spring. Dimmers were drainpipe type, worked independently. Master switches flashed when making or breaking contact, and this could be seen from the auditorium during a dark scene. Sockets were set into the stage floor for "dips" which also flashed when plugged out from. Limes were used for spotting, although these were superseded by arcs. The lens often shattered on these, sending broken glass cascading onto the stage below".[13]

---

[10] W. Beatty Kingston, "Our Musical-Box", *The Theatre*, 1/1883, p28.

[11] 62 *Lloyd's Weekly*, 3/12/1882, p6.

[12] For the opening of the Empire in 1884, there was a spectacular production of *Chilperic* which contained an electric ballet with a cast of fifty: "All London will talk of it. Nothing to compare with it of its kind has been witnessed on the modern stage." (*The Era*, 19/4/1884, p11).

[13] *Tabs* 33/3, Aut. 75, p3, and *Tabs* 15/2, Sep. 57, p16.

An unnamed illustration dated 1883, courtesy Science Museum, London/Science and Society picture library.

After The Savoy installation, every new theatre built in London was equipped with electric light, and all other theatres soon converted.[14] However, with no public supply available each theatre had to generate its own power.[15]

An unnamed illustration dated 1883, held in the Theatre Museum *Early Lighting* archive, shows a stage lit by electric lamps (see illustration above). A large stage with four cut cloths lit by overhead battens, wing booms and with footlights. There are arcs in the No. 1 wing bay from each side. A bunch-light stands in No. 4 wing to illuminate the upstage cloth. The lighting control

---

[14] in 1883 the Criterion, Grand Theatre Islington, and new Lyceum Edinburgh; in 1884 the new Prince's Theatre; in 1885 the new Pavilion Music Hall etc. The Lyric was the first to be lit by electricity alone, in 1888 (i.e. without gas as a back-up). Irving's Lyceum was the last West End theatre to convert to electricity, in 1902 (Rees, *Theatre Lighting in the Age of Gas*, p179). A public electricity supply was set up, and the Palace Theatre was the last London theatre to have its own generating supply, in use until 1904.

[15] An indication of the uncertainty of a continuous electrical supply, an early programme from the London Hippodrome (5/1903) stated the supply of electricity was "derived from two different companies in four sections, thus minimising the chance of failure" (Theatre Museum Archives, London Hippodrome file). Blackburn Starling Archives contain literature about early generating equipment.

appears to be in No. 1 wing OP and at stage level, directly above dimmers housed sub stage. Houselights are clearly on during performance and actors appear to be holding electric practicals. This system was typical of the time for a major theatre.[16]

Electric light was not universally popular, and there was a backlash principally over the extra level of brightness. An over-bright stage seemed to lessen distance and create a flat, even picture, devoid of shape, depth and atmosphere. Gas had its champions, principally Henry Irving[17], and others such as Henry Emden, Drury Lane's scene painter, who said that electric light "gave the painting a hard and cold appearance".[18] Percy Fitzgerald noted that it was common to over-light with electricity, with a resultant loss of subtlety: "now in this fierce blaze all half-tones, yellows and other tints disappear, and the painters have to paint to suit the conflagration. There is no room for shadows even".[19] He continued: "the electric light has become so profuse and glaring that all distance and mystery is lost, while the scene painters are compelled, in self defence, to make their colours as fiery as possible".[20] Later, C.B. Cochran praised gas lighting at the expense of electric, doubting "whether the harshness of electric light can be controlled to produce the subtle atmospheric effects formerly obtained by gas".[21]

It was noted that make-up should be adjusted for the extra whiteness and clarity of the electric lamp: "make-up for stages lighted by electricity should not be as heavy as in cases where gas is the sole illuminant; and, as the features in the rays of the electric light are shown up with intense clearness, care must be taken that the paints, or powder, are very lightly and finely applied; and also that all lines for shading are evenly toned by powdering".[22]

---

[16] An unusual technique common in early days of electric light was to surround the proscenium opening with lamps, often coloured red, facing the audience. These were switched on to mask scene-changes, used as "blinders" to stop the audience seeing a change without dropping a curtain in (*Tabs* 11/2, Sep. 53, p10).

[17] Irving's love of gas is well known and is a testament not only to the artistic potential of the medium but also to the lack of approval of the quality of electric light. He even gave instructions for the removal of electric facilities installed in good faith in his theatre during his absence on tour.

[18] *Tabs* 35/2, Sum. 77, p9.

[19] *Theatre Notebook* XXXIII, 3, Alan Hughes, from Fitzgerald, "on scenic illusion and stage appliance", *Journal of the Society of Arts*, XXXV 1886-7 p460.

[20] Jackson, R. *Victorian Theatre*, London: New Mermaid, 1989, p217, citing Percy Fitzgerald *The Art of Acting* 1892, p217.

[21] Cochran, C.B. *The Showman looks on,* London: Dent, 1945, p233.

[22] *Lynn's Practical Hints on Make-Up*, London, 1897, p19. Even 50 years later, Ridge noted in his 1935 book that the use of heavy make up had still not fully disappeared, except for character parts.

However, unless there was a desire to light the stage with sensitivity, it was immaterial whether gas or electricity was used. A comment in 1895 from C. Wilhelm (William Pitcher), a well known stage designer who included lighting supervision amongst his duties, further illustrated the point: "I want to see a stage illuminated with a suggestion of real sunlight, with shadows from the figures in one direction only. In processions and big spectacles, the habit of reinforcing the fiery furnace of the footlights with enormous lime-boxes, and of supplementing these by others at the various entrances, is utterly destructive of light and shade; and drapery subjected to this searching glare loses all its beauty and meaning. Again, a partiality for coloured rays of light threatens to extinguish all colour in the dress, and is greatly to be deplored".[23]

Developments in Lighting Technology, 1881-1914

Lamps

Lamp technology developed rapidly as experiments with filament types resulted in longer lamp life and brighter output.[24] By 1910 a brightness of 8-10 lumens per watt had been achieved, and by 1913 12-15 lumens per watt, about half the power of modern lamps. Lamps were available in a wide range of powers, similar to today: 15; 25; 40; 60; 75 & 100 watt versions.

Lanterns

Lanterns were manufactured to replicate gas fittings, as previously described in the Savoy installation. Limes and arcs continued in production. There were no other important developments during this period.

Colour

Prior to the manufacture of materials specifically made for the job, light had been coloured either by the use of coloured glass or coloured silks placed in the beam. Both were problematic, as safety was an issue with glass and fire a risk for silks. Light transmission for both media was also poor.[25]

---

[23] Jackson, *Victorian Theatre,* p232, citing C Wilhelm "Art in the ballet" *Magazine of Art* 1895 pp50-1.

[24] Filaments were made of carbon until 1905, then tantalum in 1906 and then tungsten in 1907, each set in a vacuum. In 1913 nitrogen or argon was added to the vacuum to get even more brightness.

[25] Ridge noted that Schwabe glass, popular on the continent, had poor transmission, and double normal wattage was required when using glass in comparison to gelatine (Ridge, H. *Stage Lighting,* Cambridge: Heffer, 1928, p84). They pioneered glass filters for their cyclorama lighting equipment, although only seven colours were available in their range.

The development of glass electric lamps allowed colouring the envelop with lacquer, called 'Lamp Dip', and a range of colours soon became available.[26] Digby produced a range of 24 lamp dips sometime after 1895, with the same numbering as their gelatine range.[27]

However, with the introduction of the hotter gas filled lamps, dipping became a less practical solution to colouring light, as hotter lamps were not suited to this process, and a new medium was required to colour light. The industry turned to a cheap, lightweight, efficient and safe material – gelatine. 'Gel' was made by dipping a glass sheet into a gelatine liquid, allowing the liquid to cool and solidify, and peeling the resulting gelatine sheet off. It proved highly successful. The sheet was cut to size and secured in the lantern with a metal frame. A range of about ten coloured Gelatine sheets, first used to tint 'Magic Lantern' shows, had been marketed in 1895 by Digby, and now these were used in stage lighting applications.[28] Gelatines may only have lasted a week, by which time they had become dry and brittle, so were changed regularly. They normally broke before they faded.[29]

Frosted gelatine was made to diffuse a light beam, and was also used as a dimmer for arcs and limes – a particularly dense No 1 frost was made for this.[30] Simple colour change mechanisms were made by mounting gelatines in a circular frame that was rotated through the beam, such as one third clear, one third red and the other third blue, with a cord to control the colour position.[31]

Dimmers

Electricity proved to be a much better medium than gas for the dimming of stage lighting. Quicker, more precise fades were possible, without the flicker

---

[26] A common trade name for lamp dip was Damarda Lacquer (Ridge, *Stage Lighting*, Ch. 4).

[27] Strand also made lamp dip, but much later (in 1928) with 33 dips in the range.

[28] The numbering of these colours gave rise to a system of identifying colours by a number that still is in use today. The colour of the gels were developed for a variety of reasons: the actress Ellaline Terriss complained her face appeared too blue under No.7 pink. A new colour, No.9 Pink was made. The same actress complained again a few years later, and No. 8 was made. Eventually No.7 regained favour. There was no overall logic to the numbering process as the range of tones expanded: in the blue family, No. 18 was double strength No.17, No.19 double No. 18, (and later others were needed to fill the gaps – Nos. 32 and 40). No.18 was known as "murder blue". There is a good story about an irate Sir Henry Irving at the Lyceum in 1899 calling at the factory of Digby at 6pm because during the matinee someone had spoilt the 18's, and he could not do the murder in *The Bells* that night without it!

[29] In conversation with John G. Holton.

[30] *Tabs* 7/2, Sep. 49, p18.

[31] *Popular Electricity*, 3/10, p32.

that was a common feature of gas lighting. The first dimmers were the liquid 'drainpipe' type, which comprised one fixed and one movable electrode set in a tube containing salt water or washing soda solution.[32] When a current passed between the electrodes en route to the spotlight, by varying the distance between them a greater or lesser resistance would brighten or dim the light.

These dimmers were cheap, could accommodate a variety of lamp loads, and required only simple maintenance. They required regular topping up due to high evaporation rates, either by a watering can or, anecdotally, urination.[33] Most were in use for many years, as liquid dimmers were robust and reliable.[34]

When wire wound resistance dimmers were introduced in the early 1900s, these were even cheaper than liquids, but worked efficiently only when equally matched to the loading of lamps for which they were engineered. Therefore this limited the potential to reallocate lanterns to dimmers, and restricted a more adventurous approach to lighting.[35]

Control Systems
The control system of the time was based on the Gas Plate, with one control per section of the lighting rig, each linked to a master control to regulate the total intensity level.

Groups of lights – such as footlights, No. 1 batten reds, and No. 1 batten blues were hard-wired to each dimmer. The dimmer required a control that allowed the operation of each one individually as well as some or all collectively. Systems were developed where each dimmer was controlled by a lever (called *handles,* the forerunner of today's fader) that could be moved to bring the light up to full or be set at any intermediate point. A master handle co-ordinated multiple dimmer fades, which were achieved by locking individual handles onto a shaft controlled by the master handle.

An early electric lighting control would have had perhaps a dozen or so handles, each one labelled as operating a set of lights such as the footlights or

---

[32] *Tabs* 6/3, Dec. 48, p23.

[33] *Focus 12A,* Aug. 92, p18. John G. Holton recalled that at a Birmingham theatre steam from boiling liquid dimmers melted the glue on a double bass that has mistakenly been left in the dimmer room, causing it to completely collapse.

[34] The liquid dimmers installed at Drury Lane in 1902 were still in use in 1949 (*Tabs* 7/1, Apr . 49, p19).

[35] The wire-wound resistance dimmer in particular was associated with portable/ temporary control systems, normally fitted internally with Dutch "Hasemeyer" wire wound resistance dimmers (*Tabs* 22/1, Mar. 64, p12).

a colour circuit on the battens. The type of cues this control could run were limited to fade up or down, to or from black, and simple crossfades between colour groups. The resultant lighting would have been crude by today's standards, as these controls worked on the principle of moving groups of lights from on to off (or vice versa), rather than the modern method of crossfading one composite set of lights to another. There was no sense of overall proportion to the fades. The light nearest to its arrival point would get there first in a crossfade, and those with the furthest distance to travel would arrive as the fade was completed.

For ease of operation, handles representing lights illuminating common parts of the stage or colour groups would be located together. Fractional intensity scales, to allow approximate balancing of intensities, were crudely indicated on each handle. As the dimmers were normally located away from the stage, they were connected to the control, which was usually situated on a perch above prompt corner, by connecting rods or tracker wires.[36]

A rare example of a fully detailed control specification from this period was published in *The London Engineer*.[37] The Earls Court control, installed in 1896, a more complex model than most, was designed to permit crossfades from one colour to another, allowed interlocking of fader handles for multiple dimmer fades from a single operational movement, and with a slow motion worm for assisted slow, smooth fades.

Projection
The arc light source used in the projector was very powerful in comparison to the overall light level on stage, which meant projected images could cut through the ambient stage light. Optical effects such as cloud and rain started to appear in about 1895.[38]

The Lighting Rig of the Period
The following are examples of electric lighting installations around the turn of the century, which indicate the typical facility found in larger theatres at this time (for technical reviews of other theatres, see Appendix ii).

---

[36] Imperial Lighting manufactured many of the first lighting control systems, including those fitted at the New Gaiety Theatre, the Theatre Royal Drury Lane, the New Theatre and the Alhambra *(Tabs* 15/2, Sep. 57, p5).

[37] *The London Engineer,* November 1896, p463.

[38] Theatre Museum Early Lighting File.

(1) In 1891, the Palace Theatre was equipped with 29 Lyons liquid dimmers, with battens wired for two colour circuits.[39]

(2) c1900, the Alhambra had battens, hanging lengths and footlights all with three colour circuits. Also there were three arcs on each perch and five on each fly rail. These fly rail arcs, instead of being fitted with lenses, unusually had large parabolic reflectors for soft-edged following work.[40]

(3) c1900 His Majesty's Theatre was equipped with Digby electric stage lighting that was amongst the most advanced in its time. There were footlights, set low into the stage floor for less restrictive sightlines, six overhead battens, two vertical rows behind and on each side of the proscenium, wing lights and portable lengths. The switchboard was calibrated to set levels of intensity from 0-10 for greater plotting precision. All lighting units were wired into three circuits for colour mixing. In addition there were at least 28 limes on stage, and more could be added, even from front of house.[41] See Chapter 4 – the work of Sir Herbert Beerhohm Tree – for an example of how this rig was used.

(4) In 1902 the New Theatre was equipped with four colour battens in white, amber, red and blue, with lacquered carbon filament lamps. The control system was sited on a stage left gallery, operating 40 liquid dimmers by tracker wire. Each circuit had its own wheel for fading, and could also be locked onto a master shaft with a self release mechanism. A contemporary account stated that: "this arrangement has the advantage of giving plenty of scope for artistic colour blending for which Sir Charles Wyndham's electrician Mr. Howey is well known".[42]

(5) In 1904 the New Gaiety Theatre was fitted with seven three-colour circuit battens, with cables fed so as not to obstruct light from the side arcs. Both resistance dimmers for fixed loads and liquid dimmers for variable loads were available, linked by tracker wires to the control. In addition, the New

---

[39] The theatre's carbon arcs (sited at the perches) were mastered by switches at the control position (Legge, B. "Stage Lighting in the Nineteenth Century", *Tabs* 26/3, Sep. 68, p17).

[40] *Tabs* 26/3, Sep. 68, p17. These would have produced a narrow intense soft edge beam, highly suited to more discreet followspot work, and may have been the forerunner to the Pageant and Beamlight lanterns developed in the 1930s.

[41] Booth, M. *Victorian Spectacular Theatre 1850-1910*, London: Routledge & Kegan Paul, 1981, p136.

[42] *Tabs* 26/3, Sep. 68, p17. The *Daily Telegraph* 6/3/02 said "it has the latest novelties in lighting…apparatus for lighting the stage is wonderfully complete, means being provided to carry out the most complicated effects on a new system, specially designed and for the first time installed in a theatre". Two power supplies were used. (Theatre Museum Archives. See *Tabs* 35/3, Aut. 72, for photo of the 1902 control).

Gaiety control had dimmer by-pass switching for each colour for snap cues.[43]

(6) In 1906 William Barbour, an employee at the St. James's Theatre, claimed it had the best control system around: "It carries 600 Amperes, four colours throughout. The electric battens can be worked from any angle. A special independent switchboard under the stage may be used to give separate control of the footlights. This means the switchboard footlights can be cut out and the number of lights and colours regulated… Mr. Barbour is a man of considerable practical experience, to whom the scientific and artistic side of his profession is attractive. His skill as an expert in stage lighting has elicited praise from some of our more famous scenic artists".[44]

The technique of flooding the stage from battens wired in three of four colour groups was the normal way to illuminate the stage, a method copied directly from the days of gas lighting practice. Primary colours (red, green and blue) were the most obvious choice in battens, as combinations of these could mix any colour. The fourth colour (in four colour systems) was usually white, to give additional brightness and subtlety to colour mixing. However, it is interesting to note that the red/blue/green for colouring lamps was not universal. In Britain yellow was often substituted for green, which was recognised as a less useful colour.[45] Also, some systems, such as Earl's Court, used red, white and green.[46] Basil Dean noted that prior to World War One most theatres used rows of lacquered lamps in footlights and battens, coloured red, amber and blue.[47] With careful use of dimmers, it was noted that the batten colouring system was capable of creating a range of acceptable temporal ambiences.

The batten lighting system was adequate if very limited. The *Electrical Review* reported that: "it is possible to achieve the following effects: bright daylight passes into evening twilight, and this again into a nocturnal effect with moonlight. This again gives place to a red morning dawn, which is succeeded

---

[43] *Tabs* 26/3, Sep. 68, p17.

[44] From an article by William Barbour, Electrician at the St. James Theatre. He started work at the age of 13 and worked for 12 years as a gas man. He gained daytime employment with the Brush Electric Light Co. to learn about electrics. Engaged by Loveday to join the Irving company, he was placed in charge of limes for the American tour of *Faust*. Later he joined the St. James's Theatre (Theatre Museum Early Lighting File: *The Era* 3/3/1906).

[45] On the continent, there was an even more unusual example of the colouring of the stage. The German company AEG electrified stages in Germany, Russia and Denmark, using a three colour (white, red and green) system.

[46] *The London Engineer,* November 1896, p463.

[47] *Sightline* 9/1, Spr. 75, p37.

by daylight".[48] Jim Laws, a lighting designer who specialises in the supply of early lighting equipment, said in *Sightline* that lighting at the turn of the century was: "compared to today, dim, very soft and indiscriminate. The arcs and limelights would have been essential to achieve any contrast on stage, and each manned spot from perch or flyrail would be a vital part of the whole."[49]

Only wealthy or larger London theatres were able to deploy multiple arcs or limes as followspots.[50] Here limes were commonly used to key into the batten atmosphere, usually following the principal actors. This is illustrated by Mr Kerr, a contractor who supplied a range of London theatres with lime-light, who said that in *Claudian* at the Princess's that "during the three principal scenes fourteen lime-lights are nightly used, and in the last scene these are subdued and coloured with blue mediums". The article continued: "by means of lime-light some of the most pleasing effects in spectacular scenes are produced... the concentrated rays of the lime-light penetrate and illumine where less potent light has little or no effect. Certainly for brilliance of spectacle we know of no effect more splendid".[51]

Basil Dean, recalling his early days from 1906, remembered that limes were usually placed upstage on either side to provide sunlight or moonlight, sometimes simultaneously from both sides. They were also installed on perches either side of the proscenium arch. They could be noisy if not kept trimmed, like the sound of an aeroplane landing.[52] David Ayliff recalled that it was common in the early days to colour limes with amber glass to simulate gas lighting.[53]

An article published in the 1950s about a young enthusiast learning the lime addressed procedures of lime operation that typified practice. The crew was called for first dress to learn the show (unpaid). The Chief described how to strike an arc, taught newcomers the ropes, and left a dayman to supervise from then on. The carbons needed feeding every minute. Vertical and horizontal alignment of the carbons was required "or there'll be a sausage shaped spot on the stage and one lime-boy less in the world." The lime had a barndoor,

---

[48] *Electrical Review* 25/8/1893, p 216.

[49] *Sightline* 20/2, Win. 86, p28.

[50] Dean confirmed there was little difference between venues, as though lighting installations were standard. He also recalled that most theatres were shabby (*Sightline* 9/1, Spr. 75, p37).

[51] Booth, M. (Ed.) *Victorian Theatrical Trades Articles* from *The Stage* 1883-4, London: STR, 1981, p42.

[52] *Sightline* 8/2, Aut. 74, p38.

[53] In correspondence with David Ayliff.

guillotine and iris, and a wheel changed the lens from spot to flood. There was a colour magazine, and focus could be changed. "Supposing I have to do all these things at once?" "Then you have to leap about a bit." The article also mentioned the technique of irising down before snapping off – a practice still common today.[54]

Developments in Lighting Technology, 1914-1935
Although initially there were few developments, some important progress was made during this period.

Lamps
A key development, the gas filled lamp, prompted much refinement in theatre lighting equipment after its introduction in 1919. Far brighter than their predecessors, by the mid 1920s lamps was available in a power range from 60-3000W, although many of these models were not suited to theatre usage. Brighter lamps prompted the development of spotlights, but these higher efficiency lamps also brought problems. Their higher heat output meant that reflector mirrors inside lanterns were not possible until the stainless steel reflector was developed in the mid 1920s.[55] Then, light output significantly increased, and the potential for new lantern designs grew.

The two most efficient lamps to become available during this period were the 'grid' or 'gate' filament 500 and 1000W 'A' class biplane, which were made for projectors and had a very short 50 hour life. Also there were 500 and 1000W 'B' Class lamps, with a longer life of 800 hours, but less efficient and less bright.[56] Although both classes were regularly used in the theatre, neither was really suitable because of the need still to manually align their filament centres precisely within the optical path for a 'clean beam'. Most lamps had a large filament that meant precise focusing could not be easily achieved. This must have lowered the incentive to move equipment from the standard rig to 'designed' positions.[57]

---

[54] "Life on a lime: first steps in theatre electrics" from *The Times* 19/12/1956 (Theatre Museum Early Lighting File).

[55] Ridge, *Stage Lighting*, p5.

[56] 2000W and 5000W lamps were also available, but with a limited lamp life of 100 hours.

[57] *Tabs* reported the difficulty in getting the filament in the right place within the optical path, especially from difficult access positions. It must have been a time consuming job, made even more difficult once the lamp had become hot. The article noted that there was a tendency to screw the lamp in and hope for the best (*Tabs* 8/2, Sept. 50, p10). The breakthrough in lamp (cont...)

Although development of stage lighting was undoubtedly enhanced by the availability of these lamps, it was inhibited by a lack of development of really suitable tungsten lamps, and there was little use of other lamp types such as discharge sources.[58] For followspots and projectors the lime and arc were still in use, and these were still the only really bright source of light available, having a sufficiently compact source for good optical projection. There is no doubt that developments in lantern optics in this country were significantly held back by a lack of investment in the production of high output compact filament lamps until the early 1950s.

Lanterns

The early batten manufactured by Strand, fitted with colour-dipped 60W lamps and lacquered white inside for reflection, was used as a footlight or overhead batten. Hotter gas-filled lamps required a more substantial construction, and the facility to accept gelatine held in metal frames. Strand rose to this challenge: their batten and footlight of 1922 became the standard lighting unit, promoted by the colour-mixing experiments of Adrian Samoiloff (see Chapter 4). These units were made with a range of different spaced lamp centres, presumably to adapt to differing stage widths, and had a high efficiency Sunray reflector behind the lamp.[59] Each compartment could be fitted with a lamp ranging

---

technology did not come until 1952, with the introduction of the "T" class Pre-focus Cap – a lamp cap that automatically placed the filament centred in the optical field, meaning that no longer had the lamp centre to be adjusted every time a lantern was focused. This development heralded the mass production of the half kilowatt profile (Patt 23) in 1953 and its sister Fresnel (Patt. 123) in 1957.

[58] *Tabs* discussed in 1949 the use of fluorescent lighting on stage, noting its potential as an excellent cyclorama light. However, at the time it was too expensive, and smooth dimming to blackout was still to be achieved. Thorn developed dimmable fluorescent lighting, aimed at the theatre, in 1950. Although it was flickery and needed careful maintenance, it pointed the way forward for soft light, colour wash and cyclorama work. A rare early example of its use was in the 1950 production of *Hamlet*, designed by Laurence Irving, which used fluorescent lighting (supplied by Thorn) as well as conventional Strand equipment (*Tabs* 7/2, Sep. 49, p11 and Theatre Museum Archives). Ridge and Aldred in their 1935 book noted the use of mercury vapour lamps on the continent, in particular the very good results when used with blue (discharge sources were mentioned as a source for lighting cycloramas in German theatres), and recommended overrunning 220v lamps at 230v to get more light output, claiming that the loss of life was more than made up for in brighter, higher colour temperature beams. The Covent Garden *Ring* of 1934 was noted for the first use of discharge lamps on stage in Britain, when a mercury lamp was used to "kill off all colour as the Goddess Freia was carried off" (*ABTT News*, Mar. 87, p14).

[59] These units gave out about 20 foot candles (*Strandlight* 8, Spr. 89, p1). As gas jets were placed as close as possible for maximum brightness, so too were electric lamps. When these became encased with a reflector (to become known as the "batten") the average stage was found to accept (cont...)

from 60-150W. These units stayed in production until 1945.[60]
Strand progressively added other lanterns to their range:

- An electric arc, suitable for followspotting, was introduced in 1915, and upgraded in 1925 to carbon-arc
- 500W focus spot with a 5" lens introduced in about 1920[61]
- 100/150W single flood, introduced in 1922
- 500/1000W 56° single floodlight, introduced in about 1924
- 150/250W baby focus spot for use in the footlight position, introduced in about 1925
- 1000W or 20A arc 13-42° focus spot, with a 6"x9" (or 10") lens was introduced around 1925, available as an optical effects projector and a spot manufactured for FOH work, fitted with horizontal and vertical shutters and an iris, and with tracker wire operated 4-colour changers
- 1000W down-light flood of medium beam angle fitted with spill rings, introduced in about 1928

By about 1930, the Strand range consisted of the following lanterns, now given Pattern numbers:[62]

- Focus spots at 250W (Patt. 27); 500W (Patt. 44); and 1000W (Patt. 23)
- Medium angle floods 500W (Patt.30) and 1000W (Patt. 49 & 30A)
- Very wide angle arena flood for down-lighting, 1000W (Patt. 35)
- Stelmar profiles 500W and 1000W (Patt. 63)
- An arc optical effects projector (Patt. 33)
- Two arc followspots (Patt. 22 & 42)
- Battens and footlights. Solenoid operated colour changers for battens were introduced in 1931

In an article in *Tabs*, Bentham recalled that before 1934 only the focus lantern could isolate areas of the stage.[63] He noted that the first Strand Patt.

---

12 compartments on a bar (hence the 12 way spot bar and the 12 way portable board) This indicates the small size of stage found in Britain. (*Sightline* 9/1, Spr. 75, p33).

[60] Legge, B. *ABTT Information Sheet*, London: ABTT, 1998.

[61] The focus spot had a variable beam angle, could accept a beam reduction mask and was fitted with a plano-convex lens.

[62] Bentham recalled that despite the crudity of early lanterns, he could remember finding one of the original Patt 23's still in use at the Savoy Theatre in 1960! (*ABTT News* Feb, 83. p3).

[63] *Tabs* 9/2, Sept. 51, p20.

23 focus spot "soon became the basic workhorse for stage lighting in this country"[64] and this was the directional light used on shows such as *Bitter Sweet* at His Majesty's in 1929,[65] *Evergreen* at the Adelphi in 1930[66] and *Cavalcade* at Drury Lane in 1931.[67] A 2kW version of the focus spot also became available, and was noted for its use on Hassard Short's *Waltzes from Vienna* at the Alhambra in 1931, *Wild Violets* at Drury Lane in 1932 and *Stop Press* at the Adelphi in February 1935. Unfortunately the beam from the focus spot was not smooth and a frost gelatine was often used to soften its unattractive beam edge.[68]

The rise of the focus spot with an incandescent lamp after 1920 prompted the decline of the lime and arc for general lighting duties. In theory, it could be hung anywhere and dimmed from the control console. The spot began to dominate the No. 1 on-stage bar, evicting the batten from this position. The ability to localise areas of the stage with light now became easier, and from a greater range of angles – a crude alternative to create a localised effect had been to split the battens and footlights onto three dimmers, left, centre, and right.

The first lantern to light the stage in a crisp, hard edged spot was introduced in 1927.[69] Called the *Stelmar*, it had a beam angle of 16½°, a 1000W lamp and the optics were of sufficient quality to give the lantern significant punch.[70] Accessories included horizontal and vertical adjustable shutters and an iris. Ridge and Aldred maintained it was the first lantern to accept a gobo, although there are no records of gobos being used during this period.[71] It was big (3'

---

[64] *Tabs* 34/3, Aut. 76, p19. It was superseded by the Patt. 43 in 1933.

[65] A production the *Daily Telegraph* of 19/7/29 described as "brilliant.. and a wealth of light and colour" (Theatre Museum Archives).

[66] Where Strand had undertaken a new installation of floods and spots instead of battens.

[67] Where 26 electrically operated colour changers were fitted to the dress circle front, driven by a special temporary control made by Strand *(Tabs* 35/2, Sum. 77, p9).

[68] *Tabs* 16/3, Dec. 58, p18. Ridge and Aldred said that frosts were commonly used to soften the edge of focus spots, noting that even the finest frost need a hole cutting in the centre so as not to over diffuse the beam. This trick could also be used to get more light in the centre of a coloured beam by making a small hole in the centre (Ridge and Aldred, *Stage Lighting, Principles and Practice*, London: Pitman, 1935, p109)

[69] It had been patented in September 1925 (*Sightline* 15/2, Aut. 81, p82).

[70] An amalgam of the names of its inventors, Steel and Martin

[71] *Cue* 31, Sep. 84, p23. Also, in their book *Stage Lighting, Principles and Practice,* the line diagrams of the Stelmar profile spot include suggestions for the insertion of "masks, cut-outs, stencils or coloured slides... which give a fairly sharp image when projected". A diaphragm or shutters could also be inserted at the gate to vary beam size and shape. This is the first full (cont...)

long), expensive and heavy by modern standards.[72] Indeed the Stelmar was so expensive that the Memorial Theatre Stratford thought it only necessary to purchase four during the 1932 refit (see Appendix ii).[73] A followspot version of this lantern appeared in the same year, fitted with a 6-colour magazine.[74]

Colour

In 1925 Digby's range of 10 gelatine colours was expanded, and Harold Ridge refers to 24 Digby colours plus three frosts in his book of 1928.[75] Digby also made thick frost for flooding, thin frost for general spotting, and a focus frost for focusing. Digby Gelatine was available in sheets 22" x 17½". Their range was progressively increased to 40 colours.[76] Lamp dip was used too, and Joe Davis recalled that about 30 lamp-dip colours were still available c1928.[77]

It is interesting to note that while the Digby range covered the full range of hues, few unsaturated colours were manufactured until the late 1930s. This is mainly due to the use of colour as a mixing agent on stage. Pale tones were achieved through additive mixing of the battens, and were not seen as important to manufacture. It is interesting to note that it was common for theatres to make their own gelatines, so it is possible that paler colours might have been home made. Ridge and Aldred noted the problems making a blue that did not fade in gelatine or acetyl-cellulose.

Little has been documented concerning the use of colour during this period.

---

reference to the use of a beam controlling device inserted into the gate of the profile. They referred to the Gobo – a lantern fitted with a "perforated metal plate" to create a moon shape, and interestingly noted that "the untrained or casual audiences - such as those we get in the West End - find it difficult to accept abstract lighting". Given the aesthetic and dramatic value this technique offered, it is suprising that there were so few mentions of this technique until the 1960's.

[72] £36 in the 1935 Strand catalogue.

[73] *Sightline* 16/2, Aut. 82, p110.

[74] An early architectural use of the Stelmar was recorded spotting Nelson in Trafalgar Square in 1931.

[75] Bentham noted that there were no very pale colours manufactured before 1938, which was surprising given the low intensity output of the lanterns of the time. The only pale gelatines were (in Strand numbers) No. 3 Straw (warm) and No. 17 (cool) until No. 36 Surprise Pink (a neutral) arrived in 1930. Colours were still produced with reference to their need to be mixed in battens to achieve a variety of colours – hence the emphasis on stronger tones. Pale colours would have been needed only for spots or front of house lighting (where more natural flesh tones are required), which of course had less of a role to play at this time (*Tabs* 22/1, Mar. 64, p63).

[76] Digby continued to manufacture gelatine until 1962, despite being merged into Strand in 1949.

[77] *Tabs* 37/1, Dec. 80, p26.

Digby's colour range	
Number	Colour
1	Yellow
2	Light amber
3	Dark amber
4	Salmon
5	light pink
6	Dark pink
7	Light red
8	Dark red
9	Magenta
10	Steel blue
11	Light blue
12	Dark blue
13	Moonlight green
14	Light green
15	Dark green
16	Violet
17	Straw
18	Middle blue
19	Middle straw
20	Middle pink
21	salmon pink
22	Purple
23	New green
24	New blue

Davis recalled that No.3 Straw was used for daylight (interior or exterior) and No.18 blue for night.[78] Adrian Klein noted in his book that that 'kaleidoscope' coloured gels could be made that when projected "makes a remarkably beautiful display".[79] This was made by mixing drops of a solution of rhodamine into the setting gelatine, which penetrated it in a tree-like pattern.

In his 1928 book, Ridge detailed more advanced colour concepts. He advocated a natural use of colour, stating that contrasting colours on either side of the face enhanced dimension. He firmly believed that colour should not be used to "merely gain a pretty effect", and should only be used when representing nature or to aid atmosphere. He talked at length of differing ways to mix colours for cyclorama work, with dimmer setting suggested to produce colour mixes. He also mentioned for the first time the problem of colour temperature change when dimming lights, although not the artistic impact of this.[80] In his book of 1935, written with Aldred, he advocated when lighting from the sides choosing the colour of the motivating light, then using its complementary from the other side at a lower level, to make "white" where the colours overlap.[81]

Ridge and Aldred still promoted the use of glass, feeling that it was the only satisfactory medium for lanterns over 200W. Referring to its colour consistency, they said that the

---

[78] *Tabs* 37/1, Dec. 80, p26.

[79] Klein, A. *Coloured Light – an Art Medium,* London: The Technical Press, 1937, p180.

[80] Ridge, *Stage Lighting,* p83.

[81] To illustrate this, they referred to Herbert M. Prentice's Cellar Scene from Toller's *The* (cont...)

advantage of coloured glass was the variety of repeatable colour mixes from the switchboard. However, they noted that glass was inefficient, and needed 50+% more wattage power than gelatine, and offered some useful advice for assessing power requirements when lighting a cyclorama: for blue, allow 4 watts per square foot minimum for gelatine, 6-7 watts for glass, and with one half of this for green and red colours.

Dimmers

There were very few developments in dimming until the 1930s. Most British theatres were fitted with liquid dimmers by the early 1920s, and these were perfectly adequate. There are few records of how many dimmers theatres were fitted with, although it seems that 12 or 18 ways of dimming was the most common. By 1930 a 50 dimmer installation would have been considered large.[82] On the relatively small number of dimmers installed in theatres in the 1920s and '30s, Bentham noted that "four-colour compartment battens and footlights were wonderful circuit economisers".[83]

Dimmers remained bulky and caused restrictions where the lighting control console could be placed. Otherwise rarely did dimmers restrict potential. If a theatre's stock of dimmers was inadequate for a show, more could be hired in. While most theatres were equipped with liquid dimmers, some installations also had the resistance versions.

Control Systems

There were no new developments in lighting control systems during this period. The existing system, where a handle controlled a colour group via a liquid or wire-wound dimmer, was simple if limited in artistic potential. This control method was now developed to its maximum capability.

The first changes were with safety in mind. Prior to the 1920s, controls had potentially lethal 'live' bus-bars exposed on the front panel, with circuitry controlled by open 'knife switches' that gave off arcing flashes during operation that would have been seen by the audience. The first safe 'dead front' control was installed at the Old Vic in 1922.[84]

Machine Wreckers - "a bare stage lit with blue from one side and yellow from the other, and the general mood of the scene, a miserable drabness, was admirably conveyed by the even greyish-white light that resulted" (Ridge and Aldred, *Stage Lighting, Principles and Practice,* p108).

[82] *Tabs* 22/1, Mar. 64, p31.

[83] *Tabs* 30/1, Mar. 72, p23.

[84] *Tabs* 42/1, Feb. 85, p3.

Strand built their first control system in 1923, installed at the New Cross Empire. It comprised four colour mixing shafts linked by tracker wire to 32 liquid dimmers. From the mid 1920s, Strand had become the most common manufacturer of this type of control. Their early models were called 'Bracket Handle'[85] and later 'Sunset', and these developed into a model called the 'Grand Master'. All worked the same way. There were many other manufacturers of control too, including Major, Blackburn Starling and Micklewright. Each copied the best features of their competitors. Many of these controls had a long life: the author recalls using a Sunset control at St. Luke's Theatre Exeter in the mid 1970s and a Blackburn Starling control at Stanford Hall Loughborough in the early 1980s.

The Sunset Control

An example of a Strand *Sunset* was installed in 1929 at the Regent Theatre Hanley, a variety-cine house. It was sited on a perch, down stage right, and controlled 18 dimmers via three shafts. These fed a typical three-coloured lighting system of battens, footlights and dips, supplemented by front-of-house arcs. The total electrical load was 36kW. This was considered adequate to light a stage 12m wide by 10m deep, which makes an interesting comparison with a contemporary installation. The control had a more advanced feature whereby the three main shafts could be linked to a second set of shafts by a worm drive to enable very slow fades. Dimmers were the wire wound resistance type. The largest capacity board made to the 'Sunset' specification was a 48 dimmer control.

The 'Grand Master' Control

The largest control built by Strand at this time was called the *Grand Master*. The first, a 42 way control, was installed at the Alexandra Hall Theatre Halifax in 1931.[86] Many Grand Masters were built, and such was their cheapness that they were still being installed well after more advanced technology had become common.[87]

---

[85] "a cheaper affair than a Grand Master" – Bentham (*Sightline* 13/2, Aut. 79, p91).

[86] The Halifax Building Society had built a commercial complex that included a 600 seat theatre. The consulting engineers on this project were Ridge and Aldred. The dimmers were Mansel and Ogan's Cecil Plate type, unlike previous Strand resistance dimmers that were made by the Dutch company Hasemeyer. The control was fitted with a reverse differential.

[87] *Tabs* 22/1, Mar. 64, p43. The last one was fitted at the Gaiety Dublin in 1955 (*Tabs* 14/3, Dec. 56, p10).

The Grand Master, which reached its peak of development in the 1930s, had some major operational weaknesses. On some versions, shafts could only move in one direction at a time, so lights could either fade up or down but not crossfade. A reverse differential was developed to allow crossfading, but some controls in major theatres were never fitted with this device.[88]

One of the largest capacity Grand Masters made was a 90 way for the Opera House Blackpool, installed in 1938. It was massive: 13'6" wide and 7'10" high, and was sited on a platform over prompt corner. Percy Corry recalled that two operators were usually necessary.[89] Bentham was quoted in 1956 as saying that the Grand Master with 80/90 dimmers represented: "the ultimate in direct operated control as far as this country is concerned... It is difficult to work up much enthusiasm over the large Grand Master board unless we approach it from a strictly historical standpoint and it now subscribes little or nothing to modern lighting techniques".[90]

Bentham was clearly not a fan of this control system, and was keen to promote emerging systems of his own design. However, he recalled in 1978 that in the early 1930s when he joined Strand, people were "perfectly content with the existing Grand Master and other direct operated manual control boards. They did not question the use of (it)".[91] He went on to say that if one person was not enough to run a cue, then more were drafted in; and if the control had insufficient capacity, temporary boards and operators were hired in.

There can be little doubt that the Sunset and Grand Master 'shaft-locking' style of controls created many problems for those who set the lighting. Bentham noted that: "it is a matter of seeing the lighting plot in terms of the board, and not asking of it what may take several men hours of practice to do".[92] The control was restricted in its capacity to run rapid multi-cue sequences, and dictated a style of design limited to a number of well defined changes. This was because of the way in which fades were executed, a problem inherited from predecessors that had not been addressed. Lanterns did not change intensity in proportion to the overall changing picture, as happens routinely today. When fading channels at different levels either up or down, those closest to their final destination arrived first, and those with the greatest intensity

---

[88] Such as the Haymarket Theatre.
[89] *Cue* 8, Nov. 80, p6.
[90] *Tabs* 14/3, Dec. 56, p10.
[91] *Tabs* 36/3, Aut. 78, p7
[92] *Tabs* 6/3, Dec. 48, p25.

difference arrived last. Thus lighting pictures would have been most unbalanced when fading in or out, with uneven pockets of colour or intensity gradation across the stage. With skilled and alert operation some of these problems could be overcome, either by 'slipping' handles on or off at appropriate moments to 'smooth out' the fade. But these were bulky, unwieldy controls, normally sited with poor vision of the stage. Most lighting must have looked very crude by today's 'dipless crossfade' standard. It is no wonder that cues mid-scene were rare, and subtle shifts in atmospheric emphasis would have been most unlikely. Fast cueing sequences also would have been almost impossible unless they involved only single circuits. It took time to lock each handle onto a shaft at the correct position, and the bigger the system, the longer this took, unless more operators were employed. Systems were often installed to allow expansion – it was not uncommon in the West End for there to be two permanent controls, as well as several portable controls, each with their own operator. While solving capacity problems, co-ordinated operation must have been difficult, and the visual result of this could not have been pleasant. Such was the crudity of lighting control that initially these controls were not even supplied with calibrated scales to allow precise setting of light levels.[93]

The size and limitations of controls from this period dictated that up to four operators was typical. "An operator had to be an acrobat or an octopus to execute crossfades or blackouts with a fast return," said Davis, who noted that the operator was critical to the success of a design, requiring much skill and extreme patience.[94] He thought that there were very few good ones, due in part to poor pay and long hours, a point confirmed by Ridge and Aldred in 1935.[95]

Temporary and Portable Controls
In 1924, Strand launched a portable control comprising 12 circuits, with wire-wound slider dimmers mounted in a teak case.[96] This made an important

---

[93] Initially they were not fitted as standard by Strand and were for a time an optional extra. However the increased use of spots meant more precise dimmer setting was required, and calibrated scales became standard.

[94] *Tabs* 20/1, Apr. 62, p4.

[95] "There should be a place, and an adequate salary, for this kind of electrician in every theatre of standing... it seems high time to revise the low scale of pay of theatre electricians. The authors know of a few progressive theatres, a very few, where the electrician ranks as engineer-in-charge with a salary on the managerial scale" (Ridge and Aldred, *Stage Lighting, Principles and Practice*, p76).

[96] Legge, B. *ABTT Information Sheet.*

contribution to lighting, as extra control could now be 'hired in', thus giving some freedom to the constriction caused by hard-wired lighting rigs. 'Specials' could now be added to a rig more easily. Temporary cabling and control became a common sight. They were usually installed under stage, and could add up to 60 ways of extra dimming for big shows. Often they remained in the theatres after the show, offering additional semi-permanent control facilities.[97]

Patch Panels

Patch panels, that offered a flexible, assignable link between lantern and dimmer, began to be introduced on a 'telephone exchange' type of system, following the installation of the first at the Parry Opera Theatre in 1925 by Strand.[98] This was in part to reduce the number of dimmers and size of control system required, but also to increase flexibility in the grouping of circuits on the control console. Another bonus was the gradual freeing of hard wired equipment to afford greater freedom to deploy equipment on the basis of design.

The Position of Controls

Although Terence Gray had advocated in 1928 that control operators should have a clear view of the stage, all controls remained positioned on stage in the wings (usually on a platform above stage level). As the operator would normally have his back to the stage, only a partial view would be possible and sensitive operation must have been tricky.[99]

Power Supply

Electricity was still being produced locally, and this created problems as there was no standard. Bob Massey recalled that there was a great range of supply voltages in the 1920s: "very little AC, with DC ranging from 75v at the Empire Cinema in West Ham, 150v at the Rialto Leytonstone, up to 500/250v at the Palace Theatre Bristol".[100] Plugs and sockets were not standardised either, creating additional work when adding equipment to the rig.

---

[97] Temporary controls installed for *Cavalcade* at Drury Lane in 1931 remained after the show, and so did controls for *The Cat and the Fiddle* at the Palace in 1932 (the programme said that Strand installed special lantern housings on the circle front and a 50 way "Dead Front" stage switchboard and dimmer regulator) and *Bow Bells* at the Hippodrome in 1932 (*Tabs* 22/1, Mar. 64, p44).

[98] *Tabs* 22/1, Mar. 64, p12. Unfortunately there is little specific information on patch panels.

[99] From *The Bookman's Journal* in the *Festival Review*, on the Shakespeare Memorial Theatre – Vol. II April 1928 No. XXXVI., cited in ABTT *Newsletter* 4/3, Aut. 70, p21.

[100] *ABTT News*, Aug. 87, p8.

The formation of a National Grid in the 1930s led to the beginnings of a standardised AC supply, although this was still at the whim of local authorities. Many of the problems encountered when touring began to ease. The move away from DC also prompted obsolete control consoles to be upgraded, although this was usually to a Grand Master.

Lighting the Cyclorama

Following Martin Harvey's experiments, British theatre adopted the cyclorama as a scenic device in the early twentieth century. Other than Jackson's brief experiments with a Fortuny cyclorama at Birmingham in 1913, Dean's introduction of the portable Schwabe-Hasait cyclorama to Britain in 1923 (see illustration), and Fagan's work at the Royal Court in the 1920s, theatres installed flat, solid plaster wall cycloramas.[101] Any other installations were temporary for one show only.

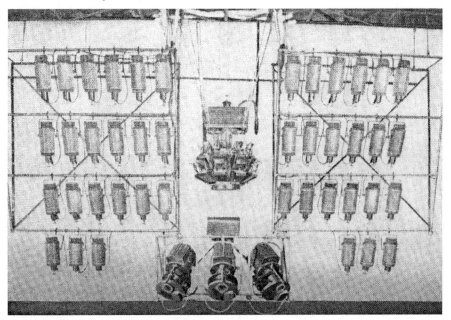

Schwabe system for cyclorama lighting.

---

[101] The Schwabe-Hasait system was not popular in Britain and few theatres invested in it, mainly due to lack of space and cost, and the fact that the painted backcloth was still the norm. It was installed at four theatres: the St. Martin's Theatre in 1923 and Drury Lane in 1924 (both by Basil Dean); the Coliseum in 1931; and Covent Garden in 1934 (but with a GKP projector).

Cyclorama lighting in Britain was more modest than in Europe. Although capable of producing sophisticated effects, the Schwabe system failed to catch on here.[102] The Strand floodlight system became more popular, even though it was less bright.[103] For economy, Ridge had recommended reducing the number of lighting colours from seven to three – red, blue and green, and this was the model for the Strand system, which was widely adopted in Britain, lighting the cyclorama from both above and below. Variation in colour was achieved through mixing at the control console. However, rigid adherence to primary colour mixing proved inefficient. Amber and pink gelatines often substituted red and green in creating sky effects. This gave a much more favourable palette for suggesting a range of atmospheric conditions, such as dawn, sunset, day and night.

Using a cyclorama meant that lights that gave out less spill than the batten were needed on stage. Floods were fitted with funnels to narrow down beam angles to 20 - 30° and these became very popular when used as down and side lights, and were deployed in large numbers. The need to control spill prompted a new range of purpose-designed lanterns to be launched in the mid 1930s.

Projection and Special Effects

The relatively small size of British stages restricted the use of projection. With the technique most effective when projecting from behind a screen, few theatres had the space to accommodate the throw of the light. Scope for front projection was limited by the difficulty in finding a suitable place to locate the projector and the vogue of masking every item of technical equipment.[104] Projection could be used to simulate effects, such as running water, fire, clouds or rain.

---

[102] An article in the *Daily Telegraph* suggested that the benefits of the Strand-Samoiloff batten system, if used with more care, outweighed the Schwabe system. In reference to Dean's system at the St. Martin's: "A lighting system that can do all these things efficiently and easily already exists, but up to present it has been put to the baser uses of engineering music hall "stunts", and in consequence its value to the theatre may have been overlooked... The Hippodrome system (Battens) is a model of ingenuity and efficiency. Wonderfully flexible and entirely independent (if need be) of lights outside the proscenium arch, it seems to me far superior to the Schwabe. The cost of installation is negligible in comparison" (*Tabs* 22/1, Mar. 64, p10 reproducing *Daily Telegraph* article 14/2/24).

[103] "only giving about 20 foot candles full up" (*Tabs* 22/1, Mar. 64, p10).

[104] Ridge and Aldred said that projection had not caught on in this country for several reasons: (1) due to the smaller size of stage; (2) the reliance on footlights and battens, which would wash out images; (3) the medium was inappropriate for touring with venues of differing stage size; (4) the cost of the equipment. (Ridge and Aldred, *Stage Lighting, Principles and Practice*, p103).

Moving effects were initially powered by clockwork motors. However, even the most realistic moving effects were considered to be of dubious artistic merit.

There was little use of projection in Britain beyond the large opera houses and 'art' theatres. The Royal Opera House Covent Garden was equipped with projection in the refit of 1934, with a Hasait cloth and a GKP projector.[105] The large scale slide format (7" x 5"), coupled with the common technique of hand painting slides, meant that it was relatively easy to overcome angle of distortion problems.[106] However, projection came to the fore in 'art' theatres, and some sophisticated work was undertaken. Notable productions include *R.U.R.* by Karel Capek, produced by George Harris at the St. Martin's Theatre in 1923. Harris projected a backcloth design for the last act, using an arc to project through four foot square gelatine frames, Linnebach-style.

There are also records of projection being used at the Westminster Theatre, for instance McArthur's *Tobias and the Angel* in 1930.[107]

Ridge and Aldred's book of 1935 offered excellent technical description of projected cloud and associated effects and for projected scenery, and discussed *The Insect Play* by the brothers Capek, directed by Dr. Hilar at the National Theatre in Prague, as a case study for projection.[108] Other effects that were used included Ultra-Violet (UV) or 'Black Light' effects, of which the first recorded use was at the Gaiety Theatre London by Leonard Applebee, probably in the late 1910s.

The Rise of Front of House Lighting

Front of house (FOH) lighting was very limited at the beginning of the twentieth

---

[105] The Viennese firm Geyling, Kann and Planer. It was initially fitted with a 100A arc light source, but later converted to a 60v 50A source.

[106] One of its first uses was for the distant palace of Valhalla in the *Ring* in 1934.

[107] *Tabs* 22/1, Mar. 64, p39. An article in the *Illustrated London News* of 3/10/1931 featured more examples. Photographs showed single and multiple projector images projected onto flat and curved cyclorama, creating both realistic and non-realistic images of the highest quality and accuracy (*Cue* 32, Nov. 84, p11).

[108] Ridge and Aldred, *Stage Lighting, Principles and Practice*, p99. The book details the use of powerful wide angle magic-lantern type of apparatus to project onto the cyclorama. Slides were painted onto glass and water cooled in the lantern to avoid fracture. They went on to describe both the Linnebach technique and the G.K.P. system: "this system was perfected in Vienna, at the Burg Theatre, and also used at the Odeon Paris and elsewhere", and picked out the work of Strobach, who was noted for projection work at Cologne Opera House. The G.K.P. system might have become common in Britain had it not been for patents and the insistence that slides were made up in Vienna.

century. Arcs and limes were commonly positioned FOH either at the rear of the gallery or in the roof, where they could be accessed for followspot operation, but fixed positioned incandescent spots were very rare. It is known Tree experimented with FOH lighting in 1910, although Dean, having used this technique from 1912, claimed that its first regular use was at the St. Martin's Theatre, where baby spots imported from America were positioned on the dress circle front.[109]

It was a long time before FOH spot lighting became the vogue. The next West End theatre to equip was the Old Vic, which had short spot bar fitted above the orchestra in late 1920s. But it was not until August 1931 that this type of lighting first hit the headlines when American producer Hassard Short used a large number of Kleigl spots, fitted with four colour changers, for *Waltzes from Vienna* at the Alhambra Theatre Leicester Square. The lighting was recorded as "outstanding" and the use of massed spots from FOH was noted as "a real first".[110] Most West End theatres thereafter installed this lighting position. For example, 26 spots were fitted to the circle front for *Cavalcade* at Drury Lane in 1931[111] and a spot bar was fitted over the orchestra at Sadler's Wells in 1931. Julian Wylie fitted FOH spots for *Bow Bells* at the Hippodrome in 1932, about which *The Times* (3/1/1932) said that public would see a new method of presentation, with "most of the lighting projected from 24 x 1kW lamps in front of the dress circle".[112] Unusually, there were no house tabs or footlights used in this production.

Davis recalled that local managements and authorities often opposed the installation of FOH lanterns, so they had to be fitted or boxed in. He believed the tour of *The Gay Hussar* in 1933 was the first use of FOH spots outside London.[113]

The developing spotlight approach to lighting the stage required more complex and refined control. Each lantern now needed to be allocated to its own dimmer and individually balanced to a precise level. The limitations of existing control consoles now became even more apparent, which should have heralded the demise of the 'Grand Master' style control, although they remained in the catalogues until the 1950s.

---

[109] *Tabs* 20/3, Dec. 62, p13.

[110] *Cue* 30, Jul. 84, p8, and *Tabs* 7/2, Sep. 49, p5.

[111] *Sightline* 12/2, Aut.78, p104. The upper circle spots were not fitted until 1958.

[112] Theatre Museum Archives

[113] *Sightline* 10/2, Aut. 76, p50.

The Lighting Rig of the Period

Bentham recalled that the lighting rig of the early 1930s would comprise following arcs from front of house and sometimes twelve or so 1kW focus spots behind the proscenium to supplement footlights and battens. Davis confirmed that arcs were still common from front of house, although they had been replaced on stage, where a man would now sit to follow, refocus and colour the Patt. 43s.[114] However, this was restricted to a few wealthy theatres and most continued to be equipped with outdated lighting. John Counsell recalled in *Tabs* that the Theatre Royal Windsor, which he joined in 1933, still had the original 1910 installation.[115] This included dipped lamps in open troughs, controlled by liquid dimmers and knife switches.[116] Bentham recalled that most theatres before 1939 still had old knife-switch DC boards with tracker wires to liquid dimmers.[117] Mervyn Gould recalled in *Tabs* that the New Theatre Boston still used water dimmers and uncovered knife switches to control the 3-colour battens and footlights right up to its demolition in 1962.[118]

The most common technique for lighting the stage was still to flood light with footlights, battens and wing floods. It was normal for London theatres to be fitted with sets of four colour battens and footlights as the standard rig. This would be supplemented by followspots to light the principals.[119] Extra equipment, such as spots, was hired in by the show, which went some way to giving a changeable look to stage lighting. It was still common for a show to return its specials to the hire company after reviews were published as a way to cut costs. However by the early 1930s hiring rigs and lanterns had become big business in the West End, and occasionally this could free a show of the restrictions of the fixed rig.

---

[114] *Sightline* 10/2, Aut. 76, p50.

[115] *Tabs* 43/1, Spr. 76, p18.

[116] Although in the 1930s this was supplemented by some spots and a six way portable control, it was not until 1938 that a new control was installed, three banks of 12 circuits made by Strand. Although it offered a great advance, it was noisy to operate and the operator could not see the stage. This system remained until 1964 when a 72 way control was installed in a FOH position.

[117] *Tabs* 38/1, June 81, p20.

[118] *Tabs* 33/2, Sum. 75, p19.

[119] Other uses of limes were that from front of house they were often set on flood focus to give a front wash to the stage (in conversation with John G. Holton). Another unusual technique was practised at the Opera House Covent Garden in the 1930s, where the limes were not used to followspot, but as repositionable lights. Following the actor was achieved by crossfading from spot to spot, and this technique was used for many years (*Sightline* 21/1, Sum. 87, p27).

Rigs were sometimes large, with the largest shows hanging as much equipment as shows in the 1960s.[120] Although lanterns might have been limited in their performance, no-one recalled shows being under lit. On the overall brightness of shows, *Tabs* recorded that "there could not have been much light, yet memory paints Short's *Stop Press* as full of glitter and colour and novel lighting effects".[121] *Cue* noted Joe Davis's recollection that this show "was the peak of what could be done with lanterns of the type common before the pageants, acting areas and mirror spots introduced in 1936".[122] To benchmark the brightness of lanterns from this period, Bentham said that a 1kW focus spot was about as bright as a 1950s 500W profile.[123]

There is little evidence to suggest that most British theatre lighting pre-World War Two made an artistic contribution beyond being merely a crude, coloured illuminant. Bentham recalled that lighting technique in the late 20s and early 30s was to "put down washes of light and use a few spots as highlights, except of course in very dramatic scenes. Even so it is amazing how telling a couple or even one spotlight then could be".[124] Joe Davis noted that lighting in the early 1930s still had no need to make shadow, as it continued to be painted into the scenery.[125] Painted cloths were the order of the day for most settings, and the general principle was that light should complement the atmosphere of the cloth, not alter it. Irving Wardle said that "good atmospheric lighting was a great rarity on the pre-war British stage".[126]

Bentham confirmed that the Strand policy of the 1930s "under Applebee's Theatre Lighting Department was to supply battens, footlights and a Grand Master".[127] The art of lighting developed at a pace governed by commerce. However, in an article in *Cue* in 1984, Davis confirmed that "it was possible to perform sensitive lighting with this type of equipment, given the will to do it",

---

[120] Bentham compared Cochran's *The Miracle* (Lyceum 1932) with *Blitz!* (Adelphi 1962) (*Tabs* 22/1, Mar. 64, p44).

[121] *Tabs* 22/1, Mar. 64, p46.

[122] *Cue* 30, Jul 84, p8+.

[123] *Tabs* 20/1, Apr. 62, p14.

[124] *Tabs* 30/1, Mar. 72, p23.

[125] *Sightline* 10/2, Aut. 76, p50.

[126] Wardle, I. *The Theatres of George Devine*, London: Jonathan Cape, 1978, p70.

[127] Bentham, F. *Sixty years of light work*, London: Strand, 1992, p68. He had earlier said, distancing himself from their commercial success, "we can never make enough; miles and miles since the originals of Samoiloff's days... in spite of all the efforts of our lectures and representatives to convince people that this is not a proper way to light a stage!" (*Tabs* 22/1, Mar. 64, p114).

citing the following as an example of effective lighting from the period:

> "I suppose that memory can play tricks but when I look back on the shows I saw and worked on in those days they were very well lit and had marvellous visual effects. I remember the last scene of Wylie's *Good Companions* at His Majesty's in 1931 when Jess Oakroyd is going off to Canada. There was a cloth painted black for the side of the liner. There were holes cut in it for portholes with two Patt 49's in amber to light them up. There was a canvas gangplank... There was a bit of smoke, the sound of the ship's siren and a few bits of rope and No.19 blue in the batten. Jess was discovered downstage with his back to the audience looking up at the great liner. A followspot in No. 17 Steel Blue picked him up and as he walked slowly upstage towards the gangplank the curtain came slowly down. So with great economy and simplicity you had all the atmosphere of a great liner leaving her berth".[128]

The most adventurous approach came from Ridge in his book of 1928. Noting that in the period up to electric light, where the stage was a shadow-less place, except when an arc or lime came on, he said that with the growing power of electric lamps, higher contrast and resultant shadow became a visual feature. He stressed the need to balance lighting angles carefully, in creating the illusion of directional lighting, such as lighting through a window, but in so doing preserving visibility. He said that shadows normally should be killed, through careful balance of lighting angles, but that natural shadows were useful to create a sense of interiors or silhouette scenes, or showing a key light such as a moon. Lanterns should be angled to avoid light spilling onto the cyclorama or background, so that this can be lit separately. He suggested that downstage should be more brightly lit than upstage. For a small stage, he said that 1100W of light was needed to illuminate downstage, 600W midstage and 400 watts upstage.[129] On the question of how bright the stage was, Bentham compared lighting from the 1920s and from the 1970s, recalling that "from contemporary press cuttings one finds an occasional remark about (Dean's) lighting being too dim in his Schwabe-Hasait days at the St. Martin's, but we read similar notices occasionally for Covent Garden today with 1¼ megawatts on call. The only certain things are that the general level of lights *everywhere* was much, much lower than today and that there were far, far fewer pieces of equipment used".[130]

---

[128] *Cue* 30, Jul. 84, p8+.

[129] Ridge, *Stage Lighting,* p76.

[130] *Tabs* 29/1, Mar. 71, p28.

With the growing use of spots on stage, lighting technique now began to diverge from flooding the stage with colour washes to lighting actors in compositions created from individual beams, although perhaps still supported by batten lighting, especially upstage. A major change in the way light was used on stage was occurring, which accompanied the growth of front of house spotlights. This new approach prompted the development of new lanterns and control, and "painting the stage with light" began.[131]

Developments in Lighting Technology, 1935-1950

Some significant new products were developed in the mid 1930s that offered a much greater potential for stage lighting. These developments included controls, lanterns and colour, and prompted the upgrading of facilities in many major venues.

Lamps

There were no significant new developments in this period, with the 'A' and 'B' class lamps still used. Arcs continued as the source for followspots and projectors. There was a theory, articulated by Bentham, that lamp manufacturers in a cartel could not see the commercial benefit in producing a lamp really suited to theatre use, and as a result such a lamp was not manufactured until 1951 when mass-produced spotlighting proceeded to take off.[132]

Lanterns

Four new lanterns were launched that heralded the arrival of the contemporary lighting rig. In the mid 1930s Strand made a profile spot for front of house and precise spotting duties, a punchy side-light to replace the arc, and a directional top-light to supplement the battens and offer a dynamic new texture from above that would also keep spill off the cyclorama. In the 1940s Furse introduced the Fresnel lantern, a focusable soft-edged area light.

These new lanterns were to form the bedrock of stage lighting for the next forty or so years.[133] However, they were initially developed only as 1kW

---

[131] Bentham noted that individual lanterns offered great artistic potential, but would demand a new generation of controls, when he said that "this is the very essence of painting with light - the balancing of intensities here and there, and then the gradual or fast change from one set of balances to another. And more dimmers will require a more flexible control system. Increase in localised light will mean increase in complexity of control" (*Tabs* 14/3, Dec. 56, p10).

[132] Bentham, *Sixty Years of Light Work*, p63.

[133] Bentham said in 1971 that there had been no fundamental progress in lantern (cont...)

instruments, in part because of the reluctance of British lamp manufactures to make a more powerful 2kW lamp. Strand recognised that tungsten spotlights needed to be brighter, and as they were unable to achieve this through increasing the power, they turned their attention to developing more efficient optical systems to get more light from the existing 1kW lamp.

The Patt. 73 'Mirror Spot'

Tabs reported that the Patt. 73 *Mirror Spot*, a profile lantern, was first used in *Young Madame Conti* at the Savoy Theatre in 1936, with six hung on the upper circle front.[134] It proved popular, and soon became the standard front of house lantern. It was the first alternative to the expensive Stelmar profile, being a cheaper, cruder version with an 8" reflector, gate and 6x9" lens. It was reviewed in the first issue of *Tabs*, which detailed all its facilities, although it made no mention of its ability to project a gobo.[135] Bentham recalled that the Patt. 73 was first made in batches of 50,[136] and was immediately advertised as being available for hire.[137]

The Patt. 50 'Pageant'

The Pageant of the Tower of London in May 1935 was the catalyst for the development by Strand's Bentham and Jack Bennett of a low cost, powerful,

---

development since the 1930s – all the lanterns of the 1970 rig were there by the mid 30s (*Tabs* 29/2, June 71, p53).

[134] *Tabs* 22/1, Mar. 64, p62.

[135] Despite the artistic potential of the gobo (and its cheapness and ease of manufacture), there was no mention of it since Ridge's book of 1935. Bill Bundy recalled using gobos at the Royal Opera House in the early 1950s, cut from tin plate (*Sightline* 13/2, Aut. 79, p114). Francis Reid in discussion recalled first use of one in 1962 at Glyndebourne, and Michael Northen's first use was in *Twelfth Night* at Stratford in 1964 (*ALD meeting*) (although this must be incorrect as the play was not in the repertoire that season. It is more likely the year was 1960 when Northen did indeed light this play). It is interesting to note that Bentham made no mention of the gobo in his book *Stage Lighting* of 1950. Bentham had incorrectly noted in 1984 that the gobo was first referred in Britain in about 1961, but it could in fact be fitted into a Stelmar and also the Patt 73 (*Cue* 31, Sep. 84, p23).

[136] *Sightline* 13/2, Aut. 79, p114. Until the launch of the Patt. 23 (manufactured by the 5,000), lanterns had been made in batches of 50 or 100, and, before 1939 lanterns other than the batten were only made a dozen at a time.

[137] Profiles caught on slowly in Britain, whereas the Leko, with wattages up to 3kW, was a great success in America. It is interesting to note that profiles caught on even later in Germany, not featuring in manufacturers' catalogues until the late 1950s. Bentham said that "no (British) theatre management bought anything in those days if they could help it". Batches of 50 indicated confidence in the product by Strand. In contrast, the Stelmar had only been made in small numbers.

narrow beam instrument. It adopted the name *Pageant*, although formally called Patt. 50. The lantern was the forerunner of the 1980s *Parcan*, and in its time made a major contribution to the look of the stage, although initially Bentham recalled that "nobody wanted it as they disliked the streaky light and only by fitting a diffuser glass could a few experiments be launched".[138] When it caught on, it was used on stage for either sunlight or moonlight – as it had the power to cut through a normal ambience. The lantern was normally hung in the wings, cross-lighting the stage and giving three-dimensional form and shape to actors and scenery.[139]

A champion of the Pageant was the director George Devine, who loved to use it as a horizontal side light to edge-light the actor. He also liked its punch for long throws, and requested a 2kW version to complement the 1kW unit. He said "the pageant is a bold and definite light. It gives the kind of clarity which the theatre needs as it emerges from the muddy gloom of naturalism".[140]

Another advocate was Joe Davis, who said that it could "punch in from fly rails or bridges for high cross or back lighting", although he too would have liked a 2kW version. He thought that often the Pageant was overpowered, and had to be run on check so as not to over-key the face. Bentham believed that the style of lighting created by the Pageant was unique to Britain at that time.

The Patt. 56 'Acting Area'

The refit of the Royal Opera House Covent Garden stage in 1934 prompted the development of the *Acting Area* lantern, called the Patt. 56, and a copy of a successful German lantern but of much greater efficiency. Although the lantern was formally listed as a flood, it had a 26° beam angle.[141] It was called "Acting Area" due to its role on stage, as it offered a controlled area lighting beam. While it often was used to supplement battens, top light could now be employed as a localising device, or, used *en masse*, to provide a blanket ambience to the stage without spill on the cyclorama.[142]

---

[138] *Tabs* 22/1, Mar. 64, p60.

[139] Bentham recalled the first theatre use of the Pageant, at His Majesty's Theatre in 1935. Two were hung off the fly rail and shone brightly down into a courtyard. He said it was "the best moonlight yet seen on any London stage" (*Sightline* 16/2, Aut. 82, p110).

[140] *Tabs* 11/1, Apr. 53, p6.

[141] The Patt. 56 was later superseded by the Patt 76, (which had a more pleasing shape), and from 1951 was available as a variable beam angle 21°-38° lantern.

[142] *The Stage* 2/6/60. Bentham's claim at the time to originality in the design of the acting (cont...)

It was initially hard to integrate both the Pageant and the Acting Area into existing rigs because of their additional power, so for a time they remained as 'specials'. It was Robert Nesbitt who first saw the potential of high-powered overhead lighting balanced by cutting side light, which he deployed to lift the performer away from minimal or poor quality war-time settings in his 'spectaculars' such as *Gangway* at the Palladium in 1941.[143] The Pageant and the Acting Area also made a significant impact on lighting ballet and spectacular productions in Britain, with their ability to pick out the artist in a bright beam of light.

The 'Frenca' Fresnel

Furse of Nottingham introduced the Fresnel, a variable focus soft edge wash light, in the mid 1940s. Called the *Frenca*, it was undoubtedly an important new development, but initially did not attract many new customers. The lantern had a variable beam angle of 5-45°, and so could work as either a spot or a flood and was made in 500, 1000, and 2000 watt versions.[144]

There were no other lantern developments of significance.[145]

Rigging

Lanterns in this era were still cumbersome to rig: the quick release hook clamp was not developed until 1959 to replace the traditional two nut and bolt 'L'

---

area flood was, years later, refuted by Basil Dean, in a letter to *The Stage* in 1960. Dean said the lantern's origin was German, developed to complement the Schwabe-Hasait system, "to secure illumination of the middle distance whilst obviating excessive dilution of the background". (Indeed, the German original had been listed by Ridge in his 1935 book). Bentham later admitted that this was indeed true.

[143] Bentham commented in 1951 on the value that these lanterns could offer revue-style presentations "High-intensity colour can be very exciting; warm amber of real kick is quite a different thing from the amber so often seen... Intense blue no longer tied to nocturnal gloom opens up a new world of experience" (*Tabs* 9/2, Sep. 51, p20).

[144] Williams, R.G. *The technique of stage lighting*, London: Pitman, 1947, p53. Furse's main business was in the midlands and the north, and had hardly any influence in London, where Strand saw little need to develop their own fresnel. When they did in the 1950s, the lantern took off.

[145] Major, although specialising in the cinema market in the 1930s, invented the rotating batten, the "Rotalux", where four colour faces rotated about the lamps, thus increasing the wattage available to light the stage by four times (*Sightline* 13/2, Aut. 79, p117). A lantern that failed to catch on was the low voltage spot (with built-in transformers), despite a large quantity being installed at the London Palladium in 1935 as a substitute for battens. The manufacturer is unknown, but Strand chose to copy them, launching them as the Patt 81 low voltage spot. Low voltage lighting was a progressive step forward, although not recognised until 30 years later (*Tabs* 22/1, Mar. 64, p61).

clamp which attached lanterns semi-permanently onto the bar.[146] It is no surprise that there was a reluctance to move lanterns once rigged: lanterns were heavy (by modern standards); the rigging attachment was complicated; the lamp would need to be re-centred; there might not be a power socket at the desired position; the plug might be incompatible with the socket in the new position; the dimmer might not accept the loading of the new lantern. And an arc could only be positioned where a person could feed its carbons. Further to this, tradition dictated that all equipment had to be masked by wings and borders.[147]

Colour

By 1935, Strand marketed a range of 32 coloured and two frosted gelatines. They are listed here in Strand's order, in an attempt to organise their product into colour sequences[148] (see table top right).

In early 1938 the first batch of pale colours for the British market was launched by Strand. These were numbered as shown in table bottom right.

These extended Strand's range to 40 colours and two frosts. The increasing numbers of colours led to the availability of swatch books, for easy colour reference choice.

The 1938 range of pale tones proved very popular, despite only comprising warm tones. British theatre had to wait many years for an equivalent range in pale cool tones.[149] Yet this range paved the way for more detailed, subtle, realistic light to be achieved, and represented a very important step towards the growth of spot lighting. However, even after World War Two, Strand still promoted the traditional method of colouring the stage with colour-mixing battens.[150]

An alternative to gelatine, a cellulose acetate medium called *Cinemoid*, emerged in 1935. It was far more durable than gelatine although it tended to

---

[146] *Lights!* 5/2, Aug. 94, p27. Despite this, Davis claimed he was always moving the kit around (*Cue* 30, Jul. 84, p8).

[147] This rule was not consistently broken until after Kenny's *Oliver* at the New Theatre in 1960 (*Cue* 32, Nov. 84, p11).

[148] Strand 1935 Catalogue

[149] Strand did not extend their pale blue range until the mid to late 1950s, and Lee Filters, whose 201+ range came to dominate this area of the spectrum, did not commence manufacture until the mid to late 1960s (*Tabs* 14/2, Sep. 56, p4 & 18/3, Dec.60, p27 and in conversation with Eddie Ruffell, MD Lee Filters).

[150] The first few editions of *Tabs* in 1946 promoted the use of colour, colour mixing theory, and colour suggestions for lighting the cyclorama, with little if any mention of more refined approaches to the use of colour, or the value of using pale colours in spotlights.

Strand's 1935 colour range			
Number	Colour	Number	Colour
1	Yellow	16	Moonlight blue
3	Straw	17	Steel blue
2	Light amber	18	Middle blue
2a	Light medium amber	19	Dark blue
4	Medium amber	20	Deep blue
33	Deep amber	21	Pea green
5	Orange	22	Moss green
6	Fire red	23	Light green
7	Light rose	24	Dark green
8	Salmon	39	Emerald green
9	Middle salmon	25	Purple
10	Middle rose	26	Mauve
11	Dark pink	29	Heavy Frost
12	Deep rose	31	Light frost
36	Surprise pink (Lavender)	27a	Samoiloff red
14	Ruby	29a	Samoiloff blue
15	Peacock blue	38a	Samoiloff mauve

Strand's 1938 tint range			
Number	Colour	Number	Colour
50	Pale yellow	54	Pale rose
51	Gold tint	55	Chocolate tint
52	Pale gold	56	Pale chocolate
53	Pale salmon	60	Grey

melt and its flame-retarded qualities needed to be improved. The full range of Cinemoid, at the time confusingly called *Chromoid*, but later known again as Cinemoid, was launched just before World War Two, and was available in all colours except Nos. 55, 56 and 60.

Dimmers

There were few important developments in dimming to reach a commercial platform until after World War One. For the most part their placing and control was still restricted by the need to be connected to the control mechanically, either by a direct rod or tracker wires. Motor driven clutch controlled dimmers were developed to accompany the Light Console (which gave their location greater flexibility), the first electrical link. After 1945, electrical links became the norm with the introduction of all-electric dimming. These changes made little difference to their artistic contribution.

Control Systems

Two significant new control systems were developed during this period: the Light Console and the Electronic. Few were sold, as the Grand Master style control continued to be manufactured and installed in the vast majority of theatres. However, theatres that invested in these new controls were at the forefront of developments in lighting design.

The 'Light Console'

The first significant step forward in control design came in 1935 when Strand introduced the Light Console, which was designed by Bentham – see Appendix vi. It was prompted by the need to cater for theatres with a larger dimmer capacity than was practical on a Grand Master style control.[151] Although the

---

[151] Bentham said that the need for a large control – such as 120 ways – prompted a change in technology, as a direct drive board of this capacity could not have been built and installed because of its size (*Tabs* 36/3, Aut. 78, p 7). He also said that "It is generally assumed that if the size of the control panel is reduced by using some form of remote control, either mechanical or electrical, the ideal is reached. This is far from the case. Sixty or more little knobs are little easier for the operator to work than sixty big handles. The only real advantage that this reduction in size gives is the possibility of the control commanding a full view of the stage. Analysis of lighting and possible developments show that in the case of a large stage most changes affect a large number of dimmers at the same time, thereby requiring, in the case of a directly operated board, constant locking and unlocking from the Grand Master. Therefore a control must be designed which enables an operator to group his circuits instantaneously as required, thus allowing him to carry out large numbers of changes in rapid succession" (Bentham, *Sixty Years of Light Work,* p78).

Light Console shared a control philosophy with the Grand Master, it offered far greater potential, in particular the ability to perform quick cue sequences. Ridge and Aldred anticipated the Light Console in their book, saying it "is superior to any system that has been invented hitherto and is likely to hold the field for many years to come".[152] Jim Laws asserted that the "Light Console was so revolutionary, that it took ages for anyone to have the imagination to buy one!"[153] He went on to say the control offered "remote control, portability (lighting sessions in the stalls), snap blackouts and flash up to full (both instantaneous and silent), cross-fades of cunning complexity, instant access to pre-planned grouping and to colour changing". The first, controlling 35 dimmers, was installed in the Strand's demonstration theatre in June 1935. The largest capacity version made was 216 ways for the Theatre Royal Drury Lane and the Coliseum.[154] However, despite the advances made by this lighting control, production was limited to fourteen British and three overseas sales.[155]

The Light Console made a radical departure from the 'handle' control, in that it was based on the cinema organ keyboard and stop console. A key represented a lantern, stops represented groups of lights, and toe pistons cued fades. The control was similar to the Grand Master in that it was based on operating a number of colour masters to which dimmers could be locked for collective movement.[156] There seems little doubt that Bentham was strongly influenced by ideas from the field of Colour Music, as his control had strong echoes of Rimington's 40 years earlier (see Appendix vi).

Ridge and Aldred quoted the philosophy behind this new control, as espoused by Bentham, in their book of 1935:[157]

---

[152] Based on Bentham's description, as it still wasn't working when it went to press (Ridge and Aldred, *Stage Lighting, Principles and Practice*, p79).

[153] *Focus*, May 94, p4.

[154] These were the highest capacity controls in Britain until Covent Garden's 240 ways were fitted in 1964.

[155] Legge, *ABTT Information Sheet*. Warsaw was the last installation in 1956.

[156] For full operating details of the Light Console, refer to either: Ridge and Aldred, *Stage Lighting Principles and Practice*, p79; *Tabs* 15/1, Apr. 57, p20; Bentham, F. *Stage Lighting*, London: Pitman, 1990, p44; Bentham, *Sixty Years of Light Work*, p81.

[157] Ridge & Aldred, *Stage Lighting, Principles and Practice*, p78. Bentham said that the control was advertised as though the operator would be playing a musical instrument, rather than operating a lighting switchboard. The caption read "lighting control at the fingertips", and this clearly suggested a radically new approach. He said that at that time he was convinced that the future of stage lighting lay with the lighting designer sitting at his console and painting the stage with light and working out his own changes directly. Bentham developed the control in part to realise (cont...)

"...the Strand Light Console, so named to avoid confusion with Colour Organs... The Light Console looks like an organ console and its standard mechanism is the same, there the similarity begins and ends. There is no equivalent to the musical scale in light, but the Light Console affords a magnificent opportunity for the artist operator to render "colour music" as an entertainment in itself. In addition to functioning as an ordinary Grand Master cross control board it is claimed that the Light Console also gives-

(1) A pre-set switchboard for 24 scenes

(2) A dimmer pre-set switchboard for 12 scenes

(3) Differential dimming

(4) Pre-selective dimmer positions

(5) Pre-selection of a continuous moving cycle of colour

(6) Portability (the control may be plotted from FOH then moved to normal position for operation), and the console will work the same for any type of dimmers".[158]

Because the Light Console controlled far more dimmers than was practical for a Grand Master, they were aimed at large theatres, and this capacity offered far greater potential for the use of spots than was previously possible.

The main drawback with the control was that the operator did not know what level a dimmer was at. Memory and guesswork were the main operating methods for assessing intensity. Bentham talked of his bluffing around this problem by stating the 'second touch' idea, which he subsequently built into the control.[159] By giving a key a second press, the intensity of the dimmer could be shown on a calibrated dial. A further problem was that lights could only fade at one speed at a time, as there was no way of fading groups of

---

his dream "to play rapid action for jazz", and also said that without doubt a lot of board operators were scared of this control (*Tabs* 16/3, Dec. 58, p28 and *Sightline* 17/1, Spr. 83, p40).

[158] The Light Console utilised the Compton cross-relay, developed for the cinema organ to select groups of stops, used here to select groups of dimmers. This was a cost effective measure, utilising equipment developed for another application to save on expensive R&D. While it may not have been ideal, it worked effectively, although sending controls down the route of group control of circuits rather than individual pre-setting, which was being developed at the same time in America. Pre-setting in Britain was discussed, but an economical way forward could not be found. While the Light Console could select groups of dimmers to be faded from a "memory", it could not "memorise" individual dimmer levels. Moss Mansell had perfected the clutch controlled dimmer movement in 1929, which meant a dimmer could be driven to a position electrically, and then would hold this position mechanically (*Tabs* 22/1, Mar. 64, p32). This new method was first used on the Covent Garden control of 1934, and then taken up in production for the Light Console (for technical information, see *Sightline* 17/1, Spr. 83, p41).

[159] *Cue* 14, Nov. 81, p14.

lights simultaneously at various speeds. The first Light Console had only three cue speeds, 'snap', 5 and 10 seconds, and of course lights still travelled in synchronised movement, with no possibility of proportional fading.[160] Bentham claimed that the development of the control was restricted by funding.[161]

Bentham maintained that the strength of the control was its playability.[162] The control found a home in revue theatres, such as the London Palladium, where smooth flowing colour change was appropriate, and it was ideally suited to lighting musicals, opera, ballet, and other spectacular productions (although this might have been an ambitious claim). It was less well suited to the precision required for drama.[163] The Light Console facilitated Bentham's interest in 'Colour Music' (see Appendix vi), admitting that it was a personalised product when he claimed in 1979 that it was "the perfect instrument for me to express *myself* in lighting", and he went on to say that the Light Console was an operator's control for painting the stage with light, that allowed for quick changes in atmosphere but without subtle intensity level control. He also said that those made were "foisted on the theatre".[164] In practice it was most suited to musical

---

[160] Joe Davis confirmed the limitations of the control by saying that the control "was designed to move banks of lights from A to B" (*Sightline* 17/1, Spr. 83, p41).

[161] Bentham, with hindsight, talked of the restrictions placed by cost and engineering. He claimed he envisaged a more sophisticated control at this time, although it was not possible to prove this to be so. He said in 1971: "in my first control of 1935 I had to make the best of what the technology, then economically practicable, enabled me to do. Ever since it has been a case, as each new development in equipment came along, of reconciling that mixture of advantages and drawbacks which make up its character" (*Tabs* 29/2, June 71, p52). In the previous year he had said "the need for dimmer memory to avoid the labour of plotting was perfectly apparent when drawing up the design of the Light Console in 1933 but the means in practical engineering and economic terms made it a hopeless proposition. Pre-setting of any kind was a difficult and expensive complication in those far-off days. Even a simple thing like a compact lightweight variable load dimmer which everyone knew they wanted had to wait until 1964 to begin to become a practical proposition" (*Tabs* 28/3, Sep. 70, p100). He also said that he considered using the telephone dial back in the '30's as a way of calling up circuits, but the idea was not developed (*Sightline* 14/1, Spr. 80, p38). A letter from Mansell to Bentham indicated concern over the expense of the Covent Garden system (the prototype for the Light Console) in development terms, needing to sell 5 at 20% profit just to recoup R&D costs. However, the Directors backed the experiment (*Tabs* 22/1, Mar. 64, p58). Bentham said that although the multi-preset thyratron control had been available from America, the cost was prohibitive (Bentham, *Sixty Years of Light Work*, p80).

[162] *Tabs* 29/3, Sep. 71, p92.

[163] Bentham said that the Light Console's natural home should have been the cinema (in the late '30's the super cinema was a much more important market than the stage) where sequences of colour-changing light were common to introduce a film. (*Tabs* 36/3, Aut. 78, p7).

[164] *Sightline* 13/1, Spr. 79, p7. Amongst the British theatres that installed the control were: The

and revue, and it informed the concept behind rock concert lighting control systems thirty or so years later. It is not surprising that so few were built as it was a complex machine to operate, and no doubt would not have enthused managements who dealt with tours or personnel used to operating a Grand Master.

The 'Electronic' Console

The modern preset board emerged in Britain after World War Two following the development of the thyratron valve dimmer in America.[165] This dimmer differed from previous types in that it required a continuous voltage from a potentiometer (fader[166]) for control, and heralded the beginning of electronic control of lighting that afforded compact, portable systems that led to today's generation of memory controls. Strand built a prototype single dimmer version in 1947, and then a six way version, and then in 1950 launched the first commercial British lighting control to utilise this technology called the *Electronic*[167] Basil Dean said "after witnessing a practical demonstration of the new Strand Electronic ..., I have no hesitation in declaring this to be the most important advance in electrical equipment for the stage that has been made since 1939".[168] *The Times* (26/10/1950), referring to the New Theatre installation of 1950, noted that the control provided for "the most delicate, intricate, and swift of effects to be controlled by one man".[169] The control also

Palladium in 1941; The Palace Manchester in 1949 (108 channels); Drury Lane 216 ways in 1950; The Stoll Theatre Kingsway in 1950 (with the control located FOH); the Festival Hall in 1951 (84 channels, and fitted with speed controls of snap; 3secs; 7s; 15s; 30sec.); and the Coliseum in 1952 (216 channels, installation No 13). The control was reliable: the Drury Lane Console was in operation until 1975 and a model at the Leicester Haymarket was still in use in 1977 (*Sightline* 17/1, Spr. 83, p47).

[165] The only pre-war example in Britain of a thyratron dimmer system was at the Leicester Square Odeon cinema.

[166] The control device – a fader – was a small, inexpensive device, meaning that many could be built into a slim unit, and in several banks to allow pre-setting. Master controls enabled cross-fading from preset to preset (presets involved the duplication of the rows of faders that allowed the incoming cue to be set up in advance and independently from the cue that was live on stage). Cross-fades could now be proportional, meaning for the first time all lights could fade smoothly in harmony with each other.

[167] The control was the first in Britain to have "dipless" proportional dimming and cross-fading, although this was dropped on the next range of control – the SP – due to technical complexity and cost (*Sightline* 11/2, Aut. 77, p43).

[168] *Tabs* 7/2, Sep. 49, p19.

[169] Theatre Museum Archives.

met the specification laid out by George Devine in *Tabs* in 1948.[170] Strand made over 30, despite reservations about their reliability.[171]

The new control and dimmers offered significant advantages. Being compact it could be sited with a good view of the stage and operated with finger-precision. The lighting rig was now free from group allocated lights, and dimmers were no longer load-dependent. Lights from any part of the stage, and at any intensity, could be smoothly faded in together and seamlessly crossfaded to a new picture. Ranks of faders could be used to store incoming or previous cues, as a simple form of 'memory store'. The coming of this control spelt the end for the Light Console, although the controls were marketed alongside each other for a time in the 1950s. When comparing the Light Console to the Electronic, Bentham said in 1950 that the preset control was best for drama, where precise individual circuit levels were required, but cues did not happen too frequently.[172]

However, the Electronic proved to be unreliable, with a reputation for lights coming on without command, and the dimmers gave off so much heat that maintaining stable conditions through ventilation were problematic. The first, installed in Iceland, was trouble-free. However, Electronics that went into British theatres had some significant problems that the Reykjavik control did not suffer from. This was probably due to the lower ambient temperature in

---

[170] Of the ideal switchboard, George Devine said in an interview in 1948 that it should be compact enough for single operation, and in view of the stage from the front. Lighting must be set precisely, to allow operator to use his "brains", but not in the sense of a "long haired genius playing the lights just as his feelings take him. Ability to see the stage should allow more precision and subtlety in operation as well as accuracy of timing". He said that at present "crude methods of control reduce what should be an orchestration to the level of driving and Underground train". He went on to say that ease of operation was paramount, and layout of controls should suit the hand. He thought that patching should be available so circuits could be grouped for ease of operation. He believed that dimmer controls should be finger sensitive with fine graduated scales, and that all dimmers should be of variable load. He advocated electrical mastering (where all circuits fade in proportion) rather than mechanical mastering (where the lowest circuit reaches black first in a fade out). He stated that fade times up to 15 seconds should be operated by hand, and beyond that by motor (he felt the longest fade time required was seven minutes) (*Tabs* 6/2, Sep. 48, p23).

[171] The first was installed in Reykjavik,1950; the last at the Riverside Studios, 1956. (Legge, *ABTT Information Sheet*).

[172] Bentham, F. *Stage Lighting*, London: Pitman, 1950, p140 and *Tabs* 9/3, Dec. 51, p5. Paget Smith recalled that plotting on the Electronic at Stratford was much quicker and more exacting, as the previous state could be recorded while the new state was being worked on. Also, being able to hold one scene "in store" allowed the producer to "go back a state" to check for continuity and rehearse cues.

Iceland.[173] Lights stuck on at $^1/_3$, $^1/_2$, or full intensity, and fuses blew violently.[174] The control proved very popular for its flexibility and ease of operation, but dimmer problems continued and in early 1954 it was agreed to cease manufacture. However, some of those installed had a long life – the one at the Memorial Theatre Stratford ran until replacement in 1972.

Both the Light Console and the Electronic broke the mechanical tie between control and dimmer for ever. As a result, controls could be better sited in the theatre, and the number of dimmers that could be driven expanded greatly. This in turn increased the number of single lantern-per-dimmer-per-control theatres, which significantly increased the potential for good lighting.[175]

An interesting control oddity appeared during this period that reflected the way in which most theatres were still lit. Such was the dominance of colour mixed lighting that dedicated controls were developed, although few theatres installed them.[176] The first automated colour mixing control appeared as a cinema lighting control in 1929, probably made by Holophane. It worked on

---

[173] Bill Bundy, who installed the first Electronic and dimmers for the National Theatre Reykjavik in 1950, recalled it was fairly trouble-free (*Tabs* 22/1, Mar. 64, p98). Following a trade show in Paris the same year, orders began to flow, and Kliegl manufactured the control under licence for the American market.

[174] For example, in 1950 the New Theatre ordered a Strand 144 way Electronic (to replace a 40 way control), as its compact size meant it could be situated in a small room at back of auditorium and the operator could have full view of stage. There were major problems keeping valves at correct temperature, which caused significant problems for Michael Northen's lighting on the opening night of Alec Guinness's *Hamlet* in May 1951. This, coupled with the control operator getting a cue behind, and then losing his nerve, was recalled by *Sightline*: "the press went to town and this led to the Electronic being taken out" (*Sightline* 17/2, Aut. 83, p48). Northen recalled his design as "dark and broody" and said that the critics noted that "the lighting was brilliant, if erratic" (Northen, M. *Northen Lights*, Chichester: Summersdale, 1997, p166). The lighting for this production was noted in the press as being "highly ambitious, erratic in execution" (unidentified press), and by the *Sunday Times* of 20/5/51 "lighting went on and off in the most unaccountable fashion. When candles were brought on the stage got darker: and the Ghost arrived in what appeared to be practically full daylight" (Theatre Museum Archives).

[175] In 1951 Strand conducted a survey of stage lighting control boards in all 41 theatres within one mile of Trafalgar Square. The average number of dimmers was 6 for direct-operated controls and for remote controlled desks 162. Eight of the 41 theatres in the survey had remote controlled controls. This survey showed that most theatres of this era still had very out-of-date inflexible control systems, where lighting design could not have flourished. The Grand Master style control still predominated, and, being built to last, would not be changed without exceptional reason. Only the artistically ambitious theatres upgraded their lighting controls. Indeed, the Grand Master style of control would probably have lasted longer in many theatres were it not for the establishment of the National Grid, and the introduction of AC supplies that Bentham recalled caused "havoc for operational logic", and forced many venues to upgrade (*Sightline* 24/4, Oct. 89, p38).

[176] One of the few was an eight selector, 24 dimmer version for the Greens Playhouse Dundee.

the principle of having colour names arranged around a dial – turn the dial and the lighting would fade to that colour.[177]

The *Delicolor*, made by Furse to the specification of Rollo Gillespie Williams and launched in 1946, was a sophisticated development of these controls.[178] It had 7 dials and 26 manual levers, all of which could be locked to a master. It measured 8'x8' and contained dimmers behind the face panel. Furse's publicity hyped the control: "It is the greatest thing in the theatre world since Talking Pictures".[179] A smaller touring model was also made.[180] This was championed by the entertainer **Jack Hulbert** (1892-1978) in *Here Come the Boys*, which toured and then came into the Saville Theatre in 1946. The show had 24 Frencas on the No. 1 bar, with each fitted with tracker wire operated four-colour changers.[181] Such was the success of the show that the control briefly threatened to take off as a theatre control even though it was unsuited to anything other than colourwash work.[182]

The Positioning of Controls

The poor view afforded by controls positioned in the wings, coupled with the possibilities offered by the portable controls now available brought this issue to the fore. Ridge and Aldred said in 1935 that "many of those working in theatres

---

[177] Strand launched a version in 1936 called the Chromolux, of which Bentham said in the 1936 Strand catalogue that it "gives pre-set colour effects at the hands of the unskilled operator". Holophane took Strand to court over this copyright violation (*Tabs* 22/1, Mar. 64, p71).

[178] Holophane sold their stage lighting division to Furse in the late 1930s (*Focus*, Jan. 97, p5). Bentham recalled that Williams who worked for Holophane was "a deadly (but friendly) opponent of Strand." He went on to say that Holophane was a company that specialised in supplying equipment to the cinema market, and led the way in three colour mixing, "the staple diet of the super cinema". Williams invented special colour mixing controls and hypnotised cinema managers and owners into purchasing lavish colour lighting installations out in the auditorium to accompany the cinema organist who was then at the height of his glory (*Tabs* 22/1, Mar. 64, p59).

[179] Bentham, *Sixty Years of Light Work*, p111. He reported in *Cue* that "lighting effects of the most elaborate kind can be controlled by the chief theatre electrician as a conductor controls his audience" and being "capable of creating 51 shades" (*Cue* 52, Mar. 88, p10).

[180] See *News Chronicle* 11/4/46.

[181] This alone meant 96 tracker wires coming down to stage level from the No. 1 bar (and this show toured!).

[182] *The Sunday Times* 14/4/46 said of the lighting "new lighting enabling the stage to present sunrise and high noon, sunset and evening-star simultaneously. Also penumbras in pear-drop and prune". Gillespie Williams, Furse and Delicolor were credited in the programme (Theatre Museum Archives). There were apparently no limits in the quest for automatic colour control. A French version of the control called a Chromoselector or Chromon, made by Clemancon of Paris in 1950, had a "joystick" style control that operated on the basis of following the CIE Chromaticity curve!

where lighting is an art rather than a craft consider that the master electrician should be able to control the stage lighting either from the orchestra pit or from some other place in the auditorium, so that he may be independent of the cues from the stage manager and be able to modify his lighting plot to suit each actual performance of the play".[183] They also noted that a front of house control position saved shouting during plotting. Bentham also loathed the positioning of controls where the operator could not see the stage: "To me, stage lighting should not be about dimmer movement but a matter of painting the stage with light. Seeing the stage before him a good operator should, in my opinion, use his keys and controls instinctively to repeat the effects of rehearsal... In this way I think the true spirit of the producer's lighting, enjoyed and experienced by the operator, comes to life at each performance; anything else is mere mechanical dexterity which an automatic machine would repeat even more accurately. We do not use a pianola in our live orchestra so why should we aim to do so for a part of our live show?"[184] Both of these comments express the role of the operator as a participant in the production, a view at odds with practice of the time, and an important step forward in the growing importance of lighting in theatre making. Theatres that acquired Light Consoles and Electronics could now respond by placing the controls front of house. Many of these theatres were at the forefront of hosting the developments in lighting design.

Power Supply

The electricity supply was slowly becoming standardised, with either a 100v/200v DC or a 200/400v DC supply most common. However, this was also being upgraded by the new three-phase AC supply as part of the National Grid. By 1950 AC had virtually replaced DC, but voltages were not fully standardised in the West End until about 1960.[185] Lack of standardisation could only have hindered the development of lighting design.

Projection

There were few developments in projection equipment in Britain as it was not

---

[183] Ridge and Aldred, *Stage Lighting, Principles and Practice,* p76.

[184] *Tabs* 7/1, Apr. 49, p19.

[185] Bentham said that tungsten lanterns were unaffected on the change-over from DC to AC, although arcs worked better on AC, and that liquid and resistance dimmers worked on either AC or DC, although transformer dimmers only worked on AC. He noted that low voltage equipment was not practical on DC. Another problem with non-standardised voltage was that various sets of lamps of differing voltages had to be toured. (Also *ALD* Lecture at the *Live!* Show, Jan 97.)

in vogue, mainly due to the smaller size of stage restricting its use. Productions where its use was noted included *Julius Caesar* at His Majesty's in 1939 and *War and Peace* at the Phoenix in 1943, both using a 1kW optical effects projector as the basic unit.[186]

The Developing Lighting Rig

For most theatres there was little development in lighting facilities in the period 1920-1950. Most stages were still lit by rows of battens, perhaps supplemented by a few spots. Footlights remained the main front of house lighting, supplemented by a couple of spots that flooded the stage. Michael Northen recalled in an ALD lecture that in the early 1950s West End theatres typically still only had six to eight lanterns located front-of-house,[187] with batten lighting still dominating the spotlight, and a more economical rig for a revue theatre.

Percy Corry said "in 1940 a reasonably well equipped proscenium stage would have had three or four compartment battens, a No. 1 twelve-way spot bar, a compartment footlight and half a dozen front of house spots... There would have been a mechanically robust and bulky board embodying resistance dimmers in 48 or 60 circuits".[188] *Tabs* reported in 1938 that the installation at Wimbledon Theatre in that year comprised four batten bars, an eight way spot bar and a Grand Master switchboard.[189] Bentham noted that the common scenic style in Britain remained the painted cloth, which perpetuated the need for flood lighting with battens.[190]

A more detailed example of a typical installation of this period shows how little lighting had progressed. Strand installed a Bracket Handle control at the Buxton Opera House in 1938. It was installed on the stage left perch, and the lighting rig comprised:[191]

On stage:
Four-colour compartment footlights

---

[186] The main projectors were still the Strand 1kW Patt. 51 or the Patt 42 Arc. It was still common for clockwork motors to drive effects wheels. Of *War and Peace*, *The Observer* 8/8/43 said the production, a 32 scene play with simple, suggestive scenery, had "its own effective simplicity. The use of platforms and of colourful, back-lit canvasses enables the vast battlescape to move at some pace..." (Theatre Museum Archives).

[187] *ALD* Lecture at the *Live!* Show, Jan. 97.

[188] *Cue* 8, Nov. 80, p6.

[189] *Tabs* 1/4, 1938.

[190] Bentham, F. *25 Years of Stage Lighting*, Institute of Electrical Engineers Paper, 1961. (*Tabs* 26/2, Jun. 61, pp79-94).

[191] *Tabs* 2/1, Sep. 38.

No. 1 bar: comprising 1000W spots

No. 2 bar: four-colour compartment battens and 2 x Patt. 56 Acting Area floods

No. 3 bar: four-colour compartment battens and a single centre Patt. 56 Acting Area flood

No. 4 bar: Patt. 60 500W floods in four colours for cyclorama lighting 1000W wing floods

Front of house:

One Arc (presumably as a followspot)

6 x 1000W Patt. 73 Mirror spots

Tabs went on to say that this rig was "sufficiently comprehensive and flexible to meet most requirements".

In 1947 Gillespie Williams published an illustration that showed a post-war stage arrangement from a West End revue theatre. There were three onstage bars, each with focus spots at about every metre, double hung with battens. Spots and battens were also arranged in each wing bay on ladders or booms. Front of house there were footlights and footlight spots, but unfortunately the diagram did not show any lights over the forestage or hung on balconies. The text indicated that a total of 76 dimmers would be needed for this arrangement, including eight dimmers for front of house spots.[192]

Francis Reid wrote in 1973 that it was still quite common as late as the 1960s to find "the battens still permanently wired in, with no possibility of substituting other equipment by means of a plug and socket". He noted also that sockets were not standardised, with lanterns, dips and fly rail sockets all being non-compatible, making it additionally unattractive to attempt more complex lighting arrangements.[193]

Even in better equipped theatres, the focus of lanterns positioned front of house had changed little, despite the publication of Ridge and Aldred's book of 1935 which detailed area isolation.[194] The first edition of *Tabs* in 1937 suggested

---

[192] For playhouse theatres, he suggested that rigs were often permanent due to the volume of shows performed in the venue and the limited fit up time to make alterations (Williams, *The Technique of Stage Lighting*, p102).

[193] *Tabs* 31/3, Sep. 73, p132.

[194] Ridge and Aldred, *Stage Lighting, Principles and Practice*, p107. This mentioned McCandless's technique of lighting from front of house at a vertical angle of 45° from both sides, to obtain a "sculpturesque effect", and with lights placed on both sides for a "more plastic aspect". However, it is disappointing that they did not adopt this system in their own installation designs; this (cont...)

that the standard front of house focus was to fill the proscenium with light, rather than the area isolation from front of house, for which the recently launched Patt. 73 would have been well suited.[195] Bentham wrote an article on the subject of front-of-house focusing in 1952, where he drew front of house lanterns' "focus edges" onto a groundplan.[196] It is clear to see that the method of focus was either still to light the whole proscenium width with each front of house lantern, or at best to focus lanterns to either centre stage and left, or centre stage and right. This shows that the McCandless method had not been taken up in this country, either in the division of front of house lantern duties to area coverage, or the intention to achieve 90° separation between each pair. Bill Lorraine pointed out that in 1958 there was still little suggestion of area cover or any sort of systematic focus to front of house light.[197] He defined its role as being generally accepted as a pleasing substitute for the footlight, although it was considered more effective if rigged to the sides of a theatre, and thus able to send light at an angle across the stage.

The growth of front of house spotlighting was slow, due in part to the expense of these new lanterns, in part to the fact that lighting installations had not the infrastructure to easily accommodate their power and control requirements, and in part to the vision and habits of those that controlled the lighting.

In 1949 Joe Davis wrote that while the standard rig in most theatres had changed little – it was still based on battens, front of house spots, arc followspots, Grand Master style control, and a spare main for temporary controls for specials.[198] He noted that since the war, lighting had got significantly more ambitious as producers saw the dramatic potential of light and wanted it in their work. Despite the lack of development in most theatre rigs, the developments in lantern technology chiefly from Strand meant that theatres which purchased or rented this equipment were noted for advancing visual standards.

Davis went on to say that demand was becoming greater for area localisation

---

technique would not be seen in this country until around 1950. In fact their recommendations for positioning lanterns on the rig was disappointingly traditional. For example, they suggested that FOH lanterns should light the whole of the proscenium width, except when required to spotlight an actor.

[195] *Tabs* 1/1, Sep. 37
[196] *Tabs* 10/2, Sep. 52, p25.
[197] *Tabs* 16/3, Dec. 58, p18.
[198] *Tabs* 7/2, Sep. 49, p5..

of the stage and less for general flooding. He said that it was very difficult to achieve area isolation in most theatres, as even if bars of spots were rigged, house dimmers may not be of the correct loading capabilities to drive these lights. Temporary boards were the only solution, subject to local authority agreement, which was not an ideal solution to the problem of running a show smoothly or sensitively. He recommended that installations needed more flexibility in their design and installation, with patching to allow freedom to hang equipment as and when and electronic control coupled to dimmers with variable loading. He believed that footlights and battens still had their place, say for comedy or farce, but that they must be made so they could be de-rigged and swapped for spots for other dramatic forms.

Bentham said in 1950 that although the flooded arc was still occasionally seen as a sidelight, the technique of spotlighting from the wings to achieve dimension with a more controlled atmospheric feel was gaining ground.[199] With Acting Areas often rigged alongside battens overhead to give a top-light punch to the otherwise soft ambience from the batten, booms fitted with Pageants were now commonly hung on the same line as the batten bar for sidelight positions. The booms stopped just above head height to keep stage access clear, as towers were found to get in the way of scene change and entrances. Pageants and Acting Areas were commonly fitted with gold, blue and pink gels which gave a range of realistic modelling tones. If the setting precluded booms, side lighting was achieved by spotting from the end of the batten bar or from the fly-rail. See the illustration of *Carousel* (1950) opposite which shows an increased use of spotlighting although battens are still in place to provide an overall colour ambience.

Bentham's book of 1950 offered a revealing insight into how the stage was lit.[200] Although he suggested a method where the stage is broken down into areas, similar to McCandless's technique but not acknowledged, he noted that few theatres would have had the facility to be able to allocate two spots to each area. He therefore recommended the tried and tested British approach to flooding the stage with batten-light, and keying into this with spots to highlight dramatic moments or the dynamics of the setting. Further to this, his lighting plans did not include important emerging techniques such as backlight or modelling light, and there was little mention of instruments such as the Pageant,

---

[199] *Tabs* 8/3, Dec. 50, p26.

[200] Bentham, *Stage Lighting*, p200.

Carousel. Tabs vol 35/2 summer 1977. Picture courtesy Strand Lighting.

capable of giving 'punch' to the lighting. His lighting examples lacked ambition and merely preserved the status quo, and did not reflect his own style of expressive lighting developed in *Colour Music* (see Appendix vi). Was this commercial interest at heart, or did he really favour this style of lighting?

He noted common uses for coloured gels, suggesting the use of the 50 range plus No. 3 for room interiors. He found No. 36 too individual for solo use, and best used modified by a second filter in the frame. He suggested as a useful guideline that daylight should be created by flooding supplemented by spotting, and artificial lighting by spotting supplemented by flooding.[201]

He went on to discuss common colours used on the cyclorama at the time, which were No. 5A deep amber, No. 16 blue-green, and No. 20 blue for a three circuit top-light, and No. 6 red, No. 36 green, and No. 20 blue for the bottom. When assessing the number of lanterns needed to light a cyclorama, he said 5 or 6 watts per square foot should be allocated for blue, and 2½-3 watts per square foot for other colours. He said that this gave "wonderful opportunities for clear sky changes".[202]

Davis said that post-war producers were more "light conscious in appreciating how lighting can evoke the mood of a scene and define the atmosphere of a play".[203] He detailed a production of *Antony and Cleopatra* at the Piccadilly in 1947, directed by Glen Byam Shaw, as an example of this more ambitious approach. Motley designed a simple multi-level setting that used swagged cloths and a dominating multi-purpose massive centre column, balcony and sliding partitions, wrapped in a cyclorama. A three colour cyclorama was used to convey time and place, such as a deep sky of Egyptian blue, noted in *The Times* (21/12/46), and onstage lighting was used to crossfade from mood and location, with live lit scene changes in the crossfades, recorded as "an excellent example of what can be achieved with flexible lighting". Scene changes were conducted in view of the audience, coupled with atmospheric crossfades of lighting and localisation of areas within the acting area.[204]

Davis noted that post-war practice was increasingly to divide the stage into areas or sections. He chose as an example of this approach the play *Our Town* at the New in 1946. Staged without scenery, with the atmosphere entirely created by light, sectioning the stage allowed two scenes to be played at the same time. He recalled this technique was also used in *Crime and Punishment* at the New in 1946, *The Glass Menagerie* at the Haymarket in 1948, *I Remember Mama* at the Aldwych in 1948, *Love in Albania* at the Lyric in 1949, and *Death of a Salesman,* designed by Jo Mielziner in 1949 at the Phoenix Theatre. He said that this approach "calls for careful planning and flexibility of control" and remembered the difficulty caused by theatres not having enough circuits.[205]

---

[201] Bentham, *Stage Lighting*, p195.

[202] *Tabs* 6/3, Dec. 48, p8.

[203] *Tabs* 7/2, Sep. 49, p5.

[204] Theatre Museum Archives.

[205] *Tabs* 7/2, Sep. 49, p5. He went on to say "the number of circuits can never be too (cont...)

Problems Encountered When Touring

Although tours depended on the equipment available in the host venue, it was common to tour some additional equipment such as spots and effects, with a portable control to avoid having to use the house system. Colour requirements (called *Colour Calls*) would be sent in advance for preparation, along with any other specific requirements. However there is little evidence that touring, while taking popular productions to the masses, was of a high visual standard.

Touring lighting equipment was dogged by problems chiefly to do with infrastructure. Because voltages varied so much, a range of lamps had to be toured with the 'specials', and without any standardisation of plugs and sockets, much labour was required to integrate touring equipment with local facilities. Minimal time would be allocated to technical fit-ups and relighting, a job usually delegated to the Stage Manager, which was hardly conducive to maintaining high visual standards.[206]

Two examples indicate the scale of toured equipment. Bill Bundy, an electrician who joined Tennents in 1941, said of his first job, *The Doctor's Dilemma*, that the show (which contained no lighting cues) toured one 12 way spot bar, complete with 12 x Patt. 43s with the lamps wired straight in to the mains without any dimmers or control.[207] His next tour, Gielgud's *Macbeth* toured more equipment: one 12 way spot bar (Patt 43s), one 12 way flood bar (Patt. 49s), and two six way booms (Patt. 43s), with three 12 way interlocking 'portable' boards to control them.[208]

Joe Davis recalled some of the problems encountered by the lighting team when going on tour:

> "If you took a show out of London on tour, or even across London to another theatre, you would be faced with different types of current, different voltages and different plugs and sockets. Varying voltages meant lamp changes to suit and the nature of the current affected the use of effects motors. All this and the continual changing of plugs used a lot of time

---

many". He recalled the difficulty caused by hard-wired rigs, and that most theatres still had insufficient dimmers to allow a spotlight approach to lighting the stage. He urged that all equipment should be on plugs for flexibility.

[206] Michael Northen recalled that it was normally the stage manager who did the re-lighting on tour (*Focus* 12A, Aug. 92, p14) – and perhaps this is why so many went on to become lighting designers.

[207] *Focus* 9, May 89, p23

[208] He also recalled that lamps, gelatine and spares for equipment were in short supply during the war (*Focus* 10, Sep.89, p26).

before you could even start to hang equipment. In those days it was impossible to visualise the uniformity of equipment and control we take for granted today". [209]

Summary

Despite the introduction of electricity, a medium with the potential to achieve Pitcher's vision of a stage sculpted sympathetically by light, it would be many years before this became possible. Indeed, for nearly 50 years the introduction of electricity barely advanced visual aesthetics. The electric rig was conceived to give a similar potential to gas, and unless there were sufficient limes and operators available to followspot to achieve the dynamics of lighting associated with practitioners such as Irving and Tree (see Chapter 4), lighting would still have been very dull and drab. Lanterns remained crude flood lighting devices, deep colours were manufactured for colour mixing, few paler colours were available, and controls were designed to crossfade one colour wash into another. Equipment was still a long way from having the potential to achieve Reid's notion of "fluid, selective, atmospheric, dimensional illumination". Until the mid 1930s, when equipment with the potential for malleable lighting was first manufactured, the lighting rig continued as a colour-wash, flooding device, pierced only by the occasional fixed or manually operated spot, and perhaps augmented by cyclorama colour washes or very occasionally projected images. Stylistic variation was very limited.

The lighting technology introduced around 1935 had potential to achieve a greater range of lighting styles, had practitioners wanted to avail themselves of it. Spots were now available, and although the control systems of the time were not favourable to a lantern-per-dimmer approach, spots could be harnessed effectively. A reasonable range of gels was now available and extra equipment could usually be hired if needed. There are enough reviews of lighting from this period to confirm that pleasing work was achieved, and there were rare examples of fine lighting. However, while Reid's definition of stage lighting may have been achieved on occasions, most theatre-goers continued to see performance lit in the traditional manner.

There is no doubt that from 1935 lighting equipment was manufactured to a standard allowing high quality visual theatre. The new lanterns offered a palette similar to today's, and while control systems did not make a major leap forward

---

[209] *Cue* 30, Jul. 84.

until the first electronic dimmers and controls from 1950, their forerunners could have been used with sensitivity, given the will of the staff to do so. In considering Reid's quotation, control now had the potential for "fluid" changes. Lanterns could offer "selective" lighting of the stage, beam qualities and colour ranges available could create "atmospheric" conditions. The gradual replacement of the batten by the spot, including the rise of front of house spotlighting, meant that Reid's "dimensional illumination" could be achieved. Of course, whether or not this lighting would be "appropriate to the style of a particular production" was still down to the vision and skill of the team creating the lighting, but the newly emerging rig now offered the technical platform from which stylistic variation could be achieved.

Therefore, from 1935 onwards one could expect to see the consistent use of lighting as a design tool, but only in theatres that had modernised their equipment. Chapter 4 details the productions and personnel associated with this work.

3 INFLUENCES FROM HOME AND ABROAD

This chapter assesses the important thinking and practice that influenced British lighting between 1881 and 1950. It includes: new approaches to producing plays, developed both at home and abroad; the influence of this on staging and technical practice; equipment developments from abroad; British practitioners who travelled abroad and absorbed new practice; and overseas practitioners who brought their work to the attention of the British public.

A New Wave of Thinking

New approaches to staging emerged in the late nineteenth and early twentieth centuries that were to promote light as a crucial component of performance values. As sufficient brightness, distribution dynamics, colour and cue control could now be achieved on stage, to free lighting from being merely an illuminant, both theorists and practitioners were quick to espouse the virtues of light as a new medium to shape performance.

Acting, directing and production style had developed since the sixteenth century in part to combat the inadequate brightness of artificial illumination. Naked flame lighting had to be deployed to maximise brightness. As a result, acting was localised near the footlights. Make up was heavy to counter up-light shadows, exaggerate features flattened by the lighting, and generally to improve visibility of the face in the gloom. Scenery comprised two-dimensional perspective painted cloths, painted even to include shadows. Highlight and shade, essential for definition and therefore good visibility, could not be adequately achieved with light alone.

However, the emergence of the limelight, and then the arc light, at last afforded the more adventurous practitioner the opportunity to experiment with a variety of hitherto unseen conditions. The actor could now be isolated from other areas of the stage and he could be followed in a sharp beam of light. 'Key' lighting could be achieved, for example the imitation of a known light source in a composition, such as sun or moonlight, and stronger colours could be effectively deployed. The potential was there for a fundamental change in production values.

Towards the end of the nineteenth century, some practitioners recognised the potential that lighting now could offer. They experimented with new forms of acting and direction and changed their settings to three-dimensional, 'plastic' scenery, to develop an overall production style that was more realistic than previously achieved. A lighting system that offered an even, overall wash of light was still employed, with the ability to vary colour to create a range of atmospheres, either temporal, seasonal or emotional, but now with the additional key light that could punctuate, sculpt and offer a sense of motivation. Special, highly dramatic or spectacular moments were well served by the (man-powered) limelight, with its piercing, focusable penetration of the general ambience.

The greater involvement in and commitment to visual presentation gave rise to the actor-manager. Actor-managers took on a much greater responsibility for the total theatrical event, either devising settings themselves or working closely with a stage designer and scene painter to create settings in harmony with the stage action. Harnessing stage lighting was a logical extension of this role.

This new potential was to develop in contrasting ways. Some practitioners utilised it to create highly realistic staging, with as close a simulation of natural lighting as possible. Others created realism on stage, but heightened by a theatricality such as followspotting principal actors. A third group used light by creating resonant, minimal, abstracted settings and environments within which the actor worked.

Perhaps the first actor-manager to utilise the full potential of the lighting system was **Henry Irving** (1838-1905). An acclaimed actor, he became an actor-manager, concentrating on staging melodrama and Shakespeare. He placed much importance on training his company to achieve high artistic values in all aspects of his productions. His recognition of the importance of lighting and stage decor in an era of realism and spectacle was demonstrated during his tenancy as actor-manager of the Lyceum Theatre London from 1878-1899.[1]

He revolutionised stage design at the Lyceum by often replacing the painted cloths with realistic environments, dispensing with the footlights for a more natural look to the lighting.[2] He made few innovations in terms of the equipment

---

[1] Wilson, A.E. *The Lyceum*, London: Yates 1952, p69. The Lyceum had developed a reputation for popular, fashionable dramas under the Vestris-Mathews company of the early 1800s, and later under the management of Charles Fechter from 1863.

[2] Wilson, *The Lyceum*, p84.

he used, although he was believed to be the first to colour limes and divide footlights into independently controlled circuits to create a sense of localised lighting and differing colour moods across the stage.[3] Indeed, he shunned the use of electricity for several years, not installing electric footlights until 1891, and then only gradually adding equipment over the next eight years until the stage could largely be lit by electricity alone. It seems curious that he preferred to work with gas, although one reason for his dislike of electricity was his concern over the effect of the lowering of colour temperature when dimming electric lamps, which gave the stage a 'muddy' look, an effect not found with gas lighting.[4]

The lighting equipment at the Lyceum was not particularly noteworthy, being similar to that in other theatres of its size. Following structural alteration to the stage in 1885 by theatre architect C.J.Phipps, the lighting system consisted of a standard gas rig, including footlights, battens, winglights and groundrows, which were fitted with simple colour changers.[5] The rig was operated from a central, one man control in the prompt corner.[6] To keylight into the fixed rig, Irving used multiple independently operated limes, fitted with a wide range of colours to highlight principal actors.[7]

While most theatre managers thought of light only as an illuminant, or at most for a spectacular effect, Irving saw light as an integral component of the art of theatre-making. His lighting attempted to capture a theatrical reality with great beauty, through a use of subtle colour tones. He demanded a greater precision in colour mixes than previous practitioners, and individually controlled colour circuits for greater precision in compositions. He used pale dyed silks to colour lights, taking care not to cut out too much light, and developed transparent lacquers for electric lamps and glasses for limes. As a greater

---

[3] See Stoker, B. *Personal Reminiscences of Henry Irving*, London: The MacMillan Co., 1906, for a full account of his work at the Lyceum.

[4] Jackson, *Victorian Theatre*, p190, citing Bram Stoker *Irving and Stage Lighting*.

[5] Booth, *Victorian Spectacular Theatre 1850-1910*, p93.

[6] "The necessity of placing the plate on the prompt side is in order that the gas man may be near the stage manager, and obey his direction for the turning up and down of the lights in the auditorium and on stage, for various stage effects" (Rees, *Theatre Lighting in the Age of Gas*, p109, citing Woodrow, Building News Vol. 66 1894 p567).

[7] In his production of *Faust* he used as many as 25 limes simultaneously (*Theatre Notebook* XXXIII, 3, Alan Hughes, from Theatrical Mechanism, *Scientific American Supplement* 22/5/1886). Including open white, red, light amber, amber and four shades of blue (Alan Hughes, *Theatre Notebook* XXXIII No.31979, p100).

control of colour hue became possible so his lighting plots became in turn more sophisticated.

Control of light on stage was aided in part by Irving's darkening of the auditorium, a device he employed not only to help draw attention to the stage, but to allow the iris to close to stage lighting levels, thus affording much greater controlled visibility, contrast range and manipulation of the stage picture. This technique was particularly well suited to the highly dramatic style of his work. Indeed, the process of adjusting auditorium lighting levels to match the mood of the play became the norm.

Norman Marshall said of Irving that "one of his favourite devices was the dramatic use of figures moving from deep shadow into a blaze of light".[8] He recalled that he dimmed lighting for scene changes, thus establishing the light cue as a dramatic punctuation device.[9]

He excelled at recreating natural lighting conditions – such as dawn, sunset and moonlight, and at suggesting geographical location – such as Mediterranean sunlight for *Romeo and Juliet* or a windy hillside for *King Lear*.[10] As well as literal interpretations, Irving used light to emphasise a character's inner feelings, or even to show a sense of irony. *The Theatre* reported that *King Lear* strayed across: "a sunny heath… such a background for so piteous an indifference to all beauty, all intelligence, heightens the tragedy unspeakably. The mind that conceived it… was the mind of a poet".[11]

Irving boldly commanded intensity levels. The storm scene from *King Lear* was played in almost complete darkness, save for a dim lime on Lear and lightning flashes: "The curtain rises on intense darkness – a darkness you can feel… blinding sheets of lightning envelop the scene, and jagged and forked flashes dart and quiver in all directions".[12] This scene was further enhanced

---

[8] Marshall, N. *The Producer and the Play*, London: MacDonald, 1957, p30.

[9] "At the Lyceum the happy idea is adopted… of lowering all the lights as the scene changes. The result is a kind of… pleasing mystery and surprise" (*Theatre History Studies* Vol. XVIII 1998 p 107 "Observations on nineteenth century lighting" by Victor Emeljanow, quoting from Percy Fitzgerald *The world behind the scenes* 1881, p19).

[10] Such was the pictorial vividness of Irving's work that it also brought some criticism. A moment in *Romeo and Juliet*: "Here we have, if anything, an excess of colour. The golden lattice, the sumptuous surroundings, the foliage of the garden, the sky showing its pinks, and oranges, and purples of a sunrise, and, at last, the golden sun itself, are all beautiful enough, but they are a trying background for the central figures" (*Theatre Notebook* XXXIII, 3, Alan Hughes, from *The Theatre*, Apr. 1882).

[11] *Theatre Notebook* XXXIII, 3, Alan Hughes, from *The Theatre*, Dec. 1882.

[12] *Theatre Notebook* XXXIII, 3, Alan Hughes, from *Licensed Victualler's Gazette* in "King Lear" at the Lyceum, 1893.

by clever use of pyrotechnics. Powders were ignited in downstage positions to create flashes, leaving a residue of smoke to hang in the air to enhance an already highly-charged atmosphere. This scene also attracted criticism for the moving lime that followed *Lear*: "Surely it is not in perfect poetical taste for Mr. Irving to be followed about by the limelight".[13] Comments such as these made him rethink his policy of using a lime as a following highlight device, but to look for more naturally motivated functions of light. His lighting style developed a greater sense of logic in an attempt to create natural lighting conditions for his actors to inhabit.

Despite working with equipment crude and simple by today's standard, Irving created stage lighting pictures that belong to a visual language of the twentieth century. He displayed an understanding of how to integrate light with design, direction and performance to create a unified theatrical event.[14] C.B. Cochran recalled the high quality of Irving's lighting, but only at particular moments rather than in its overall contribution: "I have not seen better lighting effects from the elaborate Schwabe Hazeit system than those I can recall at the Lyceum in Irving's day, though it is true that, being young, I was not then so critical."[15]

Working at the same time as Irving were the Saxe-Meiningen Players, a touring company led by **The Duke of Saxe-Meiningen** (1826-1914), who directed the company and designed the settings and costumes. He introduced a far more realistic approach in his productions, and is credited with creating much more realistic movements and groupings of actors on stage. His stage designs tended to use lighter tones for the costumes and darker tones for the settings – helping the actor to stand out – and an increased emphasis on lighting upstage gave actors a greater freedom of movement around the stage. He designed three-dimensional 'box settings' with canvas cycloramas, moving away from the two dimensional 'cut out' style of his predecessors. The greater

---

[13] *Theatre Notebook* XXXIII, 3, Alan Hughes, from *Liverpool Daily Post*, 14/11/1892.

[14] Irving developed his work with a large and loyal band of employees. He employed up to 350 technical and administrative staff at times. He entrusted much power to Bram Stoker, and his stage manager, H.J.Loveday, who functioned as a modern technical director. Stoker and Loveday worked with Irving from his entry into management until his death. His gas engineer G. Biggs ran a team of 30 (there was not a separate electrical engineer until 1902). There was a limelight team of eight. "Jimmy" Allen was the prompter (who worked with Irving for 28 years) and his chief designer and scenic artist was Hawes Craven (1837-90) (*Theatre Notebook* Vol. XXVIII No.1 1974 The Lyceum staff, Alan Hughes).

[15] Cochran, C.B. *Review of Reviews* London: Jonathan Cape, 1930, p162.

use of upstage by the actor meant that perspective scenery was no longer appropriate if proportion was to be maintained.

His company were the first to break the mould of flat, even wash lighting, and the Duke was credited with the first productions in a naturalistic style. His lighting too was more ambitious, using spotlights from the wings to enhance the actors and projections of rain and flames to make settings more life-like. His methods broke the overall wash approach by creating areas of light and shade to give tone across the stage picture.[16]

The Duke's work was highly influential and toured widely throughout Europe, including London. For two months in 1881 he performed *Julius Caesar* at Drury Lane with a company of 80. Although audience interest was disappointing (perhaps because the company performed in German), the production aroused much artistic interest.[17]

Edward William Godwin (1833-86), an architect, theatre designer and father of Edward Gordon Craig, paved the way forward for developing a freer artistic production style. While not noted for achievements specifically in lighting, he led a movement that promoted a single person as the focal point of all production activity, and questioned the artificiality of scenic methods and experimented with open staging.[18]

Hubert Herkomer (1849-1914), a Bavarian artist, set designer and musician who had emigrated to Britain, opened a little theatre at his Art School in Bushey to practice his theories. He was noted for naturalistic staging and high quality atmospheric effects made by lighting gauzes, using them as a softening device,

---

[16] An example of his use of light came in a scene from Schiller's *Mary Stuart*, where an impression of candle lighting was achieved, localised on Queen Elizabeth while reflected light caught a painting of Henry VIII in the background. A production of *Julius Caesar* drew praise from critics for its adventurous and realistic lighting – the portrayal of lightning, moonlight, and day-break with gas light combined with battery operated electrical practicals. The company employed one of the earliest lighting companies in Germany – Hugo Bähr of Dresden – to develop equipment and techniques (Osborne, *The Meiningen Court Theatre*, pp38 & 105).

[17] John Hollingshead wrote in *The Gaiety*: "in point of stage effect I have seen nothing to the crowd in the Mark Anthony scene... It is a triumph of stage management..." (Osborne, *The Meiningen Court Theatre*, p80).

[18] His production of Todhunter's *Helena in Troas*, set on a stage without a proscenium arch "for the first time in three centuries an architectural setting with only a slight element of painting was seen in Britain" (Rosenfeld, S. *A Short History of Scene Design in Great Britain*, Oxford: Blackwell, 1973, p142).

[19] "so convinced was the audience that it was seeing the actual sky through an opening at the back, that they had to be shown it was an illusion" (Rosenfeld *A Short History of Scene Design in Great Britain*, p143).

with a painted sky cloth rigged behind.[19] He a gave lecture on stage design (attended by Craig) in 1891 in which he promoted light as a key ingredient of drama, advocating a natural use of light and the deployment of lights front of house to replace the footlights. He too promoted the notion of the single figure in charge of all aspects of theatre production: "if a thousand people are needed to carry out an art scheme, it must be planned and directed by one man who stamps it as his own".[20]

Changes in the way lighting was deployed were greatly influenced by other production techniques. The staging reforms of the late nineteenth and early twentieth centuries were further prompted in Britain by a revival of Shakespeare's plays in a similar manner to their original staging conditions. Although this movement made little immediate impact on stage lighting, minimising scenery gave greater weight to the role that light was to play. Further, a movement away from the restrictions of the proscenium arch stage to an open, Elizabethan style stage brought the role of design into focus. **William Poel** (1852-1934) was the best known practitioner of this movement, and his work was sharply juxtaposed against the proscenium arch work of Irving. In 1881 he converted the St. George's Hall into a platform stage for a production of *Hamlet* and staged a range of other productions in converted halls and theatres over the next 20 years. His settings merely used curtains complemented by simple items of furniture. He directed actors to process through the audience in *The Comedy of Errors* in 1895, another revolutionary idea. Reinhardt saw his work, and was probably influenced by him.[21]

Harley Granville Barker (1877-1946) developed this idea further at the Savoy Theatre from 1912-14. For *The Winter's Tale* in 1912, with a thrust

---

[20] In a lecture on *Scenic Art*, Herkomer said that he believed that the dramatic and the pictorial were inseparable, to the point where auditoria should be built with sightlines that limited seating to positions with a correct view of the stage. He called for the same consistencies in stage design and lighting that the public demanded of the actor. He said that lighting was the key to creating scenic mood, and attacked the footlight position for unnatural and false ambience. He said that lights must be placed front of house, instead of on the floor, to create a more natural shadow on the face. He spoke of his experiments at Bushey, where he located FOH lights at about actor-head height and ten feet from the proscenium, on the auditorium wall. These lights were boxed, so they only cast light on the stage, and he said that the effect these created was "as nearly as possible that of open daylight". He went on to say that it was easier to create the feeling of sunlight rather than a diffuse light, but suggested his FOH method was a good way to achieve a diffuse feel. He recommended that all large theatres could achieve this with electric FOH light fitted with colour changers (*The Magazine of Art* Cassell & Co, London, 1892, pp259 & 316).

[21] Komisarjevsky, T. *The Theatre (and a Changing Civilisation)*, London: Bodley Head, 1935, p151.

stage backed by a white setting by Norman Wilkinson and costumes by Albert Rutherston,[22] he experimented with front of house lighting, removing the footlights and placing arcs on the dress circle front. Although this production was ground-breaking, it was not particularly well received. The non-stop scenes were uncomfortable for the audience, and the lighting was panned.[23] Wilkinson gave *Twelfth Night*, in November 1912, "a simple and direct treatment... using front curtains and built scenes". This production received mixed reviews in the press, with little mention of the lighting, other than "Mr Barker allows us to be racked in a dazzling white glare".[24] Barker's preference for using uncoloured light also drew criticism from Fagan, who said that white light lacked atmosphere.[25] He was more adventurous with colour in *A Midsummer Night's Dream* in February 1914, where he used rich coloured light, inspired, according to *The Times* (7/2/14), by the Russian Ballet's designs. However, despite his seemingly high-profile work, Cochran said "our British stage remained unmoved by all this experimentation".[26]

A radical shift in staging concepts – with an equally important re-evaluation of the role that lighting would play – occurred at the beginning of the twentieth century. This was led by **Adolphe Appia** (1862-1928).[27] Appia was inspired in particular by the works of Wagner,[28] and he looked to emphasise moments

---

[22] Rutherston presented a lecture in 1912 called *Decoration in the Art of Theatre*, that promoted an integrated approach to staging, with light as a key component (*Monthly Chapbook* 1/2 Aug 1919). In a lengthy article on staging Shakespeare in *Play Pictorial* Vol. XXI no 126, Barker discussed various staging solutions to Shakespeare, but with no mention of the role of lighting (Theatre Museum Archives).

[23] *The Times* spoke of "search-lights converging on the stage" (Beauman, S. *The RSC – a History of Ten Decades* Oxford: OUP, 1982, p58) and "rays of brilliant light thrown on to the stage from front of house. By this mode of lighting... all sense of mystery is lost" (*Daily Mail* 23/9/1912, Theatre Museum Archives).

[24] Unknown press cuttings, Theatre Museum Archives.

[25] Fagan believed that Granville Barker's productions failed because he was reluctant to use colour in his lighting, saying that although tints of light were unnatural, they created a greater range of moods appropriate to theatre work, whereas white light, Granville Barker's preferred colour, was unnatural, cold and anaemic (*Sightline* 11/1, Spr. 76, p54).

[26] Cochran, C.B. *The Showman Looks On*, London: Dent, 1945, p223.

[27] Adolphe Appia was born in Geneva, studied music, and then worked backstage at the Vienna Burgtheater and the Hofoper. In 1891 he moved to Bière in Switzerland and began working on new ways to stage Wagner's operas.

[28] Richard Wagner (1813-1883) promoted a similar theory: that all production values should be considered equally. His theatre at Bayreuth, opened in 1876 for the production of his operas, had an open amphitheatre style auditorium to encourage more integrated and symbolic settings.

that prompted emotion, movement and action. He felt that Wagner's own staging of his operas was not as expressive of the core of emotion as it could be. Through his designs he developed the stage space to portray the emotion of the music rather than the 'facts' of the story. Although his ambition was to produce operas, he proved not to have the personality to do this, restricted by a great shyness and a stammer. However, his connection with the Vienna Opera meant he was able to observe the process, especially the lighting rehearsals, and as a result gained much insight into design.

He is regarded more as a theorist than a practitioner although he did design eight staged productions between 1903 and 1925. He deployed light as a visual counterpoint to music, to underline the emotional character of the actor within the mood of the play. His published theories gave clear objective reasoning for his stage design ideas and their technical realisation. In *Die Musik und die Inscenierung* (1899) he suggested paring staging back to the minimum, to create simple settings, that when fused with powerful, dominant lighting could evoke a mood suggestive of the spirit of the performance. Colour would come from light, and its main source position would be overhead, with lanterns used as followspots to isolate actors as they moved about the stage.

Appia was one of the first to realise that it was important for the stage director as a decision-maker to harness all production elements in order to find the true meaning of a play. He placed the actor at the centre of this, with all other elements serving the actor's inner emotions. He believed that light should change in response to their emotions rather than for reasons of realism:

> "light, shade, and color, through general and specific illumination can… create artistic lighting. Light aids the actor in his interpretation of the character, it enhances the beauty of stage decoration, and as an art medium *per se* it carries to the spectator the mood, atmosphere, and emotional effect of the drama itself".[29]

He developed the idea of the lighting score, which would be designed to draw out emotional changes and emphasise dramatic and atmospheric qualities that underpinned the action. He was sensitive in his choice of material, mainly addressing his theories to opera. In *Music and the Art of Theatre*, he said that:

> "Light is to a production what music is to the score: the expressive element as opposed to external signs; and as is the case of music, light can express

---

[29] Seldon, S. & Sellman, D. *Stage Scenery and Lighting*, London: Harrap, 1930, p212.

only that which belongs to the "inner essence" of all vision... The two elements have an analogous existence. Each of them needs some external object if their activity is to be put into effect: the poet, in the case of music, and the actor for lighting".[30]

Appia differentiated clearly between the role of ambient light, which he saw as emotionless light, and moving, directional key light, which defined form, giving objects value and meaning. He promoted settings that created shadows, for light to carve new shapes within a stage space. Appia employed techniques of light and shade into his stage design, by realising that it was this combination that gave visibility and order to the visual field. This was revolutionary, as highlighting the importance of objects or ideas with light had not been explored before.

Identifying four elements that could be controlled within the visual stage picture – perpendicular painted scenery, the horizontal floor, the moving actor, and the lit space by which these are defined – he mused on ways to combine these elements in harmony to create an aesthetically correct whole. Appia realised that the physical space of the stage could be governed by light, to expand or contract the boundaries (both horizontal and vertical), to increase or decrease depth, and to separate actors or features. Through his belief that light was for the actor rather than for the setting, he dispensed with foot- and border-lights, and suggested a moving spotlight approach from above, to enhance gesture, movement and grouping of actors. He installed Fortuny's indirect lighting system for experimentation in a private theatre in 1903, aiming to create an overall ambience to key into with spotlights, and using coloured light rather than paint to tone the setting. He also proposed a significant deployment of projected imagery, especially of abstract, suggested shapes and textures, to dress the cyclorama in a more atmospheric, evocative manner. Many aspects of the stage lighting rig have developed following his lead. Arthur Kahane, Reinhardt's assistant, in 1919 summarised his style: "Lighting is the real source of decoration, its single aim being only to bring the important into light and leave the unimportant in shadow".[31]

In *A new art material* (c.1902) Appia commented on the existing practice of lighting the overall picture rather than concentrating light on the actor:

"How is the actor lit? Alas, not at all; the painting has taken all the lighting for

---

[30] Beacham, R. *Adolphe Appia: Texts on Theatre*, New York: Routledge, 1993, p51.

[31] Unidentified document, Theatre Museum Archives.

itself. Those long rows of electric lamps which run parallel to the slices of scenery, or which run right around the stage, are designed to let us see the painting clearly. No doubt they also let us see the actor clearly, lit from all sides at once... But is that *lighting*? Would a sculptor have thought of lighting in this way his bronze or marble dreams? It is useless to wish for movement without light, without real lighting that creates forms, and it is useless to seek to have light that creates forms if one remains under the tyranny of dead painting".[32]

He realised that the way in which things are seen was as important to completing the sensory image as how things are heard. Light and music for Appia became fused as one, each to complement the other. Both had similar properties: flexibility, fluidity, dynamic, colour and timbre.[33] He believed that light could clothe the actor in his emotional apparel. In *How to reform our Staging Practices* (1904), Appia said that, following a discussion on staging a scene from Wagner's *Siegfried*:

"the procedures of staging, like other artistic procedures, are founded on forms, light and colour; now these three elements are in our control and we can in consequence arrange them in the theatre as elsewhere in an artistic fashion. Until now it has been believed that staging must achieve the highest possible

---

[32] Drain, R. (Ed.) *Twentieth Century Theatre, a Source Book*, London: Routledge, 1995, p14.

[33] From 1906 he became influenced by the dancer **Emile Jaques-Dalcroze** (1865-1960), a Swiss music educationalist and composer and exponent of the system called "eurythmics", whereby a dancer responds kinaesthetically to the rhythms of the source material. Through this influence he developed and combined his interest in spatial and physical rhythm. This influence extended his design work into closer emotional links between space and the actor, with line, shape and form increasingly responsive to the moods of the work. Jaques Dalcroze started a school in Hellerau (near Dresden) in 1910, and together they built an open stage theatre there (the first in modern times) to produce Gluck's operas and explore their theories. Appia "caused a sensation with his abstract setting and directional lighting" for Gluck's opera *Orpheus et Eurydice* in 1913 (Patterson, M. *The Revolution in German Theatre 1900-1933*, London: Routledge and Kegan Paul, 1981, p40). Lighting, which in this theatre fused an overall ambience with spotlights from above for key lighting ("to reveal clearly the forms of the body in motion and the three-dimensional nature of the setting", Beacham, *Adolphe Appia: Texts on Theatre*, p122), was central to the performance, and co-ordinated music, movement and emotion. Gorelik, M. *New Theatres for Old*, London: Dobson, 1940, p290 said that the ever-changing coloured light that "suffused the walls" of the theatre inspired cinema auditorium lighting in America. Leading practitioners of the day saw his Festival performances in 1912 and 1913 at Hellerau, which ran until war intervened in 1914. Using his experiences gained in this collaboration, Appia wrote an essay titled *Eurythmics and Light* in 1912 (although it was not published until 1932) in which he explored the notion of light as luminous sound. In *Actor, Space, Light Painting*, written in 1919, he reaffirmed the fusion between the actor and the space through the medium of light by quoting the "normal established hierarchy": "the *actor* presenting the drama; *space* in three dimensions, in the service of the actor's plastic form; *light* giving life to each" (Beacham, *Adolphe Appia: Texts on Theatre*, p114).

degree of illusion; and it is this principle (unaesthetic though it is) which has barred our progress. I strive to show in these pages that scenic art must be based on the one reality worthy of theatre: the human body".[34]

Although Norman Marshall doubted "whether Appia's theories on acting and production had much influence",[35] his staging pictures in *Die Musik und die Inscenierung* clearly show a new approach to lighting, combining light and shade in varying layers of intensity.[36] Photographs of Appia's *Das Rheingold* at the Municipal Theater Basle in 1924, taken under his own lighting, confirm his credentials.[37] Marshall noted that Appia received much critical acclaim at the time for these designs, despite having only the most meagre lighting resources at his disposal: "Appia created effects which were praised for their visual splendours, the dramatic contrasts of brilliant light and deep shadow, the use of light from many angles, and the evocation of the changing mood of the music by subtle changes in the lighting".[38]

Although Appia never worked in Britain, an exhibition of his work was staged in London in 1922.

Edward Henry Gordon Craig (1872-1966), son of the actress Ellen Terry and E.W. Godwin (see p.104), was a child performer who joined Irving's company from 1899 to 1908, playing many leading roles during this period (including Hamlet), and becoming increasingly interested in production. However, as with Appia, it was his theories rather than his practice that won him respect and international influence. Published in several books, principally *The Art of Theatre* in 1905 and *On the Art of Theatre* in 1911, and although much was not original in concept, his writing articulated Appia's ideas more clearly and in turn brought Appia's work to a wider audience through his own prolific writings.[39]

---

[34] Drain (Ed.), *Twentieth Century Theatre, a Source Book*, p15.

[35] Marshall also said that it was extraordinary that such an almost unreadable book, saved by vividly revealing pictures of his designs, could revolutionise ideas about décor and lighting in the European Theatre (Marshall, *The Producer and the Play*, p29).

[36] *Tabs* 27/3, Sep. 69, p5.

[37] These are published in: Volbach, W. *Adolphe Appia, Prophet of the Modern Theatre*, Connecticut: Wesleyan University Press, 1968.

[38] The book went on to credit Appia with bringing the use of slide projection in the theatre to an international audience, and noted his interest in those that pioneered the technique, in particular the work of Loie Fuller (*Tabs* 27/3, Sep. 69, p5).

[39] He also created and edited an influential quarterly magazine called *The Mask*, which was published between 1908-1929, devoted to the art of the theatre, and set up a short-lived acting school in Florence in 1908, both of which spread his name and influence.

His approach was similar to Appia's in the sense of looking for symbolic or abstracted representation of ideas by uniting all production aspects in harmony. He too promoted the idea of the director being in total control of all visual and performance aspects, but with the actor considered subordinate to the total theatrical experience. He believed that as an artist, the theatre director should weave and weld all elements together to create an artistic whole: "He must not only produce the plays himself, but also be the designer of the scenery and the costumes, have complete mastery over every detail of the lighting, be an expert in and teacher of dancing, gesture and elocution".[40]

Between 1893 and 1928 Craig designed 17 productions, although all but five of these occurred before 1905.[41] He used simple costume shapes in bold colour, minimal settings, and swagged curtains and light as his scenic tools. However, most of his ideas remained impractical ambitions, contained in sketches of stages bigger than the largest theatres, with no notion of how scene changes might be achieved. As a result, few would employ him.

In an article published in 1911 about the establishment of a training school, Craig discussed experimentation with light.[42] He was interested in exploring the effects of a series of shafts of parallel beams of light and also the tones of colour contained in white light when falling upon a white setting. He went on to talk of having model rooms with fully dressed sets and model lighting to simulate the real stage, with mannequins to represent actors moving as actors speak their lines. This was an early practical solution to the difficulty of

---

[40] Playfair, N. *The Story of the Lyric Theatre Hammersmith* , Chatto and Windus, 1925, p119.

[41] For example, in his *Dido and Aeneas* of 1900 he employed a grey gauze in front of a backcloth lit from above and the sides to give a depth of colour, playing blue amber and green on the backcloth. For Dido's death "a rain of pink rose petals in a shaft of light fell on her..." (Rosenfeld, *A Short History of Stage Design in Great Britain*, p147). Another early example of his creative use of light was in *Much Ado about Nothing* (1903) (his last production in Britain) designed for the Imperial Theatre London, where the church scene was created with gathered curtains to represent columns and a pattern of coloured light that fell obliquely onto an empty stage. Candles flickered in the background. "the characters were lit only when they entered the acting area which was the pool of coloured light; outside it, they too became silhouettes like the columns" (Craig, E. *Gordon Craig, the Story of his Life*, London: Gollancz, 1968, p176). A later example shows a similar style – in his production of Hasenclever's *Der Sohn* in 1918: "the spotlight fell into the scanty scenery while pouring a sharp bright beam of light on the face of the speaker. Black velvet curtains that absorbed the light enclosed the bare stage..." (Fuchs, R. *Revolution in the Theatre*, New York: Cornell University Press, 1959, cit. R. Frank *Das Neue Theatre*, Berlin 1928, cit. Samuel and Hinto Thomas *Expressionism in German life, Literature and the Theatre*, 1910-24,Cambridge: Heffer, 1939). A production in 1926 of *The Pretenders* for the Royal Copenhagen State Theatre saw him deploy scenic projection.

[42] "Thoroughness in the theatre" by E.G.Craig *English Review*, Vol. 9 1911, p494.

demonstrating light at the planning stage, a concept that would prove to be very important in the development of lighting design over the next forty years.[43]

Although Appia and Craig's ideas were often thought of as impractical and not in tune with professional practice, their designs suggested a way forward in stage design, in the use of three-dimensional masses, simple bold structures and levels, and areas of light and shade. Their work was particularly influential in German and American theatre of the early twentieth century, although less so here. Initially there were only two champions of this style of production in Britain – Martin Harvey and Basil Dean. Their approach did not gain a foothold until European designers worked at theatres such as the Memorial Theatre Stratford, Glyndebourne and the other 'art' theatres which became established in the second quarter of the twentieth century.

Lighting in Europe

Lighting made a significant and pivotal contribution to the development of the staging of plays across Europe in the first half of the twentieth century. The playwrights and production styles that emerged became models of practice for many British art theatres of the 1920s and 30s, and were highly influential in establishing a more fluid, expressive style of lighting in British theatre.

Germany

German theatres were more advanced than their British counterparts at that time. Stages were bigger and better equipped with lighting, and were quick to adopt new developments in complex stage machinery such as revolves, lifts, flying and cycloramas. This offered the potential for quick scene change and multiple settings, in turn demanding more complex lighting. The ability to stage realistic scenery was significantly aided by mechanised stages, as scene changes were made significantly easier, which allowed a progression of realistic sets to be available. Further to this, sets could be more ambitious and robust as they did not need to be set and struck manually. The introduction of the cyclorama achieved far more realistic and versatile atmospheric backgrounds than painted cloths could ever achieve.

The important developments in lighting were prompted by the desire to create natural ambiences with light rather than by paint. This idea was advanced in particular by the new techniques in lighting the cyclorama.

---

[43] He wanted to call the school a "school of experiment... to develop the creative faculty", promoting drama as a collaborative, integrated human activity, citing as an example that the electrician should be involved as an equal in the making of drama. (*English Review*, Vol. 13 1913, p240).

In the late nineteenth century, German theatre was noted for the staging of classics, a policy that continued after World War One. German theatre received large subsidies from the state, so commercial pressures were less intense, allowing scope for progressive ideas to come to the fore.[44] Many practitioners adopted the theories of Appia and applied light to the stage in an imaginative way. German theatre became synonymous with adventurous staging practice and its leading practitioners were to be highly influential in Britain.

An example of ambitious lighting from the early 1900s is seen in the work of **Georg Fuchs** (1868-1949).[45] He founded The Munich Artists' Theatre in 1907 as one of the exhibits in an *Exposition of Arts and Sciences* held in Munich in 1908. The shallow stage was used for low relief scenery, a backdrop, steps and a Fortuny sky dome. He developed a sophisticated lighting rig, with bridges installed overhead for top lighting, his favoured position for dominant lighting. He deployed footlights, but only as a source for natural reflection. However, he was restricted by space from achieving the distance of throw that he wished for, and could not attain the desired levels of intensity. He claimed that the stage could be lit in "all gradations from light to dark" in five colours.[46] He found that only a little make-up was required as a result of his sculptural lighting.

When referring to the value of lighting, Fuchs said that: "light has the power to dissolve a physical object, to dematerialise it, so that an intensively illuminated expanse of canvas changes in the eye of the spectator into an illusion of infinite space".[47] He went on to say: "light is the principal factor in the presentations of the Artists' Theatre. It is light that liberates the imagination".[48] He firmly believed that: "Light is, and will continue to be, the most important factor in the development of stage design. Modern electrical technique offers possibilities that it would be folly to disregard. To use them correctly, to distribute and

---

[44] Helmut Grosser, Editor of *Buhnentechnische Rundschau*, said it was much more about education than entertainment, saying it was "a place for discussion of aesthetic, ideological and cultural political matters" (*Tabs* 34/1, Spr. 76, p5). First published in 1921 it was the official magazine of the Deutches Theatertechnische Gesellschaft (founded in 1907), and was the world's first technical theatre magazine (*Sightline* 12/2, Aut. 78, p66).

[45] A well-known drama critic and an essayist in the field of aesthetics, Fuchs promoted the theories of the emerging anti-naturalistic movement in theatre in his two key publications, *Die Schaubuhne der Zukunft* (Theatre of the Future) 1905 and *Die Revolution des Theaters* (Revolution in the Theatre) ,1909.

[46] Fuchs, *Revolution in the Theatre*, p86.

[47] Fuchs, *Revolution in the Theatre*, p80.

[48] Fuchs, *Revolution in the Theatre*, p189.

regulate these immense and manifold masses of light with artistic effect, requires the creative spirit of the sculptor. Light… governs the appearance and value of all things… including the performers themselves!"[49]

The first production, *Faust*, typified his approach, and the lighting was noted as if being under "the hand of a master musician". Instead of naturalism in the lighting there were "shafts of illumination, pools of shadow, light joyous and sorrowful, stained through with colour which seize upon our emotions".[50]

Although he was restricted by distance light could be thrown in this theatre, he was able to deploy a style whereby: "actors are always illuminated from above and from the depths. They are always represented in relief".[51] He employed designers such as Erler, Dietz and Heine, and later Bakst and Picasso. They created stylised costumes, to focus attention on the actors and help them stand out from the settings[52], three-dimensional settings and "stylised environments that suited the 'inner' nature of the play".[53]

There are many other interesting examples of lighting from this period in Germany. Perhaps the most important person was Reinhardt, whose work was seen internationally (see later in this chapter for a review of his contribution). Lighting around the time of World War One was often highly expressive. For example, in Sorge's *Der Bettler* in 1912 there was a use of directional spotlights to pick out a range of stage areas individually in a composite setting. Lighting in this production was used no longer merely to illuminate but as an expressive device to communicate meaning.[54] Leopold Jessner used a constant light that lit the setting, but allowed actors to work within it, as in *Wilhelm Tell* in 1919. He also showed character status by varying light levels. In *Richard lll* 1920 at the end of act 1 scene 2 he threw "a threatening shadow on to the stage, so warning of the diabolical power of the man". In Kaiser's *Holle Weg Erde* in 1921 lighting was used symbolically. A sunbeam casting cool blue shadows suggested the barren landscape of a character's soul, followspots were used to isolate characters, and shadows were cast to give the appearance of a

---

[49] Fuchs, *Revolution in the Theatre*, p85.

[50] Gorelik, *New Theatre for Old.* p177.

[51] Fuchs, *Revolution in the Theatre*, p190.

[52] Komisarjevsky, *The Costume of the Theatre*, London: Bles, 1931, p158.

[53] Komisarjevsky, *Settings and Costumes of the Modern Stage*, London: Studio, 1933.

[54] W. Sokel in 1959 said, "the lighting apparatus behaves like the mind. It drowns in darkness what it wishes to forget and bathes in light what it wishes to recall. Thus the entire stage becomes the universe of the mind, and the individual scenes are not replicas of the three-dimensional physical reality, but visualised stages of thought" (Patterson, *The Revolution in German Theatre 1900-1933*, p54).

skeleton. In Toller's *Masse Mensch*, also in 1921, the cyclorama was lit in a variety of colours not only for symbolic effect, but also to create silhouettes of scenery and actors in front. Felix Cziossek, in his cubist design for *Henry IV* in the early 1920s, used light from selected planes to bring architectural shapes such as steps to life. Other devices were common in German theatre lighting, such as back projection, with lighting levels dimmed to allow projections to 'read'. Hard lighting from above was another signature of this era, casting unreal shadows on the face and creating a chiaroscuro effect. UV was commonly used, and the principle of fading to blackout to denote the end of a scene was established at the Tribune Theatre.[55]

Other German producers made important contributions through their work with light. **Erwin Piscator** (1893-1966), a disciple of Reinhardt, developed the concept of the 'epic' play, and was noted for expressionistic staging, including the use of Linnebach projection. He pioneered techniques such as film projection within his theatre work in the 1920s.[56] **Bertolt Brecht** (1898-1956) worked under Reinhardt in Berlin and became one of the most important dramatists of the twentieth century. In his theory and practice light was central to forming an essential link to theatre-making, although his use of light was not noted for high drama and theatricality. His lighting was used to expose situations and actions through the deployment of bright even, uniform states. He believed that this type of lighting would dispel all illusion for the audience, so the truth of the drama would be apparent. This went as far as revealing the lighting instruments and rig; this breaking of a convention would lead to a far greater technical freedom. He also used projected words and images for commentary or documentary support, writing this into his plays. His lighting work is of great importance, despite its simple philosophy, acting as a valuable counterpoint to the imaginative, expressive progressive movements of the time, and above all else reinforcing the value of light as a simple, pure medium through which the actor communicates.

---

[55] Patterson, *The Revolution in German Theatre 1900-1933*, p102.

[56] In his *Was ich will*, Berliner Tageblatt 1927, Piscator said: "Lighting loses all dependence on space, comes alive and wanders. With many graduations and rooted in natural contrasts, it achieves an important role in the composition of the scene by first creating a focus and then spreading boundlessly across the stage" (Patterson, *The Revolution in German Theatre 1900-1933*, p134). In his *Hoppla, wir leben!* (1927) scenes imagined to be simultaneous were separated on stage and the shift between them was created by lighting one while blacking out the other, and crossfading between them. It used multiple houselight cues at the beginning, film and projection, and a filmic use of spotlights to give the feeling of "close ups" on the actors for greater intimacy. From 1955 he was noted for underlighting the stage.

However, progress in Germany was retarded by World War Two, with companies dispersed and most important theatres badly damaged. A rebuilding programme commenced in 1946 to create new theatres with advanced technical facilities, but these did not have an impact until the 1950s. Following a tour of Europe after the war, Ed Kook visited rebuilt major German theatres, noting how similar installations were from one venue to the next, with similar lavish, well equipped stage facilities, with good quality lighting instruments. Projection was particularly well catered for, and discharge sources were used to light the cyclorama.[57]

Russia

Konstantin Stanislavsky (1863-1938) began his theatre career as an actor, but a visit of the Saxe-Meiningen company to Moscow in 1890 prompted his interest in production. With the playwright Nemirovich-Danchenko he founded the Moscow Art Theatre in 1898 where he developed a more natural acting style, and moved towards three-dimensional scenery and highly detailed, realistic settings. He became a master of staging techniques, including the use of light to create and add to scenic atmospheres. As Stanivlasky became more influenced by the anti-realist movements in Europe, he founded The Studio in 1905 to explore this style further and engaged **Vsevolod Meyerhold** (1874-1942) to run it. The Moscow Art Theatre made various tours to Europe before World War One, and again after it. They toured to America in 1922, where Stanivlasky was influenced by the lavish work of David Belasco.[58]

Meyerhold's early work was influenced by Fuchs' book *The Theatre of the Future* 1905, and in particular the contradiction between the three dimensional actor and the two dimensional backcloth. His staging experiments included removing the house tabs, building a deep forestage and employing a bare stage, a single setting or sets made out of drapes. He employed an area lighting technique, probably for the first time in Russia in *The Life of a Man* by Leonid Andreev at the Vera Komisarjevskaya Theatre in St Petersburg in February 1907.[59] He also attempted to light without footlights, as in Sologub's *Death*

[57] *Tabs* 16/2, Sep. 58, p7.

[58] Marshall, *The Producer and the Play,* p97.

[59] Meyerhold staged this production with drapes rather than conventional sets. All footlights, borders and battens were removed in order to achieve a "grey, smokey, monochrome expanse. Grey walls, grey ceiling, grey floor". Each scene used a single source "sufficient only to illuminate the furniture placed about it and the actor who is near the light source" (Rudnitsky, K. *Meyerhold the Director*, Ardis, 1981, p113) The prologue is lit by "an unseen source (that) issues a weak, (cont...)

Victory in 1907.[60] However, this style was not followed in other Russian theatres, although later gaining praise.[61]

Meyerhold saw the playwright, director, actor and audience as partners in performance. He chose simple stylised settings for his platform and was skilled in the use of lighting. Huntly Carter noted that "Meyerhold composes scenes in black and white with great skill. By means of the bare walls of the stage and the limited light at his disposal he sometimes achieves Rembrandtesque effects".[62] He didn't like to conceal his lights – predating techniques often attributed to Brecht. His "two favourite lighting states were an even, overall wash effect, and sharp directional lighting".[63] He wrote copious lighting notes that illustrated a keen understanding of the theatrical values of lighting,[64] and

even light which is just a grey, monotonous, monochrome and ghostly, casting no hard shadows, no brilliant spots of light." The curtain opens "to reveal a deep gloomy expanse... After about three seconds the spectator begins to make out the shapes of furniture in one corner of the stage. Dimly visible are the grey forms of old women, their silhouettes created by a single lamp on stage." A lamp on stage just bright enough to light those around it typified the lighting (Braun, E. *Meyerhold on Theatre*, London: Eyre Methuen, 1969, citing Meyerhold, *O Teatre* pp 198-200). Other examples of area lighting and localised spotting include *Spring Awakening* (1907), with each scene picked out by a single beam, and he used a narrow beam to highlight a moment of particular dramatic significance in *A List of Assets* (1931).

[60] This production drew "grudging praise from his harshest critics for... the plasticity achieved by deploying actors on a broad flight of steps extending the full width of the stage from the line of the proscenium to the back wall." It represented a "significant attempt to break the barrier of the footlights and establish a more direct relationship between the performer and spectator" (Braun, *Meyerhold on Theatre*, p22).

[61] Footlights were normally removed for his productions, although this clearly was not in vogue in other theatres in Russia at the time: "Shameful to relate, in spite of all the attempts to abolish from the big theatre the abomination of subterranean lighting, in spite of all the experiments in this field by Craig, Meyerhold and others, not one theatre in Moscow has seen fit to throw out this outmoded theatrical remnant. Consequently we are left with that other remnant – bourgeois stage illusion" (Braun, *Meyerhold on Theatre*, citing *Vestnik teatra*, 1920 no 72-72 pp8-10).

[62] Carter, H. *The New Spirit of the Russian Theatre, 1917-1928*, New York: Brentano, 1929, p220.

[63] Examples of these include *Sister Beatrice* (1906), "where the flat unvaried lighting complemented the two-dimensionality of the compositions, and after the revolution, *The Dawn* (1920), where he used harsh white light to "dispel all illusion" in a production staged in the spirit of a political meeting, and *The Death of Tarelkin* (1922), when the harsh white light emphasised the utilitarian, and perhaps the circus, characteristics of the productions" (Leach, R. *Vsevolod Meyerhold*: Cambridge, C.U.P., 1989, p104).

[64] For example, his lighting directions for the opera *Don Juan*: "There is no need to plunge the auditorium into darkness, either in the intervals or during the play itself. Bright light infects the spectators with a festive mood as they enter the theatre". His stage directions for Act 3 detail lighting requirements: "I should like to divide the lighting into four phases: (i) At the beginning, evening (effect concentrated on the background).(ii) Gradual dimming of the proscenium lighting in order to heighten the effect of the silhouettes cast on the backdrop by the foliage of the (cont...)

had several motifs that were regularly used in his work, such as: snap cues to punctuate the start of a performance;[65] projection, from the early 1920s;[66] and only occasional use of colour.[67] His last production at the Theatre of the Revolution, *Lake Lyul* in 1924, showed how complex his use of lighting had become. He used illuminated titles and advertisements, silvered screens lit from behind, and used area lighting to switch action from one level to another, sometimes simultaneously playing two scenes in different places.

Italy

The most significant movement in performance style that was to emerge from Italy was the Futurist movement. Beginning in 1909, the movement connected the arts with industrial and mechanical developments. Two notable artists were key to this, **Enrico Prampolini** (1894-1956),[68] a painter, sculptor and

---

trees centre stage. A genuine "Schattenspiel" after the manner of the old travelling theatres. (iii) Complete darkness (the light shining through the foliage disappears in scene six when Don Juan and Sganarelle are alone on stage). The entire stage is lit by a single lantern held by Juan. (iv) Juan conceals lantern under his cloak, quick change in the total darkness, phosphorescent light on the sepulchre after the change of scene". And for Act Five:" Towards the end of scene three the sky on the backdrop is darkened (perhaps it clouds over) to make a more effective scene of the immolation and the flash of lightning which coincides with the thunder in the finale" (Braun, *Meyerhold on Theatre*, citing a letter from Meyerhold to Golovin, 30 May 1909, quoted in Alexander Yakovlevich Golovin, Leningrad and Moscow, 1960 pp159-160).

[65] He utilised snap lighting cues to increase the dramatic power of his work. Describing the opening lights in *The Forest*, "The lights on the stage go up, hard glittering lights which reveal every corner of the stage space in all its crudeness of brick and metal, paint and canvas" (van Gyseghem, A. *Theatre in Soviet Russia*, London: Faber and Faber, 1943, p17). *The Lady of the Camellias* employed a snap out of lights and back on as a signal for starting the play.

[66] In *The Magnanimous Cuckold* (1922) he used projection, otherwise lighting was relatively simple, with stage direction notes merely stating "lighting by searchlights. Coloured bulbs for Burbus's lantern". In *D.E.* (1924) he used three screens, projecting slogans and images onto each to create a complex collage of information. The screens were moved around the stage to create different locations. Most lighting was an even wash, until in a chase scene "spotlights dashed wildly over the scene as the tempo increased" (Leach, *Vsevolod Meyerhold*, p100+106). Another example of his use of projection include scene change text in *The Forest* (1924). *Earth Rampant* (1923), with the designer Popova, contained some of his most ambitious projection work, using colour that did not feature greatly in his usual lighting palette.

[67] There was little mention of coloured lighting playing a significant part in his work. An exception was *The Bedbug* (1929), in which colour was used to contrast between scenes. Reds and yellows were used to create a warm first half. The second half featured cold white and blue, "with Ilinski often in a harsh spotlight. At the moment he recognised the audience the house lights came full on, creating a sense of 'no escape' " (Leach, *Vsevolod Meyerhold*, p160).

[68] Prampolini designed over 100 settings during his career. In his book *Futurist Scenography* of 1915, he called for the abolition of the painted stage, to replace it with a "colourless electro-mechanical architecture, powerfully vitalised by chromatic emanations from a luminous (cont...)

scenographer who went on to become director of the Teatro Magnetico in Rome, and **Fortunato Depero** (1892-1960), a costume designer. However, the movement had little impact on British theatre until the 1960s.[69]

France

Practice in France followed similar lines to the rest of continental Europe. The first French producer to move to realism in performance and settings, influenced by the Saxe-Meiningen company, was **André Antoine** (1858-1943), founding the Théâtre Libre in Paris in 1887 to be a platform for his ideas. His work prompted other developments, such as at the Théâtre d'Art where **Paul Fort** (1872-1960) staged symbolist productions, believing that "theatre should be a place for fantasy and imagination".[70] He abolished realistic scenery, with settings usually comprising swagged drapes. The first attempt at productions without scenery in France was by **Jacques Copeau** (1879-1949) at his Théâtre du Vieux Colombier in Paris between 1913 and 1920. Copeau used grey side and back plaster walls with unconcealed lighting fixed to the auditorium ceiling.[71] Norman Marshall said "the atmosphere for each play was created almost entirely by the lighting".[72] Michel Saint-Denis, a young stage manager there, remembered that "each play seemed to leave traces of its pattern on the stage floor, each design unique".[73] **Antonin Artaud** (1896-1948), actor, director and poet, gave lighting a theatrical role way ahead of the times. In his thesis *The Theatre of Cruelty* (1932), he said that light should create abrupt changes, and stimulate sensations such as heat and cold. He believed that the action of

source, produced by electric reflectors with multicoloured panes of glass, arranged, co-ordinated analogically with the psyche of each scenic action" ... "on a stage illuminated in such a way, the actors will gain unexpected dynamic effects that are neglected or very seldom employed in today's theatres, mostly because of the ancient prejudice that one must imitate, represent reality" (Drain (Ed.), *Twentieth Century Theatre, a Source Book*, p23).

[69] Richard Drain said that: "Their revolutionary scenographic concepts may have taken their start from Gordon Craig, who was already based in Italy, exploring the idea of a theatre of mobile architectural forms. Prampolini and Depero outreached him, liberating scenography from the dramatic text, and devising spectacles geared to a musical or sound score, composed of moving shapes and changing light. They opened a road which branches out into the constructivists, Tadeusz Kantor, 1960s happenings, Robert Wilson, and other developments in performance art" (Drain (Ed.), *Twentieth Century Theatre, a Source Book*, p5).

[70] Marshall, *The Producer and the Play*, p25.

[71] Komisarjevsky, *The Theatre (and a Changing Civilisation)*, p151.

[72] Marshall, *The Producer and the Play*, p58.

[73] Saint-Denis, M. *Training for the Theatre*, New York: Theatre Arts Books, 1982, p28.

light on the mind was important. "We must discover oscillating light effects, new ways of diffusing lighting in waves, sheet lighting like a flight of arrows. Fineness, density and opacity factors must be reintroduced into lighting, so as to produce special tonal properties, sensations of heat, cold, anger, fear and so on." Artaud believed the stage and auditorium should become one, with scenes acted in front of walls designed to absorb light, and said that light must be capable of lighting several scenes at once, independently of each other. He knew that current lighting was no longer adequate, and in many ways predicted a visual aesthetic only achieved in the field of concert lighting in the last decade of the twentieth century.

Technological Developments in Europe

There were only two significant technical developments to come from Europe between 1881 and 1950: equipment for lighting the cyclorama, and for scenic projection.

The lit cyclorama evolved in three stages in the early twentieth century. The first attempts to create a sky with light alone were made by the Spanish/Italian painter and scenic designer **Mariano Fortuny** (1871-1949). In a quest to light the stage with a natural soft, diffuse overhead light, he developed a device called a *sky-dome*. With lights placed above the stage on gantries to allow an operator access, he lit down through bands of coloured silk, hung to create a ¼ or ½ circle above the stage. This resulted in a soft diffuse feel to stage lighting. Usually five silk colours were used – white, black, red, yellow, blue, and each could be adjusted by hand to obtain colour mixes. The system was often supplemented by spots from the wings, and footlights set at low intensity levels could be a useful addition. The sky dome also served as a reflector to direct on-stage light back down, as well as a screen for cloud projection.

He developed these ideas into a model in 1902, and his first full-scale sky-dome was installed at the Théâtre de l'Avenue Bosquet in Paris in 1906, and the following year at the Kroll Opera in Berlin.[74] However the structure proved to be cumbersome and restricted flying scenery. It was also awkward to light, taking too much power for proper effects. Nonetheless it was an important development for stage design and lighting, enabling the images of Appia and Craig to be more easily realised on stage as well as creating a more natural ambience for other stage lighting instruments to key into.

Fortuny's first attempt to create a sky with light alone had been made at La

---

[74] Bergmann, *Lighting in the Theatre*, p340.

Scala Opera House in 1902. Here he installed a cyclorama, made of a double fabric skin, with the air layer in between extracted to keep the surfaces tight. His effects were considered "sensational".[75] This work prompted the next phase of development, which was the simplification of the structure of the sky-dome system to allow better over stage access for flown scenery. The sky dome became replaced by a solid semi-circular curved plaster wall, faced with white plaster, and this, with tiny lamps set into it for a "stars at night" effect, was championed by Reinhardt.

The lighting system developed for the plaster cyclorama was called the *Schwabe System* (see page 61) after the company owner Hans Schwabe.[76] It comprised a large, high powered single light source, which could be coloured by glass sheets arranged in several tiers, mechanically operated to allow 'live' colour change. Another unit served as a projector for clouds, which could be static or animated. In collaboration with Phillips of Holland specially produced lamps of 3,000W and 6,000W were manufactured for the system, significantly brighter than previous incandescent lamps to give the system the necessary power.[77]

The most complex aspect of machinery developed for cyclorama projections of atmospheric conditions was the Schwabe cloud machine. Its single lamp fed 20 optical paths to 20 slide holders to form two tiers of ten individual projectors. The projector could fill a cyclorama with images. The whole apparatus then rotated, to give the clouds movement. A mirror, in each optical path and controlled by motors, could make individual slides move at different speeds, to give a sense of clouds overtaking each other.[78] These machines were very expensive, limiting their application. In 1926 each cost £600, although cheaper, simpler machines from other manufacturers were also available.[79]

Although the cyclorama was first used for creating an artificial sky with light, it became apparent that it offered far greater scenic potential as a screen for projection of a range of naturalistic images. On large German stages, with

---

[75] RSA, *The Journal of the RSA*, "Evolution of Stage Lighting" Vol. xciv, 2/8/46, London: RSA, 1946, p550.

[76] Stern, E. *My Life my Stage*, Camelot, 1951, p70 .

[77] "Bulbs about three times as strong as any incandescent lights used in America in 1922" (Macgowan, K. and Jones, R.E. *Continental Stagecraft*, London: Benn Bros., 1923, p71).

[78] Ridge warned that they were too distracting for the audience, but when used with imagination could be valuable.

[79] It was said that one cost "almost exactly the same cost as the whole of the stage lighting equipment, including control, at Terence Gray's Festival Theatre Cambridge, installed the same year" (Ridge, *Stage Lighting*, p60).

the cyclorama about 20m upstage of the footlights and thus clear of ambient light on stage, it was also used for more abstract images. First, colour and shadow were deployed on the cyclorama, and then projected images, both realistic and non-realistic, became common. This prompted the rise of specialist projection equipment.

After World War One, Germany moved away from the Schwabe cyclorama lighting system for coloured lighting atmospheres to using a battery of 1kW horizon floods. Each lantern was fitted with four coloured glass filters plus a blackout sheet, controlled by tracker wires to allow live colour mixes. It was noted that these created: "great brilliance... effects of great delicacy can be obtained".[80]

The Austrian **Max Hasait** (1874-1951), a master of stage techniques and technical director of Dresden Opera from 1903-1928, who later went on to teach lighting at Dresden University, explored the Swedish projection system called the *Ars System*.[81] This was a rolled canvas cyclorama hung from a semi-circular track, cleverly installed so as not to hinder other scenic elements. He built a motorised canvas cyclorama that could be set or struck in 20 seconds for the Residenz Theatre Munich, devising a method for keeping the very large cloth taut when unrolled around a stage. Schwabe developed an elaborate seven colour portable lighting system for this with both floor and grid units, which incorporated a central projector powered by a single 6000W high powered light source and a complex arrangement of mirrors and lenses.[82] This could project multiple images, such as clouds, panoramically across the whole cyclorama.[83] This system became known as the *Schwabe-Hasait* system, and became available just after World War One.

A variation was devised by **Adolphe Linnebach** (1876-1944), who gave

---

[80] Unidentified document, Theatre Museum Archives.

[81] Lester Groom's paper to the National Association of Supervising Engineers at the St. Bride's Institute in January 1925, described the system in detail: "it consists of a number of large canvas sheets sewn together and painted with a special white composition, forming a smooth screen. This screen runs on a curved rail fixed beneath the grid and is operated by an electric motor which rolls or unrolls it in a few seconds... when the whole cloth is in tension, the result is a perfectly smooth surface from which the light can be reflected evenly and without the shadows which would naturally exist if there were folds in the cloth. The function of (the cloth) is to produce the illusion of a natural sky as a background to the stage setting" (Groom, H.R. Lester, *Modern Developments in Stage Lighting*, N.A.S.E., 13/1/25) (also Klein, *Colour Music*, p176).

[82] As many as 72 were used at the Stockholm State Opera.

[83] Macgowan & Jones, *Continental Stagecraft*, p73.

his name to a form of projection still used today.[84] Taking the name *Linnebach*, the system involved placing a painted screen or slide in front of an unreflected point-source of light, which was usually an arc. Light from the front of the lantern projected the image, giving a soft semi-realistic impression of the art work. The back of the lantern was open too, aligned to illuminate the stage dome to reflect soft lighting back down onto the stage below. It is thought it was first installed in the Konigliches Schauspielhaus in Dresden in 1916. This cheap, simple system was particularly effective for projecting non-realistic images, and was used to great effect by Piscator.

Projection and associated equipment continued to be a key part of staging techniques, particularly in Germany. The company Pani from Austria, which was created in 1930 to specialise in projection equipment for scientific experiments, became drawn into stage work, soon becoming market leader, and made a significant impact with equipment installed in the Vienna State Opera and Burgtheater on its reopening in 1945.

In post-war German theatres, Bentham recalled that there was little front of house lighting, with most spotlighting tending to come from a bridge behind the proscenium. Because of the increased power and throw required in large German theatres, spots were required as batten lighting was not effective. Because overhead battens were problematic anyway when used with a lit cyclorama due to spill light, **Arthur Reiche** (1886-1956), Schwabe's No. 1 technician, developed the *Spielflachen-Beleuchtungskorper* lantern, designed to light the stage from above but not to spill light onto the cyclorama.[85] Schwabe also made a profile called a *Proszenium-Scheinwerfer* (Proscenium Spotlight) from 1920.[86] Limes and arcs were soon replaced by high powered focus spots of up to 5kW, whereas in Britain and America they never exceeded 2kW. This

---

[84] Linnebach had been educated as a marine engineer, and initially had only an amateur interest in the arts. However he combined the two in a career as a leading theatre technician. He specialised in the design of technically complex stages for the facilitation of major scene changes – such as the revolving, sinking and sliding stage at Dresden Hoftheater in 1914. He went on to become Technical Director at the Munich Opera House from 1923-44. There is conflicting evidence of his importance. Macgowan and Jones said that while once the champion of the mechanised stage, he became "contented mechanically with the devices of the electrician" (Macgowan & Jones, *Continental Stagecraft*, p63) whereas Moderwell said of the coming of Linnebach, "we can regard it as symbolic. It stands to us as a sign that the theatre of the future can choose what it needs, instead of taking what it can get" (Moderwell, H.K. *The Theatre of Today* London: John Lane, the Bodley Head, 1915, p38).

[85] The fore-runner and inspiration for Bentham's "Acting Area" lantern.

[86] *Buhnentechnische Rundschau* 6-7, 1920.

lantern could be adapted into a projector with the addition of a condenser lens. Clockwork, and later electric, powered animation slides could then be used for projection of clouds and other atmospheric effects. This led to high quality scenic projectors being developed in Germany, with slide sizes 5x5" and 7x7". Other developments included the use of fluorescent lamps to light the cyclorama, to reduce heavy loading.[87]

Lighting in America

American scenic design at the end of the nineteenth century was similar in style to European, being dominated by realistic painted two-dimensional settings. Kean had toured America with his Shakespeare productions in 1845, and his visit had been influential in promoting this design style.

There were few that proposed change. Stage workers were controlled by a union-syndicate system that tied work to local labour. This had been established in 1896 by New York producers, who considered that scenery was not important. Cost and an awkward labour force were not conducive to adventurous or progressive ideas. Richard Marston, a British designer practising in America at the end of the nineteenth century, reported on the poor overall standard of scene design.[88] Marston went on to say that Henry Irving, who visited America eight times between 1883 and 1904, was an important figure in halting a downward spiral in standards, showing managements that good scenery could be a commercial asset.

There were, nonetheless, practitioners who developed highly complex staging, coupled with stage technology of the most complex order. The pioneer of this movement was **James Steele MacKaye** (1842-1894).[89] Influenced by the emerging film industry, he was the first to bring high realism to the stage

---

[87] *Tabs* 26/2, 1961, pp79-94.

[88] Larson, O.K. *Scene Design in the American Theater from 1915-1960*, Arkansas: University of Arkansas, 1989, p17.

[89] MacKaye, a painter, actor, technical inventor and dramatist, spanned the period from gas to early electric lighting, and was the first practitioner of note to adopt electric light to illuminate the stage, working at the Lyceum Theater, New York. He was credited with a range of complex mechanical staging innovations, such as the stage elevator / disappearing orchestra pit. The platform for much of his invention focused on a World Fair held in Chicago in 1893, where he designed a huge theatre space called the "Spectatorium" for the staging of a *Son et Lumiere* "Story of Columbus" on a massive scale. The size of the venue meant that traditional fixtures such as footlights and battens had no impact on the space, and high powered directional sources were required. MacKaye was obsessed with the recreation of nature's natural light on stage, and, as an example, designed an arc lamp with the power of 50 conventional units, mounted on a track, to imitate the sun. (cont...)

through large scale productions.[90] A.N. Vardac said that throughout his career, his success came from "scenery, mass movements, spectacular action, tableaux, visions, all… thoroughly integrated by music".[91] He held patents for many lighting and stage technology developments, including the manufacture of early electric arc and incandescent lighting instruments,[92] and many special effects.[93] C.B. Cochran met MacKaye while on a visit to America in 1891 and commented on his importance: "He preceded Fortuny with machinery to produce cloud, sun, rain, wave, hail and rainbow effects, and in substituting overhead lighting for footlights".[94] MacKaye's work was technically highly complex and advanced technical theatre practice because it required centralised control of lighting and all staging effects, as well as detailed written cue sheets.

Between 1910 and 1915 there were several key events that initiated a much closer reciprocal interest in and understanding of production practice between America and Europe. **Livingston Platt** (1874-1933) was one of the first Americans to be influenced by the new European staging movements, having worked in Europe. He set up the tiny Toy Theatre in Boston in 1911. He considered his lighting a vital part of his productions, and was noted for a minimal use of footlights, and using spotlights to create pockets of light. He also experimented with scene projection.[95]

As in Germany, lighting developments were prompted by the emerging mechanised stage. However, whereas German practice was to develop the background as a lit environment both through atmospheric colour wash and projection, in America developments were to focus more closely on lighting

---

Although money ran out before the project was complete, a scaled down version was opened, and provided a forum to demonstrate his command of lighting. Fort recorded that: "his goal was a to create movement, variety, color shadings, and emotional texture of a complex lighting design by virtually projecting "moving pictures" (albeit abstract ones) across the acting area" (Tim Fort "MacKaye's lighting visions…" *Nineteenth Century Theatre*, Vol. 18 1990, p35).

[90] Mordden, E. *The American Theatre*, Oxford: OUP, 1981, p42.

[91] Vardac, A.N. *Stage to Screen*, Massachusetts: Da Capo, 1949, p139.

[92] Izenour, G.C. *Theater Technology*, New York: McGraw-Hill 1988, p108.

[93] Some of his lighting inventions are worthy of note: in 1893 he developed a colour drum called a "Colorator" that projected both colours and images, used later by Belasco to acclaim in *Madam Butterfly* of 1900; he was granted a patent on a crude form of light curtain called a "Luxauleator" that, when rigged at the proscenium, was used as a scene change device by creating an opaque wall of light; and a novel way of projecting clouds by lighting through wire scrimmed cloud shapes, tracked on wires, called a "Nebulator", that was the forerunner of the Linnebach scenic projector. His patents were taken up by the American lighting company Kliegl in 1896.

[94] Cochran, *The Showman Looks On*, p56.

[95] Larson, *Scene Design in the American Theater from 1915-1960*, p37.

the actor. The work and writings of Appia and Craig were initially less well known in America than in Europe, with Appia not being acknowledged until after the start of World War One. Craig's magazine *The Mask* was available through American theatre bookshops, and nine American editions of *On the Art of Theatre* were published between 1911 and 1914. This new thinking was further brought to America's attention through an exhibition in Cambridge (Mass.) in 1914 of European and American stage designs by Samuel J. Hume who had worked with Craig in Florence.[96] This prompted the production of more "intellectually challenging" plays, with a more experimental approach to staging following in tandem. The first 'art' theatres in America were founded in the 1910s in Los Angeles, San Francisco, Detroit, Chicago and Washington, inspired by this emerging new practice from Europe. Over the next ten years the movement grew rapidly, and by 1925 art theatres, with an artistic policy to produce challenging material, offered a substantial alternative to commercial theatre in New York, and promoted a design style tending towards simplification and stylisation.

Art theatre introduced Americans to the new movements in thought and practice from Europe, principally the work of Appia, Craig, Stanislavsky and Copeau. This prompted a sea-change in the way plays were produced, promoting the director, writer and designer as a creative partnership.[97] The hyper-realistic work of practitioners such as Belasco was swept away, and a new band of designers emerged, many from a university education (see Appendix iv), crafting simple, often highly representative or symbolic settings that were ideal to utilise lighting as a dynamic staging device. Five of this new wave, Robert Edmund Jones, Norman Bel Geddes, Jo Mielziner, Lee Simonson and Donald Oenslager, went on to dominate American theatre design from 1920 for the next 30 or so years. New York Art theatres such as the Group

---

[96] The work of practitioners such as Urban, Jones, Stern, Craig, Appia and Bakst were represented in photographs, sketches and models. There was a model theatre stage that featured a German *kuppelhorizont*, built by Hume, that was lit using colour filters made by the Boston chemist Pevear. The exhibition transferred to New York later in the same year. There, Robert Edmund Jones staged a demonstration of the lighting potential of the model stage every afternoon. The exhibition later toured to Chicago, Detroit and Cleveland.

[97] Reinhardt's *Sumürun* came to New York in 1912 and *The Miracle* in 1924. In 1927 Reinhardt brought over a German company for a repertory season, finally emigrating to America in the 1930s and going on to produce several more productions there. French theatre influence came to New York in 1917 when Jacques Copeau brought his Vieux Colombier company from Paris. Influenced by Appia, Copeau brought his staging theories to the attention of the American audience for the first time.

Theatre,[98] the Theatre Guild,[99] the Actor's Theatre and the Federal Theatre gained a reputation for work of the highest artistic and visual standards.

Whereas in Britain few stage designers actively lit their designs, in America it was usual for the designer to undertake this role. Indeed, many designers, such as Jones and Simonson, also directed. As a result, a style emerged in the 1920s of settings and lighting not only in harmony but with lighting highly influential in the way sets were designed. Generally, settings were simple and built so as to be responsive to light, in terms of openness, quality of surface textures and paint finishes, and to allow a good range of lighting angles to shape the drama. Thus design was kept 'alive' by allowing light, added at the final moment when rehearsals were complete, a fuller role. Lighting could now be deployed that responded to the director's needs and the actors' chemistry. The designer became indispensable. A growing confidence instilled through education saw them readily accepted as an essential contributor, and a strong union protected their employment and enhanced their public status to the point where the best were as well known as anyone else in the production.[100]

Lighting in Art theatres by the 1930s had become of sufficient complexity and importance, driven by the American way of hiring tailor-made rigs for each production, that they became a platform for the first lighting designers. Pioneers of this new role were Abe Feder, who gained lighting credits from 1932 including Orson Welles's production of Marlowe's *Dr Faustus* in 1935, and Moe Hack, whose first credited production *One Third a Nation* in 1938 was reported as being a "terrifying lighting plot… a triumphant statement".[101] George Izenour, who went on to become one of the most important influences on lighting in America for his technological developments, started as the lighting supervisor at the Federal Theatre in 1937.[102]

---

[98] Gorelik designed many of the Group's productions. The philosophy was that the production rather than the star was the focus of the work, and that while projects had a director, who "in turn helped form and guide the group" Clurman, R. *The Fervent Years*, New York: Hill & Wang, 1957, p33.

[99] The Theatre Guild was nearest to an established repertory art theatre in America. Set up in 1919, it had a large stage and "adequate and flexible lighting" although without a cyclorama, and presented a adventurous programme of new European and American writers (Cheney, *The Art Theater*, p71).

[100] Growing militancy amongst US backstage workers had led to the main scenic designers (still called "stage decorators" in the early 1920s) joining the United Scenic Artists union in 1923. By 1925 contracts were agreed that, amongst other issues, set the pattern of payment in three phases (on signing the contract; mid production; and first night), artistic independence from the producer and an appropriate billing status.

[101] Atkinson, B. & Hirschfeld, A. *The Lively Years 1920-1977*, New York, Da Capo, 1973

[102] O'Connor, J., & Brown, L. (Eds.), *The Federal Theatre Project*, London: Eyre Methuen, 1980, p9.

Technological Developments in America

There were many similarities between the first American and British electric lighting rigs. Each had footlights to light the faces, and battens to wash in colours and spots to pick out highlights. But in America, technical advances came much sooner. Focus spots were first developed in 1912 and front of house lighting was first recorded in 1915.[103] The technique of area lighting of the stage with spots was first claimed by Geddes in 1916.[104]

Lamps were initially dipped to achieve colour, and later, as in Britain, gelatine sheets were used. The control switchboard was normally in the wings, worked by teams of men. Cycloramas became popular after World War One, but as flown cloths rather than solid walls.[105] Projection had less impact than in Europe.

Arcs, considered harsh and with poor colour rendering properties, were less popular in America than in Europe. A range of compact incandescent lamps were developed in the early 1920s that prompted small, high efficiency spotlights.[106] This in part had been due to an easier manufacturing process when working to the American 120 volt system, but also because of a more enlightened approach to manufacture.[107]

---

[103] In *Miracle in the Evening* (Doubleday, 1960, p149 & p160) Bel Geddes claimed to have made the first ever incandescent spot in 1912, and that Belasco used FOH lighting in his production *The Boomerang* (1915), which caused quite a stir. Bel Geddes had also claimed the first use of FOH lighting in his production in his season at the Little Theatre Los Angeles in 1916, although Granville Barker had used some floods FOH (ineffectual due to their spill over the audience, as he used hooded floods rather than focus spots) in his production of *A Midsummer Nights Dream* a few months earlier. McCandless claimed he was the first to fit spotlights to the circle front (*Tabs* 21/3, Dec. 63, p39).

[104] Of the production of *Nju* in 1916, the *LA Graphic* said "a new method of stage illumination restricts light to selected areas instead of being general, so that sections of it remain in darkness when desirable. Lamps are grouped on the balcony rail at either side of the auditorium and focused on the stage in place of footlights. The skilful lighting provides swiftly moving scene changes without the lowering of curtains and long waits." The *LA Times* talked of "a play set in a new fashion, wherein the imagination is called into play rather than the photographic eye of infinite detail" (Geddes, *Miracle in the Evening*, p166).

[105] An early example of a lit cyclorama was recorded in Chicago in 1894, ahead of European practice (*ABTT News*, Aug. 85, p10, citing *Scientific American 22/2/1896*).

[106] A letter from Stanley McCandless (to whom Hartmann had been an adviser) published in *Tabs* 21/3, Dec. 63, p39 said that it was Hartmann who persuaded the lamp companies to make tight filament lamps that in turn led to highly efficient American spotlights. Dean noted during his visit in 1920 that there had been many developments in lamp technology, with 250W, 500W and 1kW incandescent lamps being manufactured.

[107] These lamps had smaller bulbs and grid filaments. At 120v DC lamps could be significantly brighter and more efficient than the British equivalents, as a smaller filament meant a smaller bulb, and a smaller bulb meant smaller housings. Light was more concentrated at a "centre" in a (cont...)

Probably the most important lantern to be developed in the twentieth century was the sharp-edged spotlight, called in Britain the *Profile* and in America the *Ellipsoid*.[108] Although the American version was launched around the same time as the Stelmar, unlike in Britain it completely reformed the way the stage was lit. It was ideal to create a style of tight area lighting, high definition spotting, with minimal stray 'spill' light into unwanted areas of the stage, and was pioneered by Geddes. The methods for deploying this instrument were first documented by Stanley McCandless in his book *A Method of Lighting the Stage*, published in 1932, a practice that modern lighting rigs still adhere to.

America was well ahead of Britain in the field of lighting control too, with the first all-electronic control installed at the vast, high profile, 6,150 seat and a 100' proscenium opening Radio City Music Hall in New York in 1933. The control was sited in the orchestra pit with full view of the stage, where Eugene Braun "devises and arranges the lighting of these marvellous shows".[109]

This lighting control marked a watershed in the development of stage lighting. Made by General Electric, probably to the design of McCandless, the control had five presets of 314 channels each. In 1971 Bentham said that it was "a quite remarkable engineering achievement for that time and it is still there and working".[110] It used the thyratron-controlled dimmer, the forerunner of the modern thyristor dimmer. Although it was very expensive, this was the first generation of controls that allowed lighting states to be preset in advance of

---

compact filament lamp, and thus was easier to focus precisely and, as more light is gathered, was significantly brighter.

[108] There is some doubt as to who first developed it, when it was launched and whether or not it pre-dated the British "Stelmar" lantern, but it appears it was developed by Bel Geddes and **Joseph Levy** (dates not known). Levy set up Century Lighting Company in New York in 1929, which really prospered with the recruitment of salesman **Edward F. Kook** (1903-1990) (Geddes, *Miracle in the Evening*, p197). In 1933 Levy and Kook took out a patent for an ellipsoidal spotlight which they called the "Leko" (*Lights!* 3/3, p6). The first model utilised a 120v 1500W lamp, and was soon followed by a 500W version. The spotlight entered the Century catalogue in 1934. Joel E. Rubin doubted the claims of Levy and Kook that this was a "first", believing that Kliegl had in fact demonstrated an ellipsoidal unit to the Illuminating Engineering Society of the USA in Chicago in 1933, confirmed by McCandless in a letter twenty years later (*Lighting and Sound International* Sep. 94, p39).

[109] *Tabs* 5/2, Sep. 47, p21. This control also prompted the relocation of controls to FOH positions. Larson noted that the Paramount Theatre New York was the first US theatre to do this in the early 1930s (the operator had to wear a tuxedo!), although Bel Geddes noted the first time a control had been located FOH had been for his production of Reinhardt's *The Miracle* in New York in 1924 (Larson, *Scene Design in the American Theater from 1915-1960*, p122 & Geddes, *Miracle in the evening*, p293).

[110] *Tabs* 29/2, June 71, p50.

their cue operation, with any lantern set to any intensity level.[111] This represented a major step forward in the type of cue that could be operated, and paved the way to the 'dipless crossfade', a cue where lights seamlessly fade from one level to another in synchronisation and without dipping their light levels in mid-cue. Other high-capacity controls were also developed at this time, in sharp contrast to the approach of British manufacturers.[112]

During a visit to America after World War Two, Strand's Leonard Applebee noted that American equipment was ahead of Britain.[113] He recalled that most lanterns were 500W spots, smaller than a British 1kW unit yet as bright.[114] He noted that three types were common:

- the Fresnel, used for general acting area light, and placed on the circle front, No. 1 bar and stage booms
- the Mirror Spot (*Ellipsoid*), with irises and shutters and in wattages from 250W to 1500W, used for spotting
- the Projector, not dissimilar to the British Pageant lantern, and normally used for backlighting

Most tellingly of all, he said that battens were only used for lighting cloths. America was also ahead of Britain in the range of colours available.[115]

---

[111] It is interesting to note that Ridge and Aldred reviewed McCandless's "proportional simultaneous dimming" board, 15 years ahead of its introduction in British theatre (Ridge and Aldred, *Stage Lighting, Principles and Practice*). It was much too expensive of a cash-strapped British theatre market, which at least knew of this control through the book.

[112] The Rockefeller Foundation put up money in 1939 for the development of a thyratron control for Yale University. Delayed by the war, it was not finished until 1943. This control, made under the guidance of George Izenour, who was to become one of America's leading theatre consultants and technologists, comprised ten presets controlling 44 twin-thyratron valve dimmers (Bentham, *Sixty Years of Light Work*, p147).

[113] Leonard G. Applebee (?-1964) was born into a theatre family that believed that "the show must go on". His grandfather was Master Gasman at Drury Lane and Alexandra Palace, and his father Master Gasman and later Electrical Engineer for George Edwardes at the Gaiety Theatre. He trained as an electrical engineer at the Birkbeck Institute and joined Edwardes at the Gaiety in 1912, and then joined C.B.Cochran in 1919. He joined Strand in 1922, and became a director in 1945. He designed most of the early equipment, including the footlight, batten and the first switchboard. He started the theatre lighting department in 1923 which he ran until his retirement. Later he became General Sales Manager. He was Chair of the Stage Lighting Committee of the IEE for seven years and became a Fellow of the IES in 1941. He retired from Strand in 1957 and in later years lectured on lighting at the RSA, the IES and at the Drama Faculty at Yale.

[114] *Tabs* 5/2, Sep. 47, p21.

[115] The first gelatine manufacturing company in America was Brigham of Vermont in 1877. Their full range grew to 95 colours, including a variegated gel, but they produced a swatch of only 24, listed in Fuchs's *Stage Lighting* in 1929. Fuchs also listed a range of forty gelatines available from the New York company Townsend, and gave detailed instructions for its home-manufacture, (cont...)

Williams listed 70 gelatines available from Century in 1947, and noted their strength, thinness and higher quality than their British counterparts.[116] Importantly, the Century range featured a full complement of pale blue colours.

Applebee also saw the advances in lighting control. He viewed an Electronic preset desk that had been developed by George Izenour. A play was staged as a demonstration of its capabilities, which contained an unheard of 273 cues in 30 minutes. He noted that the most progressive equipment such as this was to be found in the universities, where the curriculum allowed for research and development. He noted a major divergence in practice between American and British stages, saying that except for a few major resident companies, stages were permanently equipped only with a mains intake, and all equipment was hired in. It was common practice to specify lighting requirements on a show-by-show basis, rather than accept the pool of resident equipment, perhaps supplemented by some hired specials, as was British practice.[117] This approach would have undoubtedly meant that more thought and planning was required, and that there was a greater potential for good lighting.

Bentham compared British and American practice since 1945. He noted that while most British theatres still had only minimal batten rigs, dimmers and control, with supplementary equipment hired in, with only major houses such as the Memorial Theatre Stratford having sufficient permanent equipment, in America everything was hired, even the control and dimmers. In Britain this normally meant that lighting was compromised, as it was seen as an additional cost, whereas in America it was seen as an integral cost.[118] Bentham noted that Americans were 'obsessed' with patching to reduce dimmer numbers, a

---

which pointed to the fact that many theatres, in particular those remote from major cities, would routinely have made their own gelatines. Rosco of New York commenced manufacture of gelatines in 1910, claiming that "we never invented a colour, they have always come in response to a designer's or cameraman's need" (Stan Miller, President of Rosco, in personal correspondence to author). There are swatchbooks of Rosco gelatine in their German archive dating back to 1918.

[116] Williams, *The Technique of Stage Lighting*, p36. However Applebee thought they were not as robust as those made in Britain "but then they are not perturbed at having to change the colours every five or six days" (*Tabs* 5/2, Sep. 47, p21).

[117] An article by Wolfe Kaufman on American lighting practice appeared in the *New York Times* in 1952. He said that it had been normal for an American theatre to provide footlights plus a certain amount of other equipment, and an incoming show either used just this or hired extra kit, and by 1952 theatres probably owned even less, with rigs rented for each production. He felt there was a tendency in America to overvalue design and lighting, and they could over-dominate a production: "You still need technical assistance... but it has to be right... and not too much" (*Tabs* 10/3, Dec. 52, p12).

[118] *Tabs* 16/2, Sep. 58, p21.

comment that typified his own narrow, perhaps blinkered, commercial approach to lighting design.[119]

A later work of Robert Edmund Jones that transferred to London polarised the difference in lighting approach between the two countries. *Lute Song* at the Winter Garden Theatre in 1948 was lit by 107 spots (40 x Patt 73; 59 x Patt 43; 8 x Patt 50), and only two 6' battens were used. Much extra scaffold had to be rigged to achieve double stacked bars to mount the lanterns, and 96 additional ways of dimming were required.[120] This production had an equipment call greatly in excess of any British mounted production from this era.

Influential Artists Visiting Britain, 1881-1914

This section examines the contribution of practitioners visiting from abroad, set in three time periods of 1881-1914; 1914-1935; and 1935 to 1950.

American dancer **Loie Fuller** (1862-1928) became a star of the London stage around the turn of the century, bringing stunning lighting techniques to the attention of the public, synchronised into her spectacular dance routines.[121] She was best known as a solo performer, arranging her own dances and

---

[119] *Cue* 28, Mar. 84, p20.

[120] *Tabs* 6/3, Dec. 48, p18.

[121] She emerged at the *Folies Bergère* in 1893 where became a celebrity, enjoying the friendship of artists such as Lautrec and Renoir (Kermode, F. *Theatre Arts*, 9/62, p8). Although overshadowed as a performer by her contemporary Isadora Duncan, her work gained respect for the use of illusion and light. She had become aware of lighting when acting in a part that required the illusion of hypnosis. The stage was lit by green footlights, and her costume was an Indian skirt made of gauze that was much too long. She found that by gliding around the stage, holding the skirt up, that she received much approval from the audience. She defined "motion" as "not only the dancing body but the movement of light, color and silk" (Sommer, S. *Loie Fuller*, The Drama Review 19/1, Mar. 75, p54). She researched the effects of light on this costume and found that she: "obtained modulations of a character before unknown ... Finally I reached a point where each movement of the body was expressed in the folds of the silk, in a play of colours and draperies that could be mathematically and systematically calculated" (Kermode, *Theatre Arts* 9/62, p9). She performed *Aladdin* at the Standard Theatre New York in 1887, which was recorded at the time that it "offered the most spectacular lighting effects in the history of American theatre". During a scene change, coloured light played on a curtain of steam, and a rich harmony of colour was created for a sunrise effect. (In *The Black Crook*, prior to this, there had also been spectacular effects, such as the creation of a rainbow projected onto a fountain, made by projecting light through a prism) (Current, R. & M. *Loie Fuller: Goddess of Light* Boston: NE University Press, 1997, p20/1). In *Light and Dance*, published in 1908, she explained the theories behind her work: "Our acquaintance with the production and variations of these effects (coloured light) is precisely at the point where music was when there was no music... Man, past master of the musical realm, is today still in the infancy of the art, from the standpoint of control of light" (Drain, *Twentieth Century Theatre, a Source Book*, p245). She discussed the effect of different types of natural daylight on the person, and on the behaviour of a person in a conservatory glazed with different coloured panes of glass. In her (cont...)

exploiting the contrast between a darkened stage and a bright followspot, and was the first to apply chiaroscuro lighting to the stage before it was detailed as a staging device by Appia.[122] Paul Morand wrote in his *1900*: "In front of her, all artists become entranced; it is the creature enveloped in the moon; queen of indecision; goddess of evocation. In turn, light, flame, star, dragonfly, waving her extended arms from which fly polychrome gazes".[123]

Fuller pioneered many lighting techniques. It was noted that she worked in a darkened auditorium,[124] and she dispensed with traditional fixtures such as battens and footlights, and employed multiple hand held moving spots, working with both reflected and direct light in her performances.[125] She experimented with projected images, using either two lanterns or a stereopticon to impose one image on another or create changing images. As an accomplished technician, she directed a large technical crew with skill to co-ordinate spotting and colour change (see illustration overleaf).[126] Such was the extent of her lighting that the *Ballet of Light*, part of a variety bill at the London Hippodrome in September 1908 was noted for the power consumption of the lighting.[127]

Fuller was well known for the range of colour used in her performance. She used colour wheels of gelatine on the limelights, a common idea, but to her

autobiography *Fifteen Years of a Dancer's Life* (1913), she reflected on the effective qualities of colour and its relation to sound and mood. She thought of herself using light as a musician uses sound, and predicted that "there would come a time when light with all its rhythms, tones and harmonies would be played on an instrument just as music was" (Current, *Loie Fuller: Goddess of Light*, p146).

[122] Larson, *Scene Design in the American Theater from 1915-1960*, p31.

[123] Komisarjevsky, *The Theatre (and a changing civilisation)*, p134, translated by Anne Hogan.

[124] ABTT *News* Sep. 85, p11, citing *Scientific American* 20/6/1896.

[125] 34 were used on *Salome*.

[126] Fuller was happy for electricians to be in full view of the audience, a stage style that was to prompt a new approach to the role of the technician in the twentieth century (Drain, *Twentieth Century Theatre, a Source Book*, p26) and was rigorous in rehearsal: "I would say, "tell No. 1 to put on blue: now tell No. 2 to put on red; No. 3 yellow" and so on. My eyes would recognise a false combination at once, and alter it until I got what was right. Then my Stage Manager noted it down. I arranged the rhythmic fall of colors one after the other in the same way…" (Sommer. *Loie Fuller,* p60, citing articles from *The Theatre Collection*, Lincoln Centre Library, and Carter, A. *Dance Theatre Journal*, Nov 98).

[127] 1000 amps were used to power the lighting "enough to light a whole town of 30,000 inhabitants". This was seen by Henry Russell, director of the Boston Opera, who invited her to give advice on lighting arrangements in his new theatre. This she did the following year, recommending no footlights, spotlights scattered around the theatre, projected scenery and a glass floor above the stage floor to light through (Current, *Loie Fuller: Goddess of Light*, p194 and Theatre Museum Archives).

Skirt Dance. Scientific American 20/061896. Courtesy Scientific American.

own secret colour specification, trusting few with the chemical mixes.[128] She chose colours with great care, and rehearsed the lighting meticulously, using strong tones from side arcs in classic dance lighting manner, as Ridge and Aldred recorded, to "obtain rainbow effects".[129] Her costumes were designed and manufactured to interact with light – in *La Danse Blanche* from *Salome* at least ten hues of light were used, carefully choreographed to echo and enhance the costume".[130] In 1902 she experimented with radium, having been introduced to it by Pierre and Marie Curie, applying it to costumes to experiment with its luminous qualities. In the *Radium* dance, slides of colour were projected onto silk, crossfading from one to another, and overlaying the slides for complex effects.

Perhaps her best known work was *Danse du Feu*, which used one of her signature devices. Taking the idea of underlighting from a fountain she saw in Paris in 1892, she incorporated a glass panel in the stage floor, through which a red spot was projected:[131]

"Heavy black chenille curtains are hung all around the stage and a jet black carpet laid over the entire floor except over a glass plate which has been sunk into a space about four feet by four cut in the centre of the stage. Ten feet below this plate stands Burt Fuller guarding his two lamps. Four step ladders are arranged in the left and right wings nearest the audience, and on each stands an electrician, with his searchlight in his hand. Revolving in front of each of these lights is a round piece of pasteboard, from 12-16" in diameter, with a border of disks of different colors. Some of these disks are solid, others show a combination of 2, 3, 4 or more colors, and the men work them rapidly and harmoniously. The two principal lights underneath the stage are of great power, and they alone produce more effects than of the side lights put together".[132]

"Powerful red lights were thrown on Miss Fuller as she danced above the glass plates in the stage, waving an enormous scarf, a great flood of fire seemed to envelop her, illuminating her drapery beneath, from the interior of

---

[128] In 1892 spectators were impressed by the "diamond like brilliance" and the "constantly changing colours that came from the electric lamps" (Current, *Loie Fuller: Goddess of Light*, p46).

[129] Ridge and Aldred, *Stage Lighting, Principles and Practice*, p108.

[130] Current, *Loie Fuller: Goddess of Light*, p95-7.

[131] Kermode, *Theatre Arts*, 9/62, p16.

[132] Sommer, *Loie Fuller*, p60, citing *The New York Blade*, 11/4/1896.

her skirts as well as exteriorly. She seemed a mass of living fire and her scarves great tongues of flame."

"In the Fire Dance, the two principal lights are used almost exclusively. The dress worn in this dance is a simple full slip made of plain white thin material... But no sooner does she rest on the glass plate then the hem seems to catch fire. Up the flames creep... The more she fans the gauze... the higher the flames leap and the redder they glow, until she finally snatches a gauze scarf from her neck...beats at her draperies until the scarf too catches the glowing color, and in an instant nothing but inky blackness is left to tell the tale".[133]

Fuller performed regularly in London. When touring Britain in 1889, she became heavily influenced by the Gaiety Girls and their skirt dancing, and developed a dance called the *Serpentine Dance* where light was projected onto a flimsy skirt which could be manipulated by extending batons from her arms. One costume, for *Le Lys du Nile* in 1895 was made of 500 yards of silk and extended into space ten feet around her body.[134] She visited London again in 1923, and her troupe had great success with a shadow ballet called *Ombres Gigantesques,* where light yet again was a key part of the staging (see illustration overleaf). Fuller was without doubt a great influence on British theatre, and she was the first to bring showy effects lighting to the attention of the British public.[135] She perhaps did not however receive enough tributes for her pioneering work in stage lighting. Richard Drain said that her work "opened the way towards the experiments of the futurists, Kandinski and the Bauhaus".[136] She was seen as a showman rather than a purist, and therefore

---

[133] Sommer, *Loie Fuller*, p60, citing articles from *The Theatre Collection*, Lincoln Centre Library.

[134] Such was the popularity of the *Serpentine Dance* act that it was parodied by "Little Tich", a popular Parisian music hall act. Apparently Little Tich "appeared in the voluminous shirts of La Loie, chasing the coloured lights from the projectors, the delight of the spectators surpassed all bounds" (Cochran, *The Showman Looks On*, p46).

[135] It was claimed that the Lyceum pantomime regularly copied her work, and that Mr. E.J. Nicol, a member of her company, said "our whole modern system of projected stage lighting owes its origin to her ingenious mind." Nicol also suggested that she influenced Edward Gordon Craig (Frank Kermode, *Theatre Arts*, September 1962, p14). Adrian Klein was a great admirer of her work. In his book, he said that Fuller was one of the pioneers in the use of coloured light and "her original inventions have been imitated all over the world". He remembered one particular effect *(Danse du feu?)* where three lights were placed under the stage shining through the floor, and with rapidly changing colours gave her figure the feeling of being "enshrouded in a silent and iridescent column of flame". He said she must have been one of the first to use light as an integral part of the emotional scheme of the ballet, and that she always attempted to interpret the mood of the music in her lighting (Klein, *Coloured Light – an Art Medium*, p179).

[136] Drain, *Twentieth Century Theatre, a Source Book*, p228.

Ombres Gigantesque, The Sketch, 12/12/1923 courtesy Illustrated London News picture library.

sat outside mainstream theatre, which lessened her status as an artist of light.

An exhibition titled *"Loie Fuller: Magician of Light"*, held at the Virginia Museum of Fine Arts in Richmond in Spring 1979, was one of the few extensive tributes to her work. Sally Sommer reflected that "she dreamed of a theatre of the future to be called "The Temple of Light". The dancers would have been the only forms, the music arising from an invisible orchestra. Light would palpitate from all around through the walls of glass....", and went on to record that Fuller had said "I consider my work to be the point of departure of the great light symphony which will transform the theatre of the future. We don't know enough about the infinite resources of light, and how many treasures are enclosed in a simple ray of a projector".[137]

Fuller influenced many of the British practitioners credited with the rise of the lighting designer.

Several of **David Belasco**'s (1853-1931) productions transferred to London, such as *Madam Butterfly*, which transferred to the Duke of York's Theatre in

---

[137] Sommer, *Loie Fuller*, p67.

1900.[138] His Chief Electrician and trusted companion the Russian **Louis Hartmann** (1877/8-1941) thought that this was his most successful production, in particular the scene where Cho-Cho-San waits for Pinkerton to come home with her child.[139] While her vigil was supposed to represent a whole night, in fact it lasted fourteen minutes in stage time. He employed a changing lighting atmosphere to hold the audience's attention and steer their imagination through the scene.

Belasco, with Hartmann in support, formed perhaps the first true lighting design team, combining their respective viewpoints on art, vision and technology to produce work that significantly pushed the boundaries of stage lighting forward.

Belasco strove to achieve realism on stage with a level of detail previously unseen, and he wanted light to play a key role in this by attempting to recreate as natural a lighting feel as possible.[140] He did not approve of the work of

---

[138] Belasco was the most prominent actor-manager, playwright and producer in New York theatre at the turn of the century. He drew his influences from European trends and in turn was influential in Europe. He visited London in 1885, and having served his apprenticeship as a stage manager in a variety of American theatres (including being under MacKaye at the Lyceum between 1885-1890), he made his debut as a Broadway producer in 1890. He went on the produce over 300 plays, and was a prolific writer on theatre matters. Two theatres were named after him.

[139] In 1896 he joined Tairov's Kamerny Theatre in Moscow, admiring their use of light and colour. With the coming of political upheaval in Russia he left for America, becoming lighting advisor and technician to David Belasco in 1901. He remained his Chief Electrician until 1929. Belasco described him as: "a genius... expert in lights shading and coloring, an artist who paints with light beams and diffused glows instead of pigments and brushes". *Tabs* in 1976 asked the question if Hartmann was the first ever lighting designer, suggesting that "he must surely be, at least, one of the first". His book *Stage Lighting*, New York: DBS, 1930, contained quotes that, in *Tabs'* view, underpinned this claim. These quotes certainly enhance his credentials, suggesting a mature understanding of his craft. He believed in a well researched, planned approach coupled to an understanding that often it is the simple image in the context of a clear visual aesthetic that speaks most clearly: "The man with "theatre sense" will get more actual results with crude apparatus than a highly trained technician, who lacks this gift, with elaborate paraphernalia". "So many units were used that the scenery was virtually burned up with light. Quantity and not quality was the result." "To obtain good results the men must be trained. It is just as necessary to coach the men who work the mechanical effects as it is to rehearse the actors. It is far better to do things in a simple way and do them well than to attempt to do them spontaneously in an elaborate manner and make a bungling job of it". "Knowledge acquired by experience is a great asset if we use it to guide improvement and new development; but if we try to use it as a standard or formula it is apt to hold us back".

[140] In his book, he detailed his production process and the value he placed on lighting: "the all-important factor in a dramatic production is lighting the scenes. Night after night we experiment together to obtain color or atmospheric effects, aiming always to make them aid the interpretation of the scenes. Lights are to drama what music is to the lyrics of a song. No other factor that enters a production of a play is so effective in conveying its moods and feeling. The greatest part of my success in the theatre I attribute to my feeling for colors, translated into effects of light. (cont...)

Appia and Reinhardt,[141] and was keenly aware of the importance of the effect changing light could have on the actor, and worked in detail to fuse performance and atmosphere through heightening the awareness of light with his performers.[142]

Belasco used multiple following limes, and he preferred soft edge following. He deployed a traditional batten rig, but with only occasional footlights, retracting them into the stage when not in use. He allowed overhead lighting to dominate on stage, used front of house positions, and also experimented with indirect reflected light from above.[143]

The lighting effects on my stages have been secured only after years of experiments and at an expense which many other producers would consider ridiculous" (referring to his production of *The Girl of the Golden West* in 1905). "Sometimes I have spent five thousand dollars attempting to reproduce the delicate hues of a sunset and then have thrown the scene away altogether" (Belasco, D. *The Theatre Through its Stage Door*, New York and London: Harper and Bros., 1919, p55).

[141] He did not speak highly of experimental approaches such as those of Reinhardt and Craig: "and yet I am told that all this is not art, that art consists of pink and yellow and blue splotches upon a curtain, or draperies illuminated from above by shafts of white electric light. I reply that when you use false lights and colors you do not stimulate imagination, you only distort reality. And when you distort reality you have destroyed truth" (Belasco, *The Theatre Through its Stage Door*, p232).

[142] He said that: "The spell produced by light is an incalculable aid to the art of the actor. Light has a psychological effect which perhaps the actor is not able to understand or explain, but he feels it instantly and responds to it, and then the audience just as quickly responds to him. I have sometimes doubled the persuasiveness of a speech.... by increasing the value of the light in which the character stands." (Belasco, *The Theatre Through its Stage Door*, p74).

[143] At the Belasco Theatre he was able to specify a lighting rig that was developed out of his years of research and experiment. He had a rig installed where footlights could retract into the stage when not needed. He was open minded about the use of footlights, finding occasions when they were both invaluable and obsolete, and principally used them as a means of creating the feeling of reflected light when a sense of key or shadow was not required. He used overhead and sidelight, and also developed a system of reflected light placed overhead to aid realistic lighting. He used "bulls-eyes" (focus spots) placed on the balcony front. All his equipment was home-made in his theatre work-shops. Belasco recommended reflected light to give an exterior feel, and Hartmann (his chief) built reflector units to facilitate this soft light. Commercially available gelatine colours in those days were quite saturated, so he specialised in making pale colours for a more natural toning of the set. He also treated gelatine sheets to obtain a graded colour effect. Under his guidance, colour control advanced to a level whereby in a later production of *Madam Butterfly* in 1910 live colour changes were achieved with the use of colour scrolls. He deployed battens with lamps wired in three groups (rather than four) to keep colours very closely spaced to achieve an even greater softness to their light. He was keenly aware of the need to balance light and create areas of light and shade within a set, and had manufactured a wide range of lens spotlights in a variety of intensities. If actors moved towards a lamp, then the operator would be instructed to dim it to keep the balance of the picture. He required control systems to be small enough for a single operator, laid out with thought for ease of groupings of colours and areas of the rig. He recommended that 30 x 3kW dimmers were adequate for the average production. Controls were calibrated in five main positions (off, quarter, (cont...)

The Viennese scenic artist **Joseph Urban** (1872-1933) was another important practitioner to visit Britain. His work with paint and light made him an important figure in the development of visual aesthetics on stage. He became artistic director at the Boston Opera in 1911, having previously worked extensively across Europe (including the Royal Opera House Covent Garden), and then at the Metropolitan Theatre New York from 1917. He deployed a design style noted for "imagination, simplicity and impressionism".[144] When dancers from the Russian Ballet appeared in America in 1911, with designs copied from the original productions, Urban noted and developed the multi-colour lighting that richly enhanced scenic colour more effectively than white light. In about 1915 he introduced sponging and spattering scene painting techniques, developed to create a *pointillage* system of painting for the stage, which, when lit with coloured spots, brought out or suppressed the colours in the setting.[145] Moderwell said that "the result to the observer is nothing short of a miracle".[146] The use of 'broken colour' soon became the norm in scene painting, and the associated lighting technique was taken into the commercial domain in Britain a few years later with great success by Samoiloff.

Founder and artistic manager of the Russian Ballet **Serge Diaghilev** (1872-1929) became an internationally known figure for high quality classical ballet productions that toured the world. Diaghilev developed a staging form at odds with the progressive trends in drama, reverting to a style of cloth settings, painted to the highest artistic standards by leading painters of the day. The company also employed the leading dancers of the day (such as Nijinsky and Pavlova), and leading artists as designers (including Bakst, Benois and Picasso).[147]

Diaghilev was deeply committed to high quality lighting for his ballets, and was renowned for the detail he applied in plotting and his flair for the use of coloured lighting. He understood that the eye becomes fatigued, and developed techniques to counter this.[148] While his rig was typical of the period, he experimented with front-of-house lighting positions with lamps placed on the

---

half, three-quarters and full, plus intermediate positions). Control operators normally could not see the stage, and were given cues. There were some experiments with the control operator under the forestage with a hood (similar to the prompter), for better operational visibility.

[144] Larson, *Scene Design in the American Theater from 1915-1960*, p42, citing Kenneth MacGowan.

[145] Cheney, S. *Stage Decoration*, London: Chapman and Hall, 1928, p67.

[146] Moderwell, *The Theatre of Today*, p103.

[147] Rosenfeld, *A Short History of Stage Design in Great Britain*, p167.

[148] Beaumont painted this picture of him at work on *The Sleeping Princess* in 1921: "...the (cont...)

Dress and Upper Circle front at the Coliseum when his company visited London in 1918. He did not use footlights in *Pulcinella* in 1920, much to the distress of the dancers who could now see the audience.[149] He deployed limes from the wings, which proved particularly effective for ballet.

In 1911 Diaghilev first visited the Royal Opera House Covent Garden with Alexandre Benois as director and designer. Through the use of flamboyant painted scenery and symbolic costuming, he created a sensation with movement, music and décor as one. *Shéhérazade* (1912) by Rimsky Korsakov, designed by Bakst, used bold, bright colour never seen before on the stage. Beaumont noted that when the curtain went up the scene "almost took my breath away" with a lavish setting richly augmented by light. Cochran said that the Russian Ballet's arrival in London "did more to stimulate the purely visual art of the theatre than anything else which has happened in the twentieth century".[150]

Diaghilev's repertoire was a celebration of the lavish art of the scene painter, setting new standards in the quality and vitality of painted cloths. He obtained a wonderful sense of infinity on the stage with layers of gauze and carefully controlled lighting. Although he did not develop new lighting techniques, he heightened the awareness of the potential of visual art on stage, making significant demands on the lighting installations of the stages to which the productions toured. It is interesting to note that the installation at the Royal Opera House Covent Garden was not up to meeting his technical demands.[151]

business of lighting. Diaghilev would remain hunched in his seat with an electrician to relay his instructions to the stage, first, pink in this flood, amber in that, then the whole "washed" with white. He would spend hour after hour dimming this, "bringing up" that, until he was satisfied and the weary light men could plot the lighting. Even then he would have the curtain lowered and, after a few minute's interval to banish the memory of the lighting from his mind, would order the curtain to be raised again so that he might judge how the effect appealed to him, when revealed afresh" (Beaumont, C. *The Diaghilev Ballet in London*, London: Putman, 1945).

[149] *Dance Chronicle* 14:1, 1991, p15.

[150] Cochran, *The Showman Looks On*, p223.

[151] It was said that the production of *Pavillon d'Armide* was rendered meaningless by poor lighting. Scenes demanding vitality were played in semidarkness, with great shadows cast across the set, a background flooded in a sickly amber lime. In *Carnival* as colours moved upstage costumes "lost their meaning" through colour distortion (Carter, H. *The new spirit in drama and art*, London: Palmer, 1912, p23). This painted a sad picture of the state of British theatre, where one of the largest and best known stages in London could not stage work such as this to appropriate standards. This contrasts starkly with a press quote from the American tour of 1917. MacDonald quoted the American critic Ernest J. Hopkin, who unusually commented on the lighting following a perform-ance of the Ballet Russe in San Francisco. Hopkin gave the lighting high praise for its colour, ability to control the space, and integration with setting and costume. She noted that Diaghilev (cont...)

The Austrian director and actor manager **Max Reinhardt** (1873-1943) dominated German and European practice in the early years of the twentieth century.[152] Established as a leading practitioner in his home country, he toured Europe and America and his work received the highest critical acclaim.

Reinhardt had a keen interest in lighting. He studied Fortuny's ideas in 1905, and was key to developing the portable cyclorama that could be set and struck

used side light for the principle source, and used footlights to provide colour. She also noted that Diaghilev removed the borders. Hopkin said that the lighting for this production "attained the ultimate". She also noted the rigour that Diaghilev rehearsed his lighting plots, to the point of becoming unpopular with theatres he visited (MacDonald, Nesta. *Diaghilev observed by Critics in Britain and the USA 1911-1929*, London: Dance Books Ltd. p206).

[152] He started work in the theatre in his teens and by the early 1900s was a prolific director at a range of important German theatres, including the Deutches Theater working under **Otto Brahm** (1856-1912), the most important director at the end of the nineteenth century in Germany, specialising in naturalistic productions (notably of Ibsen) with very high production values and noted for his use of atmospheric lighting at Der Kleines Theater, Der Kammerspiele Berlin and Der Künstler Theater Munich (Patterson, *The Revolution in German Theatre 1900-1933*, p32). His influence was extensive, with his productions touring to Europe and the US. In later lifer he moved to Hollywood to direct films. German theatre at the time of Reinhardt was a platform for safe, "educational" productions of classics. He injected a level of visual excitement into production work, although at the expense of critical damnation. His work was pivotal to twentieth century German theatre, prompting a higher standard of performance and production values. He produced plays on their own merit, rather than imposing a personal style upon them. He was greatly influenced by Craig's thinking, and came closest of all to practising his philosophies: "For the audiences, going to see a performance directed by Reinhardt always meant a festive experience and a delectation in a world of illusion, where reality was transformed and poetically heightened through the specific meaning of theatre. Reinhardt's productions appealed to the audience's senses and stimulated their feelings through new and daring theatrical devices. He employed the most up-to-date theatre technology and trained his actors in new performance styles, placing particular emphasis on the mimic and gestural element in acting.... While novel lighting designs and the use of atmospheric music created a sensuous mood and the scenic designs effused a beautiful and captivating quality. Movement, colour, light and music were tightly knit together and used in a non-naturalistic way, not expressing specific meanings but rather interpreting the general ideas behind the plays" (Bergaus, G. *International Directory of Theatre 3*, London: St James Press, 1996, p651). Influenced by naturalism, he harnessed the potential of the mechanised German stage to great effect. The most famous display of the impact of mechanisation on realistic staging was his *A Midsummer Night's Dream* in 1905 where the whole forest was built on a revolve. This production proved a turning point for Reinhardt, who thereafter directed non-realistic productions, the first of which was *Ghosts* in 1906, designed by Edward Munch. Reinhardt's staging was also of great importance to the development of the auditorium in the twentieth century. He favoured breaking the artificial barrier of the proscenium arch between the actor and audience, and was noted for open stage productions. The building of Der Kleines Theatre in 1906 established this signature. A critic wrote that: "It seemed that when the curtain rose the players and the spectators were together in the small intimate, discreetly decorated room rather than in a theatre" (Marshall, *The Producer and the Play*, p221). Stern recorded that Reinhardt had no great practical understanding of scenery or technical matters, or of their cost (Stern, *My Life my Stage*, p120). However, it is interesting to note that Stern was not enthusiastic about 3-D scenery, seeing great advantage in using 2D painted flats, citing the disadvantage (cont...)

with ease.[153] He particularly favoured sharp lighting accents and follow-spotting his principals, which in turn allowed independent control and treatment of the remainder of the stage and the scenery. He was probably the first to apply to drama the technique of chiaroscuro, introduced by Fuller, highlighting a principal actor in a followspot on an otherwise unlit stage.

An early comment from 1901 typified his approach to lighting: "lighting must replace the decorations, which we want to do almost without".[154] **Ernest Stern** (1876-1954), who first designed for Reinhardt in 1905, said of him that he tried to paint with light: "only emphasising that which is essential".[155] Reinhardt went on to work regularly with Stern, and created a reputation for a dynamic use of light.

Reinhardt was particularly influential in Britain as several of his productions were staged in London. His work was introduced to the British audience through a wordless mime play *Sumürun,* comprising eight tableaux taken from *The Arabian Nights*, at the Coliseum in January 1911.[156] It was designed by Stern, who recalled that actors were placed in silhouette for some scenes against a white background lit in with coloured light, and that the production utilised a revolving stage.[157] Each scene was 'colour-coded' with light, and much

---

of 3D scenery as cost, storage, and lack of versatility. When watching ballet at Covent Garden, he saw an opportunity to convince Reinhardt that painted flats was superior to 3D décor of the revolving stage: "at once I took advantage of Reinhardt's admiration and enthusiasm to try to convert him to my point of view, and I hammered it home that light and shade was produced purely by painting, that the whole magnificence was nothing but lath and canvas painted!"

"...I treated Reinhardt to a practical demonstration in an attempt to clinch the matter. I put two columns on the stage. One was plastic and three-dimensional, complete with capital and base, and perfectly made. The other was an exact copy, but painted and its contours silhouetted. This painted pillar was provided with light and shade and did not disappear when it was illuminated. When the plastic column was lighted from one angle only, it, of course, also had light and shade, but when it was lighted from all sides, all light and shade disappeared and the plastic column looked two-dimensional, whilst the painted two-dimensional column looked plastic and realistic. My demonstration showed quite clearly that in stage lighting, which must come from all sides, plastic, three-dimensional scenery no longer looked plastic, whilst painted, two-dimensional scenery looked plastic." However, Reinhardt was not convinced.

[153] Bergmann, *Lighting in the Theatre*, p342.

[154] Bergmann, *Lighting in the Theatre*, p342.

[155] Bergmann, *Lighting in the Theatre*, p345.

[156] Theatre Museum Archives.

[157] William Prichard Eaton said of *Sumürun* that the settings were simple, using drapes and properties, and the mood of the play was dependent on the careful grouping of actors and lighting: "the effectiveness of such a set depends upon the ability of the stage manager to light it right, and to keep his actors composed in pictorial groupings, as well as on its suggestibleness of the weird dark to the imagination" (Larson, *Scene Design in the American Theater from 1915-1960*, p40).

emphasis was given to finding appropriate colours in the compositions.[158] The beauty of this was recorded by the magazine *English Review*.[159] Cochran recalled that the black and white scenery "caused a sensation... and really it could be looked upon as a pioneer movement in the London theatre towards improvement of stage décor".[160] However, the production was not universally praised. Huntly Carter noted that some scenes were over-lit and garish, with "vibrating coloured atmospheres overdone" and "an over-imposing yellow lamp that looks like a lighthouse beacon".[161] He recorded that the acting style and moves also attracted criticism. Yet despite this, the production marked a great advance in stagecraft seen in London.

Reinhardt, with Stern as designer, went on to produce an arena production of *The Miracle* at Olympia in December 1911, transforming the venue into the interior of a cathedral. Stern recalled that the production was seen as a pivotal work in the development of staging techniques in this country, saying that "*The Miracle* is not only a triumph of stagecraft, it is also an artistic work of deep significance was a fair example of the praise the critics gave our work".[162] Ernest Short recalled that it "showed that a new force was at work in the theatrical world".[163] The production was entirely new with a cast of 1500, and was staged with the audience surrounding the action, a ground-breaking concept that would initiate much twentieth century work.

---

[158] "The fantasy is divided into seven scenes, and the varieties of colour themes illustrated are in accordance. Each scene has its dominant colour theme... Rich oriental colours, not tones, flow in, meet and compose, never failing to achieve a definite unity. In consequence the scenes are saturated with singing coloured atmosphere created by the harmonies of contrast. One of the most beautiful effects is obtained in the darkened interior of the hunchback's theatre, by the dome focus-light and the coloured mediums on the perches in the prompt corner being concentrated upon a mass of draperies where the slave makes her quick changes of costume. At the same time the footlights of the bijou theatre are diffused softly over the coloured forms and faces of the audience in the darkened pit" (Carter, *The New Spirit in Drama and Art*, p15).

[159] "rarely have more beautiful effects of light and scene been seen on the stage... each scene takes us out of the theatre as by some fairy spell. For this is a strangely beautiful performance. It has the joy in it of a great painting, a glow of spring and colour like an African sunset" (*English Review* Vol. 7, Dec 1910, p745).

[160] When Cochran saw the production first staged in Berlin he said: "it gave me supreme delight to stumble quite unexpectedly against something of extreme beauty in a theatre... a good deal of credit must go to Ernst Stern for his costumes and scenery" (Cochran, C.B. *Secrets of a Showman*, London: Heinemann, 1925, p162).

[161] Carter, *The New Spirit in Drama and Art*, p15.

[162] Stern, *My Life on Stage*, p100.

[163] Short, E. *Sixty Years of Theatre*, London: Eyre and Spottiswoode, 1951, p265.

The Miracle was such a vast production that lighting control had to be divided into sections, with each operator having a number of instruments under his control. This was co-ordinated by "carefully planned cue sheets or "light score" under the centralised control, by telephone, of the "lighting conductor" in the person of the chief electrician".[164] Cochran recalled that "miles of cable were laid. Huge lighting bridges had to be built. Hundreds of lamps of varying kinds had to be bought; a myriad of electricians employed".[165] Reinhardt used a spot lighting technique with limes high in the Olympia roof to highlight principal actors, allowing contrast between them and the crowd, who were lit in an ambient atmospheric lighting.

1911 production of The Miracle. The Sketch, 21/02/1912. Illustration by permission of the Illustrated London News Picture Library.

The Sketch (21/2/12) published a picture taken from the roof showing the beams of light on the principals and the dressing for the crowds (see illustration).[166] *Punch* (10/1/12) made fun of the distance between the characters in such a large theatre space, especially when two characters were lit in spots at either end of the arena. However, the article concluded that the staging "was a thing to wonder at". Reinhardt used the GKP system for projecting architectural styles and images of landscapes[167] and Schwabe created the flame effect.[168]

---

[164] The programme credited Cochran as General Manager, Baron von Gersdorff as Stage Manager, George Taylor as Chief Electrician (Theatre Museum Archives and Fuchs, *Stage Lighting*, p282)

[165] Cochran, C.B. *I Had Almost Forgotten*, London: Hutchinson, 1932, p172.

[166] Theatre Museum Archives.

[167] Fuerst and Hume *Twentieth Century Stage Decoration Vol. 1*, p113. *The Times* said the scenery was "prejudiced by the weak employment of transparencies", but overall gives the design high praise (Theatre Museum Archives).

[168] *The Sketch* 3/1/1912 published photographs of this (Theatre Museum Archives).

In 1912 Reinhardt staged *Oedipus Rex* at the Lyceum, with simple, bold scenery by Stern and Alfred Roller. Lighting was noted for the creation of white light through colour mixing the limes.[169] Reinhardt brought other large scale productions to Britain including *Venetian Night* in 1912 at the Coliseum and *Helen* in 1932 at the Adelphi. His reputation in this country was based on "showmanship, vastness and quantity", although Norman Marshall accused him of being "vulgar and tasteless, achieving splendour without grandeur, size without style." However, his spectaculars were only a small part of his output, as he produced a wide range of "classics", including 22 of Shakespeare's plays. Marshall was more favourable to this work: "the productions I remember most were not his vast spectacles but his subtle and intimate work at the Kammerspiele Theatre".[170]

A notable design from Stern was for *White Horse Inn* at the Coliseum in

White Horse Inn. The Sketch, 06/05/1931. Courtesy Illustrated London News picture library.

---

[169] "The scene was lit from all parts of the theatre according to the new methods, whereby coloured limes are thrown on neutral surfaces, and the desired effects obtained by mixing the coloured rays as they fall on each object. The principle aim of the lighting was, however, to keep a blinding white light beating upon the palace, and to break it up with vivid bits of colour" (Gorelik, *New Theatres for Old*, p294, quoting Huntley Carter).

[170] Marshall *The Producer and the Play*, p50 & 52.

1931, which ran for fourteen months and 651 performances. The design featured elaborate settings mounted on the revolve with painted backdrops.[171] The show was generally heralded as "sensational" in the press, with Stern noted for his dazzling costumes and settings. The *Play Pictorial* (May 1931) described Stern's lighting as "often quite beautiful". A photo from *The Tatler* (1/7/1931) under show lighting conditions, showed a night-time scene, with the principal lit by a followspot, the chorus lit by the floats and a little set dressing lighting, probably from above (see illustration).[172]

Influential Artists Visiting Britain, 1914-1935

The showman **Adrian Samoiloff** (1877- not known), a refugee from the Russian revolution, became known for his trickery with light in his revues, which led to his name being given to the technique of lighting in primary colours to hide or reveal visual information encoded into scenery.[173] His sets, costumes and make-up were carefully painted so as to reveal information under certain colours of light, and upon a crossfade to a new colour, to reveal new information and hide old. This required much skill and precision; special lighting even had to be installed in his dressing room to get the correct shades of make-up for these 'transformations'. Samoiloff's work was first seen in London in September 1921. His revue *Round in Fifty* at the London Hippodrome in 1922 was highly successful and "enabled coloured light to first hit the British newspaper headlines".[174] This success prompted a working relationship with Strand, who designed the high efficiency battens suitable to create these effects. The battens soon became an industry standard piece of equipment, due in part to the exposure Samoiloff gave to Strand through his shows. Strand also manufactured three gelatines specifically to create the "Samoiloff effect": 27A Samoiloff Red; 29A Samoiloff Blue; 38A Samoiloff Mauve (although these colours did not transfer into the Cinemoid range).[175]

---

[171] Stern, *My Life my Stage*, p200+. Norman Marshall recalled that it was the first show to make use of the triple revolve in the 27 years since its installation, and it was used to the full (*Tabs* 28/1 Mar 70). Venreco of Neal St. London, under Schwabe-Hasait patents, was credited for the lighting.

[172] Theatre Museum Archives.

[173] He was according to Strand employee Applebee "a mixture of electro-technician/artist, though not of Royal Academy standard" (*Tabs* 22/1, Mar. 64, p8).

[174] *Tabs* 7/1, Apr. 49, p16. *Punch* 22/3/1922 said "excellent fun alternated with lovely or fantastic colour-schemes and scenic designs" (Theatre Museum Archives). The show also involved cinema-style projection of a moving sea and moving high road.

[175] Hall, M. *A Brief History of Colour in Theatre and Film*, London, Hall, 199, p27.

An article in the *Daily Telegraph* in 1924 publicised the lighting for the revue *Brighter London* at the Hippodrome:[176] "Mr Samoiloff shows what can be done in the modern theatre with light and its twin sister, colour... the Hippodrome installation is a model of ingenuity and efficiency. Wonderfully flexible and entirely independent (if needs be) of lights outside the proscenium arch".[177]

The technique of changing the appearance of an object's colour by illuminating it in changeable coloured light was already known, having been documented by Luckiesh in *Color and its applications* (1915). Adrian Klein noted in his book that three Russians may have developed this technique, either independently or in collaboration.[178] Samoiloff may well have borrowed ideas from Madame Boutkovsky, who demonstrated similar techniques in Paris three months earlier, or even from Lipsky, who performed in New York one month later.[179] Although his work never moved beyond the music hall stunt, he illustrated a potential for lighting, and also the limitations of equipment available at that time.

After World War One a number of productions transferred from America, bringing with them production values that were far more sophisticated than those practised here.

Gilbert Miller (1884-1969), a British actor who worked from Toronto and later New York, returned to London to produce plays from 1915 onwards.[180] He took on the role of manager at the St. James's Theatre in 1916. As well as staging his own productions, he brought shows over from America. Working with ReandeaN (see Appendix iii), it is known that some American equipment was imported for the St. James's Theatre, but little of his achievements with lighting seems to be recorded.

The American actor **John Barrymore** (1882-1942) brought a production of *Hamlet* to the Haymarket in 1925. The design was by **Robert Edmund Jones** (1887-1954), one of the twentieth century's most important stage designers.

---

[176] the programme credits "Stage Lighting Installation by Samoiloff's Lighting Scheme Ltd." and "Electrical effect in *What's to become of the fairies?* by Adrian V. Samoiloff.

[177] *Daily Telegraph* 14/2/24.

[178] Klein, *Coloured Light – an Art Medium,* p180

[179] Ernest Short also recalled that Madame Boutkovsky, based in Paris at the same time, was well known for her use of coloured light on scenery (Short, E. *Introducing the Theatre*, London: Eyre and Spottiswoode, 1949, p245).

[180] MacQueen-Pope, W. *St. James's: A Theatre of Distinction*, London: Allen, 1958, p201.

Influenced by Craig, Reinhardt, and experimenting with model theatres,[181] he became a master of expressive lighting, and was probably the first to plan schemes on paper, drawing detailed plots that compare with schemes today.[182] His first production to transfer to London was *Anna Christie*, which Cochran brought to the Strand Theatre in 1923. This was O'Neill's first major play to be staged in London and was potentially an influential production. Having seen it "superbly produced in America by Arthur Hopkins", Cochran believed this to be one of the best ever settings.[183] However, although the acting and production were widely praised, his setting attracted criticism for not being

---

[181] He graduated from Harvard in 1910. Initially he had little success as a designer, but travelled to Florence to attend Craig's school in 1913. However he was rebuffed by Craig, and later that year travelled to Berlin to observe Reinhardt at work. This made him aware of the power of fusing acting, setting and lighting into a dramatic whole. Jones returned to America in autumn 1914, and came to attention in the theatre scene for his operation of a model lighting stage at a stage design exhibition. In November of that year he published an article in the *New York Times* on cyclorama lighting. In January the following year, his break came at an important event in New York. A performance of Shaw's *Androcles and the Lion* was directed by Granville Barker (who was seen as the vogue producer in New York) and designed by Norman Wilkinson (on invitation from the New York Stage Society, third choice after Craig – too high a fee demand – and Reinhardt – blockaded in Germany). Jones' production of *The Man Who Married a Dumb Wife* was added to the programme to fill up time. This production was seen as a triumph, with settings in white, grey and black, and costumes in primary colours, and heralded a new movement in American stage design. Jones went on to bring the new movements prompted by Appia, Craig and Reinhardt to the attention of the American audience. Jones remained at the centre of American design throughout his career, although he gained few specific notices for his lighting work. He travelled to Europe in spring 1921 with Kenneth Macgowan, seeing about sixty productions in a range of countries (although not in Britain). This visit was the basis for the book *Continental Stagecraft* that was to be a highly influential report of European practice. In 1925 he exhibited his designs in New York and recorded them in a book called *Drawings for the Theatre*, published by Theatre Arts Books. In the 1930s he made the memorable quotation on the art of stage lighting, that it "is putting it where you want it and taking it away from where you don't". In 1932 he was appointed Art Director of the Radio City Music Hall, with responsibility for the visual side of productions staged there. He didn't gain his first lighting design credit until May 1940, for Laurence Olivier's *Romeo and Juliet* designed by Motley, at the 51st St. Theatre.

[182] His symbolist designs for *Macbeth* in 1921 (three large bird-like masks, lit by spots from the footlight position, hung over the stage and dominated the otherwise simple setting. Spots around the proscenium dominated the rest of the rig. Jones made much use of actors appearing from out of darkness) may have been panned by the press but were highly influential due to the lighting. His sketches (recorded by Larson in *Scene Design in the American Theater from 1915-1960*, p65) represent what was probably the first set of lighting designs to be planned on paper. Twenty elevations exist that show the rig plan for each scene, and note lantern position, colour, focus and some intensity notes. Each scene specified the lanterns to be used, with beam angles drawn in section to show the centre of focus and actor groupings. Where such light was set within an overall ambience, battens (in three sections: left, centre and right) were shown that included colour descriptions.

[183] Cochran, *The Showman looks on*, p225.

"as good as the author's direction".[184] Cochran recalled difficulties maintaining the integrity of the design in London, as he feared both the subdued lighting and the subdued acting meant the audience could not hear or see facial expression:

"I asked Mr. Hopkins if he could give us more light in the fog scene, without destroying Mr. Jones' scenic effect; and I begged him to ask the players to speak up. But Mr. Jones was jealously anxious about the artistic completeness of his stage settings. Mr. Hopkins was afraid of disturbing the realism of the drama by an increased volume of noise. My theory is that, in a theatre, the audience must see and hear; nothing can excuse failure in either of these two respects. In the celebrated fog scene it would have been wiser to have let the curtain go up on as thick a fog as the producer liked. As the action of the scene developed, the stage should get lighter. The audience, in the meantime, would still maintain a mental impression of the fog and its influence on the drama".[185]

Jones's second production to come to London was *Hamlet* at the Haymarket Theatre in 1925. *The Times* (20/2/25) noted that the "scenery throughout was of austere simplicity" and *The Bookman* (19/2/25) recorded that "the setting is unsurpassed in its rugged magnificence". An unknown press cutting said it was "the finest ever seen in London … lighted superbly".[186] Ridge and Aldred recalled in 1935 that the production used spotting techniques rather than floods, with all the lights and control system imported from America.[187] There was a large battery of focus spots behind the proscenium, and instead of footlights, ranks of spots on the gallery fronts. They noted that American practice was to do away with battens except on the No. 1 bar, and use more spots, and tall side lighting towers, again containing spots. An example of the type of detail this spotlight approach could create was noted in the lighting of the King and Queen's thrones, which were lit in a frosted dark blue, to tone into the scenery, overlaid with a lightly frosted medium blue on the thrones, and a pink spot to bring out costume colour and a spot on the faces alone. This is the first recorded production in Britain that used spots extensively, positioned both front of house and on stage (see illustration).

The spotlight approach to stage lighting was seen again in London when

[184] *Daily News* 11/4/23.

[185] Cochran, *Review of Reviews*, p407.

[186] Theatre Museum Archives.

[187] Ridge and Aldred, *Stage Lighting, Principles and Practice*, p109.

Hamlet at the Haymarket, 1925. The Times 20/2/1925. By permission of the British Library.

Hassard Short (1877-1956), a British actor who became a stage director and was discovered in New York, hit the headlines in the early 1930s for several productions that he brought to London. *Waltzes from Vienna*, at the Alhambra Theatre in 1931, was described in *The Morning Post* (18/8/1931) as "a dream of moving colours and lights… scene, colour, light and song all in one".[188] He employed a number of Kliegl spots rigged on the circle front, each fitted with a four-colour solenoid-driven changer. An article in the *Daily Mail* commented on the impact the lighting had on staging techniques of the times: "I do not want to depress our scenic artists…but it sometimes seems to me that as stage lighting develops more and more the scenic artists will become superfluous. I grow more and more convinced that lighting has hitherto been in its infancy and that it is rapidly taking its place as far the most important of all the ancillary arts of the theatre".[189] He also introduced a colour new to Britain in this

---

[188] Settings by Albert R. Johnson and costumes by Doris Zinkeisen, and "all lighting and mechanical effects devised by Hassard Short". The programme also credited Strand for supplying the lighting (Theatre Museum Archives).

[189] *Tabs* 22/1, Mar. 64, p34, citing Alan Parsons, *Daily Mail* 18/8/1931.

production – No. 36 Surprise Pink – which was interesting as it was the first pale pink manufactured that was suitable for realistic drama. The colour had a peculiar quirk in that it could appear to be both warm and cool. *Tabs* reported that this colour: "soon became a favourite of everybody".[190]

Short's production *Wild Violets* at the Theatre Royal Drury Lane in 1932 was reviewed in the *Daily Mail* (1/11/32), describing him as "a master of lighting and scenic effects", and noted his use of "soft foot-lighting-less lighting… a constant joy".[191] The production made much use of a revolve (the first at the Theatre Royal Drury Lane) and sliding scenery. Ernest Short recalled that he brought cinematic scene change to the stage, staging 16 scenes by the use of the revolve and clever lighting effects.[192] Wonderful lighting pictures were published in the *Illustrated London News* (5/11/32), showing the control, wing towers, follows, stage bridge, etc. It said the show used 120 lanterns, many with colour changers, plus hundreds of small lamps built into the sets and backdrops (see following illustration).[193]

Stop Press, at the Adelphi in February 1935, was noted for its lighting in the use of tableaux, lit in sepia, coming to life as lighting changed to a more natural tone. Many papers praised Short's ingenious lighting skills – the *Daily Telegraph* (22/2/35) headlined the show "Lovely lighting at the Adelphi". Mirrors combined with clever lighting to transform a few dancers into a room full. A photograph from the production show characters localised with an interplay of light and shade. James Agate in the *Sunday Telegraph* (21/2/35) said "the evening varies from dazzling to dim and the superb lighting exploits the whole gamut of imaginative sensitivities." He noted a range of techniques used to create contrasting atmospheres, such as cross lighting, actors stepping in and out of pools of light, and key scenes lit in a "blaze".

Anmer Hall (real name A.B. Horne, 1863-1953), opened the Westminster Theatre in 1931. Hall was influenced by Gray's work at Cambridge, and his productions gained much critical acclaim, and the theatre became one of the most high profile in London in the 1930s.[194] The Westminster was the only

---

[190] *Tabs* 7/2, Sep. 49, p18.

[191] a musical comedy operetta set in Switzerland, with settings designed by Aubrey Hammond and costume by Doris Zinkeisen, and "scenic and lighting effects devised by Hassard Short" (Theatre Museum Archives).

[192] Short, *Introducing the Stage*, p238.

[193] Theatre Museum Archives.

[194] Belden, K.D. *The Story of the Westminster Theatre*, London: Westminster Productions, 1965, for a general account of the theatre.

Wild Violets. The Illustrated London News 5/11/1932. By permission of the Illustrated London News Picture Library.

professional London theatre with a permanent plaster cyclorama, despite its shallow stage. This gained much press attention for the way in which it was lit "with remarkable effect" in the opening years by the Australian designer **Molly McArthur** (1900-1972), especially for her experiments with projected imagery.[195] A production of *The Unquiet Spirit* in 1931 used Linnebach projection. *Tabs* noted that: "a woodland scene projected by light was most effective in the second act... The slide was specially painted by the scene designer and gave a realistic impression of the atmosphere of a late November afternoon".[196] Two James Bridie plays staged in 1932, designed by McArthur, *Tobias and the Angel* and *Jonah and the Whale* also utilised Linnebach projection. In *Tobias*, a projection of a growing angel was achieved, painted on a slide in distortion by McArthur. Her work was praised in the press, but *The Observer* (13/3/32) noted the lighting "is frequently unkind to the players by throwing shadows and obscuring the speaker". *The Sunday Times* (18/12/32) said of *Jonah* "perhaps the best actor in the piece is the electrician who, doubtless after consultation with that highly imaginative producer Mr Henry Oscar, has devised a glow of lighting which turns the stage pictures into coloured plates. In the last scene, with the sun rising upon and the lark singing over Nineveh, he and Mr Oscar exactly produce the atmosphere of Grieg's "Morning". McArthur has found her tasteful scenery partly in her own clever imagination, and partly in the canvas of Holman Hunt".[197] For a technical review of the theatre see Appendix ii.

Influential Artists Visiting Britain, 1935-1950

Theodor Komisarjevsky (1882-1954)[198] was a Russian director and designer who worked under Meyerhold. He emigrated to Britain in 1919, worked at major theatres in London, and came to attention for his studio productions of classic Russian plays at the Barnes Theatre in 1925/6.[199] He joined the Shakespeare Memorial Theatre Stratford in the 1930s, produced in the West

---

[195] Bentham, *Sixty Years of Light Work*, p75.

[196] *Tabs* 22/1, Mar. 64, p39.

[197] Theatre Museum Archives.

[198] He was half-brother to Vera Komisarjevsky, actress and manager. Having trained in architecture and worked at his sister's theatre under Meyerhold from 1906, he began to direct in 1907. His apprenticeship at her theatre exposed him to ideas at the forefront of radical drama. He worked in a range of theatres in Moscow, including 3 years producing (on average one play a month) at the Nezolbin Theatre (1910-13), the Maly Theatre and the Bolshoi.

[199] Komisarjevsky, T. *Myself and the Theatre*, London: Heinemann, 1929, p42.

End, taught at RADA, but later went to America, disillusioned with British theatre. He wrote five important books on the theatre.

Komisarjevsky's production style was to explore a stage space without scenic accessories – which became known as Synthetic-Realistic theatre. This led out of the movement, promoted by Fuchs, Appia and developed by Meyerhold, whereby the producer would choose single important items in a set and highlight them with light.[200] An example of Komisarjevky's emerging style can be seen in his own recollections of *The Idiot* at the Nezolbin Theatre. Minimal settings were used, and the following notes show how detailed his thinking in terms of the use of light had become:

"The action of the play started in darkness, as though it was a continuation of something which had already happened just as the novel itself begins. First, only a window of the railway carriage appears, lit from behind, and then the figures of two men sitting on both sides of it. In the following scenes I had only one plain backcloth and different sets of furniture necessary for the action; each scene was lighting according to its mood, and the lights were arranged in such a way that all the settings seemed to be surrounded by a semi-circular frame of darkness. The garden was suggested by a bench and a backing made of threadbare green sack-cloth hung so that the uneven folds gave an impression of trees, and the spaces between them, with steel blue lights behind, of misty depth".[201]

His style developed to be one where all production elements worked in harmony with each other:

"Actors, costume, props, scenery, lighting sound and music, *all* these elements of a theatrical performance must together form a synthetic composition, idealistically and emotionally united with the acting, and expressive of the interpretation of the play".[202]

All the arts utilised on the stage of a synthetic theatre should convey simultaneously the same feelings and ideas to the spectator. The rhythm of the music must be in harmony with the rhythm of the words, with the rhythm of the movements of the actors, of the colours and lines of the décors and costumes, and of the changing lights... Experimenting with dynamic décors I found that lighting afforded the best means by which to realise my ideas and that, until

---

[200] Komisarjevsky, *Settings and Costumes of the Modern Stage*, p13.

[201] Komisarjevsky, *Myself and the Theatre*, p94.

[202] Komisarjevsky, *The Theatre (and a Changing Civilisation)*, p21.

the seventeenth century "baroque" stage and auditorium, still used in modern theatres, are abolished, the best possible "décor" is a high plain screen or wall at the back and sides of the stage and a floor, the levels of which can be changed... We need quick action in the theatre without any intervals occupied by the present antediluvian way of shifting scenery and props. We no longer want ...regular acts or scenes. We need, sometimes, in the midst of a scene a flash into the past or the future. We need action happening simultaneously in various parts of the stage... and of moving lights from the front, the back, the sides, above and below the actors... Before I came to this conclusion I employed moving sets, transparent sets, changing colours and varying intensities of lights, gauzes in front of the stage to diffuse and reflect the lights, etc., but have always been handicapped by the deficient equipment of theatres".[203]

"A production can do very well without scenery..." But levels, steps and traps are needed, 3D and of real materials, not "faked"... "The scenery must reflect the lighting"... the world beyond the actor must be suggested by "the acoustic perspective and the light perspective. The sounds and lighting... had to reveal the unseen to the imagination of the public and stimulate their emotions".[204]

The Barnes Theatre was a cinema converted by Philip Ridgeway in 1925, who appointed Komisarjevsky as its producer.[205] He produced a season of Russian plays that were in complete contrast to Dean's realistic productions which were in vogue at the time. Marshall recalled that his productions contained little realism, with settings more concerned with "mood than detail... and his lighting, soft, rich and mellow, was romantic rather than realistic, and with the skill of a painter he made dramatic use of highlights, shadows and half-tones to give emphasis to his beautifully composed groupings and ensembles. I have seen nothing more lovely in the theatre than the stage pictures Komisarjevsky created on that cramped little stage at Barnes".[206] One of his most notable successes there was *Three Sisters* where he: "conveyed Chekhov's inner meaning and made the rhythm of the "music" of the play blend with the rhythm of the movements of the actors, giving the necessary accents with the lighting..."[207]

Komisarjevsky's work at Stratford occasionally drew praise for its lighting,

---

[203] Komisarjevsky, *Myself and the Theatre*, p149+.

[204] Komisarjevsky, *The Theatre (and a Changing Civilisation)*, p23.

[205] The theatre reverted to a cinema in 1926 due to financial pressures.

[206] Marshall, N. *The Other Theatre*, London: Lehmann, 1947, p 218.

[207] Komisarjevsky, *Myself and the Theatre*, p174.

such as Bridges Adams' *A Midsummer Night's Dream* in 1933, with set and costumes by Norman Wilkinson, where he deployed localised sidelight from opposing sides to create expression and depth within a tight, high contrast field.[208] Other notable productions including *Macbeth* (1933), *The Merry Wives of Windsor* (1935) and *King Lear* (1936). A good example of his lighting can be seen in *King Lear*. Kemp and Trewin recorded that he caught the "cosmic quality of the Lear's desolation", noting that the short scenes "were played in pools of light which swirled in changing colour until the whole setting was embraced for the purposes of crowded court or open heath. He flecked ... a sky of serene blue... with moving clouds, ...created a stormy sky against which he silhouetted the actors" and he used smoke to enhance the battle scenes. In the closing moments, "when the light faded out slowly in the sky, and darkness descended step-by-step down the stage, line by line the motionless soldiers and courtiers faded from view. The light lingered for a moment on the dead Lear and Cordelia before they too dissolved into the dark. The rolling drums died away, and the curtain crept slowly down to cover the darkened stage".[209]

However, the limited scope for expressive lighting at the theatre (for a technical review of the venue see Appendix ii) may well have curbed his instincts. He was concerned that British theatre was generally hampered by lack of resources, and that lighting suffered from often having only the dress rehearsal with the set, so that time pressures meant that lighting was often "arranged during the interval of performances".[210] Komisarjevsky thought productions in Britain were generally of a poor standard. He rated only the producers C.B. Cochran, Bronson Albery, Alec Rea, and Barry Jackson,[211] the stage designers/painters Norman Wilkinson, Charles Ricketts, Lovat Fraser, Oliver Messel and Augustus John,[212] and the only British theatre he noted as "artistically merited" was Nigel Playfair's Lyric Hammersmith in the late 1920s.[213] "Otherwise the West End was dull and pictorially tasteless".[214]

---

[208] Komisarjevsky, *Settings and Costumes of the Modern Stage*, p21.

[209] Kemp, T. & Trewin, J.C. *The Stratford Festival. A History of the Memorial Theatre Stratford*, Birmingham: Cornish Brothers, 1953, p178.

[210] Komisarjevsky, *Myself and the Theatre*, p155.

[211] Komisarjevsky, *The Theatre (and a Changing Civilisation)*, p160. He said that Cochran and Reinhardt combined a rare combination of business and artistic success (Komisarjevsky, *Myself and the theatre*, p21).

[212] Komisarjevsky, *Settings and Costumes of the Modern Stage*, p9.

[213] Komisarjevsky, *Myself and the Theatre*, p42.

[214] Komisarjevsky, *Settings and Costumes of the Modern Stage*, p9.

Komisarjevsky was one of the most influential practitioners of the inter-war years. Joe Davis said that he had aroused his interest in what could be done with lighting when he worked for him as a young man.[215] He remembered him as a stimulating producer, a designer in his own right and a creative and exciting lighting man and a skilful mixer of primary colours.

Jo Mielziner (1901-1975)[216] had the reputation of being the finest American lighting designer in the first half of the twentieth century.[217] Joe Davis, greatly influenced by Mielziner, re-lit many of his productions that transferred to London after World War Two. He recalled that Mielziner was the first to include detailed lighting plans with his designs.

Mielziner liked to design minimal, skeletal scenery, allowing light the opportunity to penetrate as much as possible, to afford the greatest potential for change and illusion. He was noted for introducing to the theatre the film technique of backlighting, and used large rigs with multiple instruments per area to create complex light interplay. He was a master of projection, and revived the use of follow spots in 'serious' plays, a technique last seen in Belasco's work.

Two of his productions that transferred into London, *The Glass Menagerie* at the Haymarket in 1948 and *A Streetcar Named Desire* at the Aldwych in 1949, were particularly memorable for their designs. He integrated scrim into the settings that could be made to appear or disappear with lighting, although this gained mixed press in Britain for its effectiveness (see illustration).[218] His *Death of a Salesman* at the Phoenix in 1949 showed his integral use of lighting to capture the mood of a scene. Except for a couple of long static moments,

---

[215] *Cue 30* Jul. 84, p8.

[216] Mielziner was born in Paris into an artist's family, who moved to New York in 1910. He decided to pursue a career in scene design having seen Jones' *Dumb Wife* production and graduated in scene design from the Philadelphia Institute of Fine Arts. He met Craig in 1920, became apprenticed to Urban in 1921, and then left for Europe to study Stnard and Reinhardt's work in Vienna. He returned to the America in 1923, where he became a design apprentice to the Theatre Guild. Here he was influenced by Edward F. Kook (later the founder of Century Lighting) on the value and potential of lighting. His first credited lighting design was for *Panic* in 1935. Mielziner had always designed set, costume and lighting (until about 1960 when he gave up designing costume due to work load and scheduling). He always said he could not see how one could be designed without the other. He led and typified the approach of many US scene designers, specialising in set, costume and lighting design, by being able to weld all three disciplines seamlessly together. Mielziner had said in 1936 that the first thing he did before reading a play was to delete all the playwright's instructions, to let the words of the author speak for themselves.

[217] Larson, *Scene Design in the American Theater from 1915-1960*, p151.

[218] Theatre Museum Archives.

A Streetcar Named Desire souvenir programme. By permission of V&A Images/ Victoria and Albert Museum London.

the lighting was remembered for being in a state of near constant flow, with 69 cues running through the desk.[219] Kitty Black recalled that the show used the "American way" of having "batteries of lanterns hung in view all over the stage and auditorium, superseding the old fashioned idea that lighting sources should always be invisible".[220] Lighting was used to guide the audience's eye around a multi-scene composite setting, and a cinematic style that was not particularly well received by the London press. The play featured the rare use of a "leafy fringe", a gobo, which was projected onto the background to "symbolise hope," and the production required an additional 30 ways to supplement the in-house 98 dimmers.[221]

Summary

London had an early opportunity to see the work of overseas practitioners that

---

[219] *Cue* 14, 1981, and *Tabs* 7/3, Dec. 49, p3.

[220] Black, K. *Upper Circle, a Theatrical Chronicle.* London: Methuen, 1984, p165.

[221] *New Statesman* 6/8/49.

was significantly more complex and technically ambitious than work generated at home. Artists brought influential productions from America, Germany and Russia, promoting a more sophisticated and integrated use of light than was in vogue at home. These visiting companies were highly influential in developing the art of lighting in Britain. It is also interesting to note that many of America's leading stage designers visited Europe, especially Germany, but few came to Britain. Those that did stage high profile productions in London provided much inspiration for the growing 'Art Theatre' and 'Stage Society' movement (see Chapter 4).

Britain, although this really means London, was exposed to a wide range of production styles, including the realism of the Duke of Saxe-Meiningen and Belasco, the sumptuousness of Diaghilev, the stage spectaculars of Reinhardt, the trickery of Fuller and Samoiloff, the showmanship of Miller and Short, the art of Komisarjevsky and Jones and their interpretations of Appia and Craig, and later the Broadway spotlight style of Mielziner. As well as more advanced production styles, these practitioners brought new technologies and techniques to the attention of the British, such as the lit cyclorama and the area lighting approach with spotlights. Enlightened British practitioners such as Irving, Dean and Cochran travelled abroad to see work, met these people and engaged with their ideas. From these influences a growing band of British producers emerged, committed to using lighting in a sensitive manner, matching lighting to production styles for the first time and building on the platform of techniques established pre-1881. From these producers and their teams of workers the first specialist lighting practitioners emerged.

4 THE LIGHTING DESIGNER EMERGES

This chapter considers the impact of the work of British practitioners that established lighting design as an essential component of modern theatre practice. Details of their influences and partnerships are recorded where information is known, and their productions. Their credentials are assessed with reference to contemporary press reviews.

The chapter divides into three sections: 1881-1914; 1914-1935; and 1935-1951.

British Lighting Practice and Practitioners, 1881-1914

The main influences on British practice during this period came from abroad: from America through Belasco and Fuller; from Germany through Reinhardt; and from Russia through the Russian Ballet. Each showed that high quality stage presentations could be achieved despite the limitations of the technology available, whether the production style was realism, spectacle or sumptuous beauty. In Britain, few initially responded to this work. The theories of Appia and Craig were also slow to be adopted by British practice, despite being highly influential abroad.

In Britain it was the custom for actor-managers, perhaps with their scene designer/painters, to set the lighting. At the turn of the century, production style commonly promoted the work of the 'star' actor-manager, with settings and costumes commissioned from fashionable painters. As a result, direction, acting and scenic design often did not form a unity. There are no records of British practitioners applying the exacting standards of their American counterparts of the time, such as Belasco.[1]

---

[1] Belasco spent much time during the production week setting and rehearsing lighting routines, and he greatly valued the skill and input of his technical team. His lighting rehearsals might last a week, whereas those of other producers might last a session or two: "It may take hours, or, perhaps, a whole day and a night... for the timing of lights is quite as important as the timing of the movements of the players. The perfect lighting of a stage can be accomplished only when the electricians become as familiar with the play as the actors themselves. Having comprehended the spirit of the play, they are as dextrous with the appliances for the regulating of lights as musicians with their instruments." When lighting the stage, Belasco set the atmosphere first before bringing on the actors. Often he would follow with soft edged light, normally with two units from either each side or from the proscenium bridge. (Belasco, *The Theatre Through its Stage Door*, p80). In (cont...)

Only two actor-managers from this period, Beerbohm Tree and Martin Harvey, were particularly noted for their use of light. However, their lighting styles diverged. Whereas Tree followed Irving's methods, Harvey progressively adopted a more minimal approach.

The actor-manager **Sir Herbert Beerbohm Tree** (1853-1917) was perhaps the first important figure in Britain to establish electric lighting as a creative component of theatre, continuing Irving's tradition of Shakespeare productions with elaborate and realistic staging.[2]

Tree's lighting method was to follow the principals in a moving lime, overlaid on an ambience created by battens and footlights. A good example of this is his production of *Henry VIII* at His Majesties, painted by Joseph Harker, in 1910, which received great critical acclaim.[3] Lighting ranged from a cold, blue stage for the 'River Gate' scene to a brilliant, yet softly coloured for 'The Banqueting Hall'. For the 'Hall in Blackfriars', twenty-one limes were deployed, all in dark amber gelatines. Eight limes lit through stained glass windows. Lighting took on a symbolic role in the 'Ante-Chamber', where it was noted that: "King and servant stand in full light backed by the brilliant dresses of courtiers... As the sun of his powers sets at the bidding of his master, the robbed and broken Wolsey staggers into the darkness of the sanctuary". He employed lanterns in the auditorium dome to light the forestage as well as positions further upstage, which he said were a "device for throwing light

---

Germany it was the province of the scenic artist (Stern, *My Life on Stage*, p162). It was common for the German technician to be intimately involved in a production, attending rehearsals, contributing to the process and learning a plot to be performed without notes or cue sheets (Moderwell, *The Theatre of Today*, p55).

[2] Tree became Manager of the Haymarket Theatre in 1887, installing electricity under the supervision of Chippendale and built His Majesty's Theatre in 1897. (W. MacQueen-Pope *Haymarket: Theatre of Perfection* Allen, 1948, p376). Irving's decline in 1898 was in part due to illness, in part due to a major fire that destroyed or severely damaged many of his sets, but also due to Tree's work at His Majesty's, "which became as fashionable as Henry's had been in the eighties and early nineties" (Ellen Terry *Memoirs* London: Gollancz, 1933). However, Basil Dean, who began his career under Tree, in his memoirs did not speak favourably of Tree's presentation standards, saying that production methods at His Majesty's were "a sort of Royal Academy of presentation...extremely conventional." (*Tabs* 20/3, Dec. 62, p10).

[3] **Joseph Harker** (dates unknown) was the resident designer/painter at His Majesty's, and he lit the scenery for Tree (in correspondence with Brian Legge). The Theatre Museum Archive file said he took over from Craven as "the best". He went on to design for **Oscar Asche** (1871-1936), who joined Tree's company as an actor in 1902 and took over management of His Majesty's in 1907, continuing Tree's tradition of high visual standards. Harker was probably best known for his settings for Asche's production of *Chu-Chin-Chow* of 1916, which ran for five years, a record at the time. The show gained good notices for its effects: It "will appeal to those who appreciate spectacular effects" (*The Sketch* 27/9/1916).

upon the faces of those on the stage". This was probably the first example of front of house lighting in Britain.[4]

The first British practitioner to show the influence of Reinhardt, Appia and Craig was **Sir John Martin Harvey** (1863-1944). Having worked for 14 years for Irving, whose production style he described as "archaeological", Harvey was drawn to the work which represented for him the "new cult" or "reformed theatre".[5] Through this influence Harvey found a simpler staging style. He became manager of the Lyceum in 1899 and installed a permanent semi-circular plaster cyclorama, similar to the one used by Reinhardt at the Deutches Theater, Berlin. He called this "the drum", and used it as a canvas for atmospheres created by light.

Harvey's productions showed great understanding of lighting. Two productions from before World War One illustrate this. *Great Possessions* by Karl von Rossler at the Adelphi in January 1907 won praise for the staging and especially the lighting, "lighting finer than anything seen on the stage... like a Tintoret or a Titian".[6] In *Oedipus Rex* at the Royal Opera House Covent Garden in January 1912 he utilised Reinhardt's trademark lighting. Bright, stabbing beams picked out the principal actors in an overall gloom to create the feeling of a vast space. The production used large crowd scenes and simple architectural settings, although not to great critical acclaim.[7] Harvey continued to develop his staging and lighting style which is detailed in the next section of this chapter.

There were few others of note. **Herbert Trench** (1865-1923) took over the management of the Haymarket in 1909, opening with *King Lear*. Simple, impressionistic staging was designed by Charles Ricketts (1866-1931), and the lighting was notable for novel use of storm and cloud projected effects.[8] In January 1911 Trench attempted to imitate Diaghilev's gauze techniques, seen in the work of the visiting Russian Ballets**,** in *The Blue Bird*, but could not achieve a similar level of finesse. He lacked the skill of the Russians, and the ideas were not well received.

---

[4] Booth, *Victorian Spectacular Theatre*, p128, 139 &149, citing *The People* 4/9/1910 and *Pall Mall Gazette* 20/8/1910.

[5] Harvey, Sir J.M. *The Book of Martin Harvey, Autobiography*, London: Henry Walker, 1933, p62.

[6] Harvey, *The Book of Martin Harvey, Autobiography*, p150-3.

[7] The *Weekly Times and Echo* 21/1/1912 said that elaborate stage effects were praised but over dominated the production as a whole.

[8] *The Sketch* 15/9/1909 recorded the production as having "poetic and imaginative settings that featured swagged cloths and angular jutting rocks and architecture that would have lit well".

British Lighting Practice and Practitioners, 1914-1935

The actor-manager system was challenged as the influence of Appia and Craig and continental practice slowly began to permeate British theatre. The start of World War One marked an end to the era when, according to *Tabs*, "stars were follow-spotted throughout a play, on the basis that they were the reason the public had come".[9] The new concept of the 'producer' emerged, whereby a single figure took overall artistic control for production, in theory giving equal weight to all production values.[10] In response to this, scenic artists began to develop as stage designers, and established artists such as George Harris, Oliver Messel, Norman Wilkinson, Charles Ricketts, Lovat Fraser and Augustus John became noted for their design work and formed collaborative partnerships with the leading producers.[11]

Other than the work of Irving, Tree and Harvey, productions with a high visual artistic standard did not feature in the West End, where the economics of theatre rental dictated that the theatre must be full every night and the ethos was "give the public what they want". The pressure of work schedules dictated by the weekly touring/weekly repertory system militated against quality work. There was little enough time to rehearse actors, let alone design and build good quality sets and create sensitive lighting. British theatre was at a low point in the years immediately after World War One.[12]

---

[9] In April 1914, Shaw persuaded Mrs Patrick Campbell, playing Eliza Doolittle in his *Pygmalion* at His Majesty's (alongside Herbert Tree as Professor Higgins), to forego her follow spot by telling her that it made her look like "a suet pudding in which two prunes had been embedded" (*Tabs* 41/1 Mar. 84, p2).

[10] This was perhaps most clearly articulated by Komisarjevsky in his writings around 1930. He said: "the work of a producer on a production is a matter of composition just as in any work of art. It is like devising an animated coloured talking and moving sculpture... Unless the producer can find an artist who can express his ideas, he must design the sets and the costumes and light the production himself. A real production is in the first place psychological, and pictorial only in the second place. The producer first gets a broad conception of the production, of its form and style. Then he conceives – visualises and hears – each character, and then puts all of them into rhythmical movement. Only then does he visualise the environment best suited for the expression of the movement, and invents the sets, their ground plans and levels, the colours and directions of his lighting etc. In constructing the sets the producer should not lose sight of the fact that the life *in* them is connected with the life *around* them; and this helps to create what is called an atmosphere and make the sets seem "alive" " (Komisarjevsky, *Myself and the Theatre*, p164 and Komisarjevsky, *The Costume of the Theatre*, p154).

[11] Komisarjevsky *Settings and Costumes of the Modern Stage*, p9.

[12] Cheney said in 1925 that: "Since Craig's leaving and Barker's lapse into inactivity, Britain has shown only these few too timid thrusts toward the established creative theater... For the most part the country seems satisfied with the fare it finds in its older conservative theater, varied (cont...)

The Stage Society had been formed in London in 1899 to present better quality drama to the public on Sunday evenings (without charge), but production values again fell foul of time constraints. However, such was the demand for this type of work that it continued until the outbreak of World War Two, and it was movements such as this, and practice from the continent, that were the catalyst for the rise of the Art Movement in the theatre.

In 1923 St. John Ervine began a campaign against "the pernicious system of weekly repertory". In his book *The Organised Theatre*, and in an article in *The Observer*, he suggested grouping local theatres together to combine repertory and touring, so each theatre only needed to produce a show "every three or four weeks".[13]

In 1928 Norman Marshall continued the debate, and articulated the role that lighting could play in setting new aesthetic standards in the theatre:

> "No art can flourish without intelligent criticism.... Audiences are already becoming keenly critical of the antiquated stage-craft and lighting which still prevail in many theatres. Recently in the West End I heard the audience openly laugh at a stupid piece of lighting which a year or two ago would have been completely unnoticed... The first duty of stage lighting is to help the actor... I have seen lighting which was sensationally beautiful but criminally selfish, because all the time it was fighting against the actor, calling attention to its own beauty instead of to the faces of the actors. The real test of stage lighting is the extent to which it succeeds in combining visibility with atmosphere and pictorial effectiveness".[14]

A number of small or 'fringe' venues opened in the 1920s to address the need for better quality productions. Their repertoire was drawn from European writers, plays and playwrights that had been successful at Stage Society performances, and the new British writers that appeared after 1918. Art theatres, from fringe theatre to major house, emerged, with artistic policies that placed emphasis on high production values. In the inter-war years, the best known in London were the Barnes Theatre, The Gate Covent Garden, the Lyric Hammersmith and The Everyman Hampstead; and the Birmingham Rep, the Cambridge Festival Theatre, the Oxford Playhouse and the Shakespeare Memorial Theatre Stratford in the regions. Selective West End

---

with brief Sunday excursions by the Stage Society. Theatrical leadership of the British-speaking world has shifted to New York" (Cheney, S. *The Art Theater*, New York: Knopf, 1925, p60).

[13] Cited by Marshall in *The Other Theatre*, p191.

[14] Ridge, *Stage Lighting*, Preface.

theatres also contributed, either for a single show or for the period of a particular manager. This movement was particularly important as it took work of high production values into the provinces for the first time.

These theatres became a platform for many of Britain's leading twentieth century playwrights, actors, producer/directors, designers, stage managers and eventually lighting designers. They played a crucial role in the establishment of performance values for lighting and in turn prompted changes in technique, involvement and recognition that led to the formalisation of the title 'lighting designer'. In 1946 Laurence Irving, the chair of the Royal Society of Arts, in his introduction to a speech entitled *Evolution of Stage Lighting* by Leonard Applebee recalled the breath of fresh air that the Art theatre movement brought to performance values and, in particular, he noted how an educated audience could appreciate the dynamic style of lighting employed in these small venues.[15]

In the mainstream commercial sector the shortage and expense of technicians to man the multi-follow spot approach that characterised the best work from before 1914 meant a rethink as to how the stage was lit. Battens of much higher efficiency were developed in response, and the economical style of lighting offered by these became the norm. Spotlights were first introduced to Britain by Basil Dean in 1920, and soon after this Strand Electric Ltd. began their manufacture. However few theatres invested in them as they were not ideally suited to the dimmers and control manufactured at that time. Also, to use spotlights required a more considered approach to lighting the stage that few were prepared to engage with. There were not many significant technical developments during this period to challenge the rise of the batten. The incandescent lamp began to oust the lime and arc, and gelatines replaced the

---

[15] "If you go to little art theatres you often see the most beautiful and imaginative lighting effects, which, by comparison, when you come to London, may cause you to be disappointed in what you see. The point is that the lighting of a small art theatre and the lighting of a commercial theatre are two entirely different things. Since the auditorium of the small art theatre is small, it is possible to go in for half-lighting and atmospheric effects while the actors still remain visible to almost everybody in the audience. Moreover, the audience in a small art theatre is a specialised one which understands that kind of thing and is prepared to see less of the actors and a little more imagination in the production. That is not so, however, in the commercial theatre. In London there are theatres with large auditoria and high proscenium arches where everyone has paid to see the actors. Although people criticise the unimaginative lighting in the average commercial theatre, I think that the managements are justified in demanding that their stages should be fully lit. The actors in this case are of paramount importance and must be seen and heard. Therefore the problems of lighting in the two kinds of theatre are quite different and must be judged on their own merits. I think that the lighting experts and the designers of lighting effects are equally valuable in both these branches of the theatre" (*RSA Journal* 2/8/46).

crude lamp dip. Perhaps the most important advance abroad, lighting the cyclorama and projected effects, had limited impact in Britain.

There were fewer influential visiting companies from abroad during the inter-war years. Robert Edmund Jones brought highly praised productions to London in the 1920s that utilised front of house lighting, and around 1930 Hassard Short and Gilbert Miller brought productions to London from New York that deployed spotlights *en masse* both on stage and front of house. This practice had a great influence on British thinking and spotlighting was soon adopted here in high profile venues.

The early 1930s saw the first wave of major electrical refits in key British theatres. The Royal Opera House Covent Garden and the Shakespeare Memorial Theatre Stratford were fitted out with the latest equipment, although looking back it did not match the exacting facilities provided for American productions. Glyndebourne opened with a world class technical facility, although its equipment had been imported from abroad (see Appendix ii).

The Process of Lighting

The practice of setting the lighting (*plotting*) is documented in several sources. Lighting was plotted during the technical rehearsals, where the producer, perhaps assisted by the stage designer and stage manager, sat in the stalls to set and record each lighting state and cue once the set was installed. Peter Godfrey, in his book *Backstage*, was probably the first to detail the procedures for plotting from the early 1930s. He recorded that lighting was plotted before the dress rehearsal, and decisions about colour and the final look of the show were taken at this point. The producer called out his requirements to the stage manager, who passed on information to the unseen electricians. Godfrey quoted the following exchange:

"I want more light on the back," cries the producer.
"Two more floods up-stage, Bill," says the stage manager.
"What mediums, sir – amber or pink?"
"Neither," says the producer. "I want to try white."
"How's that, sir?"
"No good. Check them down. That's too much. Bring them up again. What are they now?"
"Half-check, sir."
"Not enough. Bring them up….slowly. *Slowly!* More yet."
"They're full up, sir."
"Oh, all right; put in a pink."

"How's that, sir?"

"No good. Try an amber. *Hmm…* I don't like it. Try the pink again. Now try a straw. Let me see the amber again. That's not rich enough. I want a number four."

"Put in a Number Four, Bill …Eh? Oh! That *is* a Number Four, sir."

"Then frost it. All right, that'll do"

…and so on".[16]

It is interesting to note the subservience of the crew to the producer, their lack of involvement in the artistic process, and the amount of time wasted due to a neglect of planning.[17] Michael Northen recalled that "lighting in those dim days wasn't considered of any importance", and this extract confirms low ambition.[18]

John Sommerfield described a similar style of plotting session. The producer and stage manager sat in the stalls, and the chief electrician organised their instructions. Once the producer said "Plot this!", then the chief wrote down all the settings. The stage manager might make suggestions, but the producer set the lighting and confirmed how the cues would run. The stage staff walked as plotting dummies, apparently reluctantly. There was no mention of refinements to the lighting during dress rehearsals. He went on to say that during the show lighting was cued by red and green "Warn" and "Go" lights from the stage manager, with cues recorded in the prompt copy.[19]

Ridge and Aldred attempted to define the principles of plotting. While recognising that there were several legitimate approaches to doing this, they recorded the exacting procedures used at the Cambridge Festival Theatre as a model for others to adapt. Plotting involved the creation of a log book for each production, detailing the hanging position, beam angle, focus and colour for each lantern on the rig. To record cues, the percentage level of each lantern's intensity was recorded, along with operational fade times noted in seconds. Written notes would often be included to describe how the cue was to be executed, and how the control was to be set up for the next cue.[20]

If the operator could see the stage he would not normally be cued by the

---

[16] Godfrey, P. *Backstage*, London: Harrap, 1933, p90.

[17] The Chief was usually an ordinary man, with responsibility for all technical and engineering matters in the theatre, including the boiler room and all the house electrics. They were not men of art. And you got no "thank yous" for doing the lighting (in conversation with John G. Holton).

[18] *Focus* 12A, Aug. 92, p14.

[19] Sommerfield, J. *Behind the Scenes*, London: Nelson, 1934, p9, 93 & 108.

[20] Ridge and Aldred, *Stage Lighting, Principles and Practice*, p119.

stage manager, and would be expected to operate in a sensitive, responsive manner as set in the technical rehearsals. If the operator could not see the stage, either he would follow hand signals for cues or follow the text and work sensitively. The prompt copy would contain "Warn Electrics" and "Electrics Go" points.

They said that it was common for colours to be chosen during the technical rehearsal when the costumes arrived on stage.[21] The Producer asked for a colour to be tried and, if it was not suitable, changed. Actors were rehearsed to "play to their lights", and they said professionals were adept at finding the "hot spots". However, they acknowledged that this approach was not the norm, as time was too limited for matching the art and science of lighting with the demands and potential of a production.

However, it appears that Ridge and Aldred's system, which may have been based on the detailed American procedures for planning and plotting lighting introduced to London in the 1920s by Jones, had little influence on British practice.[22]

Key Practitioners of the Period

Despite the limited facilities in most British theatres, there were several noted for their use of light during this period. In the commercial sector, Harvey's work reached a peak, and Basil Dean and C.B. Cochran became known internationally for their high visual standards. Many art theatres developed a reputation for imaginative creative lighting, and this served as a training ground for many important lighting artists.

Harvey's work increasingly matured, influenced by the new approaches to staging. His production of *Hamlet* in 1916 typified this. He used minimal scenic elements to give better continuity, and made much use of a lit cyclorama to create location and atmosphere, drawing curtains across it for interior scenes. The production attracted considerable press interest that analysed how his staging and lighting style suited the complexity of the play.[23]

---

[21] Colour samples were made from the 1920s framed up in a single card for ease of use.

[22] Jones had adopted a style of producing sketches that would suggest lantern placement, beam angle and colour. He was assisted by his Chief Electrician George Schaff, who would help realise his instructions and find the best solution to his demand. Jones closely supervised the plotting of the lights. **Lee Simonson** (1888-1967), principal designer and artistic director of the New York Theatre Guild from 1919-1940, talked of the lighting plot "akin to the score of an opera" (Larson, *Scene Design in the American Theater from 1915-1960*, p167).

Harvey's production of *Via Crucis* at the Garrick in 1923 was noted for featuring striking lighting moments. "When the curtain went up ... the stage was draped with curtains, and mysterious blue light. Two figures were haloed with two circles of vivid phosphorescent green, and a shaft of light from the limes picked out their heads and shoulders".[24] *The Nation* said it was "a spectacle of rare beauty", and the *Manchester Guardian* praised the designs of Sir Aston Webb which "give a massive spaciousness ... behind which is a vault of blue".[25]

There is little doubt as to the importance of Harvey as a progressive staging practitioner. Building on his experiences with Irving, he incorporated influences from Europe to establish a visual language ahead of his time. He was knighted

---

[23] Harvey described the value of the cyclorama thus: "when illuminated it becomes space, air, the sky. The time of day, or night, the weather - calm or stormy - can be suggested on this 'drum' by modern methods of light: and by these means we get the impression of being out of doors. Sometimes we are there at the solemn hour of midnight when the ghost of the old king stalks along the ramparts of the castle at Elsinore; at another time when the floor of heaven is strewn with stars and, in the mysterious glimpses of the moon, Hamlet is seen waiting for the spirit of his father; and yet again when, in the sombre twilight, the corpse of the distracted Ophelia is laid to rest on what appears to be a lofty windswept eminence below which the sun is sinking in angry blood-red clouds". Interior scenes also were made to work within "the drum", with curtains lowered. "In my production they reach up to a height of about fifty feet and give the dignified perpendicular lines, with occasional glimpses of the sky beyond, which all who are familiar with the designs of Gordon Craig will recognise". Arthur Machin wrote about the staging of *Hamlet*: "it seems to me that (Harvey) has solved a very difficult problem of the stage. I mean the problem of the scenery of the poetic drama. There were two schools of scenic presentation. The old school tried to put actuality into its cloths and wings and flats... helped vigorously by the floats, by half a dozen battens, by three electric "bunches" and six limelight boxes on each side of the stage. (The scene) stands out in a blazing furnace of light... and it will go far to dim the drama and extinguish the actors. In the new school, the whole material universe was translated into curtains... the Blasted Heath, the Forest of Arden, the Battlements of Elsinore and Olivia's Garden. This is better than the old way. A dark curtain is a quiet, unobtrusive sort of property. It does not distract the mind from the play. (In the performance) all the lights went out. The black square of the proscenium began to glimmer. It only brightened so far as midnight may be said to brighten; there were no "blue limes" as in the old language of the stage. We looked at the dim and misty space, and beyond it the vast dim circle of the sky, and the vague shapes like battlements showed against it... Everything was suggested, nothing was declared. The mind could not be distracted by detail, since no detail was visible. The stage picture was just the sufficient background and atmosphere for the great action which now began. The best scene of all was the graveyard. Again the great dim circle of the sky, but now against it in black vagueness rose very old tombs and ancient crosses... The air was all twilight; and indeed the action of this Hamlet seemed to me to proceed at twilight and dawn and midnight, at hours which have more of mystery than of earthliness about them, hours which are consonant with doom" (Arthur Machin, *Evening News* 12/5/1916 cited in Martin Harvey, *The Book of Martin Harvey, Autobiography,* Henry Walker, 1933, p 93 & also see p63-4).

[24] *English Review* Vol. 36 1923, p 266.

[25] *The Nation* 19/2/23 and the *Manchester Guardian* 9/1/23.

in 1921 for his services to the theatre, and his work showed the British public the potential role lighting could have as a dynamic staging device.

Two men, Basil Dean and C.B. Cochran, dominated theatre production in the first half of the twentieth century, consistently creating high quality visual work set in a commercial environment. Both had travelled abroad, which resulted in a far greater awareness of trends in theatre presentation.

Basil Dean (1888-1978) became a leading producer in London and was known for exceptional skills in lighting.[26] He developed a style here influenced by his travels abroad, and imported equipment and ideas in equal measure. He gained a reputation for creating lavish theatre spectacle that combined sound business sense with high artistic standards – a truly commercial artist. Ernest Short summarised his approach when he said that "Dean's characteristic as a producer lies in his passion for accuracy in detail".[27]

He first became involved with theatre in 1906 working as acting ASM at the Gaiety Theatre Manchester. A chance to produce provided the opportunity to explore staging and lighting, and he went on to be appointed Producer at Kelly's Theatre Liverpool in 1911. In the same year, drawn by the desire to view German theatre, he travelled to see Reinhardt's *Oedipus Rex* at Frankfurt and *Sumürun* in Berlin.[28] He was so impressed by Reinhardt's lighting of the plaster sky dome that on his return to the Liverpool Repertory Theatre he plastered the back wall to try to re-create these ideas.

Dean's first season was ambitious, with Goldie recalling that "he had seen the importance of lighting in the new stage craft and was eager to experiment with it and the methods he had seen in Germany".[29] In 1912 Dean returned to Germany with George Harris, his designer, to continue a study of the latest developments in stagecraft. Back in Liverpool he produced Ibsen's *Pillars of Society*, using the cyclorama to great effect to create swiftly changing sky effects, complete with thunder, lightning and rain. The play did good business. In Wilde's *A Florentine Tragedy* that autumn Goldie recalled that "lights were

---

[26] In later life he became an MBE, CBE in 1947 and was the first honorary member of the ABTT for his work with theatre technology.

[27] Short, *Introducing the Theatre*, p223.

[28] Of *Oedipus* he recalled "an open stage performance, a company of 100 or more, imaginative lighting..." (*Sightline* 8/2, Autumn 74). Of *Sumürun* he recalled "colour, light and movement combined to such a brilliant effect followed closely upon the enormous upsurge of interest in stage decor that had been aroused in Western Europe by the designs of Bakst, Benois and others" (Dean, B. *Seven Ages, an Autobiography 1888-1927*, London: Hutchinson, 1970, p81).

[29] Goldie, G.W. *The Liverpool Repertory Theatre*, London: Hodder and Stoughton, 1935, p70.

thrown on to the stage from the auditorium", one of Dean's early experiments with front of house lighting.[30] His Christmas production that year, *Fifinella*, co-written with Barry Jackson and noted for Harris's fine designs, was full of lighting tricks. The first Chairman of Liverpool Repertory Theatre, Charles Really, described Dean's work in his autobiography thus: "he nearly ruined the theatre financially … he not only included more serious drama than in any two successive seasons, but with the help of that very genuine artist of the theatre, George Harris, broke what was at that time fresh ground in this country in decorative scenery and lighting effects".[31]

The lit cyclorama was crucial to Dean's early thinking. He was asked to advise on stage technology for the building of the new Birmingham Repertory Theatre in 1913, with Jackson, the Director, insisting on the most modern lighting equipment, including a "well equipped electrical board". He installed a Fortuny cyclorama, "painted in the very lightest tint of blue. For night scenes stars had to be arranged for, and some care was taken with these" and lit by automatic arcs, with silks on tracker wires for colour change.[32] *Tabs* reported that "the effects… were extraordinarily soft and beautiful".[33] Birmingham Rep. was the only British theatre to install a full Fortuny system, and it remained in use until sometime during World War One.[34]

Dean joined Tree at His Majesty's Theatre for a year, where he encountered a very traditional stage with wings and borders, although normally lit with a lot of arcs. Dean suggested bringing "more life and colour" to the stage, but his ideas were rejected. He recommended a Fortuny system to Tree, but was again ignored.[35]

In 1919 Dean formed ReandeaN with **Alec Rea** (1878-1953), the former chair of Liverpool Repertory Theatre, to manage and produce shows, a partnership that lasted until 1926 when he went solo as a producer. They established themselves at the St. Martin's Theatre, ideal for the production of realistic plays, but too small and shallow for imaginative use of light and space.

---

[30] Goldie, *The Liverpool Repertory Theatre*, p81.

[31] Really, C. *Scaffolding in the Sky*, London: Routledge, 1938. (see also *Tabs* 30/1, Mar. 72, p35)

[32] Matthews, B. *A History of the Birmingham Repertory Theatre*, London: Chatto and Windus, 1924, p160.

[33] *Tabs* 22/3, Dec. 62, p9. Differing sources report the height of the cyclorama between 40' to 60'.

[34] However, the installation was not suited to the general stage layout, which was quite shallow. Also, it proved difficult to get the carbons for the arcs, which had to be imported from Italy. The system was dismantled after the war (*Tabs* 21/1, Apr. 63, p4). See also Theatre Museum *Early Lighting File*.

[35] Dean, *Seven Ages, an Autobiography 1888-1927*, p103+.

Dean travelled to Germany again to view latest lighting equipment used by Reinhardt, and invited his chief technician Arthur Reiche to London to prepare a similar lighting scheme for the St. Martin's. He witnessed front of house incandescent spotlighting which he specified for the St. Martin's – the first front of house installation of incandescent spotlights (rather that arcs) in Britain. Bentham said of Dean: "he pioneered the use of German stage lighting and methods in so far as our cramped stages permitted".[36]

Dean's production of *The Blue Lagoon*, at the Prince of Wales in August 1920, gave him an opportunity to experiment with a more continental approach to staging and lighting on a larger stage. "An enormous cyclorama for wide skies and bright sunlight, lit with automatic arcs in semi-circular housings with grooved fronts to take colours" was used. This was home made, copied from the Schwabe system.[37] Complex stage design by Harris involved "heaving seas, boats adrift around a burning ship, fog, a storm with rain and thunder." One review noted that the play itself was "rather less convincing" with action held up by too many delays with the curtain down to reset the stage, although another recognised the importance of the stage effects, which were "the crowning accomplishment of this production". [38]

In 1920 Dean visited America. He was greatly influenced by the work of David Belasco, whom he met on this and a subsequent visit. Dean spent many hours with Louis Hartmann, Belasco's Chief Electrician, who had built effects such as "indirect reflectors" to create a softlight that could be moved to track an actor. Hartmann gave him a reflector and a copy of the paint formula to take home. Dean installed some of these units on the No. 1 bar and in the footlight position at the St. Martin's. He recalled that "we certainly obtained some intimate and elusive effects by these means".[39] He also returned with 250W baby spots, high efficiency batten reflectors called "X-rays" (which may have been the inspiration for Strand's new batten launched in 1922) and slider-type dimmers.[40] In 1923 Dean installed a Schwabe-Hasiat cyclorama, and three days after opening A.A. Milne's *The Great Broxopp* gave a public

---

[36] Dean, *Seven Ages, an autobiography 1888-1927*, pp140, 154 & 164 and *Sightline* 16/2, Aut. 82, p110.

[37] Dean, *Seven Ages, an Autobiography 1888-1927*, p141.

[38] Uidebtified press review, Theatre Museum Archives, and *Morning Post* 30/8/20.

[39] Dean, *Seven Ages, an Autobiography 1888-1927*, p169.

[40] *Sightline* 9/1, Spr. 75, p38.

demonstration.[41] He ran the lighting control himself from on stage, "a modest Prospero in spats," a reporter wrote. Bernard Shaw warned: "I'll take good care ye'll not use any of those contraptions in my plays, young man. The audience would be so busy staring at your clouds they wouldn't listen to my words".[42] Dean said: "of course he was right".[43] The system also had its critics: *English Review* reported that: "we saw it making perfectly naturalistic clouds and sky effects – a result hardly worth spending ten months and £13,000 to achieve".[44]

Dean experimented with scenic projection in Capek's *R.U.R.*, designed by Harris, at the St. Martin's in April 1923, believing this to be the first use of projection in Britain.[45] Frames to hold the projection material, made of linen, gelatine, silk and net, were cut to angles to cope with distortion and placed in front of floods and projectors. The *Sunday Times* reported that: "Dean may regard the production as his greatest triumph. With the help of Harris, and the Schwabe-Hasait lighting system, he has not only done the fullest justice to the author's own daring, but provided some of his own that lend the finish of perfection to the work".[46]

Hassan at St. Martin's in September 1923 was also reported to be a major success. With music composed by Delius and settings by Harris, lighting supplied by Schwabe, Digby and GEC, the production gained much attention in the press. Reviews noted "camels apart… (a) full-blooded, gorgeous production…" …"light was used for the purpose of indicating the passage of time. In the final scene… the dawn of day …slowly the light grew stronger (revealing the setting)… the sun was now shining brightly… they departed in a blaze of glory…" …"the scenery was very beautiful and gave effects of vast space… the general effect showed the genius which Basil Dean has for stage production…" [47] Dean experimented with a dozen spots fitted with broken

---

[41] Dean was invited by GEC, the Schwabe agents in the 1920's to be their stage lighting technical advisor.

[42] Dean, *Seven Ages, an Autobiography 1888-1927*, p191.

[43] *Sightline* 9/1, Spr. 75, p38.

[44] *English Review* Vol. 36 1923, p354.

[45] Dean, B. *Mind's Eye, an Autobiography 1927-1972*, London: Hutchinson, 1973, p66. The Schwabe-Hasait was operated by Walter Veness, with H. McDonnell as Master Electrician (Theatre Museum Archives).

[46] *Sunday Times* 29/4/23. The sentiment of the last act was noted by the *Manchester Guardian* 25/4/23 as being "drenched…in a salmon-pink sunrise".

[47] Programme notes, *The Times* 11/8/73, *Dancing Times* Jan. 1924, *The Star* 21/9/23 all Theatre Museum Archives.

lenses set at 45° to the lamp, to create a dawn effect through prismatic striations on a set painted in whitening with ground mica mixed in to reflect the light. *Sightline* recalled that the effect of this prismatic light on the broken surface was: "quite wonderful. I shall always remember the gasp of astonishment from the first night audience...". However, it was also noted that this production was dogged by over-long scene changes, with ten different locations required.[48] Dean believed that the secret of success, as illustrated by *Hassan*, was to "weld all the elements of production into some degree of artistic unity - speech, music, light and movement - like the conductor of a symphony. Without such unity the production would fall apart as a rather ill-judged spectacle".[49] Thus Dean positioned himself as the first modern producer, controlling an integrated team to deliver all production elements in harmony.

Dean also brought back scenic techniques from America, such as clever gauze lighting, stippling paint techniques and the use of better quality scenic fabrics that were much more responsive to changes in lighting tones. In the production *The Forest* at the St. Martin's in March 1924, Harris designed a set as a simple arrangement of cloths, which "backlighted in yellow and green, created such an effect of density and vastness it made the shallow St. Martin's stage look as deep as Drury Lane".[50]

Dean installed a Schwabe-Hasait system at the Theatre Royal Drury Lane in 1924 for a famous Christmas ballet production of *A Midsummer Night's Dream*. The music was composed by Mendelsohn and Harris designed elaborate stage settings. Dean projected scenery onto gauzes and a created "solo on the cyclorama for Mendelssohn's *Dawn*". The production was remembered as being "superbly lit", although other press comment was mixed, with suggestions that it was visually overproduced.[51] The *Daily Telegraph*

---

[48] Dean, *Seven Ages, an Autobiography 1888-1927*, p184 and *Sightline* 9/1, Spr. 75, p38.

[49] Dean, *Seven Ages, an Autobiography 1888-1927*, p234.

[50] *Sightline* 9/1, Spr. 75. The programme for this production notes that again Veness was in charge of Schwabe – Hasait system, with McDonnell the Master Electrician (Theatre Museum Archives).

[51] *The Times* criticised this for "scenic over-emphasis. Concentrate on the acting, refuse steadily to be diverted from it" (Theatre Museum Archives, *Sightline* 12/2, Aut. 78, p108 and *Cue* 30, Jul. 84, p13). The *Manchester Guardian* 29/12/24 recorded "the forest, when not being submitted to the over ambitious efforts of the electrician, blazes with stars". The *Daily Mail* of 3/1/25 noted that the woodland scene was played in "semi-darkness". The *Observer* 28/12/24 was more flattering, rating Harris's work his best, although: "the forest scene was lovely, and only spoiled once when, over one-half of its delicate grey-green moonlight, with its tall trees climbing up into the vastness of Drury Lane's darkness, a distracted lightman let loose a flood of brilliant violet limelight like an extreme toothache or the mercury vapour lamps they use in cinema studios. As I presume (cont...)

summed up the production style which even if considered brash at least included the possibilities for lighting and ambitious stage effects: "It is probable that many people will complain that Shakespeare himself becomes somewhat lost in the crowd of his interpreters: the best answer to that is, that if this gorgeous medley of colour schemes, lighting effects, flying ballets, scenic transformations and the like is not quite the fantasy that Shakespeare wrote, it can hardly be believed that Shakespeare would not like it if he saw it".[52]

Although there is little noted of Rea's contribution to the partnership, when ReandeaN broke up in 1926 there was a noticeable change in relationship between Dean and theatre managements. He experimented less, and a move into film production restricted his theatre activities.[53] Dean's contribution to this period of British theatre is well summarised by Adrian Klein, who had ridiculed the use of light on stage except for the work of a few, and most notably Dean. Klein observed that Dean "manipulates his lighting resources in such a way as to assist the whole artistic conception in the mind of the dramatist. He is as much prepared to create an illusion of "plein air" as to indulge in poetic fantasy or pretty light-patterning, all depending upon his interpretation of the dramatist's intention".[54]

Charles Blake (C.B.) Cochran (1872-1951), after a variety of jobs in the theatre, started his career in America, first producing in 1897 in New York. He returned to Britain, and went on to be associated with some of the most important productions seen to date in London. These included: *The Miracle* with Reinhardt in 1911, and its revival at the Lyceum in 1932; intimate revues at the Ambassadors and the Vaudeville and spectaculars at the London Pavilion between 1918 and 1931, for which he was hailed a master showman; and important new productions of Noel Coward plays. He wrote five books on his life in the theatre and was knighted in 1948.[55]

Cochran travelled widely, bringing work from Europe and America to the London stage, and his influences included Fuller, MacKaye and Reinhardt. Like Dean, Cochran embraced the role of the producer, building a strong creative

---

Mr. Harris interviewed the lightman after the performance and killed him, I shall say no more on this score..." (Theatre Museum Archives).

[52] The *Daily Telegraph* 29/12/24.

[53] Rea remained in artist management as lessee of the St. Martin's until 1937, and then was based at the Apollo.

[54] Klein, *Coloured Light – an Art Medium*, p179.

[55] His reviews marked "the beginning of a new era in the history of the London stage": an account from *Play Pictorial* Vol. 33 No.199, reported in *Sightline* 13/2, Aut. 79, p119.

team around him, although both still retained a style dictatorial by modern standards. He believed in a strong visual literacy and a detailed command of all aspects of production.[56] He employed leading designers and artists of the day, including Oliver Messel, Augustus John (1878-1961 – "the finest symbolic designer"), William Nicholson, Doris Zinkeisen, Gladys Calthrop, and Norman Wilkinson. He long courted Craig to design for him, and claimed he nearly achieved this unique liaison. He used a regular production team led by Stage Supervisor/Director Frank Collins and Stage Manager Dan O'Neil, whom Cochran rated the best.[57]

On his use of designers, Cochran said that: "the visual side of the entertainment has a strong appeal to me, and I take great care in my selection of designers for the scenes and costumes. I suggest to them what I require and they go away to return later with their detailed development of these general ideas".[58] Sir Nigel Playfair confirmed that "he has a real love of beauty and of colour, and he is always anxious and ready to call to his services the best stage decorators and musicians and writers".[59] Cochran believed sets should be appropriate to the production, saying that this defined a good setting. He believed that illusion was all, and that the eye must be pleased and the intelligence satisfied. He felt that: "the best examples are when a play departs from actuality and from realism… into purely imaginative scenic design", first seen in Britain by the Russian Ballets.[60]

Cochran was dismissive of theatre design in this country, except for the

---

[56] In correspondence with Theodore Komisarjevsky: "On the function of the producer: needs to be multi-skilled. But most important he is an artist who gives an imaginative interpretation on the stage of a written play or of an improvisation through the ensemble of actors and with the aid of all the means of expression which the stage possesses." The mis-en-scene requires a similar imaginative interpretation. "the stager of a play… gets a conception of the story, of its idea, of its emotional movement… of the whole dynamic… A good stager of plays must have a strong and subtle sense of rhythm and be musical. He devises how the characters should act, and then devises the settings, lighting and everything else which forms the actor's environment on stage. The sets, furniture, props, lighting etc. cannot have an absolute value and be admired by the public independently of the acting. The work with the actors is the most difficult part of a producer's job. To be able to work with them he must be a psychologist… The power of a show lies not only in words but in action. What matters most on stage is the life that lies hidden beneath the lines and also between the lines." (Cochran, *Review of Reviews*, p62).

[57] Cochran, C.B. *Cock-a-doodle-doo*, London: Dent, 1941, pp110, 226 & 248, and Cochran, *I had Almost Forgotten*, p125.

[58] Cochran, *Cock-a-doodle-doo*, p122.

[59] Playfair, N. *Hammersmith Hoy*, London: Faber and Faber, 1930, p182.

[60] Cochran, *The Showman Looks On*, p223.

stylised settings for Granville Barker's *The Winter's Tale, Twelfth Night,* and *A Midsummer Night's Dream,* designed by Norman Wilkinson and Albert Rutherston at the Savoy between 1912-14.[61] Only occasionally did he think that the public showed an awareness of stage design, such as the production of *The Beggar's Opera* at Hammersmith, designed by Lovat Fraser in 1920.

Cochran placed great value upon lighting. Bentham, not being one to praise lightly, noted in *Cue* that: "all Cochran's shows were properly lit", and MacQueen-Pope said that he "produced lovely scenes and was addicted to pastel tints rather than high colours... A Cochran show became a yardstick for others". Cochran claimed that "by skilful use of light, mystery and romance are created".[62] Davis remembered that Cochran was fond of gelatines No.36 and Nos.7-11 range for ladies.[63] An example of the quality of the lighting can be seen in *The Silver Tassie* at the Apollo in 1929 (see illustration below).

Three major productions from the early 1930s illustrate Cochran's commitment to the highest standards and innovative use of lighting. Firstly, a notable success was the lavish, spectacular production of Noel Coward's

The Silver Tassie, The Sketch, 22/11/1929. By permission of the Illustrated London News picture library.

[61] Cochran, *The Showman looks on,* p223.

[62] *Cue* 30 p13; Macqueen-Pope, W. *Nights of Gladness,* London: Hutchinson, 1956, p240; and Cochran, *The Showman looks on,* 1945, p233.

[63] Tabs 37/1, Dec 80, p26.

Cavalcade, The Sketch, 18/11/1931. By Permission of V&A Images / Victoria and Albert Museum, London.

Cavalcade at the Theatre Royal Drury Lane in 1931. The production was designed by **Gladys Calthrop** (1897-1980), for whom Cochran had the highest regard: she "had done brilliant work for me... she sees the thing through... and lighting rehearsal even if it lasts 24 hours. She has acquired during the years I have known her in the theatre a really fine sense for lighting effect". The design employed rising and falling bridges, and the play called for 22 scenes in a wide range of locations, with times and places from New Year's Eve 1899 through to New Year's Eve 1930.[64] *Play Pictorial* No. 357 published stunning photographs of *Cavalcade* (see illustration above). One featured the

---

[64] Such was its size, Stage Manager W. Abingdon needed 200 stage hands to run the show. "*Cavalcade* is an example of wonderful stage management. Everything is superbly timed". On viewing the show from the wings, a reporter noted "all the stage hands stand to attention when the National Anthem is played" (*The Observer* 10/1/32, and Cochran, *I Had Almost Forgotten*, pp142 & 148). Cochran was known to be critical of the quality of stage staff, preferring an enthusiast rather than a Union man. In a letter from St. John Ervine, advising on working to a limited budget: "I should engage members of the middle class to shift my scenery and work my lights, and I am certain that I could obtain better results from them than are at present obtained from working men who have deposited their brains in their Union. If the worst came to the worst, I should expect my players to be able to shift scenery and operate lights. Why should they not? A player who has twenty five words to say in a play ought to be glad to be given the chance to occupy himself interestingly for the rest of the evening" (Cochran, *Review of Reviews*, p30). Lighting, with Strand credited in the programme for the equipment, was critical to the staging. Cochran said that the show "necessitates the best modern lighting equipment available and a full week of dress rehearsals, Frank Collins for Stage Supervision and Dan O'Neill as Stage Manager".

cast on stage on a simple setting of levels, with nine narrow beam spots picking out each actor. Other photos showed highly charged, realistic urban environments. The overall impression gained from these photographs is that of modern, stylised lighting.

Secondly, the production of *Helen* at the Adelphi in 1932 was the first of two highly successful collaborations with the designer **Oliver Messel** (1904-1978)[65], whom Cochran thought a genius.[66] Messel's style, whilst showing echoes of Craig and Appia, was firmly rooted in the designs of the Russian Ballet.[67] *Helen* was best known for the all-white bedroom scene, which Zinkeisen recalled was "brilliantly successful. Oliver Messel handles light and delicate colours better than almost any designer for the stage".[68] The *Daily Telegraph* (1/2/32) recorded that the lighting was "a feast to the eye." Alan Parsons in the *Daily Mail* (1/2/32) noted that "those familiar with Reinhardt's work will continually recognise the master hand... in the lighting. There was one moment in particular where the whole stage is bathed in green light, save for the solitary figure of Helen, 'spotted' by a sapphire-blue arc light, hidden, in typical Reinhardt fashion, in some dim and lofty upper box. I only hope that it may not prove too sophisticated for the general public. Beauty is not too frequently met in these drab days" (see illustration). At an ALD lecture, Michael Northen recalled Messel's fondness for pink and blue gels, using them solo and in combination: nos. 17 and 54, and also used double 17 and 17+54 split in a frame.[69] Sadly Messel's autobiography contains no helpful references to his use of light, except that he regularly used lighting specialist Bill Lorraine as his assistant.[70]

Thirdly, twenty-one years after it was first seen in London by Reinhardt, Cochran revived *The Miracle* at the Lyceum in April 1932, with settings

---

[65] Messel was perhaps the most important British stage designer of the century learning his craft at the Slade, and as apprentice to the artist John Wells. Soon after graduation he made a major impact on the theatre scene for his mask work first with Diaghilev and then for Cochran and later he worked for Glyndebourne, as well as for a variety of other managements.

[66] *Helen* and *The Miracle* established him as "the only British designer who can "steal the notices" from the actors and author" (Cochran, *The Showman Looks On*, p225).

[67] Roy Strong, Director of the Victoria and Albert Museum, in his exhibition catalogue said that his work "always had that slightly unreal, transparent, bleached out effect, as though we were being presented with an hallucination of a previous century" (Pinkham, R. (Ed.) *Oliver Messel Exhibition Catalogue*, London: V&A, 1983, p7). His designs offered the British public a "colourful escapism after the tragic reality of war" (*Cue* 24, July 83, p12).

[68] Zinkeisen, D. *Designing for the Stage*, London: The Studio, 1938, p72.

[69] *ALD* Lecture at the *Live!* Show, Jan. 97.

[70] Castle, C. *Oliver Messel a biography*, London: Thames and Hudson, 1986, p124.

Helen.

designed by Oskar Strnad and costumes designed by Messel. It was reported by *Tabs* as being "very elaborate indeed" and a "far bigger fit-up task than the recent production of *Blitz!*"[71] Unlike the original, an end stage format was

---

[71] *Tabs* 22/1, Mar. 64, p44.

used, with auditorium gangways used for entrances. Perhaps the most notable aspect of the lighting rig was that no battens were used. All lighting was provided by spotlights. The rig contained 108 lanterns: on No. 1 bar there were 48 x 1kW arena floods and 12 x 1kW Patt. 23 focus spots; on the perches 3 x 2kW spots (with 6" lenses) a side; front of house there were 26 x Patt. 23 and 16 x 2kW spots. The 2kWs were either manned or refocused during the production. Backlighting was used to great effect to light stained glass windows. The production used 185 candle fittings and 100 torches. Control was by an 80 way Grand Master.[72] The lighting unusually gained press coverage, with the use of spotlights, rather than battens and footlights, praised, and the emotional intensity of the scenes was noted as "astonishing".[73] Other press reported that the show was "the finest production ever seen on the theatre stage".[74] However, *The Times* was critical, saying that the scenery was "prejudiced by the weak employment of transparencies", but overall gave the design high praise.[75]

Dean and Cochran set standards that few could reach or even aspire to. The gulf between the quality of their work and that of their contemporaries was huge. However, another commercial producer worthy of note was **Julian Wylie** (1878-1934). A theatre manager, agent, and accomplished illusionist, he was described by Hartnoll as "one of the best technical producers of his day" and was known as "The King of Pantomime".[76]

---

[72] *Cue* 36, Jul. 85, p17. Bentham records the Arena Floods as Patt. 35's, although these were not being manufactured at the time of this production. The rig was supplied by Strand

[73] "Spot-light Halo: Illumination marvels of *The Miracle*": "Probably the most interesting and elaborate experiment in theatrical illumination ever carried out in this country is the lighting of *The Miracle*. The lighting is so subtle, so full of variety, that few visitors to the Lyceum Theatre realise that throughout the performance the stage is illuminated by spot-lights and nothing else. Footlights, of course, are out of the question with an apron stage in use. It is astonishing how skilfully the lighting is used to vary the emotional intensity of the scenes, especially since it is so unobtrusive. One feature of particular interest is the glass trap door in the floor of the stage. It is on this spot that the Nun dies and a light shining through provides a beautiful and amazingly natural halo. The striking stained-glass effects are obtained by spotlights shining through the coloured screens. Not the least beautiful of the lighting achievements is the golden radiance behind the altar, with the scores of burning candles in front. Hypercritical people have complained that the candles are electric lights. But real candle are prohibited by the regulations against fire" (*The Evening News*, 28/4/1932).

[74] An unidentified newspaper article 11/4/32, Theatre Museum Archives.

[75] Theatre Museum Archives.

[76] He was Producer at the London Hippodrome from 1920-25, at the time when Samoiloff's shows were staged there. A notable production from this period was the revue *Round the World in Eighty Days* in 1922 in which a film was used to show various sequences, such as the approach of a (cont...)

Wylie was another producer to see the potential for front-of-house lighting, first using it for *Bow Bells* at the Hippodrome in 1932.[77] The *Daily Telegraph* (5/1/1932) said the show contained "a kaleidoscope of colour and movement", and the *Daily Mail* of the same day published a photograph taken under the stage lighting, noting that "a new lighting system, a moving stage and a new method of hanging scenery are employed in the production." The production was also noted for its lack of footlights. Davis remembered that Wylie's favourite gelatine colour was No.17 steel blue.[78]

Outside commercial theatre, a number of practitioners were noted for their contributions and achievements in lighting in the emerging Art theatre movement, which set out to provide an equally valid counterpoint to the best of mainstream practice.

Perhaps some of the most adventurous lighting during the 1920s was to be found in a student theatre. The 600 seat proscenium arched **Parry Opera House**, located within the Royal College of Music in London, was built in 1921 for the staging of operas. The stage was of modest size and fitted with a curved cyclorama but the lighting installation was far ahead of its time. It was designed so that any lantern could be rigged anywhere on stage and plugged to any dimmer via a patch system (the first in Britain, made by Strand).[79] This offered the potential for very complex yet flexible lighting by maximising the number of dimmers available. Harold Ridge claimed that this venue was "the best equipped building in London in which to practice the art of the theatre".[80] Each production was rigged from scratch as no set scheme of lighting was established.

Archives detail that "before long two ingenious students, **Michael H. Wilson** (a violin student – dates not known) and **Humphrey Proctor-Gregg** (dates not known), were turning their talents to providing scenery and lighting. Proctor-Gregg went on to be the resident scene designer and producer".[81] Wilson

---

liner and a race along the Portsmouth Road. Audiences thought this "remarkable" (the *London Hippodrome File,* Theatre Museum Archives and Trewin, J.C. *The Gay Twenties,* London: Macdonald, 1958, p47).

[77] Its programme credited Strand for the special lanterns on the dress circle front (*Tabs* 22/1, Mar. 64, p36).

[78] *Tabs* 37/1, Dec. 80, p26. Wylie had a strong relationship with Strand, and used technicians such as effects specialist Percy Boggis, who had worked as an electrician for Loie Fuller and joined Strand in 1919, and Strand employee Jack Madre as his touring electrician.

[79] *Strandlight* 8, Spr. 89, p 1.

[80] Ridge, *Stage Lighting,* p118+.

[81] Warrack, G. *Royal College of Music* ,Vol. 1, RCM Archives, p145 (not published).

apparently designed the control, which was located on the stage right perch with "an excellent view of the stage".[82] With high quality hydraulic-operated dimmers, it offered a level of control hitherto unknown: smooth fades of up to half an hour could be achieved, and differential dimming was possible, meaning that each dimmer could travel at its own speed, independent of others.

An example of the style of lighting typically produced in this theatre can be gained from the review of *Pelleas et Melisande* contained in Harold Ridge's book, quoting Proctor-Gregg, the Producer:

> "*Pelleas* was about the most difficult scene to light I have ever known: it took more time than the remaining twelve scenes of the opera altogether. Also the 'check' has to work smoothly and accurately to the score, arriving at particular points at particular bars - twice out of six times it got mistimed by a few seconds. In this most Maeterlinckian of scenes atmosphere is everything – miss the subtle effect of twilight going breathlessly into a night heavy with storm – opening too with a calm sunset – miss all that, and your audience had better keep its eyes shut and listen to the words. Three people meet on a terrace overlooking the sea and discuss the weather, two of them lovers meeting *for the first time:* they allude only to the weather, lighthouses, ships setting sail, the bustle of mariners in the port far below, but the unfolding of the whole drama is symbolised meteorologically in that seven minutes at most!
>
> This is how we tried to do it, scorning the discreet 'general check' of the opera house – I give an untechnical précis of the plot.
>
> Scene: a break in a pine forest giving on to a terrace, sea supposed far below: steps descend that way. All top lighting dark blue, three shades, one patch of green which checks first. Two circuits of orange (spots and floods) set to throw long pools of sunset light through the branches on to the stage and pick up the figures on the terrace, and set low, to throw long shadows. Horizon dark blue above a green blue below. (a little reflected light from the orange circuits striking stage etc. helped this). The orange checked first, to out, one circuit at back changed to green to pick up the two figures left on the terrace. Meantime everything else 'to out' working front to back, leaving only one cloud lantern to light the whole sky with a judicious 'leak' arranged to drop a faint, unseen ray on the lovers descending from the terrace.
>
> The difficulties of all this were of course: timing; keeping a balance and avoiding unintended shadows; setting the spots accurately in the rapid scene change preceding". [83]

---

[82] Very little can be found about Michael Wilson's career, except that he went on to be a well known figure in Bentham's *Colour Music* group (*Sightline 21/1, Sum.* 87, p28).

[83] Ridge, *Stage Lighting*, p118+.

If this example was typical, then the work was clearly well ahead of the time. Indeed, Ridge concluded that "the work done at this theatre is at an immensely high level". However, it is interesting to note that the standards achieved in this theatre appear to have had little if any influence.

In the 1920s **Terence Gray** (1885-not known), director, designer and playwright wrote a number of mime plays that utilised only movement and lighting. To try out this work, with **Harold Ridge** (not known-1957), author and amateur actor, they took on an old Georgian playhouse in Cambridge, rebuilding it in part and opened it as the Cambridge Festival Theatre in 1926. Ridge designed the lighting installation. (See Appendix ii for a technical review of the theatre.)

The Festival was Britain's first modern open stage theatre, and Gray introduced numerous staging innovations during his tenancy. The theatre was based on an eighteenth century horseshoe theatre, the auditorium of which was kept intact. The stage had no proscenium, was the width of the auditorium, and had a cyclorama. It ended in steps falling into the stalls with no obvious division between actor and audience. The theatre was refined with comfortable seating, and had a restaurant that served quality wines.[84] (For a technical review of this theatre, see Appendix ii.)

The team Gray formed at Cambridge with Ridge also included **Herbert Prentice** (1890-c1965) as the first Producer and **Norman Marshall** (1901-1980) as the first Stage Director.[85] They were to become perhaps the most influential creative team in the development of British theatre production this century. Their achievements may have been variable and received a mixed

---

[84] In 1928 Gray detailed his thoughts on theatre architecture, stating arrangements that were essentials for a modern stage, features that he tried to incorporate into his scheme at Cambridge. He said that ¼ the acting area should be in the auditorium, surrounded to an extent by audience. Actors should be able to approach the stage by the eight points of the compass. Light (with sources invisible to the spectator) should be able to come from anywhere. Every spectator should be able to see the action backed by a cyclorama. The orchestra or musicians should be invisible to the spectators. Stage management and lighting operators should be in a central position with an uninterrupted view of the stage, and the stage floor should be on hydraulics to sink and on palettes to slide into the wings in sections, with the acting area able to be raised into multiple levels (from *The Bookman's Journal* in the *Festival Review*, Vol. II April 1928 No. XXXVI., cited in ABTT *Newsletter* 4/3, Aut. 70, p21).

[85] Prentice had worked at Northampton and Sheffield, and after Cambridge directed at Birmingham and Stratford. J.M. Barrie said he had "an adroitness in stage effects that is beyond the author's skill who knows what he wants but not how to get it" (Trewin, *The Gay Twenties*, p121). Marshall was an Oxford graduate, author of *The Other Theatre* and *The Producer and the Play* and from 1961 the first Chair of the ABTT until 1977 when he became its first President.

reception, but their pioneering work was noticed, highly regarded and the inspiration for many to follow.[86] Gray introduced a European and American expressionist and symbolist repertoire and a programme of classics staged in a highly controversial manner. Inspired by Craig, Appia and Meyerhold, he set the plays with simple geometric structures on split levels and used lighting as a key dramatic ingredient. He saw the play text to be just one element in a total theatre event. His approach was new to Britain, although already well established on the continent. His productions were daringly experimental and, although criticised for self-indulgence and at odds with British theatre of the time, he challenged the status quo. The artistic policy dictated that it was not the choice of play that mattered but the manner of the production. Marshall said it was to "attack the realistic tradition of acting and production which in Britain at this time had been brought to a pitch of almost photographic perfection by Basil Dean at St. Martin's."[87]

The theatre was not designed to accommodate box sets, and progressive staging techniques were employed such as revealing lanterns and doing away with wing masking completely. Gray designed the scenery out of screens and simple stock scenic items. All plays were given the same treatment. However, this approach often oversimplified the play and subtlety was lost, and Gray's virtual abolition of props often only confused the audience as to what the actor was doing or referring to.

Gray placed great importance upon lighting, as indicated in his writings of 1927:

"of all the factors that have emerged in the exploration of the artistic possibilities of play production, the most potent, the most vital, is that of light. It has been maintained that a play could be performed adequately with the aid of light only, but at least it can be certainly said that not less than one third of the power and expression which can be got out of a play can be obtained only by an inspired use of this medium".

However, he qualified this when he said that a controlled colour scheme was not yet possible with light. "Lighting is not yet an art, it is a science, and its only function in the theatre as yet is to make the movement, form and colour visible".[88] Prentice indicated both his interest and depth of understanding of the use of

---

[86] His work inspired Tyrone Guthrie, who directed at the Festival in 1929/30, to influence a range of theatre building designs later in the century, such as the Festival Theatre Chichester.

[87] Marshall, *The Other Theatre*, p53.

[88] Holme, G. (Ed.) *Design for the Theatre*, London: The Studio Ltd, 1927, pp7&8.

light when he said: "this whole matter of lighting is one of great importance in our theatre today and the future. No longer must it be mere illumination, but light and shade must be brought to help the changing feeling of the play. It is possible for your lighting to take as important an emotional part in your play as your actors".[89]

The theatre was equipped with one of the most elaborate and up to date lighting systems in the world. Lighting was used to show the changing moods within a play, to focus on the important and to ignore the peripheral. Marshall said that "at its best it continually achieved effects both dramatic and beautiful".[90] Bentham suggested that the style of lighting employed at the Cambridge Festival Theatre was the ideal approach for open stage settings of Shakespeare.[91] Three examples indicate the scope and ambition of lighting at the theatre.

Firstly, in *Masses and Man* by Ernst Toller, Prentice worked exclusively with limes against a background of black curtains and with only a black rostrum on stage. The whole setting and emotion of the play was put over by the swing of the beams of light and the throb of the varying intensity:

> "a pulsing of the light can work upon your audience as much or more than your best actor, and should be treated as a necessary part of the movement of your play and not as mere illumination..."[92]

Secondly, in *The Judge of All the Earth*, with a cubist-style setting, lighting was used to show the characters' journey through the play:

> "these masses, orange coloured, stood out against a background of blue light, obtained by strong hidden floods shining on to light coloured curtains. So your figures are seen largely in silhouette and very much two-dimensional. This should give a certain unreality to the figures for the earlier part of the play, and not until they really find themselves at the end do they appear as wholly real, when a white spot-light picks them out seated on the throne..."[93]

Thirdly, the lighting for *The Immortal Hour* indicated the complexity of a lighting plot from this creative team:

[89] Ridge, *Stage Lighting*, p166.
[90] Marshall, *The Other Theatre*, pp42&53.
[91] *Tabs* 16/3, Dec. 58, p30.
[92] Ridge, *Stage Lighting*, p166.
[93] Ridge, *Stage Lighting*, p166.

"the pillars were emerald green with the centre steps in gold and the throne scarlet and gold. The cyclorama was flooded with orange. The steps were lit from the spot-batten with a mixture of red and blue. A spot-light on the batten immediately above the thrones projected a pool of white light on the throne steps. The central entrance at the back was by a flight of steps from the cellar to stage level, lit by a vertical shaft of green, coming from a focus lamp below.

At the beginning of the scene the acting area was flooded with amber and was gradually dimmed after the entrance of Midir. As the scene progressed and Midir influenced Etain and drew towards the central steps away from the King, the light changed very gradually to green, this in turn fading as the two mounted the steps at the entrance. By the time they had reached the top they were standing in a pool of green light, then as they descended into their own "realm" the light from the pit was increased so that they were, in effect, swallowed up in a blaze of green light. This was dimmed gradually as they disappeared from view, leaving the stage almost in total darkness, a concentrated white spot being brought up rapidly on the dimmer to pick out the King as he stood on the steps of his throne, until Dalua's shadow passed over him and he falls dead".[94]

These examples show the complexity and vigour of the lighting, and were in advance of any other theatre or practitioner from the period.

In his book Ridge illustrated many examples of the creative use of light to set atmosphere and create a highly individual, non-realistic style. In *The Oresteia of Aeschylus*, the acting area was a mixture of greens and blues, with actors picked up in "severe and concentrated" shafts of bright green light. Curtains through doorways were lit in violet. It was common for actors to be lit in strong colours, or highly localised by a single spot with the rest of the stage in blackout. UV was used, as in *The Adding Machine*, for a graveyard scene, where the actors too wore UV make-up. *The Pleasure Garden* demanded a more realistic approach, but creativity was brought to bear with light falling on the stage broken by perforated screens. Actors lit in a spot from either side in contrasting colours was used as a technique, to create an additive colour to the face yet retain rich colours in the shadows.[95]

Lighting the cyclorama was a key component of most settings, with a similar bold approach taken to the use of colour. In *On Baile's Strand*, it was lit to suggest mist rising from the sea. In *And the Tomb was Found*, a lit cyclorama

---

[94] *Tabs* 20/1, Apr. 62, p14.

[95] Ridge, *Stage Lighting*, Ch. 8.

set action into silhouette, with no general stage lighting throughout. *Richard III* used only focus lamps, to create areas of distinct light and shade: "characters in conflict picked out in surrounding darkness". Blues and violets were used to "emphasise an atmosphere of plotting and deeds of darkness".

With reference to the lighting at the Festival Theatre Cambridge, Bentham said: "Inevitably, this early installation provoked the question: is all the lighting we use today really necessary?" He suggested two answers: firstly, that we have become more used to higher levels of artificial light, in all fields; and secondly, as a backlash against even flooding of the stage, local spots with sharp edges with clear cut shadows would stylistically have been acceptable.[96]

The Festival Theatre Cambridge ran for only eight years because, with new writers not forthcoming, the repertoire became exhausted.[97] In a farewell letter, Gray said: "Cambridge has supported our work magnificently, for we have compromised with none and pandered to nobody's prejudices. Whatever we believed to contain truth and to be worth saying or doing we have done without hesitation; for a theatre that considers everybody's feelings, seeks to please all and offend none, will get nowhere, for it can have no policy."[98]

Ridge retired early due to poor health. In his obituary in *Tabs*, L.G. Applebee said that he: "greatly influenced the art of stage lighting, quick to see the enormous potential of directional lighting made possible by the installation of the incandescent spotlight in the early 1920s. His association with Gray was at the time considered rather revolutionary, but the Festival Theatre Cambridge did an immense amount to encourage the use of lighting as a very necessary and essential part of dramatic expression".[99]

Sir Nigel Playfair (1874-1934), educated at Harrow and Oxford, bought the Lyric Theatre Hammersmith in 1918 and ran it for 14 years. He gave

---

[96] *Tabs* 20/1, Apr. 62, p14.

[97] Gray was a rich man, prepared to subsidise the box office takings in a quest for experiment and realisation of his artistic vision. His decision to leave the theatre ultimately was due to his poor leadership and man management, and his inability to take people with him. His casting was bizarre, although often most effective, taking amateurs and inexperienced actors and bullying them into performing the way he wanted. His programming was intense, and big cast productions worked long hours to maintain the repertoire. The theatre tapped into local amateur companies for extras and a local ballet company for dancers, such as for choruses in Greek productions, choreographed by Ninette de Valois, Gray's cousin, who had a rare combination of imagination and emotion and went on to form Sadler's Wells (Marshall, *The Other Theatre*, p139). Gray retired from theatre in 1933 to live abroad, become a winegrower and breed racehorses.

[98] *Tabs* 20/1, Apr. 62, p14.

[99] *Tabs* 15/2, Sep. 57, p5.

design opportunities to **George Sheringham** (1885-1937), **Doris Zinkeisen** (1898-1991), **Norman Wilkinson** (1882-1934) and **Claude Lovat Fraser** (1890-1921), of whom he said was "the first designer in Britain to give serious attention to the problem of designing for the small stage".[100]

A rarely documented example of Playfair's work at the Lyric was *The Fantasticks* in 1933, with lighting by Ridge and Aldred. They created a soft, unobtrusive feel, without sharp contrasts in colour or intensity. Cues responded to the emotional landscape of the plot through delicately toned ambiences, with the overall aim to create a fairylike mood for the production. One special moment included the use of a tree gobo projection from front of house that also incorporated a split colour to obtain a range of hues across the projection. Silhouette was also used to separate characters between foreground and background.[101] (See Appendix ii for a technical review of the theatre.)

Sir Barry Jackson (1879-1961) founded the Birmingham Repertory Theatre and was the first director, from 1913 to 1923.[102] He promoted the highest standards of acting, production and design, set in an experimental context. He went on to work at the Festival Theatre Malvern and the Shakespeare Memorial Theatre Stratford, and many of his productions came into London.

Jackson designed the settings for the opening seasons, and productions such as *Twelfth Night* in 1916 received much critical acclaim. His style was to use simple scenic shapes and a cyclorama for atmospheric lighting. In a production of *The Merchant of Venice* in 1919, he experimented with fabrics "to catch the opalescent tones of the lagoons and palaces as he had observed them in

---

[100] Playfair said that Fraser's work was an inspiration to British stage design, coming at a time when standards were so low, characterised by – according to Playfair - elaborate, extravagantly realistic scenery that tended to look flimsy, with dull unrelated costumes. His early death was a great blow to British theatre. He said of Fraser's designs for *The Beggar's Opera* (1920, running for 3 years) "I thought them perfection" (Playfair, *The Story of the Lyric Theatre Hammersmith*, p96). Of Fraser's *La Serva Padrona* "for the first time that extraordinary simplicity, combined with what our grandfathers called *elegance*, for which he became famous, appeared on the British stage" (Playfair, *The Story of the Lyric Theatre Hammersmith*, p31). He got his effects by "*not* spending money, and designed scenery which was not only very much better than the conventional stuff – it was mechanically ten times as efficient, and financially at least several times as cheap" (Playfair, *The Story of the Lyric Theatre Hammersmith*, p32). It was said that one of his great strengths was that he "had a wonderful grasp of stage mechanics and, without ever sacrificing a visual effect, could always find the most practical and economical way of securing it" (Fraser, G.L. *In the Days of my Youth*, Cassell, 1970, p244).

[101] Ridge and Aldred, *Stage Lighting, Principles and Practice*, p112.

[102] A trained architect, a founder of the Repertory movement in Britain and knighted in 1925 for services to the theatre. He stayed at Birmingham until the mid 1920's despite never fully winning public confidence. After a couple of years in London he founded and directed the Malvern (cont...)

the brightness of early spring." He observed in *Shakespeare Survey 8* in 1955 that: "these experiments remain in my memory as efforts to use colour to enhance atmosphere. I need hardly add that I never heard any reference made to them by members of the audience".[103]

Jackson recognised the need to collaborate, and **Paul Shelving** (1888-1968) became his regular designer. His approach was summarised by comments expressed in *The Beacon* in 1923 that: "scenery is best regarded in terms of background to the actors. It should not "shout" unduly or take the spectator's attention from them".[104]

Jackson set high standards in his theatre. One of those that rose to this challenge was **H.K. Ayliff** (1872-1949), an actor before becoming Stage Director and Producer at Birmingham Rep from 1922. Having trained as a painter he took great pride in lighting his own productions, and used a full range of colour and controlled beam direction "to give full value to the colours in the sets and to make it unnecessary for the actors to use the heavy make-up that they had to use before".[105] He was probably best known for directing a modern dress *Hamlet* at the Kingsway Theatre in 1925, designed by Shelving. The set comprised traditional staging using levels and individual pieces such as statues, played against a lit cyclorama for outdoor scenes or flattage for interiors. The production was criticised in the press for being too dim to see that it was in modern dress.[106]

Peter Godfrey (1899-1970), partnered by actress Molly Veness, opened the tiny 96 seat Gate Theatre Salon in Floral Street, London in October 1925.[107] It was the first private theatre club in London, in part because the premises were not up to licence standards, in part because of the nature of the plays Godfrey wished to present. The theatre was a "barn-like apartment that was both stage and auditorium".[108]

Festival from 1929-37, and later directed at The Memorial Theatre Stratford and the Opera House Covent Garden. His considerable personal wealth allowed him to subsidise his work as he despised commercial theatre. Birmingham soon became the leading playhouse for Shakespeare outside London, attracting leading actors of the time.

[103] Trewin, J.C. *The Birmingham Repertory Theatre 1913-1963*, London: Barrie and Rockliff, 1963, p53.

[104] *Sightline* 21/1, Sum. 87, p11.

[105] Personal correspondence with his son, David Ayliff.

[106] Theatre Museum Archives.

[107] Above Strand's main "ramshackle warehouse". There was no flying space, or even room to stack scenery (*Tabs* 27/1, Mar. 69, p39).

[108] *The Observer* 17/1/26. It also had a small library and art gallery, and was reputed to serve (cont...)

Godfrey was the first to bring expressionistic theatre to the London stage, and his policy took off when in spring 1926 good press for *From Morn to Midnight* by Kaiser launched the theatre. Marshall said: "I still count this production as the best I have seen".[109] Each subsequent production ran for two weeks, and with a low budget design approach, 'house style' comprised a permanent black background with minimal props and furniture to indicate the location. He relied on unrealistic lighting for atmosphere and effects. Production output was impressive with 23 challenging plays produced in the first season.

In 1927 the theatre moved to Villiers Street. This theatre measured 55'x30', with the stage about 18' deep and 18" high, with steeply raked seating.[110] eighteen productions were presented in the first season. The intimacy of the theatre meant movement and vocal work could have far subtler 'filmic' dynamics, and this was true too of the lighting. The theatre continued to build in confidence, with a peak reached by the sixth season, 1930/1.

Licencing problems, and a constant battle with the censor, eventually undermined the venture. On closing the theatre in 1939, Peter Godfrey wrote to members, stating the object had been to give London the "chance to see the amazing experiments that were being made in theatre all over central Europe and America just after the war." His output had been prolific, with over 350 plays staged. The building was bombed later in the same year.

James B. Fagan (1873-1937) opened the Oxford Playhouse in 1923, and presented an ambitious programme of classic plays, staged with simple settings, to attract the student market. He used the designer McArthur from 1923-25 and attracted named actors, including John Gielgud, Tyrone Guthrie and Flora Robson. However, the theatre closed in 1929 unable to sustain itself.[111] That year Fagan became a director at the Festival Theatre Cambridge as well as producing in London. Later he became a director at the Royal Court.

Fagan had a keen interest in lighting. In a paper titled *The Art of Stage Lighting* given to the Illuminating Engineering Society at the Royal Society of Arts in April 1919 (which both Marshall and Bentham attended), he said that, based on 25 years' experience, the most important thing was always the play, second the acting, third the lighting, fourth the scenery, and fifth the dresses. He defined stage lighting "as the art of placing, of graduating, of colouring light

---

the best coffee in London (Marshall, *The Other Theatre*, p42).

[109] Marshall, *The Other Theatre*, p42.

[110] *The Gate Theatre* file, Theatre Museum Archives.

[111] Marshall, *The Other Theatre*, p16.

and shade". He talked of two lights in nature – direct and diffuse, and was keen to use a system such as the Fortuny, which he was later able to do to a degree during his time at the Royal Court. He also noted the emotional values of light, and predicted that the role of the operator would one day be as another company member, playing lighting to accompany the changing mood of the play.[112] If he had seen some of the early *Colour Music* experiments, he was surely linking this notion to theatre practice (see Appendix vi).

Ridge and Aldred used Fagan's Oxford University Dramatic Society production *King John* in February 1933 as a case study in their book, for which they had created the lighting plot.[113] The play was lit to reflect the mood of the scenes within the boundaries of realism, with an active cue sequence that responded to reflect the rhythms of the play. Colour work was ambitious, and the lighting synopsis detailed in the book suggested that light was a key driving force behind the production. The production was characterised by directional lighting that complemented the stylised settings with bold brushstrokes of light. (For a technical review of the theatre, see Appendix ii.)

Fagan rated few contemporary producers for their use of light. He noted the work of Tyrone Guthrie, Robert Atkins, Charles Hickman, and Hilton Edwards at the Gate Dublin: "whose lighting of *The Picture of Dorian Gray* is one of the finest examples of directional lighting I have ever seen".[114] He also noted Owen Nares' *Rebecca* (1940) for colour and directional light, and Wilhelm's ballet *A Midsummer Night's Dream* at the Empire (c1900), and Oscar Asche's *Kismet* (1911) for excellent lighting, and the lighting of Fuller and, interestingly, Samoiloff.

Norman MacDermott (1890-1977) started as a scenic designer at Liverpool Repertory Theatre and then produced in the provinces until founding the Everyman Theatre Hampstead in 1920, where he made a name for himself as one of the pioneers of the Art Movement in Britain. He ran plays in pairs back-to-back for a month with about 15 plays produced a year, marking the

---

[112] "The stage lighting artist, like the painter, must go to nature in her softer moods, and select those which harmonise best with his subjects. He must change with the emotional changes of the play – melting one mood into another. The day is not far off when we shall see the electrician an artist as well as a technical expert – seated at his switchboard like a player at an organ – sending forth rhythmic harmonies of light that shall be as music to the eyes, swaying strange sub-conscious moods in the audience, in perfect tune with the unfolding of the drama in which he himself is playing a part of no mean importance." (Reproduced in *Sightline* 11/1, Aut. 77, p52).

[113] Ridge and Aldred, *Stage Lighting, Principles and Practice*, p112.

[114] Theatre Museum *Early Lighting File*.

beginning of modern repertory performance patterns, in contrast to the norm of weekly short run plays and long run West End star productions. In a programme note he said he practised a continental and American scenic style based on simplicity, placing "only the essentials on stage, and by careful lighting, a beauty more in accord with the growing taste of today can be secured".[115] MacDermott attracted leading figures in design and an accomplished backstage team.[116]

The building was revolutionary, with a single steep raked audience, flat stage floor and no footlights, a variable proscenium opening, and a shallow projecting forestage. The theatre had its own scene shop, prop and wardrobe provision and a permanent company of cast and crew. The artistic policy was one of experiment. MacDermott, committed to high production standards, said that "staging and lighting must show forth the new principles". Design and production was agreed to be a collaborative process. Choice of scenic methods were dictated by limited budgets of £30 per production. All scenic items were built in units of 1' to create stock items and to allow inter-changeability.

The lighting installation was simple, but arranged to give the potential for highly expressive composition and included a cyclorama. There were no footlights, and MacDermott believed that the installation was one of their main innovations:

> "Small floods and spots were used to highlight aspects of the stage. For a backdrop the gable wall was cemented with three circuits of fifty or more torch lamps for stars wired for control by separate circuits on the switchboard. The wall was sprayed white, and then under-sprayed in light green, and over-sprayed in light blue. It was lit from the top with blue and green floods, and from a trough below with deep blue floods on the ends, then pinks, ambers and whites in the centre".[117]

(See Appendix ii for a full review of the installation.)

The first performance, *The Bonds of Interest* by Benvente in September 1920, designed by John Garside, was noted for: "brightly-lit white scenery (which) was such a contrast to anything in the depressed post war theatre".[118]

---

[115] Theatre Museum Archives.

[116] This included H.W.Craven, the son of the great prop maker and scene painter Hawes Craven, Martin as chief electrician, and Veness as electrician, who transferred from Dean and later set up a supply business as a subsidiary of ReandeaN.

[117] MacDermott, N. *Everymania*, London: STR, 1975

[118] MacDermott, *Everymania*, p21.

MacDermott designed the sets and lighting himself for the second season. A press notice for *Arms and the Man* in 1922 said: "the setting and lighting was a triumph of simplicity and beautiful effect... Rarely indeed does one see so beautifully simple or so simply beautiful a scene on the London stage as Raina's Bedroom".[119] Perhaps the most important production mounted at the theatre was Noel Coward's *The Vortex,* designed by Gladys Calthrop, which transferred to the Royalty Theatre in December 1924.

The Glyndebourne Opera House opened in 1934. The actor **Carl Ebert** (1887-1980), producer for the opening season and a disciple of Reinhardt, insisted on complete artistic control. Francis Reid recalled that Ebert did his own lighting over "a series of lighting rehearsals of legendary length, followed by fine tuning, over many dress rehearsals". Reid continued: "lighting at Glyndebourne, especially in the 1930s and in the immediate post-war period, had a degree of artistic and technical sophistication that was well ahead of the norm for the time".[120] However Roy Strong noted the tendency towards conservatism in design, due to the cost of the settings and costumes, and also that traditionally Glyndebourne attracted an upper and middle class audience. Neither of these factors was likely to promote experiment: "an adventurous design policy was not part of the initial Glyndebourne concept".[121] Unfortunately Strong makes no references to lighting. There are few pre-war records from this theatre, as many of its own archives were lost during the war.[122]

Hamish Wilson (see page 198), the first designer who went on to light many productions, was regarded by Strong as amateurish. Production photos support this, with no obvious use of the progressive lighting rig. The first 'named' designer was Casper Neher (1897-1962), whose debut production *Macbeth* in 1938 was regarded at the time as groundbreaking. However, the intervention of war, and then the establishment of Glyndebourne at the King's Theatre, Edinburgh in the 1940s, meant that work did not recommence in Sussex until 1950. It was this era that heralded great design work of Messel and Osbert Lancaster.

John Christie, Glyndebourne's owner, had stipulated that it should have the most modern lighting system in Europe, and was advised by Wilson on the

---

[119] MacDermott, *Everymania*, p44.

[120] *Cue* 30, Jul. 84, p4,

[121] Higgins, John (Ed.), *Glyndebourne, a Celebration,* (London: Jonathan Cape, 1984), p90.

[122] Glyndebourne Theatre Archives. Much was lost to paper recycling during the war.

installation.[123] British manufacturers were either unable or apparently unwilling to supply what Wilson required, and so Christie went abroad or had equipment made in his own workshop.[124] The first Glyndebourne prospectus described the lighting installation:

> "It is no exaggeration to say that the technical equipment of the stage is second to none in the country... Particular attention has been paid to the lighting installation, which is of the most complete and modern description, and contains many features still unknown in the theatres of this country... The proper lighting of operatic productions, in which British opera houses have hitherto lagged badly behind, will bring new and unsuspected beauties to the most veteran opera lover".[125]

Bentham grudgingly recalled that at Glyndebourne everything was German except for the Strand battens – a sad indictment of British manufacturing.[126] (For a technical review of the theatre, see Appendix ii.)

British Lighting Practice and Practitioners, 1935-1950

Theatre lighting made significant advances during this period, to the extent that by 1950 the first lighting credits had been posted. This recognised the improvements that had been achieved in the standards of lighting and the contribution of the lighting specialist to the overall production arts.

The period commenced with a significant new family of spotlights and a radical new control, all made by Strand. Some of the spotlights made an immediate impact. Although few of the new controls were sold, the art of lighting was undoubtedly furthered by this equipment. Fuller ranges of coloured gelatines, now made in a more robust cellulose-acetate, became available. Motor-driven dimmers meant that the control system could be placed more appropriately in the theatre space, and a front of house operating location became increasingly common. However, lighting facilities were refurbished in very few theatres.

---

[123] Ironically the managing director of Hill, Norman and Beard, organ manufacturers, which may have led to some friction between him and Strand. Bentham believed that his opposition to Strand was due to their collaboration with Compton Organs, and claimed that Carl Ebert (Christie's first producer) had, in 1948, sat at the Light Console in the London Palladium and said "all my life I have dreamed of something like this" (*Cue* 30, Jul. 84, pp13-16 and *Tabs* 35/2, Sum. 77, p3).

[124] Hughes, S. *Glyndebourne, A History of the Festival Opera*: Newton Abbott: David and Charles, 1981, p35. Christie said that Strand boards were "years behind the times" (*Tabs* 22/1, Mar. 64, p55), boasting that his lighting was the most modern in the world (*Tabs* 35/2, Sum. 77, p3).

[125] Hughes, *Glyndebourne, A History of the Festival Opera*, p54.

[126] Bentham, *Sixty Years of Light Work*, p74.

Practice from abroad enhanced British theatre less during these war-dominated years. Then several important plays and musicals transferred to London from New York from 1946 and British practice responded to the more advanced technological and creative thinking that accompanied this work. Thyristor control, pioneered in America, came to British theatre in 1950. This completed the palette of technology that essentially remains in place today.

Training in stage design, lighting and stage management had commenced just before World War Two, resuming in 1946. The status of these crafts was greatly enhanced by this. The use of models to plan lighting was adopted by a few enlightened practitioners, and Colour Music experiments confirmed the expressive potential of light (see Appendix vi). The lighting expert became established as producers and stage designers finally realised that specialist knowledge, as well as another pair of hands, was needed as stage technology and production arts became more complex.

The above summarises a range of factors that led to the emergence of the lighting designer in the middle of the twentieth century. The most crucial was the relinquishing of lighting responsibilities by producers. Expectations that a high visual aesthetic could be achieved on stage had risen, and the producer could no longer take on the role of lighting to the necessary standard, when coupled with other duties. Equipment and control was by now sufficiently sophisticated to allow precise, repeatable lighting, and complex enough to require expert dedicated attention.

By the 1930s most producers had reached their limits with lighting. The producer required some technical lighting knowledge, although it was more important to know what could be achieved, and what was or was not appropriate. Now assisted by able designers and experienced production teams, they increasingly maintained an overview. Sir Nigel Playfair, director at the Lyric Hammersmith in the 1920s illustrated this with the following comments. Having chosen the play, he engaged a pictorial artist to design scenery, costumes and lighting "three jobs, one man. This is essential, for the three things are, or should be, indivisible".[127]

Ridge and Aldred had said that "until stage directors and producers are trained in the technicalities of lighting, and until they can visualise what the effect of it will be, they will continue to pursue the safe, but uninspiring course".[128] Brian Legge recalled that producers such as Cochran, Dean, Asche

---

[127] Playfair, *The Story of the Lyric Theatre Hammersmith*, p123.

[128] Ridge and Aldred, *Stage Lighting, Principles and Practice*, p110.

and Marshall had recognised the extent of their knowledge: "they knew what they wanted in visual terms, but when there was some doubt in their minds about how to achieve it, would cajole (rather than employ) Digby, Strand or Furse (and individuals on their payroll, usually within their Hire Dept.) to solve the problems without any credit. People such as Applebee, Lorraine and Bundy all started out this way".[129] David Ayliff, a stage manager at the New Theatre just after World War Two, thought the title 'Lighting Designer' did not arrive until the 1950s, and probably came from America, as a result of the increasing diversity and sophistication of lighting equipment. Directors, used to a standard basic rig, now needed more technical assistance than the Chief Electrician could provide. This created the opportunities for people like Davis and Northen.[130]

The grip of the producer loosened slowly. Joe Davis, on the relationship between producers and lighting technicians in pre-1939 theatre lighting, said:

"the most important preoccupation for me in the pre-war years was the development of a relationship with the producer whose control of the production was absolute. It took a long time and people were suspicious because it was an age when the producer liked to and did his own lighting and often very well. Even if it took a long time, labour was cheap. He was after all the only one who knew where his actors were going to be, what the mood was and what was going to happen at what time. Many of them were wary of the technical innovations in equipment and began to see that there was a benefit to having someone technical, and perhaps artistic, to allow them to concentrate on directing the actors". [131]

Because the producer had a tight control on the lighting, it was rare for any sort of credit to be given to anyone else. Even Davis, the first high profile lighting specialist, found it hard to get credits. He recalled that Hugh Beaumont, the General Manager of Tennents said: "I do not want you to have separate credits. Everybody knows who lights my productions and that should be good enough. As far as I am concerned we all work with the director".[132]

Davis claimed that the first time his name actually went on the bill outside the theatre as the person responsible for the lighting was for *Blackbirds* at the

---

[129] In correspondence with Brian Legge.

[130] In correspondence with David Ayliff.

[131] *Cue* 30, Jul. 84, p10 and *Tabs* 21/3, Dec. 63, p10.

[132] *Sightline* 10/2, Aut. 76, p50.

Gaiety in 1936.[133] Northen recalled that "as more sophisticated lighting equipment came on to the market, directors, and designers began to realise that they could make the best use of it by employing a lighting designer...Gradually it became accepted practice to engage a lighting designer who would be given a credit as such in the programme".[134]

Although some producers continued to do their own lighting, it was now normal for a more collaborative approach to prevail. Bundy recalled that for Gielgud's *Macbeth* in the early 1940s, the lighting seemed to be decided on by a "committee of three: John Gielgud, the director, Michael Ayrton, the designer, and Ian Dow, the stage manager.[135]

There were respected practitioners who continued the tradition of not seeing a need for the lighting designer, preferring the producer and designer to do this work. **Tyrone Guthrie** (1900-1971), who had directed at Cambridge under Gray and went on to become Director at the Old Vic in 1933, in an interview for *Tabs* in 1952 said that "we have become altogether too 'fancy' on the whole visual side of theatrical production." For Shakespeare, "you should put on all the white light you have, and leave it on. Shakespeare does all the painting in the text, and far better than anyone can do with lighting".[136]

In his autobiography he said that he didn't like coloured light, as colour was the job of the stage designer. He believed that open white light was best on the face, and perceptively believed that it was the angle of strike and intensity that made light give a 'hard' impression, not colour. He went on to say that he abhorred the American technique of top lighting from the No. 1 bar, which he believed was poorly placed for face lighting, hardening the look of the stage with strong shadowing of the face.[137] He said the standard of lighting in London was better than in other countries, but still the separation of the actor from the setting could be better.

The designer **Roger Furse** (1903-1973), who worked under Komisarjevsky and later with Guthrie at the Old Vic, typified the commitment of many designers to lighting. Furse believed that the designer must be in a position to understand the producer's problem, the actor's outlook and at the same time lend a

---

[133] This is unconfirmed as he received no mention in the programme (Theatre Museum Archives).

[134] Northen, *Northen Lights,* p179.

[135] He couldn't confirm who laid out the rig, thinking it was a combination of Dow and the touring Chief Electrician Jack Eagan (*Focus 10*, Sep. 89, p26).

[136] *Tabs* 10/1, Apr. 52, p10.

[137] *Tabs* 19/1, Apr. 61, p14.

sympathetic ear to the stage carpenter, stage director and electrician. On lighting, he said he was particularly keen to plan lighting from the outset of a project. He liked to visit the venue to see in particular the angle that front of house lighting would strike the actor and to work out how far back settings should ideally be placed to avoid shadow from the actors. He believed the producer should do the lighting, although he would expect to contribute to discussions both at the planning stage and the plotting session. "I personally think that in America, for example, the designers have far too much say about the lighting".[138]

The Process of Lighting

With tours increasingly becoming more complex, the need to record lighting plots in greater detail was required, a practice that had already been established in America.[139] Joe Davis claimed he was the first person to plan lighting rigs on paper in this country. Davis, influenced by Jo Mielziner, recalled that Mielziner was the first to include detailed lighting plans with his designs, having experimented with colours and angles in his workshop.[140] He again recalled the production of *Blackbirds* in 1936 where "it was the first time I started to do drawings or layouts of what I was going to use before I went into the theatre".[141] Davis said that Peter Brook, with whom he worked many times, made a very shrewd remark: "the lighting of a production is only as good as the design". Davis went on to say that the point he was making was very important, as if the equipment was of the right type and hanging in the right position one could achieve anything, but that you couldn't produce the right results without the right layout and then "you are in trouble". This confirmed the need for planning if lighting was to achieve a high artistic standard. Although Davis was probably the only person to regularly plan lighting on paper before 1939, this became more common after 1945. Planning procedures became

---

[138] Furse said of Komisarjevsky that he "knew what was possible and what was impossible" (*Tabs* 10/2, Sep. 52, p5).

[139] **Abe Feder** (1909-1997) the first American to specialise in the discipline of lighting design, is credited for starting, in the late 1930s, the system of referring to lanterns by number, and using plotting sheets and schedules to detail instrument positions, focus, colours and intensities. **Jean Rosenthal** (1912-1969) gained her first drama lighting credit in 1943, and went on to develop the lighting notation system established by Feder, inventing symbols for lanterns and drawing up detailed hanging plots.

[140] *Tabs* 37/1, Dec. 80, p26.

[141] *Cue* 30, Jul. 84, p8.

formalised, leading to *Tabs* first publishing a lighting plan of a Pageant in Nottingham in 1949.[142] This showed lantern type, hanging position, focus and patch, and paved the way for others to copy. The next edition saw the first stage lighting plan published in Britain, Davis's plan for Mielziner's *Death of a Salesman*.[143]

Plotting procedures too required an increasingly complex detail and accuracy. While it was still common to refer to a light by its position and a fraction of intensity, such as pink No. 1 batten at three-quarters, this began to change in the late 1940s with a move to call lanterns by their circuit number. Applebee confirmed in 1953 that referring to circuits as numbers rather than names came in "during the last four years. The cue sheet (now) merely gives the number and the degree of dim".[144] Davis remembered that producers never referred to circuit numbers, only "give me the reds". It is interesting to note that in *Stage Lighting* Bentham's notes on plotting are less full than one might have expected, probably because of his interest in composing light live and in the principles behind Light Console operation, rather than regular exact reproduction required by more serious drama. However, it must be remembered that the norm for rig design and plotting was, as recalled by Paul Weston, that "nothing was ever written down in those days".[145] However, there were exceptions to this, and the following illustrations show the rig and lighting for *The Birds* at the Sadler's Wells in 1942. It is believed that this is the work of Henry Robinson, then the stage manager at Sadler's Wells, who also undertook the lighting duties.[146]

Two leading theatres, the Shakespeare Memorial Theatre Stratford and the Royal Opera House Covent Garden, illustrated how these procedures developed at different rates. Peter Paget Smith, Chief Electrician at Stratford, said that by 1950 the producer, outside consultant, or member of staff who designed the lighting at Stratford attended all rehearsals. Plans were produced detailing the focus, colour and circuit number for each lantern (not lantern position), to allow resetting when working in repertoire or for maintenance. He said that thirty hours were normally allowed for rigging, focusing and plotting. The show would be plotted from the stalls, with the production team in contact with the

---

[142] *Tabs* 7/2, Sep. 49, p15.

[143] For which he was credited as Chief Engineer (*Tabs* 7/3, Dec. 49, p16).

[144] *Tabs* 11/2, Sep. 53, p26.

[145] Interview at the Theatre Museum 22/11/01.

[146] Sadler's Wells Archives.

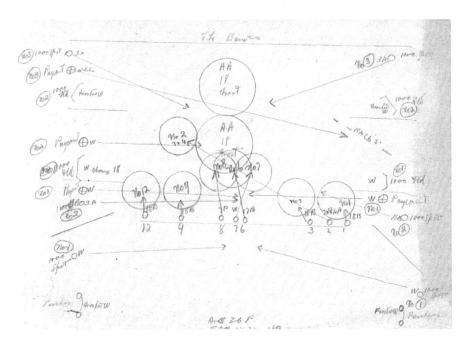

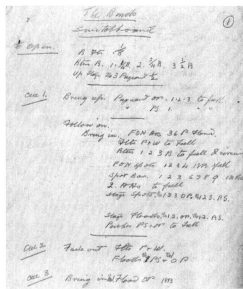

Lighting plan and plot for The Birds, 1942.

board operator via a talk-back system.[147]

At Covent Garden the lighting was still supervised by the producer, stage director, or production manager in 1950, and it had to be established during rehearsals as only new productions were allocated lighting time. Bundy remembered that "in the early 1950s lighting designers were a fairly unfamiliar species" at Covent Garden.[148]

If the operator had a good view of the stage, they too were

---

[147] *Tabs* 9/3, Dec. 51, p5.

[148] Procedures for co-ordinating the performances at this theatre (cont...)

charged with an enhanced responsibility. George Devine said in an interview in 1948 that while the stage manager should still 'warn' and 'cue' lighting, if the operator had good stage visibility, he should use own judgement to find the exact moment and pace.[149]

However, it is interesting to note that lighting practice was slow to respond to the new potential offered by one lantern per channel operation that the Light Console and Electronic offered. Where these controls existed, lanterns still tended to be plotted in 'block groups' (many lights plotted at the same level intensity), and front of house lanterns were often treated as though they were still grouped on a single dimmer. For example, in *Oklahoma* (1947) and *Carousel* (1950), both at the Theatre Royal Drury Lane, all front of house lighting still moved as a single unit, and in Mielziner's *Mr Roberts* at the Coliseum (1950) about half the front of house was used for 'block' lighting and the rest as spotlights.[150]

Planning Lighting with Model Theatres

Working with model theatres was developed as a way to plan lighting for productions. While few practitioners adopted this method, they achieved great success. The usefulness of lighting the set model on a well equipped scale stage was that it allowed colours, lighting positions and cues to be tried out in advance of the technical rehearsal, and for the director/producer and designer to see and discuss the effects of light and experiment.

Lighting models as peepshows from the eighteenth century had been an important part of the development of an aesthetic role for lighting in creating atmosphere and effect. The first to link lighting models with full scale designs were Americans. Belasco set up a model stage for experiment in 1902. Bel Geddes started to use models as a planning tool from 1912, and a lit model stage, operated by Jones, was the central attraction in an exhibition in 1914.[151]

---

were poor by modern standards. Shows were cued by the Stage Manager, who cued the Chief Electrician, on "Standby" and "Go", and the Chief, who then cued the appropriate operator via a voice tube to the switchboard, cue lights or telephone to other operators. Bundy noted the lack of a good communications system recalling that at times five control desk operators were required (*Sightline* 22/2, Apr. 88, p12).[149] *Tabs* 6/2, Sep, 48, p23.

[150] *Tabs* 35/2, Sum 77, p9. The *Theatre Newsletter* 15/7/50 recalled that the setting, that used the revolve to bring on five interior sets from out of the ship, cost £10,100, and the lighting used over 275 spots and "a highly complicated lighting and cue-plot" (Theatre Museum Archives).

[151] Bel Geddes developed an interest in theatre as a young man, and in about 1912 built a model stage (in 1:24, with a 15' proscenium opening) to stage designs for his own devised production called *Thunderbird*. He built the model to help work out how to stage a play. The model also helped him to gain an understanding of the potential part lighting could play, and he realised that if (cont...)

In Germany, Hartmann noted that Adolf Winds recorded a model stage used for lighting experiments in a book *Bühne und Welt* in 1910.[152]

In Britain, the use of models came later. While Craig had discussed the value of experimenting with lighting on models in 1911, Fagan was the first to use a model stage to plan lighting for the Royal Court in the 1920s. Bentham set up a complex model stage in the late 1920s, and advocated the building of models in his writings, encouraging experiment to practice colour mixing and the effect of colour on scenery and fabrics, and to try out ideas before technical rehearsals. He also suggested practising composing lighting to music, and, imaginatively, to build a suitable set in advance of a radio broadcast of a Shakespeare play, and try to light it on the hoof.[153] Another important user of a model was Devine and the design team Motley, who first utilised one in the early 1930s. Ridge and Aldred recalled in 1935 that the Cambridge Festival Theatre used ½"-1' models to help familiarise stage staff with the fit up, and their own model stage, made in the 1930s and described in their book, was placed on show in the Science Museum, Kensington. The public could experiment with the lighting on the model, with some dimmers available for hands-on practice.[154] In 1947 *Tabs* detailed a fully lit model of a proscenium stage by J.P Bannister, featuring a full rig of spots, floods etc, with dimmable control. The accompanying photograph suggested that it would have been a very useful tool.[155] In 1949 *Tabs* featured a range of miniature stage lighting made by the toy makers Pollocks.[156]

After World War Two, Michael Northen constructed a fully equipped model theatre at his home in Chelsea, built to a scale of ½" - 1'. It had a variable size proscenium opening and 60 counterweight lines. With assistance from Robert Stanbury, a stage director who manufactured the scale lanterns and a control

---

narrow beam spots could be used to highlight details, rather than the normal flat, wash lighting, it would be far more effective. This was in an era when shadows were always painted onto the scenery, and shadow caused by lighting was unheard of. He built his own model spots and fitted them two a side in each wing bay. From this model he worked out that a 45° angle was the most suitable for a natural feel to the lighting, and that this angle also modelled the face well and enhanced the face's features. He noted too that an actor's shadow would not fall onto the scenery with this angle of light (Geddes, *Miracle in the Evening*, p135).

[152] Hartmann, *Theatre Lighting*, p118.

[153] His model theatre, which began with three dimmers, ended up with 87 (Bentham, *Sixty Years of Light Work*, p13)

[154] Ridge and Aldred, *Stage Lighting Principles and Practice*, p109.

[155] *Tabs* 5/3, Dec. 47, p17.

[156] *Tabs* 7/1, Apr. 49, p14.

system, a comprehensive facility became available for directors and designers to try out ideas, local to the West End.[157] The model received much acclaim and many prestigious visitors. When the Royal Opera House Covent Garden started to use it, Northen added five stage lifts to replicate its stage, and worked on the lavish settings for *La Traviata* with designer Sophie Fedorovitch. This was followed by work for the Shakespeare Memorial Theatre Stratford with the designer Audrey Cruddas. From then on he received regular work to try out designs for both Stratford and the Opera House.[158]

Nomenclature in Use at the Time

The combination of high expectations and increased complexity of equipment gave rise to the need for a specialist. All production personnel became more focused on their own specialist areas. The producer retreated from overall production control to focus on directing, the stage manager became more focused on running rehearsals and the actors and the stage designer focused increasingly on settings and costumes. A new role was required to command the stage technologies. The *Stage Director* was the first new role to appear consistently and was first noted in the early 1940s. This role normally included lighting duties.[159] Other names that were sometimes given to the lighting specialist included *Chief Electrician* and *Electrical Engineer*.

These positions became consolidated and clarified after 1950 when the phrases *Lighting designed by* or *Lighting arranged by* or *Lighting by* or *Technical and lighting direction by* or *Lighting Consultant* became established, recognising this specialist contribution. Thereafter, the Stage Director focused on the organisation of all staging matters in production, the Chief Electrician ran the rig and the show, and the Lighting Designer solely focused on the creation of the lighting.

The Last Producers Noted for Their Lighting

Basil Dean came back to the fore with his production of *Johnson over Jordan* by J.B. Priestley at the New Theatre in February 1939. A play about

---

[157] Stanbury also started building a high quality ½" - 1' model in 1950. The control operated 100+ dimmers, with miniature versions of mirror spots, pageants, acting areas, floats, battens, and cyclorama lights (*Tabs* 10/1, Apr. 52, p29). It is believed this model is stored at the Slade School of Art, London.

[158] Lighting for Michael Benthall's Opera House production of *Aida* in 1948 was first seen on his model.

[159] For example, Hamish Wilson gained many "lighting by" credits in the 1940s as a Stage Director.

Johnson Over Jordon. The Sphere 11/03/1939. Courtesy Illustrated London News picture library.

life flashing before a man at the moment of death seemed to him an appropriate play to revisit experiment with indirect light, which he believed was "quite the right atmosphere for this eerie play" (see illustration).[160]

Designed by Craig's son Edward Carrick, the set, backed by a Hasait cyclorama, was a simple, open arrangement of undyed hessian drapes with a centre-parting blue silk cloth in front. Dean recalled in *Sightline* that "each was lighted as though the other did not exist".[161] Only direct spotlighting was used to light downstage, as Dean wanted to use reflected light for the main source onstage. Having played a key part in the introduction of spotlights to Britain twenty years earlier, in this production Dean reverted to a more minimal lighting rig, reacting against what he saw was "the multiplicity of lanterns of various shapes and sizes, each with a separate dimmer, that had followed that introduction".[162] Much experiment went into the reflected lighting. Strand designed 12 special reflected light projectors, each with a colour changer controlled by tracker wire. Each reflector was 2' wide x 4' long, fitted into a trunnion arm for tilting, and painted with Hartmann's original formula. It was planned to rig these all centre stage to give the impression of source-less light, but the rig would not take the weight, so they had to be distributed about. Strand also made the cyclorama lighting

---

[160] Dean, *Mind's Eye, an Autobiography 1927-1972*, p266. In *The Observer* 29/1/39 Dean had been quoted predicting "the mood of the various scenes will be heightened by the dramatic and romantic use of light" (Theatre Museum Archives).

[161] *Sightline* 9/2, Aut. 75, p35.

[162] He complained that despite an increase in the quality and quantity of technology, aesthetic principles had not always developed in tandem: "today there are occasions when contrasts of light and shade appear to be employed solely to cancel each other out" (Dean, *Mind's Eye, an Autobiography 1927-1972*, p266).

based on that devised for *The Blue Lagoon* at the Prince of Wales in 1920, fitted with semi-circular slides of glass imported from Germany.

Dean recalled that "we literally painted our draperies with light in sympathy with the mood which Johnson was experiencing. In the night club they took on ruby red, against which shadowy figures wearing grotesque masks danced".[163] In particular, Dean recalled the last scene for memorable lighting.

> "The play ends as Johnson – in his dream – all the struggles and hopes and fears of his past life over – turns to say farewell to the porter. Taking from him his rolled umbrella and his bowler hat, he mounts a steep ramp between the two cycloramas... As he does so to the inspiring music specially composed by Benjamin Britten, a 5000 W German projector beams his ascent. The light in front fades as the sun lamp picks him up between the cycloramas, the silk one being lighted an iridescent bluish-green, and the rear one a deep blue. The effect was indescribably beautiful and was so referred to by the press..."[164]

He went on to say: "from the results achieved I was convinced that an entirely new concept for the use of light on stage was in course of evolution. But the interruption of the Second World War put a stop to further advance in that direction".[165] *Johnson* signalled the end to Dean's lighting work, thereafter leaving lighting to the job of a specialist. The play did not do good business and was withdrawn after 16 performances.

The producer **Robert Nesbitt** (1906-1995) came to the fore just before World War Two for his revues staged at the London Palladium, and he went on to be known for stylish spectaculars for the rest of his working life.[166] Michael Northen said that his name on a poster "would instantly inform the

---

[163] Dean, *Mind's Eye, an Autobiography 1927-1972*, p267.

[164] *Sightline* 9/2, Aut. 75, p37.

[165] Dean, *Mind's Eye, an Autobiography 1927-1972*, p267. However, his interest in the subject continued, and he met Reiche in Berlin in 1945 who told him of the advances he had made in projection.

[166] As a child he was brought up on the fare of the Coliseum and the Palladium, and had seen Fuller's work (In correspondence with Brian Legge). He learned the art of revue under French producer Andre Charlot (1882-1956) at the Alhambra in the 1930's, and then produced his own revues at the Palladium for the next 30 years (where he also directed 35 Royal Variety performances). He became known as the "Prince of Darkness", due to his booming voice from the darkened stalls during technical rehearsals, rather than his lighting. His first production as a director was *Ballyhoo* in 1932. He kept his interest in theatre technology throughout his career, and in later life became President of the ALD.

public that the show would be gloriously glamorous, with utter taste, and have great showmanship", and he set and expected the highest standards from his work force.[167] His usual production credit was "devised by" rather than "directed by", and he used lighting as the key design tool, and deployed effects such as gauzes and revolves for emphasis. He developed a style with minimal front of house lighting, except for followspots, and used top-light onstage, focused away from the cyclorama, and cross-light to achieve a crisp, clean look that afforded rich colouring. This he contrasted against a lit cyclorama.[168] He was probably the first practitioner to champion the Pageant lantern, which Bentham recalled he used on booms in the wings, with row upon row of Acting Area floods overhead. This created "a style of installation peculiar to this country… which became *'the way'* to do any kind of stage spectacular. Graham Walne described his lighting style as "full of chiaroscuro".[169]

The production that launched his name in lighting was a revue called *Gangway* at the London Palladium in December 1941. Bentham recalled that it relied on drapes and orthodox scenery, minimal due to the very limited offstage space in this theatre and to the fact that scenery was scarce in war-time London. The show was a mixed variety revue, and was remembered for "pace and sparkle, tuneful music with striking lighting effects", although *The Times* (18/12/41) recorded that "it depends a good deal on spectacle".[170] Nesbitt asked Strand for a Light Console to operate the show, and the rig comprised three bars of top-lighting Patt. 56, Pageants and six 2kW Fresnels cross lighting from the wings. This show marked the professional debut of the Light Console.

Nesbitt instructed Bentham, who plotted the show, to 'ad lib' on the console for some routines, and these improvisations were developed further by Hilary Gould, the house operator. Bentham, who operated the console on the opening night, got a stage call from Tommy Trinder for the lighting.[171] After this production, the Robert Nesbitt method of top and side light, which he said was

---

[167] *Focus 12A*, Aug. 92, p13. Through his "complete inability to tolerate anything other than the highest of standards, (he) required both stars and crew to push their own boundaries further" (*ABTT Update 13*, Mar. 95, p28).

[168] *Focus*, Jan. 95, p5.

[169] *Lighting and Sound International*, Jan. 95, p6.

[170] *Tabs* 43/1, Feb. 86, p20, and Theatre Museum Archives.

[171] Bentham recalled receiving a "best wishes" telegram from Nesbitt on the opening of *Gangway* that said "the public debut of yourself and console" (*Sightline* 12/2, Aut. 78, p110).

to "light, with high intensity, specific areas of the stage and simultaneously leave other areas dark, contrast colour with colour, and thus secure an interesting pattern of highlights and shadows, expressive control of the light rays being considered to aid *atmosphere*", became the standard for spectacle.

He was also well known for his use of colour – especially pinks such as No. 13 Magenta and No. 36 Surprise Pink. Julian Williams recalled that "his combinations of colours, some thick and dense washes, were carefully complementary and well thought out. He lit his scenes with non-repetitive 'conditions' as he called them; no wishy-washy splashes of light added from assorted directions".[172] Nesbitt continued to produce work of the highest visual standards, such as the series *Latin Quarter* (1949, 50, & 51) at the London Casino which the press recorded as: "gorgeous costuming and lighting effects" (*Performer*) and "the best of the lavish productions Nesbitt has devised" (*News of the World*).[173]

Most producers lit their own work, and many did this very well. Some even had the confidence to name themselves as lighting either their own or even others' productions. **Frank Adey**, a stage director and production manager gained two lighting credits for *The Student Prince* at the Stoll in 1944 and *Gay Rosalinda* at the Princes in 1946. **Harold Arneil** (1902/3-1959), a stage director, gained a lighting credit for *The Little Dry Thorn* at the Lyric Hammersmith in 1947. **Michael Benthall** (1919-1974), a director at the Old Vic for much of his career, lit *Job* at the Royal Opera House Covent Garden in 1948 and 1949, with settings by John Piper. **Charles Hickman** (1905-83), a highly experienced director who also acted, was credited with lighting *Annie get your Gun* at the Coliseum in 1947. **Jack Hulbert**, an actor/producer, lit *Here come the Boys* at the Saville in 1946. **Albert Lock,** stage director at the Royal Opera House Covent Garden, lit *Pilgrim's Progress* in 1948. **William Mollison** (1893-1955), a director and production manager lit *Lady Behave* His Majesty's in 1941. These productions did not receive any press notices for the lighting. **Frank Collins** (1878-1957) a highly experienced director and producer, lit *Ghosts* at the Duchess in 1940. *The Observer* (2/6/40) said the setting was far too light and "the rain (or snow) effects merely fidgeted the eye".[174]

---

[172] *Lighting and Sound International*, Mar. 95, p31, and *Focus*, Feb.95, p10.

[173] Theatre Museum Archives (neither dated).

[174] Theatre Museum Archives.

The First Specialists

George Devine CBE (1910-1966), was educated at Oxford, where he was President of Oxford University Dramatic Society. Having developed his interest in lighting through reading Ridge's 1928 book, he built a model in the early 1930s based on the New Theatre stage in the Motley design studio for lighting experiments.[175] He was one of the first British practitioners to see the value of experimenting and planning his lighting. He went on to be a key figure in establishing the role of the lighting designer in theatre training. Marius Goring said that "from 1937-1939 there was nobody on the British stage to touch him as a lighter".[176]

He started his career as an actor, and was in Komisarjevsky's production of *The Seagull* at the New Theatre in May 1936. In the same year he joined Michel Saint-Denis at the London Theatre Studio as Assistant Director. Here he taught stage lighting, probably the first professional in Britain to do this.[177] After 1945 he continued to teach stage lighting at the Old Vic Theatre School, and gave a speech titled *Theatre Lighting and Dramatic Expression* to the Society for Theatre Research at Strand's premises in March 1949. In 1950 he became one of four Directors of the Old Vic, working with the influential design group Motley.[178]

Devine's first lighting of note was for the production of *Richard II* at the Queen's Theatre in September 1937 (see illustration). The programme stated: "Lighting arranged by George Devine", which I believe is the first specific credit for a lighting practitioner in Britain. The production was directed by Gielgud and designed by Motley, and was praised for having an "atmosphere like a thundercloud".[179]

The next production he lit was *Three Sisters* at the Queen's in 1938. The production gained much praise in the press. The *News Chronicle* (1/2/38) said that the lighting for the last garden scene, highly charged with atmosphere, and autumnal fading light was "a diffused and fading beauty – as is all Devine's

---

[175] The designer Margaret Harris also used the model (Wardle, *The Theatres of George Devine*, p42).

[176] Wardle, *The Theatres of George Devine*, p69.

[177] An actor, director and producer, he mixed lighting with other roles in his early career, and went on to establish the English Stage Company at the Royal Court Theatre in 1956 and became a director of the Old Vic. Lighting tuition was first offered by Devine at the London Theatre Studio from 1936-39. See Appendix iv for further details of his teaching career.

[178] He married Sophia Harris, one of the Motley designers, in 1939.

[179] *Daily Telegraph*, 7th September 1937.

Richard II. The Sketch, 15/09/1937. Courtesy Illustrated London News picture library.

lighting throughout the play". *The Observer* (30/1/38) echoed this, saying "four acts of superb performance... in the last where the breath of autumn's being plays so lightly on the silvery branches and drives so heavily into the heart of youth".[180] Irving Wardle praised Devine, quoting from *The Times*: his "control of lighting, particularly in the garden scene... was among the production's chief assets." Wardle went on to say that the designer Margaret Harris confirmed that Devine "took immense trouble with exact colour" and experimented to get the correct tones, perhaps a reference to his model theatre work.[181]

Devine did not light many public productions as his energies mostly went into acting and directing after the war. He was credited for lighting *The Merchant of Venice* at the Queen's in 1938 (in which he also played the part of Launcelot Gobbo), and *Hamlet* at the Lyceum in 1939 (the last production before the theatre closed). Both were directed by Gielgud and designed by Motley, but neither drew specific press comment for the lighting. He also lit *Dear Octopus* at the Queen's in 1938, *The Corn is Green* at the Duchess in

---

[180] Theatre Museum Archives.

[181] Wardle, *The Theatres of George Devine*, p42.

1938, and *Rhondda Roundabout* at the Globe in 1939. The lighting received no press notices for these productions. Later he was noted for his lighting and use of Pageant lanterns in *Dark of the Moon* for Peter Brook in 1949 at the Lyric, Hammersmith. Bentham recalled: "a ~ Chorus of Pageants ~ ought to have been listed along with the cast. They were used in extraordinarily large quantities for such a small stage".[182]

Hamish Wilson (dates unknown), started work in the theatre in 1929 as a stage manager, and worked at Glyndebourne as a designer from its opening in 1932.[181] As a stage director, he was credited with lighting many productions during the 1940s, yet gained little favourable press coverage for his work.[182] *The Beggar's Opera* at the Haymarket in March 1940, a Glyndebourne production directed by Gielgud and designed by Motley, was noted for lighting being too dark for the style of the piece, "the lighting needs lightening".[183] Production photographs of *A Midsummer Night's Dream* at the Haymarket in 1945 indicate a rather crude use of spotlights.[184] Hamish Wilson continued lighting during the 1950s, and became Stage Director at Sadler's Wells in 1955. It is believed Wilson remained a stage/company manager into the early 1960s.[185]

Osmund "Ossie" Willson (1896-1967), having trained at RADA started as an actor at His Majesty's in 1914, joined Birmingham Rep for nine years and became a stage director at the Duchess in 1933.[186] He gained credits for lighting many productions, with most written and/or directed by Emlyn Williams, including: *Morning Star* at the Globe in 1941; *Watch on the Rhine* at the Aldwych in 1942, with décor by Michael Relph; *The Little Foxes* at the Piccadilly in 1942 for Tennents with set and costumes by Ruth Keating; *David's Rest* at the St. Martin's in 1944; *Wind of Heaven* with set by Alick Johnstone and costumes by Motley at the St. James's and *Spring 1600* with set and costume by Michael Weight at the Lyric in 1945; *Animal Kingdom* at the Playhouse, *Ever Since Paradise* at the New with décor by Michael Weight

---

[182] *Tabs* 11/1, Apr. 53, p30. Kitty Black claimed that this production featured the first use of U.V. light – although this seems not true, it perhaps shows how rare the use of such an effect was. (Black, *Upper Circle, a Theatrical Chronicle*, p146). William Walton was recorded as the Chief Engineer (Theatre Museum Archives).

[183] *The Observer* 10/3/40.

[184] Theatre Museum Archives.

[185] In correspondence with Graeme Cruickshank.

[186] Willson became a founder member of the ABTT, and was noted working as a company manager for Players Ventures Ltd. in the early 1960's (in correspondence with Joe Aveline).

and *Trespass* at the Globe in 1947; *Bred in the Bone, Davy Dick,* and *Crime Passionnel* at the Lyric in 1948; and *The Seagull* at The Lyric in 1949. His work attracted no press comments.[187]

Stanley Earnshaw (dates unknown), son of one of the co-founders of Strand Arthur Earnshaw (? – 1940),[188] lit *Arc de Triomphe* at the Phoenix in 1943, of which *The Times* (10/11/43) said the production was "magnificently spectacular." He also was credited for lighting *Alice in Wonderland*, designed by Gladys Calthrop, at the Scala in 1943 and the Palace in 1944 (no press comments), *A Night in Venice* at the Cambridge in 1944, which *The Times* (25/5/44) called "a lavish spectacle", *Perchance to Dream*, with décor by Joseph Carl, at the Hippodrome in 1945, of which the *Daily Mail* said the production was "tastefully expensive", and *Cinderella* at the Casino in 1947, a highly praised production. He did not undertake any more lighting work for which he was known to be credited.[189]

Others who had worked as production or stage managers also lit shows, and these were sometimes credited. Stage manager **William Conway** (1914/5-1950) lit *Lady Windermere's Fan*, directed by Gielgud with décor by Cecil Beaton at the Haymarket in 1945, and *A Bell for Adano*, with décor by Motley, at the Phoenix in 1945. **Gordon Crier** (dates unknown), a singer/dancer who became a production manager and then a director, gained a lighting credit for *Inherit the Wind* at the Playhouse in 1948. **Charles Miller** (dates unknown), an ASM at Sadler's Wells, alternated singing with lighting. He lit the Sadler's Wells touring season, directed by Tyrone Guthrie, in 1941. Productions included *The Marriage of Figaro, La Traviata, Madam Butterfly, Die Fledermaus, Dido and Aeneas,* and *Thomas and Sally*, for which the lighting was praised by *The Times* (5/7/41).

Anthony Pélissier (1912-1988) designed the set and lighting for one show, *Duet for Two Hands* at the Lyric in 1945. The play required various times of day to be indicated, and the *Evening Standard* (4/8/45) described the play as being atmospheric. **Joan Riley**, stage manager and stage director, lit *Still She Wished for Company*, a Sunday Night Society production at the Whitehall in 1947. She was probably the first British woman to receive a lighting notice. **Henry Robinson**, a very experienced stage manager and stage director, and

---

[187] Theatre Museum Archives.

[188] Stanley Earnshaw joined Strand becoming a Director in 1935, and Joint Managing Director in 1945.

[189] Theatre Museum Archives.

Alec Shanks (1904-87), principally a prolific costume designer, gained the occasional lighting credit in the 1940s. The production manager **Maxwell Wray** (1898-1972), a production manager, was credited for lighting *Hi de Hi* at the Palace in 1943. None of these productions gained press attention for the lighting except where indicated.[190]

Eric Wolfensohn (dates unknown), a stage director, lit many productions in the late 1940s for the New London Opera Company, with Carl Ebert as the Producer, and the Under Thirty Theatre Group. The opera productions included, at the Cambridge, *Rigoletto* and *Don Giovanni* in 1947 and *Falstaff* in 1948, and a season of operas at the Stoll in 1949 including *Falstaff*, *The Barber of Seville*, *La Bohème*, *Tosca*, *Rigoletto*, and *Don Pasquale*. Many were designed by Joseph Carl and attracted praise. For the Under Thirty Theatre Group, he lit *The Wanderer* at His Majesty's and *Blood Wedding* at the Playhouse in 1947. He was also lighting advisor for Ram Gopal at the Princes in 1948.

John Moody (dates unknown) worked as production manager at Sadler's Wells after World War Two where he lit the ballet productions. During the seasons 1946-49 he lit 24 ballets.[191] Many of these were highly praised in the press for their set and costume designs, and many were designed by leading figures such as Motley and Fedorovitch. The only production where his work was specifically mentioned was *Khadra* in 1946. *The Evening Standard* of 27/5/46 described this as being "beautifully lit". A photograph from *Valses Nobles et Sentimentales* that appeared in *The Dancing Times* of November 1947 shows his talents to the full (see illustration). Moody continued to light at the Sadler's Wells into the 1950s, although most of his work was as a producer, the role for which he was best known.[192]

John Sullivan (c1910-c1975), born in Birmingham of Irish descent, started as an actor and stage manager in the early 1930s. He joined the Sadler's Wells Ballet company and was part of the company's escape from Holland as

---

[190] Theatre Museum Archives.

[191] The full list of the ballets Moody lit at Sadler's Wells between 1946 and 1949 is: *Assembly Ball; The Catch; Façade; Khadra; The Gods go a-begging; Les Sylphides; The Vagabonds; Promenade; Le Spectre de la Rose; Mardi Gras; The Dance of the Tumblers; The Nutcracker; The Haunted Ballroom; Bailemos; La Fete Etrance; Le Carnival; Valses Noble et Sentimentales; Les Rendezvous; Parures; The Haunted Ballroom; Children's Corner; Capriol Suite; Selina;* and *Etude*.

[192] Arundell, D. *The Story of the Sadler's Wells 1683-1977*, Newton Abbott, David and Charles, 1978, p220

[193] In correspondence with Mrs. Pat Walker and Kitty Fitzgerald.

Valse Nobles et Sentimentales, The Dancing Times, Nov 1949.

the Germans invaded in 1940.[193] From 1942 he worked at the New Theatre as Stage Director, and gained his first 'lighting' credit for *Richard III* in 1944 for the Old Vic Company then in residence there. Produced by John Burrell, with sets by Morris Kestelman and costumes by Doris Zinkeisen, *The Times* said of it "some of the sombre pictures, though they strain the eye, are grimly effective".[194] He went on to light several Old Vic productions over the next five years: *Henry IV 1&2* in 1945, which the *Evening News* and *News Chronicle* (27/9/45) reported was "a very dark production" with "lighting superb". Later in the same year he lit *Oedipus* (see illustration over page), and in 1947 gained lighting credits for: *The Alchemist* produced by John Burrell, with set and costumes by Morris Kestelman, *Richard II, The Taming of the Shrew*, and *St. Joan*, and in 1948 for *The Government Inspector, Coriolanus, Twelfth Night, The Way of the World*, and *The Cherry Orchard*. He then was credited as Stage Director until *A Month in the Country* in late 1949.[195] He lit *Twelfth Night* again in the reopening season of the Old Vic in 1950, with set and costumes by Furse, before moving on to become Production Manager the Royal Opera House, where Bundy recalled that he lit the ballet productions

---

[194] *The Times* 14/9/1944.

[195] Theatre Museum Archives.

[196] *Sightline* 22/2, Apr. 88, p12. Between 1953 and 1965 he lit 62 operas for the ROH, 47 in the main house and 15 touring (Royal Opera House Archives)

Oedipus, 1945. Picture courtesy of John Vickers, London.

in the early 1950s.[196] It is believed that he also worked for Sadler's Wells Ballet at this time but little else is known of his career.[197]

Joe Davis (1912-1984) started work for Strand at the age of 13 in manufacture and was soon going out on shows. By 1928 he was working as a fit up electrician for managements such as Cochran, Wylie, Clayton and Waller and Komisarjevsky, who particularly inspired him. Davis joined H.M Tennent as a lighting engineer in 1935, and his interest in lighting got him noticed. Once, when the producer of Kate O'Brien's *The Anteroom* at the Queen's in August 1936 was delayed, he lit the show from his rehearsal observations, recollections of discussions with the producer, and his instinct. Despite "nobody lights my plays but me" from the producer, it was a great success and secured his

---

[197] Apparently be disappeared from the theatre scene following a row with Bill Bundy in the Model Shop at the Royal Opera House. His work was remembered as being meticulous and of a very high quality. (In conversation with Bill McGee and Kitty Fitzgerald).

[198] Press recorded the play as being lit too darkly until light is allowed to stream in through windows at the end (*The Observer* 16/8/36, and *Sightline* 10/2, Aut. 76, p50). H.M.Tennent Ltd. and its manager Hugh "Binkie" Beaumont were associated with the production of highly successful star-studded plays with lavish settings and costumes in the West End. Most of the plays were considered to be of a high artistic merit, and attracted leading established actors such as Edith (cont...)

position at Tennents. From 1936 he became their Lighting Director.[198]

Other than a spell in the RAF, he stayed with Tennents until 1972 although he went freelance in 1960.[199] During the war also he lit far-east tours of Gielgud's *Blithe Spirit* and *Hamlet,* and other notable productions include most important West End shows in the period 1945-55 including *The Lady's Not for Burning*, directed by Gielgud and designed by Messel, at the Globe in 1949 and *Ring Round the Moon* directed by Brook and designed by Messel, at the Globe in 1950.[200] As Chief Engineer he re-lit work by the Americans Mielziner and Jones, adapting Broadway shows to "British conditions". These shows included *Oklahoma* at Theatre Royal Drury Lane in 1947, *The Glass Menagerie* at the Haymarket and *Lute Song* at the Winter Garden in 1948, *A Streetcar Named Desire* at the Aldwych in 1949, *Death of a Salesman* at the Phoenix in 1949, and *Mr. Roberts* at the Coliseum in 1950.[201]

His death came just after conducting a lighting rehearsal for *42nd Street*, by which time he had lit nearly 600 shows. *Cue* noted that he was the first British practitioner to regularly be credited with the title 'Lighting Designer.'[202] Lew Burroughs, an electrician who worked with him from the 1930s said he was "a perfectionist in his field and always made sure his lighting was first class in every way".[203] Bill Cousins, an electrician who worked with him from the 1940s, said that he used lighting most creatively, using groups of pageants to 'bash' in through windows, and doubled up colours such as nos. 3 and 53 to make new tones. "Fit up and lighting were always planned meticulously in advance. Joe was a true lighting artist, painting with light to bring the setting to

Evans, Vivien Leigh and John Gielgud, and launched the careers of many future stars such as Richard Burton. Leading designers of the day were employed by Tennents, including Messel and Calthrop. From 1936-1973 Tennents produced over 400 plays, once with 15 running concurrently (for more details, see Black, *Upper Circle, a Theatrical Chronicle*).

[199] It is interesting to note that, despite his pioneering job title, he was not mentioned at all in Black's book on Tennents, a book that records most aspects of Tennents backstage work. (Black, *Upper Circle, a Theatrical Chronicle*).

[200] Using a single Winter Garden setting, "an effect of more than one scene is gained by clever lighting and rearrangement of the few stage properties and the show ends with a magnificent display of fireworks" (*The Sphere* 11/2/50).

[201] In 1953 he became the lighting designer for Marlene Dietrich, which continued for over 20 years. In later life he became the founder Chairman of the SBTLD in 1961, and subsequently was elected Life President. He was the first elected chair of ABTT *Lighting Committee* in 1961, and a founder member of the ALD in 1963 (*ABTT Bulletin No.1*, Apr. 61, p1).

[202] *Cue* 30, 1984, p8

[203] *ABTT News*, July 84, p6.

life and complementing the artiste's features, always softening harsh shadows using frost filters of all shapes and sizes".[204] David Ayliff recalled that "we used to say, rather sarcastically, that Joe Davis used more lights on one window backing than you usually had on an entire set! But then we were used to seeing a window backing lit by just one flood on a stand".[205]

Nat Brenner (1915-1993) left a university science education to start as an actor at the Unity Theatre, and after World War Two, where he had combined radar duties with producing camp shows, worked at the Midland Theatre Company and then the Salisbury Playhouse as Stage Director from 1948-50.[206] He joined the Bristol Old Vic company, becoming General Manager in 1951 and in 1963 become Principal of the Bristol Old Vic Theatre School. A tribute recalled that "during his long career as actor, director, stage manager, production manager, general manager and inspired teacher, he mastered every skill. He was a superb lighting designer and a wizard at filling the stage with magic on a tight budget".[207] His first show to receive a lighting credit was Goldsmith's *The Good-Natured Man"*, designed by Hutchinson-Scott, at Bristol Old Vic in September 1950.[208] Many of his Bristol productions transferred to the West End.

He regularly gained press coverage for his work at Salisbury. For example, the production of *Murder in the Cathedral* in April 1949 recalled "the clever use of darkness from the very beginning, …creates an atmosphere of quiet reverence… Seldom if ever have I seen better use made of lighting. The effects are too wonderful to describe…", and for *Musical Chairs* in November 1949 "the lighting and effect deserve special mention", and for *At Half Past Eight* in February 1950 "the noises off and the lighting together with the acting … make this a memorable production".[209]

Christopher West (1915-1967), who had worked with John Sullivan as Stage Manager on three productions in 1948, gained his first lighting credit for *Much Ado About Nothing*, produced by John Gielgud and designed by Mariano Andreu, at the Shakespeare Memorial Theatre Stratford in 1949. West was a

---

[204] *ABTT News*, Aug. 84, p3.

[205] In correspondence with David Ayliff.

[206] Salisbury Playhouse Archives.

[207] From a tribute "To Nat at 6.30" Bristol Old Vic 21/11/1993.

[208] Williamson, A. & Landstone, C. *The B.O.V.- the first ten years*, London: Garnet Miller 1957, p89.

[209] All quotes from the *Salisbury Journal*, held in Salisbury Playhouse Archives.

member of the stage management team at the time. Unfortunately little is known of West's work and there are no press comments to confirm his credentials.[210]

Cecil Clarke (c1890-c1980),[211] a shy but well liked stage manager, became the stage director at the Old Vic in 1946, and also taught on the technical training course. He gained a lighting credit for *Bartholomew Fair*, directed by Devine and designed by Motley, at the Old Vic in December 1950, the second production in the newly reopened theatre. The staging was focused onto the forestage and involved multiple separated acting areas.[212] He also lit *Electra* at the Old Vic in March 1951, produced by Saint-Denis with scenery and costumes by Barbara Hepworth (see illustration over page). A *New Statesman* of the time noted that the challenging setting "allows the producer the most effective possible use of a very imaginative lighting".[213] He lit *King Lear*, produced by Hugh Hunt, in November 1951. *The Stage* reported "that the man responsible for the darkness was Cecil Clarke", although Clarke had said that Hunt had had him take the lighting down on every scene in the play.[214]

Hilton Edwards (1903-1982) was to be one of the most important lighting practitioners of the first half of the twentieth century. He was born in London, became an actor and director who worked at the Old Vic from 1922-24, but

---

[210] Two other members of the Stratford Stage management team also gained lighting credits shortly after the period this book covers. **Julia Wootten** (dates unknown) was credited for lighting *As You Like It* and *Coriolanus* in 1952, and *Othello* in 1954. Northen, who worked at Stratford during this period, recalls her as a first class stage manager, and excellent cook, but makes no mention of her lighting skills (Northen, *Northen Lights*, p102&106). **Peter Streuli** (dates unknown) had been introduced to lighting by Ridge's books and became a Stage Manager at Birmingham after the war where he was greatly influenced by H.K. Ayliff, and he also directed there. By 1952 he was at the Old Vic, where the School's theatre brochure lists Streuli as Assistant Director to the acting courses, and also lighting the shows. He lit *Toad of Toad Hall* at the Princes Theatre in January 1953, noted for requiring five operators, three on the Grand Master, and two for portable controls. He went on to be Stage Director at Stratford, where he was credited for lighting several productions between 1953 and 1957 including *Antony and Cleopatra* in 1953 and *Romeo and Juliet* in 1954 (in conversation with Peter Streuli and in correspondence with Douglas Cornellison).

[211] In conversation with Christopher Burgess.

[212] Wardle, *The Theatres of George Devine*, p134.

[213] It is interesting to note that it did not recognise the work of the specialist practitioner (Theatre Museum Archives).

[214] It is believed that the last production he lit for the Old Vic was *The Italian Straw Hat* in Nov. 1952 (in correspondence with Denis Groutage). Clarke left at the end of the 1952 season to help Guthrie set up the Shakespeare Festival at Stratford, Ontario (Guthrie, T. *A Life in the Theatre*, London: Hamish Hamilton, 1961, p285), and later worked in senior management in ATV (in correspondence with Douglas Cornellison).

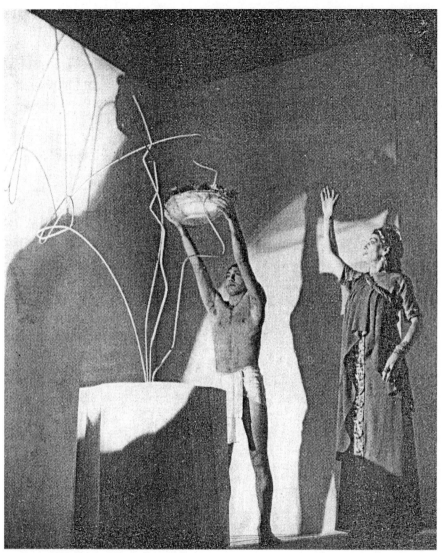

Electra, The Stage, April 1951.

then moved to Ireland in 1927 and founded the Gate Theatre Dublin in 1928 with Michael Macliammoir, becoming Director and Producer. After World War Two he toured his company to Europe and America.

Edwards became highly experienced at lighting, going on to light over 400 of his own plays. In an article in *Tabs*, he discussed his approach and some of the pitfalls he had identified.[215] He thought each show presented different problems, and thus the job never became easy, believing it was dangerous to say "this idea worked well before". He said he was no electrician, but "once the juice enters the dimmer and therefore under my control... I know where I am". He noted the difficulty in balancing lighting between the set and the actors, and thought it vital to understand the limitations of the switchboard in order to set cues that could be operated. He was one of the first producers who learned gel numbers and lamp positions, and plotted his shows with precise intensity settings.[216] He restricted his colour palette to about 16 different colours plus frosts, and found that rarely would these not provide a solution. His palette included: (Cinemoid) Nos. 3; 4; 5; 6; 7; 14; 15; 16; 17; 18; 19; 20; 24; 26; 27; and 32. He said that he had yet to find a use for the others. Edwards was responsible for equipping two theatres in Ireland with Strand installations – Galway and The Gate.[217] The lighting rigs did not feature battens, as he preferred the spot and flood system to give better distribution and control across the stage picture. He specified one dimmer per lamp, and he had the control consoles calibrated to set half-point intensity levels. Both theatres featured a cyclorama, although he did not rate the Schwabe system "because I believe this makes of the cyclorama a tyrant".[218]

Few of Edwards productions came to Britain. His Gate Dublin season at the Westminster Theatre London in 1935 comprised three productions: *Yahoo*, *The Lady says "No"*, and *Hamlet*. Although the season attracted much praise overall, only *Hamlet* attracted comments for his lighting, and these were not favourable. *The Times* of 18/6/35 expressed a good awareness of lighting:

"The stage is too darkened, particularly when the Ghost enters upon Hamlet and his mother; to concentrate the light on the Ghost and abandon the living players to blackness not only contradicts lines which clearly imply that these two were visible to each other but obscures the whole terror of

---

[215] *Tabs* 4/1, Sep. 46, p22.

[216] When plotting, he believed that "lighting is half darking: knowing where not to put your light" (*Tabs* 4/2, Dec. 46, p8).

[217] The Gate was a small stage, with a 20' proscenium opening, and with no footlights or fly tower, with the lighting control (a bracket handle type) located in the wings. *Tabs* recalled that "in this theatre...Edwards presented his miracles of staging and lighting" (*Tabs* 4/2, Dec. 46, p21).

[218] Tom Kelly, a Dublin-based producer and TV lighting man, in 1971 said that Edwards was "perhaps the best stage lighting designer to work in Dublin. It was he who introduced spotlights into general use in the city" (*Tabs* 29/2, Jun. 71, p46).

the scene. Elsewhere, when there is light, it falls too often from above so that the actor's eyes are looped in their brows' shadow and their performance is deadened as it were by blinkers".

His *Ill Met by Moonlight* at the Vaudeville in Feb 1946 (in which he acted as well as directing) attracted no press comments for the lighting.

William "Bill" Lorraine (1909-1990) joined Dean as a youth at the St. Martin's and soon became interested in lighting, developing a deep knowledge of, and enthusiasm for its Schwabe system.[219] Dean recalled that: "the more I increased my demands the better Bill was pleased, even though it often meant working all night".[220] He went on to become Dean's Chief Electrician in the 1930s, and was the Supervising Electrician for Dean's *Johnson Over Jordan* in 1939 and *The Wizard of Oz* at the Winter Garden in 1946.[221] He also worked for Oliver Messel on the Cochran revues and at Glyndebourne. On Messel and Cochran's attitude to lighting, Lorraine is reported to have said that when sitting in the stalls during a lighting rehearsal, on his enquiry as to how the lighting looked, they would invariably answer "if it's alright with you Bill, it's alright with us".[222] After 1945 he joined Strand, and then went freelance, lighting *Wizard of Oz* at the Winter Garden in 1946, a season of three plays, *Private Enterprise*, *All This is Ended*, and *Happy With Either*, directed by Basil Dean at the St James's in 1947/8 (he received no press notices for this work), and revivals including *Hassan* at the Cambridge Theatre in 1951 and the *International Ballet Season* at the Royal Festival Hall in 1951, the first use of the new installation.[223] He became a specialist in projection, lighting circuses, ice shows, non-theatre venues and exhibitions, and also regularly contributed to *Tabs*.[224]

Michael Northen (1922-2001) is generally acknowledged to be the first British lighting designer and remains today amongst the most distinguished representatives of the profession he started in this country. He was one of the original six founder members of the SBTLD in 1963, and achieved the highest professional honour when elected President of the ALD in 1995.

---

[219] In correspondence with Douglas Cornellison.

[220] Dean, *Mind's Eye, an Autobiography 1927-1972*, p267.

[221] the programme for *The Wizard of Oz* credited "Lighting and Effects by SwanAvon Ltd.", whose chief technician was Bill Lorraine (Theatre Museum Archives).

[222] Pinkham, *Oliver Messel Exhibition Catalogue*, p55.

[223] *ABTT News* Jun. 90, p6. Also see Appendix ii for a technical review of this venue.

[224] *Focus 10*, Sep. 89, p29.

Born into a family of theatre-goers, his early influence in technical theatre was stimulated, like Bentham's, by the effects in the Theatre Royal Drury Lane pantomimes and cinema presentation lighting. He built a model cinema at his home where he projected short films, complete with simulated lighting sequences.

He joined the 'Q' theatre in 1938 as an apprentice Stage Manager. This small venue at Kew Bridge had a reputation for artistic excellence and was a 'try-out' house for the West End. Working under the director Jack de Leon, designer Tanya Moiseiwitsch, and stage manager Sara Wilson, he showed an aptitude for combining the technical demands of theatre production with a creative sensitivity. Northen's lighting education began at the 'Q', where de Leon lit shows off a modest rig, recalling that de Leon was "the master of getting the maximum effect with the minimum equipment", a principle that characterised Northen's lighting work and a technique well suited to touring.[225] He picked up the technical knowledge required from working as a stage manager and the artistic insight from working alongside colleagues in an open and inquisitive manner. He was transferred into the West End and despite the interruptions of the war and National Service soon established himself as one of the most creative stage managers. His talent was spotted by Guthrie, who invited him to join the Old Vic company in 1942, and soon his services were in demand from Glyndebourne, the Royal Opera House Covent Garden, and the Shakespeare Memorial Theatre Stratford.

Feeling his future lay in lighting, and following a call from Gielgud to light *King Lear* at Stratford in 1950, he went freelance. This proved an astute decision. Of this production, Northen recalled that "Leslie's (Hurry) sets were wonderful to light as they were strong both in colour and outline, so that it seemed to me that I should follow his lead and provide strong lighting on the actors with the intention that this would be sufficient to light the scenery as well". He also was quoted as saying it was a "a bloody difficult show to light". He recalled his work on this production as being a "lighting designer... I was quite proud of my first efforts to light a big production... it seemed likely that in the future lighting designers would have an important role to play in a production".[226] He was credited for "technical and lighting direction", and for

---

[225] This efficiency was noted by the Globe theatre management in 1986, who queried Northen's credentials with Strand when submitting a minimal hire order for the production of *Lend Me a Tenor* (Northen, *Northen Lights*, p29).

[226] Northen, *Northen Lights*, p95&102, and *Lighting and Sound International*, Jan. 88 p31.

Measure for Measure.

being part of the design team for Peter Brook's *Measure for Measure*, the first production of the 1950 season (see illustration).[227]

In August 1950 he lit his first play in the West End, *Rosmersholm* at the St. Martin's Theatre, directed by Michael Macowan and designed by Tanya Moiseiwitsch, for which he received billing "lighting designed by...". Other than "beautiful settings" the lighting and design received no press coverage. This is the first known association of the words 'lighting' and 'design' in a production credit.[228] Later in the same year he lit *Don Giovanni*, designed by John Piper, at Glyndebourne. He recalled that:

> "the sets were painted in true Piper tradition and I didn't have an idea in advance how I was going to light them. It wasn't until I actually started that any ideas came to me. I found that the sets, which were bold in lines with dramatic colours, actually didn't need any help from my lights. The scenery

---

[227] Brown, I. & Quayle, A. *Shakespeare Memorial Theatre 1948-50*, London: Reinhardt and Evans, 1951.

[228] Theatre Museum Archives. The decision to credit Northen was in part due to his reputation and in part to the fact that the leading Swedish actress Signe Hasso, who had worked in New York took the lead in *Rosmersholm*. The management felt it important to use a professional lighting designer, as American actors working in London expected the services of a lighting designer.

rejected any direct lighting upon it and in fact seemed to resent the intrusion of a lighting designer! Quite by chance I found the solution by lighting the scenery entirely by light spilling over from the acting areas onto the floor of the stage. This bought out as much of the colour as was required to achieve a stunning effect. I used this technique on all John's productions except for *Billy Budd*'.[229]

From 1950 he continued also to stage manage and be a technical assistant, but from 1957 his sole employment was in lighting design. He was to become one of the most important figures of his time, with his most high profile work *The Mousetrap* still running in the West End, while continuing to work on major productions at Stratford and around the country. Later in life he lectured on the art of lighting and the relationship between creative team members.

His design process became the accepted way to light a show. He placed much importance on early discussions with the director and designer, and planning out the design on paper (as well as experimenting on his model stage). He built up a file of equipment information on regional theatres to aid planning. He sent out lighting plans in advance for the venue's Chief Electrician to prepare the show. His clear plans speeded up focusing to maximise plotting time. He established the routine of the designer setting the lights for the director's approval, with adjustments made over the following dress rehearsals.

Northen did much to establish the professional status of the lighting designer. Fees for lighting designers and technical consultants were uncharted waters, and he had to negotiate without the support of an agent, as Messel had previously done for designers.[230] Initially there was confusion over whether the director should pay the lighting designer as an assistant or the management as an employee, and he managed to negotiate for the latter. He also established all aspects of contractual arrangements, including appropriate billing, with the same size lettering as the designer, and fees, although he was not able to establish the precedent for royalties. He established new methods of working that were a significant development from those of previous stage managers or chief electricians.

Although it is thought a private income allowed him to be selective in the work he undertook, his interest in the art of theatre and his relationships with

---

[229] Northen, *Northen Lights*, p130. At an *ALD* lecture he recalled his favourite gels were nos. 9; 17; 17 doubled; 18; 40 & 50 (The *Live!* Show Jan. 97).

[230] As well as setting new standards on stage, Messel set new standards for design fees, demanding by far the highest wages to date for his services, also establishing the principle of royalties for someone other than the leading actor (Castle, *Oliver Messel, a biography*, p124).

leading directors and designers of the day afforded an ease which allowed him to marry technology and art. His model theatre provided a platform for common understandings and shared goals. He worked on different performance genres within the fields of drama and opera, which would have challenged and honed his deployment and use of light. His technical knowledge was sound, and his all-round professionalism placed his services in high demand.

Summary

As theatre lighting moved into the electric era, and following on from the standards and style set by Irving, Tree continued to present plays to a high visual standard, albeit governed by the limits of technology available at the time. Flexibility in spotlighting and control was compensated for with multiple manual follow spots. Harvey's work marked the end of this era of production style, and began to show influence of the minimal, expressive staging styles from abroad. His work introduced a new way of thinking to British theatre, set new standards and bridged the realistic, highly theatrical work of Irving and Tree with the more stylised approach of Cochran and the Art Movement practitioners that emerged after World War One.

The period from 1914 to the mid 1930s heralded significant advances in lighting. While technology did not advance significantly during this period, equipment became more refined and more readily available, and hire became a practical way to address deficiencies.

In mainstream theatre Dean and Cochran showed that high artistic standards were compatible with profit, and the art theatres in London and the provinces attracted growing support for more intellectually challenging work, even if often produced with minimal resources. While producers continued to light their own work, their growing trust in stage designers meant this duty was now often shared. Their slow relinquishment of control heralded the rise of the specialist around the time of World War Two.

The period 1935-1950 saw great changes in the role of lighting in Britain's major theatres. Shows from abroad, commanding a high visual standard, were highly influential and promoted the importance of the lighting specialist. With good quality spotlight and control equipment now available that required a more skilled and imaginative master, producers were finally persuaded to relinquish control of setting the lighting. The specialist emerged.

Yet despite the work of the first specialists, Brenner, Davis, Northen, Sullivan and their colleagues, most theatre-goers still saw visually uninspiring work.

Dorian Kelly, lighting designer and consultant, recalled in 1982 a depressing picture of British stage lighting:

> "Thirty years ago when the lighting was 'done' by the producer, design was largely a matter of setting levels for the battens and floats, and choosing between amber, straw, pink or steel for the very few focus spots. The mirror spots in the front of house were generally left untouched, focused in a double cover, warm and cool, which seemed to satisfy most requirements. The odd special was procured and rigged for very special occasions, but this was a matter of much discussion and practical consideration".[231]

The lighting designer was not regularly employed in most major British theatres until the 1960s, when the multi-lantern installation finally became the standard. Francis Reid commented in 1970 on why there was little actual need for a lighting designer until theatres became more fully equipped:

> "The need for a lighting designer arose mainly from the evolution of lighting techniques with complex multi-lantern rigs, which a director would find difficult to control without ignoring his primary responsibility for the complete production".[232]

Therefore lighting design in the 1940s and 50s was restricted to a few progressive and better equipped theatres. The fact that when the Society for British Theatre Lighting Designers was formed in 1963 there were only six members gives a clear indication of the scale of operations at this time.[233]

For a final comment, I quote from the youngest of these six. Richard Pilbrow at the age of 30 wrote a positive forward-looking assessment of lighting in an edition of *Tabs* in 1963.[234] He said:

---

[231] *Cue* 15, Jan. 82, p14.

[232] *Tabs* 28/2, Jun.70, p63.

[233] The six were: Charlie Bristow, Bill Bundy, Joe Davis, Michael Northen, Richard Pilbrow and John Wickham. It is interesting to note their backgrounds, and the fact that they were not "educated" as lighting designers. Mielziner was critical of lighting design training in America, saying that "would-be designers take to lighting when they find they cannot draw". He went on to say that it made sense to come into lighting design from another discipline, because "there is too much artistic... improvisation in the craft to make it a good discipline to train in". This offers an interesting insight into the need for the lighting designer to be able to adapt and juxtapose ideas to a changing environment that will be driven by a range of various artistic inputs. This also serves to comment on the six founders of the SBTLD. Each came from a sister discipline, although all technically or managerially based rather than artistically rooted: Davis, Bristow and Bundy began as electricians, and Pilbrow, Wickham and Northen as stage managers (*Tabs* 28/3, Sep. 70, p77).

[234] *Tabs* 21/2, Sep. 63, p12.

"the use of dramatic lighting in the theatre has in the last thirty years revolutionised stagecraft and staging methods. The appearance of our stages has been radically altered by the creative use of light, and the current... experiments in various audience stage relationships, are powerfully influenced by this *new lighting*. As awareness of the dramatic potential in lighting has been realised, and as technical resources have been developed, so the position of an individual, the lighting designer, has been established."

He went on to say that while it could be argued that the job of lighting should be down to the director or producer, then often they did not have the technical skill: most technicians do not have the artistic skill. The lighting designer married both fields of expertise.

5 CONCLUSIONS

This chapter draws together the main issues that led to the emergence of the lighting designer, and then goes on to assess who could claim to be Britain's first.

While there was much evidence of experiment, ideas, and an aesthetic potential for lighting emerging throughout the history of artificial light being used in the theatre, many factors held back the development of the lighting designer until the middle of the twentieth century. The key reasons for this fall into four distinct categories:

- the quality of equipment available
- theatre architecture and facilities
- commercial dictates
- a tradition of the actor-manager, and then the producer, "doing everything"

The Quality of Equipment Available

This was probably the main reason why the lighting designer was not required until the mid twentieth century. The three most important items of equipment required were the high powered, compact electric lamp, a precise spotlight that could penetrate the overall lighting ambience, and a control system that allowed smooth fading from one state to another. Of lesser importance, was a full range of coloured gels and stages with rigging facilities that afforded flexibility.

The development of the lamp and spotlight went hand-in-hand. It was not until the tungsten filament lamp became available just after World War One that the individual lantern could dominate the mass. Although the man-powered lime and arc had offered this possibility, rising labour costs and restricted rigging possibilities limited this technique of lighting the stage.

The tungsten lamp had power coupled with a small filament, lending itself well to being sited within an optical system for efficient light projection. First generation lanterns of the 1920s were relatively poor, and it was not until the second generation lanterns of the mid 1930s were developed that the potential for a stage lit by spotlights alone became possible, despite the lamp requiring a positional adjustment every time a focus operation was made. However, no sooner had these products started to make an impact than war intervened.

A new generation of controls introduced in the 1930s offered a greater sophistication in control methods, although it was not until 1950 that the Strand Electronic was launched, the first control desk capable of achieving a dipless crossfade, essential for smooth lighting operation. Other controls could achieve this if only a few luminaries were involved, but not for full states. Cost had prohibited the development of this essential component of control, and British theatre had to wait for the technology to be developed in America before it was adopted here.

The ranges of coloured gelatine and cinemoid available for purchase were expanded in the late 1930s, although there remained a shortage in the range of pale blue gels due to production difficulties. However by this time the palette available was adequate to achieve a good control of colour.

Theatre Architecture and Facilities

The architecture of theatre buildings was very important in offering potential for lighting design. British theatres tended to be small in comparison to their European and American counterparts, and the small stage was more favourable to a floodlight-style installation than a spotlight approach. Existing theatres proved difficult to convert to facilitate spotlights, and there were many instances where local authorities were hostile and obstructive to the placing of lanterns front of house, which were bulky, ugly and awkward to get power to.

Innovative lighting work therefore tended to be found in newly-built theatres that were designed to accommodate the latest technical equipment. As a result, buildings such as the Memorial Theatre Stratford and Glyndebourne became important venues, although few significant theatres were built during the inter-war years. Many larger theatres, particularly in London, enhanced their lighting facilities, although many remained unsuited to facilitating the new techniques being developed.

Lanterns were semi-permanently mounted to lighting bars, not being designed to be moved about the rig. The quick-release hook clamp that enabled this was not introduced until 1959. Lamp filaments in early focus spots needed to be re-centred every time they were refocused, a time-consuming and tedious job that was not overcome until the arrival of the pre-focus cap in 1951. Rigs hardwired to the dimmers meant that it was difficult to add more equipment or move it around. Resistance dimmers had limited load variation which afforded little flexibility. Plugs and sockets had not been standardised, so moving equipment often meant time-consuming changes to the plugs. Also there were many local variations in voltage supply to complicate matters further.

Lighting controls were operated from the wings and this was a major factor that hindered design ambitions. Poor sightlines must have alienated the keen operator from fully integrating with the performance. Most reports suggest that lighting operation was functional rather than responsive, and the operator would not routinely have improved intensity levels by subtle visual adjustment. Controls first moved to a front of house position in the 1940s, but only theatres that invested in the latest generation of controls had this possibility.

Commercial Dictates

Economic factors too contributed. Ambitious lighting took time to rig, focus, plot and rehearse, and production schedules traditionally did not allow for this. High theatre rents meant minimal 'dark' time was more important than artistic experiment. Once a stage was equipped with lights, economics dictated that money would not be spent again. Therefore most theatres had a basic batten-style rig, and any supplements had to be hired. But lighting was costly to hire, and equipment was not readily available outside London, meaning additional costs and inconveniences being added to a touring budget. Managements did not want to pay extra for a lighting designer when the existing staff would do the work. The public and the critics did not expect a high visual standard.

Equipment was often in poor condition, which would not have been conducive to precise lighting. Bill Bundy recalled that when he joined the Royal Opera House Covent Garden Electrics team in 1951 the stage electricians lacked basic electrical skills and "couldn't see the point of preventative maintenance".[1]

There was little incentive to invest in the new controls such as the Light Console and Electronic. Existing systems such as the Grand Master were very robust, and changing to these new systems would have been expensive, as new dimmers would have also have been required. This would have caused much upheaval and down-time in the theatre, and may have posed problems over staff training for their operation, and the fear that visiting staff (perhaps on tour) would not be able to operate them.

Manufacturers preserved the status quo. Despite the fact that more sophisticated equipment was being imported from Germany and America, Strand, having tooled up for the footlight and batten stage, effectively strangled

[1] ABTT *News*, Dec.89, p10.

the market, partly by cleverly promoting a culture that 'Strand knew best', and partly by monopolisation in the major venues. Strand spotted the commercial value of hire, and equipped few theatres with more than the basics, hard wired back to a control system that didn't allow scope for additions. This meant that companies would run up potentially high bills for the rental of 'specials' and control. It is interesting to note that American theatres, while typically not equipping their theatres with any luminaires, meaning that all had to be hired, nonetheless installed infrastructures based on patchable dimmers, far more conducive to lighting design by allowing greater flexibility in the choice and positioning of equipment. Strand carefully promoted the hard-wired approach through its house magazine *Tabs*, which had a veneer of independent authority. Rarely did it refer directly to Strand's products, but it regularly suggested that the only way to light the stage was the Strand way, and it never reviewed the work or practice of non-conformists or other manufacturers. Bentham, their leading man, noted European and American practice but belatedly introduced new products, and had a greater interest in serving his own Colour Music projects than in giving British theatre the standards of equipment available abroad.

Stage lighting design only emerged as the style of lighting inherited from the gas era and continued for many years by Strand – the even, flat wash of batten light – until finally ousted by a dynamic style first mooted by Craig and Appia and first championed in this country by Ridge and Dean and the art and fringe theatres.

Claimants to the Title – the First British Lighting Designer

Although many practitioners had been crucial to developing the art of lighting, several candidates emerged around the time of World War Two, receiving lighting credits for their work. George Devine was the first to receive public recognition, but despite much acclaim from the press he lit few shows as his career diversified. Had he gone on to become a specialist, he may well have claimed this title.

John Moody and John Sullivan worked in leading London theatres, with renowned production personnel, gained very favourable press coverage for their work and Sullivan in particular went on to have a substantial career in lighting. It is a pity that little can be found to confirm their credentials, and that magazines such as *Tabs* made no reference to their achievements at the time.

Joe Davis may have made unsubstantiated claims to have been credited as early as 1936, but he was best known for his work as a re-lighter of others' work, principally Americans. There is little recorded about his career other than his prolific work-load. His time with Tennents enhanced his credentials as a lighting practitioner of the highest standing, but press reports did not allude to an exceptional creative ability. It appears Davis belonged to the school of 'problem solvers' rather than being an initiator of ideas – a practitioner who lit the show at the plotting session rather than in his mind during rehearsals.

Michael Northen was probably the first we can be sure met the ALD definition. Northen lit in theatres with an appropriate facility that would offer consistent opportunities and production time for creativity, and worked alongside others that were supportive to high visual standards. He served an apprenticeship in an 'art' theatre and fully understood the role of design and stage management through practice and assistantships. He actively promoted experiment and planning through his sophisticated model theatres, engaging producers in constructive dialogue *before* the production was staged, thus meeting the terms of design as a predicted, collaborative solution. He worked across a range of production styles and genre. Perhaps most importantly, he had the social gifts necessary to be at ease in the company of leading producers, managers and artists of the day, to be taken seriously, trusted and valued for his contribution. He soon built up an accomplished C.V. At the end of his autobiography, he recalls Joe Davis saying in the early days of SBTLD meetings: "Don't you boys forget, it was Michael and me who started this lighting racket", one of the few published tributes to his ability.[2]

Others could have claimed the title. Wilson and Willson established good profiles, but gained little or no acclaim and did not continue as lighting designers; Lorraine gained good experience working with Messel, but his career diversified. Clarke and West also gained some credits, but soon moved into other aspects of the profession. Brenner gained much credit for his work at Salisbury but also diversified his career.

Three other lighting men, Bentham, Ridge and Williams, should be noted for their contribution. All three were key to the development of the art of lighting through their writings. Bentham and to a lesser extent Williams developed key items of equipment. Ridge lit many shows in the 1920s and 30s, but ill health curtailed his work and no record of him lighting in the 40s or 50s can be found. Williams lit very few shows. Bentham lit only one, concentrating his creative

---

[2] Northen, *Northen Lights*, p251.

energies into Colour Music demonstrations for which he gained much critical acclaim, playing a key role in developing the profile of lighting.

Could earlier practitioners have claimed the title? Nesbitt represented the last of the old school of producers who lit their own shows to acclaim, and Britain had others too before him (such as Cochran, Dean, Gray and Tree) for whom records show very high visual standards. However, these people didn't work in a collaborative team, and had varying standards of technical knowledge. Some good work was also noted at fringe theatres and at specialist theatres such as the Parry Opera Theatre.

The most influential practitioners from abroad who brought their work to the British audience were the dancer Fuller, producers Reinhardt and Short, and the designers Jones and Mielziner. These set standards in artistic achievement, technical competence and professional practice that the more enlightened British practitioners noted. Theorists such as Appia and Craig had a more limited and lower profile influence in lighting practice. While their work was acknowledged as important, practicalities prevailed, and their theories only prospered in art and fringe theatres.

By the time of the first British 'lighting design' credits, Britain was 20-30 years behind America in thought, technology and practice. America had been quicker to adopt the new continental European ideas that emerged in the late 1890s, which proved to be the catalyst for the modernisation of theatre equipment and progressive design ideas. Two world wars inevitably restricted development in Europe, whereas they had much less impact on developments in American theatre. Artistic development in German theatres, ahead of all at the start of the century, was significantly retarded by these wars, in particular the second when many major theatres were destroyed, and many leading artists fled to exile. It was not until the mid 1950s that German theatre began to recover from the effects of war.

The lime and the arc had prompted lighting developments in the mid and late 1800s, and introduced the keylight, which gave chiaroscuro, separation, definition and delineation to the visual picture. This was in contrast with most early electric techniques which were based around creating diffused light to light the cyclorama or flood the acting area. Companies such as Schwabe promoted the former across Europe and Strand in Britain the latter. While Schwabe promoted equipment that aided the development of visual aesthetics, much of Strand's influence was detrimental to this. Schwabe prompted the development of spotlights to light the actor, an approach that developed more or less in parallel but independently in America. American and European designers and producers developed the art of spotlighting pioneered in the era of the arc and lime, whereas in Britain few saw the point in any form of lighting other than flooding with colours.

End Note

The rise from the first credited designs in the 1940s to today's high sophistication, as in the 50 years before, has more to do with technological advances than thought and ambition. Soon after the first British credits the 'baby' profile spotlight, the Patt. 23 was launched in 1951 by Strand, the first affordable mass-produced lantern that reformed stage lighting. This lantern went on to sell over one million units. The following years saw technological advances through refinements in optical and luminaire design associated with the production of lamps with smaller, tighter filaments that burned brighter with higher colour temperature and that lasted longer before failure. The introduction of the Tungsten Halogen lamp in the early 1960s finally brought high intensity, near 'daylight' quality light to the stage, and with the advances in complex manual control at the same time leading to the beginnings of 'memory' recall of lighting states by the end of the 1960s, a new palette of potential became available. The durability and refinement of this technology made great advances in the 1970s, and by 1981, with financial investment from the rock super-group *Genesis*, the first automated luminaire (with the ability to pan, tilt and change colour to predetermined positions, all controlled remotely by a computer), hit the concert stage. Several product generations later, and driven by the latest high speed digital processors, the technological picture is now complete. The lighting designer now has the full palette available to control, and at last has parity of expressive potential with the musician, sculptor or painter.

The post-war wave of new theatre building in Britain established many regional centres designed for and equipped with this latest technology. These gave a greater platform on which lighting design could be practised, and exposed high quality visual work to a much wider public. In 1950 there were only a handful of specialists: ten years later their numbers had increased significantly, with many of these – such as Charles Bristow, Bill Bundy, John Bury, Jim Laws, Richard Pilbrow, Francis Reid, Peter Streuli and John Wyckham – going on to gain significant recognition for their work in lighting, and fully consolidate the place of the lighting designer within the creative team.

Today's designers have continued the traditions established by their predecessors. Internationally known names such as Rick Fisher, David Hersey, Max Keller and Jennifer Tipton show in their work that the techniques developed in the early days of lighting, and honed by the practitioners emerging in the 1940s, still lie at the heart of theatre lighting design. Davis's choice of the word 'racket' to describe his profession remains a good descriptor today, with many professional lighting designers still having to work outside their main function to make a living, manufacturers pressing designers or managements for their products to be used, and nearly all jobs being awarded by 'word-of-mouth'.

Yet the last fifty years has seen a boom in the number of people engaged as lighting designers. The Society for British Theatre Lighting Designers, which became the Association of Lighting Designers (ALD), was formed in 1963 over informal lunches at Rules Restaurant with a membership of six (Charles Bristow, Bill Bundy, Michael Northen, Richard Pilbrow and John Wyckham under the chairmanship of Joe Davis).[3] The admission criteria was "must have lit 13 West End shows" (a number set to ward off the threat of the growing number of specialists?) and the aims of the Society were to "advance the standards of lighting in the British theatre, to establish a code of professional conduct, and to act as an advisory body to the profession as a whole."

Today the Association is over 600 members strong, although criteria for entry are somewhat more relaxed.[4] Proof indeed of the attraction of the medium to creative artists today.

---

[3] Northen, *Northen Lights*, p251.
[4] ALD Membership, 2003.

APPENDICES

APPENDIX I

ALD Education Policy Document:
Recommended Syllabus Outline for a Course in Lighting Design

The ALD recommends that any course in lighting design should cover a prescribed range of topics, a knowledge and understanding of which, when set within a practical and vocational framework, might be considered pre-requisite for achieving professional status as a Lighting Designer. These topics fall into five distinct areas, called *units*. It is for the training provider to set the depth of detail and length of study for each *unit* in accordance with the academic level of the qualification.

Unit (1): **Cultural reference:**
(1.1) Understanding movements in performance style and stage design and their relationship to social, cultural and political history.
(1.2) Knowledge of the historical development of lighting design styles and conventions in all forms of performance.
(1.3) The aesthetics of lighting, as a component of visual art.
(1.4) Recognition of style and trends in other art disciplines, such as music, literature, painting, architecture etc.

Unit (2): **Creative thought and practice:**
(2.1) The role of lighting within the objectives of a production.
(2.2) Understanding and manipulation of a dramatic structure.
(2.3) Drawing developmental information from a range of sources.
(2.4) Developing an appropriate lighting scenario.

Unit (3): **Techniques:**
(3.1) Translation of lighting scenario images into technology.
(3.2) Realisation of ideas in a variety of stage formats.
(3.3) Working within constraints.
(3.4) Manual and computer-aided plan drafting and production paperwork.
(3.5) Pre-performance routines, such as rigging, focusing and plotting.
(3.6) Performance and post-performance routines.

Unit (4): **Technology:**
A detailed understanding of the workings and safe application of equipment
and plant such as:
(4.1) Lamps, optical systems and luminaires.
(4.2) Dimmers and electrical systems.
(4.3) Control systems and protocols.
(4.4) Stage technology and rigging systems.
(4.5) Special effects and ancillary equipment.

Unit (5): **Professional skills:**
(5.1) Appropriate communication skills to all production personnel.
(5.2) Professional etiquette.
(5.3) Industrial context.
(5.4) Knowledge of current regulations, codes of practice, health and safety.
(5.5) Understanding freelance working practices, contracts of employment,
agents, unions and professional bodies.
(Courtesy *ALD,* 27th August 1998)

APPENDIX II:
TECHNICAL REVIEWS OF SELECTED VENUES

This appendix charts the technical lighting facility at the venues featured in this book that were key to the emergence of the lighting designer.

Many major theatres were significantly developed or refitted during the period 1935-1950. The three really large stages in London, the Royal Opera House Covent Garden, The Coliseum, and the Theatre Royal Drury Lane, each still had scenic limitations, with limited wing space, relatively low grids, and limited mechanisation of lifts, bridges etc., although each was equipped with a cyclorama. The lighting installations in these flagship theatres were far from being cutting edge. Covent Garden's rig was modernised in 1934, but drew little notice for the role of lighting in its productions.[1] Artistic triumphs achieved at the Coliseum and Drury Lane were down to hired rigs and portable controls, not the antiquated "hotchpotch of out of date veterans" that belonged to the theatres.[2]

Bentham cited the installation of a good lighting control as key to realising ambitious lighting, and said that while a management would not balk at spending £10-15,000 on an organ for a concert hall or cinema, a similar sum for lighting would have been out of the question. Other than Covent Garden, he said that only the Memorial Theatre Stratford could stand comparison with a continental theatre, in terms of scenic and mechanical facility, although this too was very limited until the 1950 refit. He made no mention of Glyndebourne, probably the most sophisticated rig in Britain, as it was not a Strand installation.

The lighting facilities at these five major theatres was as follows:

The Theatre Royal Drury Lane[3]
There are few records of the lighting facilities at Drury Lane before 1950. Electricity replaced gas in 1898, and the stage had five 45' front battens, each

---

[1] Of lighting at Covent Garden in the mid 1930s, Bentham recalled that "there was not any memorable lighting for ballet" at that time, although he spoke more favourably of the lighting for operas: "Of course light levels were very low then and in opera even more so. The abiding memory for many years was of darkness rather than light... and an over-reliance on those perch spots". Bill Bundy recalled that stage designs at the Opera House ran for many years – for example the *Tosca* set of 1898 ran until 1964 – and that although built to last were tatty and benefited from dark lighting! (*Sightline* 22/1, Jan. 88, p23).

[2] Bentham, *Stage Lighting*, p13.

[3] *Tabs* 35/2, Sum. 77, p9.

containing 250 lamps, and six 38' back battens. The new control, which allowed each colour group to be faded up or down, alone or together, had a very poor view of the stage, but was located next to the prompt corner. It had many live elements with exposed wiring amongst the switching and fusing, and was on a 100volt DC supply. An (unknown) student commented in his college notes of 1904 that the "the regulator gear is coloured according to the lamps it controls and is arranged as on the switchboard viz.- white, red, blue. The regulators again are capable of being worked all together, each separately, or one after the other."

The lighting rig was subsequently improved. Schwabe cyclorama floods had been fitted for Dean's *A Midsummer Night's Dream* in 1924, which comprised 36 floods coupled to 36 dimmers. Strand fitted 'Sunray' battens and footlights in 1927, and 26 spots with colour changers were fitted front of house for *Cavalcade* in 1931. The original 1898 control lasted until March 1950, when a 216 channel Light Console was fitted. This was positioned in the same place as the old, still with no view of the stage. However, it had an extra-long control cable to allow it to be positioned in the stalls for plotting, although *Tabs* noted that it was never moved there.

The Coliseum

The Coliseum opened in 1904, having the largest stage in London.[4] The theatre was opened as a variety theatre, although it also staged some more adventurous productions. When it first opened, four shows a day were performed (one at noon and 6pm, and another at 3pm and 9pm). With such a schedule, it is no surprise that lighting was never noted for its art! However, some highly complex technical shows were regularly staged using the revolving stage, such as the *Derby Day races*, where 12 horses galloped against the turning revolve. The original installation had been by Blackburn Starling, although their archives contain no further information.

Lighting remained simple for variety work: typically a soloist was follow-spotted before a front cloth, with a floodlit stage revealed when the cloth opened for a full production number. Sir Ernest Stoll, the theatre's owner, staged many high quality acts, including leading actors of the day such as Bernhardt, Tilly, Terry and Langtry, Fuller and the Russian Ballet. He brought Reinhardt's production *Sumürun* to the Coliseum in 1911, and the following

---

[4] Designed by the architect Frank Matcham (1852-1920), the stage was 130 feet wide and 85 feet from footlights to back wall, with a proscenium opening of 55 feet wide and 34 feet high.

year another German production *Rialon*, which was noted "for the effect created by having the stage lit only by a row of candles (placed) behind the actors".[5] Symbolic stage design also came to the theatre in the same era through regular work of H. Kemp Prosser. However, despite these artistic diversions, variety ruled in the Coliseum, with a public appetite for dog racing, a cricket match, Highland games and the Rodeo.

Tabs said that there was nothing noteworthy concerning the Coliseum lighting rig before a refit in 1952.[6] Then, a 216 way Light Console was placed at the rear of the stalls, to replace the Grand Master which had been sited on a bridge on stage which Stoll recalled "required nine operators".[7] However, an oversight by *Tabs* was that Adrian Klein had been commissioned by Stoll in 1921 to build a coloured light projector for use at the Coliseum for "spectacular events, change of scene".[8] Klein had already demonstrated an expertise with this type of projector through his *Colour Music* work (see Appendix vii) and Stoll thought it could add something to variety theatre. However, it never happened, due to the cost of multiple projectors required for such a size of stage space. Several expensive, elaborate and well regarded musical productions were staged in the 1930s. A Schwabe cyclorama lighting system was installed in April 1931 for the first musical, *White Horse Inn*, but there are no records of other permanent additions to the rig.

The Shakespeare Memorial Theatre, Stratford

A major fire at Stratford in 1926 prompted the development of an ambitious replacement theatre. When it reopened in February 1932 the *Architectural Review* heralded the theatre as a triumph. On the fabric of the building "no expense had been spared,"[9] and it was fitted with a system described as "typical deluxe Strand Electric of the time".[10]

However significant mistakes were made in a quest for complexity and flexibility in the technical facilities, despite much research into stages across Europe. Many were consulted on the design, and Sir Barry Jackson and Norman Wilkinson acted as advisors. The proscenium arch was too low (21')

---

[5] Barker, F. *The House that Stoll Built*: London: Frederick Muller, 1957, p104.

[6] *Tabs* 26/4, Dec. 68, p10.

[7] Barker, *The House that Stoll Built*, p237.

[8] Klein, *Coloured Light- an Art Medium*, p27.

[9] Beauman, *The RSC – A History of Ten Decades*, p13.

[10] *Tabs* 22/1, Mar. 64, p40.

and too narrow (30'), particularly for a stage 40' deep; the audience too remote; and stage lifts did not fall enough or rise out of sightline. The theatre had a moveable plaster cyclorama, included at the last moment and built on a stage not engineered to take its 200 ton weight. Yet despite these problems, the theatre served as a benchmark of the aspirations for theatre design in the 1930s.

Harold Ridge, assisted by F.S. Aldred, were the consulting engineers for the lighting installation. The installation they specified was almost identical to that at Cambridge. It is no surprise then that the lighting installation was limited, but Ridge significantly mismatched the potential of the rig with the artistic policy of the theatre. On stage, lighting was from three four-colour compartment battens, split left, centre and right for dimming and using 36 dimmers in all. There was also a five way spot bar in the No.1 position, three perch spots a side and some dip plugs. Front-of-house there were eight spots on the circle front and a four colour arrangement, similar to battens, over the forestage. Four Stelmars were fitted in the ceiling slot. The cyclorama had 30 lamps set into it as stars.

The opening performance of *Henry IV* gained mixed press: "it was as if the Memorial Theatre had stood still... Each location of the play had a different, relentlessly literal set, made of canvas flats and curtains. The lighting, presumably because Bridges-Adams (the director and designer) had insufficient time to work on it, was murky. It was a dull, bad, depressing performance..."[11] However, the *Daily Telegraph* (25/4/32) was more encouraging, saying that "the settings throughout were magnificent. So was the lighting, except for some refractory shadows on the backcloth and a tendency to keep the stage too much in darkness".[12]

The theatre had been designed for a remote control system, yet was allocated a standard 56 way Grand Master switchboard "that was awkwardly crammed" on a platform behind the proscenium.[13] The main shafts were assigned to colour mixing, with a lower shaft (with poor access) for spots. This Grand Master was only the second to be made, and it had cross-gearing, allowing lights to come up and go down simultaneously on the same shaft. Initially the handles were not calibrated for intensity levels, a mistake that soon had to be

---

[11] Beaumann, *The RSC – A History of Ten Decades*, p117.

[12] Theatre Museum Archives.

[13] Marshall, *The Other Theatre*, p147.

rectified. Also a design fault meant that it was hard to tell if the handles had been locked onto the shaft or not. Bentham said that the thinking behind the layout of circuits on the switchboard was poor, even allowing for electrical considerations and space limitations.[14] Dimmers were clutch driven automatic Mansell type.[15] One novel feature was that the elaborate house-light controls that allowed the lights to be dimmed in three stages from rear house to stage, creating a sense of flow into the stage as lights dimmed.

Komisarjevsky, one of the first producers to use this new facility, was very particular about lighting, and considering the obvious limitations, lighting in this era at the theatre gained better press than one might have thought. However, *Tabs* reported that "spotlights were used extensively in only very advanced productions".[16] It is interesting to note that a theatre where the expectation for producing 'advanced productions' would be high, saw their number of spotlights to be adequate. The worst fault with the lighting installation was that only 24 circuits were dedicated to spots for the whole stage, a very small number, particularly when considering the size of the forestage. The whole system seemed at odds with the approach Ridge developed at the Festival Theatre Cambridge – which, as Bentham said in *Tabs*, was "a theatre where spotlighting was virtually the rule".[17] He continued that "one would have thought that Ridge and Aldred would have known better".

To accommodate a modest increase in the use of spots, the Grand Master was supplemented by a twelve way board for the spot bar and six way board for fly rail circuits in 1945/6. Michael Northen recalled that the rig had about 50 lanterns, which were fixed although they could be recoloured and refocused for each play in repertoire.[18] Northen, noted for his minimal use of equipment, confirmed that there were enough lamps to light the stage.

The Royal Opera House Covent Garden

Covent Garden underwent a major stage refit in 1934, undertaken by Strand, their first major commission. Bentham said this installation was the largest in Britain for many years, and served, with the addition of a couple of twelve-

---

[14] *Tabs* 30/1, Mar. 72, p25 reported full circuit details for the control.

[15] Dimmers had 100 contacts for added smoothness (the norm was 80, although Strand fitted 120 contacts per dimmer in their demonstration theatre).

[16] *Tabs* 14/3, Dec. 56, p10.

[17] *Tabs* 30/1, Mar. 72, p15.

[18] Northen, *Northen Lights*, p103.

way temporary desks, until the 1964 refit.[19] The refit received much attention, and the equipment was even illustrated and described in the *Illustrated London News* (7/7/34). Ridge benchmarked the re-equipped theatre, saying that it "compares favourably with any other theatre or opera house in the world so far as the stage lighting plant and flexibility of control are concerned".[20]

Only nine Stelmars were installed, due to their expense.[21] They were positioned three a side on the perches, manned for redirecting rather than following. The remaining three were in the dome, fitted with remote 4-colour change. Bentham recalled that there were a lot of side lighting wing floods, there were 14 focus spots under the bridge, overhead onstage there were five batten bars supported by poor quality Acting Area floods (the early Strand copy of the German versions), and floats. The huge Hasait cloth cyclorama was lit from above by 148 x 1kW floods (80 in No. 20 blue, 34 in No. 6 red, and 34 in No. 39 green), and from below from a truck that housed 72 x 500W floods, with the same colours in the same ratio. A GKP and arcs were used for projection.[22]

The previous 1902/3 control had been sited under the stage: the new control was located on the prompt side perch, which Ridge described in detail, built as a 'one-off' by Strand and having many useful features.[23] It was designed to be locatable anywhere in the theatre, although it was never actually moved from its perch position.[24] *Tabs* noted the control as "the first really large board – 130 ways".[25] The control worked in the manner of a Grand Master, with each circuit switching to a shaft for either an up or a down fade. The masters

---

[19] *Sightline* 21/1, Sum. 87, p27. The total load was a colossal 700kW AC and 150kW for the 100V DC arcs, with the cyclorama alone requiring 222kW (which was half as much again as the total load at Stratford).

[20] Ridge and Aldred, *Stage Lighting Principles and Practice*, p77. In the 1960's it became clear that the architecture of this theatre had an important bearing on the development of the rig – in particular FOH. It was hard to locate followspots that would cover the whole stage, and control was problematic to locate due to space restrictions – in those days they were still large by modern standards. However, there was never any suggestion that architecture held back the rig in the earlier days (*Sightline* 22/3, Jul 88).

[21] Bentham, *Sixty Years of Light Work*, p53.

[22] *Sightline* 21/1, Sum. 87, p23. Although the Pageant was available, it was not used at the Covent Garden until after 1945.

[23] Ridge and Aldred, *Stage Lighting, Principles and Practice*, p77.

[24] "It is but one step farther to the *Strand Light Console* which has just made its appearance"- this system hinted at the Light Console, which had been developed just too late for the 1934 installation (Ridge and Aldred, *Stage Lighting, Principles and Practice*, p77).

[25] *Tabs* 22/1, Mar. 64, p55.

were manually driven – surprisingly no motor drive was fitted, given that opera often requires very slow fades. Circuit levels were indicated by a Rolls Royce petrol gauge that showed the percentage of intensity. This must have allowed far greater accuracy in setting and recording lighting compositions. Ridge remembered the control as offering "independent control …to every light or group of lights, allowing a very wide range of blending with fading and brightening to be effected gradually or rapidly".[26] Connection to the resistance-type dimmers was via 12v DC electric lines that operated the Mansell clutch system. This was the first example of electric dimmer control in Britain.

Reflecting on the quality of the 1934 lighting refit, Bill Bundy, who joined the Opera House in 1951 recalled that little additional equipment had been added since 1934.[27] The control had been supplemented by a twelve and an eight way temporary control, and other temporary controls were also located on the wing floors to operate float spots, practicals, etc. A pool of stock, including profiles and pageants, was available to be deployed according to the needs of the productions.

Glyndebourne Opera House

Glyndebourne Opera House opened in 1934. Sadly it appears there are no exact records of the original installation. However, Francis Reid recalled that the rig was still virtually unchanged when he joined the company in 1959.

Reid recalled that access to every part of the rig was excellent, allowing a lighting design to develop in a free and experimental way. The rig was full of German 500, 1000 and 2000 W focus spots, and a couple of Strand battens. The cyc was lit by Horizon floods and a large two-tier Schwabe cloud projector. There were very few front of house spots, as early photographs confirm.[28] The lighting control was a 60 way Micklewright interlocking desk, similar to a Grand Master. It controlled via tracker wires a 48 way Siemens Bordoni transformer dimmer imported from Germany, which gave each patchable

---

[26] Ridge and Aldred, *Stage Lighting, Principles and Practice*, p77.

[27] Save for 12 x focus spots FOH, 4 x focus spots a side to cross-light the forestage, and 3 x arc followspots in the dome. The 14 bridge spots had been changed to (Strand) Acting Areas, the Acting Areas on the batten bars had been changed to Patt. 76's and a sixth 4-colour batten bar had been added. Six 1kW spots supplemented the Stelmars from the sides. Bundy introduced six Patt 53 profiles FOH, controlled by another temporary control, which were the only refocusable FOH spots until 1964. Soon after 1950 a programme of lantern replacement was put in place (*Sightline* 22/1, Jan. 88, p23, and *Sightline* 22/2, Apr. 88, p12).

[28] Theatre Museum Archives.

dimmer a variable load from 40W to 6kW.[29]

These five major theatres compare and contrast in an interesting manner with the lighting facilities at other venues noted for their importance in the emergence of the lighting designer pre-World War Two:

The Parry Opera Theatre at the Royal College of Music

In total there were 120 stage circuits that patched into 32 switch and hydraulically operated dimmers mastered by three main dimmers with remote control switches. Single or multiple circuits could be patched to the same dimmer. Dimmers were both liquid and resistance types for flexibility and were connected to the desk by tracker wires. Gelatine was used throughout the theatre for colour: no lacquered lamps were used.[30]

The lighting circuits were distributed as follows:
Cyclorama top: 20 circuits;
Cyclorama bottom (in a trench): 10 circuits;
No 3 batten: 7 plug points;
No 2 batten: 8 plug points;
No 1 batten: 15 plug points;
Proscenium perches 5 plugs a side, and usually 2 or 3 lanterns;
Stage dips: 9 plugs per side;
Floats 18 circuits (3 sections of 5 colours each plus 3 for specials);
FOH 5 circuits;
Arcs were only used for special effects.

A new lighting system was fitted in 1950 with a grant of £2,000, replacing the original system. As far as can be ascertained, there had been no significant upgrades or investment in lighting since the original installation.[31]

---

[29] The Bordoni system was at the time considered the best available, although it soon was found to be limiting. A similar installation at the Josefstadt Theater, Vienna in 1956 attracted criticism because it could "no longer follow the modern production style with its demand for ultra quick lighting changes" (*Tabs* 40/1, Aug. 83, p18). The control allowed for pre-setting of up to 36 intensity levels (rather confusingly the controls were up for off and down for on). It had some more quirks: it could not do an instant cross fade or blackout, due to its design (fortunately rarely needed in opera). It was situated in a side box with a partial view of the stage. Michael Northen recalled that the control was "erratic" (Northen, *Northen Lights,* p130).

[30] Ridge, *Stage Lighting*, p118+.

[31] Warrack, *Royal College of Music* Vol. 2, p366.

The Festival Theatre Cambridge[32]

The stage was a proscenium arch arrangement, with a permanent curved cyclorama 40' high, projecting out into the auditorium, joining the audience with a flight of steps. The lighting installation was designed by Harold Ridge, in association with his electrician Leslie Steen. The forestage was lit by six 1kW focus lamps, one from each side and four from the front (although not fitted with colour change magazines which was common elsewhere) plus footlights. The on-stage acting area acting area was lit from a red, green, and blue batten bar and a spot bar comprising five 1kW and two 500W focus spots located behind the proscenium. Portable equipment consisted of two 1kW and two 500W focus spots, two baby spots and six 500W floods. Portable lanterns were served by six dips.

There was a lighting bridge to light the cyclorama and a pit to light it from below. The cyclorama top was lit by twenty 1kW Schwabe flood lamps in seven colours: six dark blue; four mid blue; two light blue; two daylight blue; two green; two yellow; and two red. The cyclorama bottom lighting used a three-colour system: eight 250W red floods; eight 250W green floods and seven 300W blue floods, arranged alternately, with glass (made by Hetley's) as the colour medium.

The interlocking style lighting control worked electrically rather than mechanically, thus allowing selective lamps from anywhere on stage to be faded up as a group. It controlled 35 dimmers, allocated thus: six for front of house; three for batten colours; seven for the spot bar; six for stage dips; one for each cyclorama top colour; three for the cyclorama bottom; and three for decorative front of house.

Although progressive ideas were being practised in this theatre, the lighting facility appears limited and must have been extended regularly to match ideas such as those quoted in the main text, despite the relatively sophisticated control.

The St. Martin's Theatre

It is known that Dean imported American equipment for the St. Martin's theatre around 1920, but detailed lists are not available. He also installed a cyclorama that was lit by 1kW Horizon floods, coloured with glass. This was supplemented by a complex projection arrangement: a 3kW projector for projecting multiple moving, rising and falling slide patterns (usually used for cloud projections), with direction and speed regulators for complex images, and a further three

---

[32] Ridge, *Stage Lighting*, p110.

3kW projectors used for projecting either clouds or landscape onto the cyclorama, with positions set by motors, used either in conjunction with the single unit or alone. Control was from a console connected by wires to the apparatus.

The Lyric Hammersmith
Despite the reputation of Playfair and Lovat Fraser for adventurous work, the theatre had only the most modest equipment. Kitty Black recalled that even after 1945 "the theatre still used the original liquid dimmers for the footlights, and the lighting system was "antiquated".[33] In the 1920s Ridge and Aldred had recorded that the rig was a conventional rig of battens and footlights, supplemented with about eight 1kW spots on the No. 1 bar, and five 1kW acting areas on the No. 2 bar, angled to avoid lighting the scenery. There were arcs on the perches, arc projectors, and some front of house spots.

The Everyman Hampstead
McDermott remembered the lighting had "no footlights, revolutionary at the time" (1920). The theatre initially used floods from either side front of house as licencing officers objected to lanterns in the auditorium – "they would explode and terrify the audience who would panic and jam all exits..." plus some centre floods from the roof, to provide front of house face lighting. It was ugly but effective. This lighting was replaced in 1923 with a 'Phoebus' system from Germany, complete with lever controlled dimmers, one per circuit "that was a miracle of smoothness, and evoked envious comment from even highly technical electrical engineers who came to see them". Also, there was a single large lantern, a modified searchlight, from Germany (nicknamed *Big Bertha*), fitted with a reflector and lenses, with a maximum output of 26,000 ft cnds. It was hung in the roof in a position that meant all spill from actors would fall on the stage floor, and then the front of house floods were withdrawn".[34]

The Westminster Theatre
The lighting installation of 1931 was typical of the period. There were four 1kW spots from front of house and two 1kW spots per side for sidelight. Footlights could disappear into the stage, and battens (with sunray reflectors) were fitted on stage with two 1kW spots centre stage behind the proscenium.

---

[33] Black, *Upper Circle, a Theatrical Chronicle*, p122.
[34] MacDermott, *Everymania*.

The cyclorama was lit by a Strand system. Control was by "Strand's latest system…with sunset dimmers".[35]

Three installations completed around and just after 1950 are included to indicate how a greater understanding of the potential of lighting was now being incorporated into theatre facilities. These venues, all noted for ambitious artistic policies, are the Old Vic, a refit at the Shakespeare Memorial Theatre Stratford, and The Royal Festival Hall.

The Old Vic

Little appears to have been recorded of the lighting installation at the Old Vic before a refit in 1950 following wartime damage. A very progressive lighting system was fitted by Strand in 1950, in particular its front-of-house lighting arrangements and control where 60 circuits were installed, a very high number for those days.[36] Mirror Spots, with remote colour change, and Pageants were fitted both on the circle ends and centre. The forestage roof, rather unusual in that it formed a 'sky-dome', concealed a lighting bridge fitted with Mirror Spots and Acting Areas for down lighting. There were also perch positions for side lighting the forestage. This front of house installation suggested that area isolation would be the technique employed in the theatre. Onstage the arrangements were more traditional, with a spot bar, two batten bars, and a cyclorama bar, although no footlights were installed. There were many dips at stage level and the fly rail. The control (a 120 way Electronic, with the capacity for future expansion to 144 ways) was placed at the rear of the dress circle in a glazed booth with a full view of the stage. The dimmers (2kW each) were located under the stage.[37]

Royal Festival Hall

A good example of the new style of lighting rig achievable with the post 1935 lanterns was that installed at the Royal Festival Hall for its opening in 1951.[38] 33 x 1kW Acting Area spots were rigged over the stage to light concerts, each individually dimmed to allow the size of the lit stage to adjust to the demands of the concert. For ballet, a further 31 x 1kW Acting Area floods were available

---

[35] *Tabs* 22/1, Mar. 64, p39, citing *The Kine* 15/10/31.

[36] *Tabs* 8/3, Dec. 50, p24.

[37] The theatre reopened with *Twelfth Night*, with set and costumes by Roger Furse. Unfortunately there was little press comment of note on the visual presentation (Theatre Museum Archives).

[38] *Tabs* 9/3, Dec. 51, p18.

from overhead, 22 of which had remote controlled colour-change units fitted. A flood bar was available should a cyclorama be required. For front light, 16 x Mirror Spots were rigged on the balcony front, all with remote control colour change. Side lighting was achieved with Pageants, four a side with colour changers. 45° front lighting was also achieved with four pageants a side, again with colour changers. Two 5kW scenic projectors were also available. The rig was controlled by an 84-way Light Console, positioned front of house with a good view of the stage.

The venue was used primarily as a concert platform as the stage facilities were not designed for complex drama productions. Despite this the lighting facility was ambitious and would have served drama well. This suggests that drama theatres could, given the money, have been better equipped than they were.

APPENDIX III
THE GROWTH AND IMPORTANCE OF
LIGHTING COMPANIES

The First Lighting Companies

Electric stage lighting equipment was not widely available commercially in Britain at the turn of the century – although the component parts, including the lamps, could be purchased. It fell upon a theatre's own gasmen to make the lantern bodies and wire their own electric lights and to add these to the theatre's stock. These men naturally evolved to become the first "electricians", and a course started at the Birkbeck Institute in London to train people in the new skills of Electrical Installation.[39] A growing number of stage technicians became electricians. With lighting equipment expensive, the managements that installed electric systems were not prepared to invest in anything more than a basic system and perhaps the occasional 'effect'.[40] Indeed many theatres remained without their own electric lighting equipment. Due to a booming demand for electric equipment, manufacturing companies and hire and fit up suppliers soon emerged and theatres became the province of contractors who supplied equipment for each show. However, wages were poor and often had to be supplemented by other means, so commitment to theatre was limited. Show staff in the West End often worked in the Covent Garden fruit market to supplement their wages, a principle that remains today.[41]

R.R. Beard of Trafalgar Avenue, Peckham was probably the first British lighting company. Formed in 1882, it manufactured limelight and carbon arc mechanisms, and went on to make arcs, floods, footlights, battens and spots.[42] The General Electric Company (GEC) was founded in 1886, specialising in the manufacture of tungsten lamps.[43] W.J. Furse of Nottingham, formed in the 1890s, made a full range of equipment but was mainly influential in

---

[39] *Tabs* 15/2, Sep. 57, p4.

[40] *Tabs* reported in 1956 that at the turn of the century the cost of lighting was very expensive in comparison to the 1950s. A catalogue from 1899 of the company Messrs. Verity states that a 21' batten "costs a couple of pounds more than today" (and required 84 lamps, as opposed to 28 in the 50's.), and a 21' footlight cost £20 more than today (and used 54 lamps against 28 today) (*Tabs* 14/2, Sep. 56, p5).

[41] Around 1900 a Head Gasman or Chief Electrician received a fairer wage of about £6 per week (*Tabs* 11/2, Sep. 53, p10).

[42] They still continue today as Photon Beard (see their website for company history).

[43] The lamp division became called OSRAM in 1909.

cinemas.[44] Other early companies included Digby's, founded in 1895; Verity; Imperial; Holophane, founded in 1896 but ceasing trading during World War Two;[45] Blackburn Starling of Nottingham, manufacturers of generators, control and dimmers, incorporated in 1899;[46] Curtis of Hammersmith, founded in 1910, making resistance dimmers and control systems; Micklewright of Alperton, who made control systems; and Strand Electric, founded in 1914.

Digby's

Thomas J. Digby of Hammersmith was the first influential theatre lighting company in London. By the early 1900s Digby controlled a monopoly within West End theatres, supplying equipment, gelatines and staff. His style was to use a lot of hand operated follow arcs of his own manufacture, and up to 40 lighting men were commonly used in a show.[47] This system was initially very popular, but suffered during and after World War One through labour-shortage and was in terminal decline by the mid 1920s due to labour cost.[48] By the 1920s Digby had moved to Gerrard Street to be in the West End in an attempt to revive fortunes. Notable clients for Digby were Tree and Dean.[49]

Digby contributed much to early electric lighting, both in terms of developing the "key light within an overall ambience" style, as well as much technological development. He was the first to use pattern numbers to indicate a lantern type in his catalogue of 1908, a system later copied by Strand.[50] As well as

---

[44] Furse's most influential period was just after the start of World War Two, when, with Rollo Gillespie Williams joining the company from Holophane, the company launched the Delicolor control system. Furse for a time secured a foothold in theatres, and are credited with the launch of the first Fresnel in Britain in the 1940s and indeed even exporting Delicolors to America. But they did not anticipate the move away from floodlighting and colour mixing into the spotlight methods of stage lighting that began to dominate from the 1950s, and the company declined. (*ABTT News*, Aug. 87, p8).

[45] It was founded three years after its French parent company that developed lenses for lighthouses, and was well known for its manufacture of equipment for coloured lighting displays for cinemas in the 1930s (*Lighting Equipment News* Mar. 96).

[46] Blackburn Starling were heavily involved in the theatre lighting industry in the early part of the 20th century up until the mid 1950s, providing a whole electrical service. Important installations included the Coliseum and Leicester Square Empire in the 1920s. The company also supplied Strand products. Unfortunately company archives hold no product catalogues of the early days (in correspondence with Mike Gutteridge, Deputy Chair, Blackburn Starling and Co. Ltd.).

[47] *Tabs* 22/1, Mar. 64, p2.

[48] *Tabs* 22/1, Mar. 64, p24.

[49] Digby gained a programme credit as Electrical Engineer for Dean's production of *The Blue Lagoon* at the Prince of Wales Theatre in 1920.

[50] Tabs 34/3, Aut. 76, p19.

arcs, Digby also made a Patt. 56 batten, arranged in colour groupings – red, blue and yellow for three circuit, and an extra open white in four circuit, and a Patt. 85 Optical Attachment (a lens and slide carrier) for an arc.[51] Along with George Applebee, electrician at the Gaiety, in 1908 he patented devices to dim an arc with a shutter. Digby's were taken over by Imperial in the late 1920s.

Strand Electric Ltd.

Strand Electric Ltd. was formed by practising theatre electricians Arthur Earnshaw, Philip Sheridan and Jim Woolnough to provide an alternative to Digby. When Strand first opened, they marketed Digby's gelatine and lanterns, but they soon gained independence, having recruited a small team of specialists as business took off.[52] Strand promoted a cheaper approach to lighting the stage with the predominant use of battens – in contrast to Digby's labour-intensive approach. Whilst good for business, this approach did little to advance the art of lighting, continuing the bland, even illumination of gas light days.

It is thought that Strand initially made a 400W lens spot, a flood, an arc and a batten.[53] Manufacturing success started with the launch of a high quality batten and footlight in 1922, which were both significantly better than Digby's. The Strand batten was championed by Adrian Samoiloff in his "totally forgettable" show *Round in Fifty* at the Hippodrome in 1922.[54] This show "created a sensation in the papers" and soon all theatres were fitting these battens praised for their high light output.[55] Strand took off.

Initially Strand was based at premises in Garrick Yard, moving in 1924 to Floral Street. Both premises were located in the heart of the West End, another key to their early success. With many of its employees working for the company by day and for theatres in the evening, Strand was well placed to give advice

---

[51] *Tabs* 34/3, Aut. 76, p19.

[52] Strand expertise grew as technicians joined them. For example, Percy Boggis joined them from Loie Fuller. Boggis had a big reputation as a technician: Bentham described his wave effect, in Arthur Bourchier's *Treasure Island* at the Strand Theatre 1922, as "probably the most intriguing of all optical effects" (*Tabs* 22/1, Mar. 64, p5). In the programme for Samoiloff's *Brighter London*, Boggis was credited for a lighting effect in *Send Me a Bluebird*, and there is an advert for details of the *Boggis Effect*, "apply to sole agents Westminster Advertising Service Ltd., 7 Leicester Sq. WC2". Boggis also specialised in U.V. Frank Weston, who worked for Boggis, also moved to Strand, taking with him much technical know-how, particularly of U.V. techniques with discharge lamps.

[53] Believed to be used for one of the first times by Earnshaw on Gilbert Miller's *The Willow Tree* at the Globe Theatre in 1917 (*Tabs* 22/1, Mar. 64, p7).

[54] *Strandlight* 8, Spr. 89, p1.

[55] *Tabs* 22/1, Mar. 64, p8.

on equipment for hire or purchase. Strand had a natural market and staff on hand for immediate feedback to the client.

With many theatres still owning only the most basic of lighting rigs there was a growing market for hire. With few manufacturers of lighting equipment Strand made their own lantern hire stock, which matched the sales business as an immediate success.[56] In the early 1920s they started to manufacture controls, and also diversified into illuminated signage, exhibition, architectural and trade show work.

With Digby in decline, Strand became the leading theatre lighting company by the mid 1920s. Led by commercial interests, they preserved the status quo of the colour mixing batten stage. There were few practitioners that demanded a more adventurous approach to lighting, and those that did imported equipment from Germany or America, or made their own.

ReandeaN

Alex Rea and Basil Dean formed a company called ReandeaN in 1919 that offered an alternative approach to the batten stage of Strand. With an eye on the type of equipment being manufactured on the continent, they imported lighting equipment and lamps. Amongst the imports were 500 and 1000W American grid filament lamps, 250W baby spots, and X-Ray batten reflectors. This equipment had a far greater efficiency than British equivalents and was installed at Dean's St. Martin's Theatre, along with a Schwabe cyclorama lighting system imported from Germany.

Although they sold few products, their influence was to be enormous. Their equipment promoted a style of lighting that laid the foundations for the emergence of the lighting designer thirty years later, and helped Dean become one of Britain's few world-class producers.

GEC[57]

GEC became actively involved with theatre lighting in the 1920s, having formed a relationship with Harold Ridge, and publishing the first British lighting pamphlet

---

[56] Kitty Black, who joined Tennents as a secretary and went on to become a leading agent, recalled that "London theatres possessed only skeleton lighting – some of the touring houses seemed to have even less than that – so extra equipment was hired from Strand Electric, and their tiny managing director, Stanley Earnshaw, was a frequent visitor to the office" (Black, *Upper Circle, a Theatrical Chronicle*, p18).

[57] In the 1920s GEC was a very important company, at the forefront of establishing the National Grid (*Everything Electrical, a Brief History of GEC*, GEC Archives, 1999)

in 1923 – see Appendix v. They gained sole British rights to market the Schwabe-Hasait system. Strand, concerned about this threat to what they perceived to be 'their market' went some way to curb the import of German equipment with an agreement in June 1931 that GEC would also supply Strand equipment, in return for Strand using GEC lamps. As a consequence, Bentham said that only a trickle of equipment thereafter found its way to this country, notably 'specials' such as controls or scenic projectors from the German company Reiche and Vogel.[58]

To raise their profile GEC organised a discussion at the Theatre Royal Drury Lane in June 1925. This coincided with Dean's installation of a Schwabe Hasiat cyclorama, and the meeting was led by H. Mather, the theatre's Chief Electrical Engineer. Mather compared the performance of limes with gas-filled lamps, and demonstrated batten and cyclorama light. A comparison between the British and the Continental methods were discussed. The agenda went on to Klein, who used the meeting to discuss linking lighting to colours, and the potential for projected scenery.[59]

GEC closed the theatre lighting department in 1932, shortly after the Strand agreement. By the mid 1930s Strand were by far the largest and best known firm for the supply of stage lighting equipment. Their main competitors in the West End were Major, founded in 1931, and Venreco. Micklewright and Blackburn Starling still made control and dimmers, and W.J. Furse had a strong presence in the midlands and the north. Holophane also made equipment, although mainly for cinemas. ReandeaN had minimal commercial impact, and Strand took over Imperial Lighting in 1949.

The Importance of Strand Lighting

As the largest manufacturer of stage lighting equipment, Strand was undoubtedly of great importance in the development of stage lighting in this country. The company employed many people who worked in the theatre, and their relationship with the profession was generally very strong. Perhaps this was the company's greatest strength, extended through its personnel, catalogues, magazine, lectures, and network of hire shops and agents throughout the country. However, the company was often timid about investing in new ideas, and was often overtaken by overseas companies in implementing new

[58] *Tabs* 22/1. Mar. 64, p65.
[59] *ABTT News,* Mar. 86, p10.

thinking. For details of Strand's publications, see Appendix v.

Strand believed their role also lay in educating customers. Bentham said "Strand have tended to train our customers to accept what we feel they need rather than what they think they want... The only place the young lighting enthusiast can train is by attending Strand lectures, reading *Tabs* and other Strand publications".[60] He cited an example of the controlling influence of Strand when Furse introduced the Fresnel in the mid 1940s: it was not until Strand deemed them a replacement for the Pageant and Acting Area lanterns that they took off.

Strand's Demonstration Theatre

Gillespie Williams persuaded Holophane to open a demonstration theatre in Vincent Square, Victoria to display his cinematic colour change displays "wherein", Bentham recalled, "damsels cavorting in coloured light was said to be the attraction".[61] This prompted Strand to do likewise. In 1933 they opened their first demonstration theatre in Floral Street, in part to nullify this competition.[62]

The theatre was used to demonstrate equipment and effects to both professionals and amateurs. It was to be a key part of Strand's growing role in education, and within a few years had a significant impact on the technical theatre world. With a simple arrangement of swagged drapes, gauzes, legs and borders, Strand (or perhaps more accurately Bentham) chose to illustrate their products by setting light to music – *Colour Music*, as it was later to be called.

Set in the heart of the West End, the theatre promoted Strand as an advisor as well as a supplier. As well as showing Strand's lighting equipment and effects, it also stocked Hall's stage curtains, and thus was able to demonstrate a complete stage arrangement. At the inaugural party on 18th March, opened by C.B.Cochran, a range of lighting effects were demonstrated, including UV and Samoiloff. Optical effects were projected to accompanying sound effects. The programme finished with the first Strand Colour Music solos on the curtains.[63] See Appendix vii for full details of Strand's Colour Music recitals.

---

[60] *Tabs* 22/1, Mar. 64, p66.

[61] *Sightline* 16/1, Spr. 82, p41.

[62] The theatre was equipped with a (chrome plated!) Grand Master that controlled 30 dimmers, with footlights in four colours, and a single Patt. 43 focus lamp with four-colour change front of house (*Sightline* 17/1, Spr. 83, p43).

[63] *Tabs* 22/1, Mar. 64, p49, & *Sightline* 16/1, Spr. 82, p41.

Strand's architectural and environmental work

Strand became increasingly active in the architectural world, lighting major public events and exhibitions from the mid 1920s. This must have broadened their company profile and influenced the public to the power of lighting. Significant initial projects included the Empire Exhibitions of 1924 and 1925 at Wembley, which included the construction of a theatre on the site called the Admiralty, prompting a long association between the Government and Strand for lighting public events that culminated in sophisticated war-time model simulators for training purposes. Other important exhibitions for Strand pre-war included every *Daily Mail Ideal Home Exhibition* from 1930, the *Glasgow Exhibition* of 1938 and the *New York World Fair* of 1939. Post war exhibitions included *Britain can make it* at the V&A in 1947, and the South Bank *Festival of Britain* in 1951. 1931 saw the first floodlighting of a public building, the National Gallery façade and Nelson (by two Stelmars), and later Strand even lit the first floodlit football match in Britain (Arsenal versus Rangers at Highbury) in 1951.[64]

Strand's influence abroad

Strand exported little before World War Two. The first significant overseas orders were for controls, in 1939 for the first Light Console from S'Carlos Opera House, Lisbon and in 1950 for the first electronic desk and dimming installation at the National Theatre, Reykjavik. Despite limited overseas market penetration even as late as the mid 1950s, Strand had offices in most European countries, Australia and Canada.

Strand's legacy

Strand effectively strangled the lighting market through deals, take-overs of competitors who struggled to compete, subcontracting out work, and continuing to promote a lighting system that preserved the status quo and their own commercial interest. Strand copied the best ideas of its competitors – such as lanterns, control, the Demonstration Theatre and the magazine. However, they also made a very important and positive contribution to creating a thriving theatre scene in this country. Perhaps one of the best tributes to the invaluable service that Strand offered the theatre profession was from Basil Dean, who said that "Earnshaw and Sheridan set up a hire business called Strand that

---

[64] *Strandlight* 8, Spr. 89, p3.

never quite lost its paternalistic attitude towards its clients. Therein lay the secret of success".[65]

[65] Dean, *Mind's Eye, an Autobiography 1927-1972*, p266.

APPENDIX IV
EDUCATING THE LIGHTING DESIGNER

For the British practitioner interested in gaining an education in lighting in the first half of the twentieth century, there were few options beyond learning 'on the job'. Formal training courses, while well established in America, began tentatively in 1936, and in greater earnest after World War Two. Other than occasional lectures on the subject already referred to in the main text, or visits to see manufacturers' Demonstration Theatres or Bentham's *Colour Music* experiments, books were the only source of knowledge.

Training in Britain

There had been occasional short courses that featured stage lighting. Stagecraft courses ran at the Little Theatre, Citizen House, Bath from about the mid 1920s, and in 1931-35 Easter and Summer Schools, and autumn evening classes were held at the Everyman Hampstead as well as at Bath, offering tuition in scene design and lighting. Sadly there is no record of the curriculum.

Formal training in lighting did not become available in Britain until the 1930s.[66]

Lighting tuition was first offered by George Devine at the London Theatre Studio from 1936-39, a school founded by Michel Saint-Denis in 1935. Saint-Denis had worked as a stage manager and administrative assistant under Copeau at the Théâtre du Vieux Colombier in the early 1920s, and became the first director of the influential Compagnie des Quinze between 1929 and 1934, whose ethos promoted integration between all production elements. The company appeared at the Arts Theatre in London in 1931, and, feeling that he was now "in the country that best understands my work" set up a training company with Devine and the Motleys that opened as the London Theatre Studio in 1936, with 64 students on four different courses. However, production students only had one class a week due to a shortage of space.

---

[66] Actor training was well established, with schools such as LAMDA starting in 1861, RADA in 1904 and Webber Douglas in 1926. Bristol was the first University to offer a drama course, in 1947. Theatre Design, despite Craig's writings in *The Mask* and his unfulfilled ambition to set up a design school alongside his acting school in Florence, was first taught at Wimbledon School of Art (founded in 1890) in 1932 under Morris Kestelman, and forming a Theatre Design department in 1948 under Peter Bucknell. (See *Wimbledon School of Art* website). LAMDA was the first drama school to offer technical training, in 1965. In associated professions there were also limited opportunities to learn. A *Tabs* article in 1956 said only 2 out of 18 Schools of Architecture in Britain offered any instruction in lighting, and the article highlighted the lack of understanding architects had of lighting, and the lack of design and visual training in lighting engineers.

Better, larger premises were opened in the autumn, with a stage 32' wide by 22' deep, large enough to take shows that could transfer into the West End (although none ever did). Saint-Denis and Devine both wanted to abolish the idea that a stage manager was a menial worker, and introduced the term "artist-technician". Devine taught lighting and sound, and lit all Saint-Denis' shows. The LTS was wound up when war broke out.

In 1946, Saint-Denis set up the Old Vic Theatre School, based at the Old Vic in London. There were three courses: Acting; Technical Production and Stage Design (one year); Advanced Production and Stage Design (three years). Production was led by stage manager Cecil Clarke, with Margaret Harris in charge of Design. Wardle said that about 30 technical students were recruited a year, but most left at the end of the first year, equipped to be stage managers. Usually about 12 progressed onto the advanced course, considered a director training, which included a broad view of the arts, civilization, theatre history and "the discussion of ideas". Lighting featured in the first two years, and in the final year the student could specialise in Design and Direction. The course focused on three periods – Shakespeare, Restoration, and Modern Drama. The success of a design was judged by its ability to "assist the actors in articulating the play's rhythm". The technical students and the actors joined together at the end of the year for a production, designed by second years with first years in all other capacities. The School ran into financial difficulties and closed in 1952.[67]

British Books on Lighting

For most students of lighting, books and magazines provided the only way of learning other than "hands on experience", and many leading practitioners noted the value of the best books in their own learning.[68]

Before World War One virtually nothing had been written about backstage and technical theatre. The only previous book of note on staging practice at the end of the gas era was Percy Fitzgerald's *The World Behind the Scenes* (London: Chatto and Windus 1881). It reviewed all technical theatre practice

---

[67] Saint-Denis, *Training for the Theatre*, pp43 & 219-236, and Wardle, *The Theatres of George Devine*, give an account of the School.

[68] For example, **Richard Pilbrow** (1933-), the internationally renowned lighting designer and theatre consultant, who learned his trade in part from reading the texts from this era, said that Ridge and Aldred's book was his "Old Testament", Bentham's his "New Testament" and Rubin and Watson (an American book published in 1954) his "Book of Revelation", and that he had "devoured *Tabs* since my schooldays. What a debt we owe to *Tabs*" (*Sightline* 20/1, Sum. 86).

of the time. Fitzgerald provided both historical and contemporary accounts of stage lighting, although the strength of the book lies in his writings on stage technology.

After Fitzgerald, there were five British books of particular importance written during the period 1881-1950. These were by GEC in 1923, Ridge in 1928, Ridge and Aldred in 1935, Williams in 1947, and Bentham in 1950. The other important publication was the magazine *Tabs*.

The first British lighting publication was by GEC in 1923, a 32 page pamphlet entitled *Modern Stage Lighting*. Although the author is not credited, it appears to be by the hand of Ridge. The booklet proposed an approach radical by British standards, and compared the 'old fashioned' way of painted atmospheric backgrounds with the 'new method' of lit cycloramas. Lighting the stage was discussed with emphasis on lighting the acting space and lighting the background. Traditional footlights were treated with disdain, and 'reflected light' was promoted through the use of tubular lamps in the footlight position. Front of house lighting, with lanterns hung from the theatre roof, was suggested as the best way to light downstage or forestage areas of the stage. There was much detail concerning lighting technique for lighting the 'horizon' (cyclorama), with colours suggested for particular atmospheric effects. Cloud projection and special effects such as lightning and how to obtain a rainbow effect were detailed.[69] Photographs included a Schwabe cloud projector and a Schwabe cyclorama lighting system, and there were other useful illustrations of equipment.

When discussing control, the author intriguingly likened the control desk to a musical organ: "its function being to regulate the quantity and intensity of light, just as the volume and quality of sound in an organ is modified by keyboard, stops and pedals".[70] Rehearsing lighting routines and plotting compositions was encouraged "in order to obtain known results".

The booklet ended by promoting the Schwabe system, stating that: "the artificial and somewhat crude attempts at nature effects which we have seen in the past are completely eliminated, a new field is opened up to the producer, who now has at his command resources enabling him to represent within the four walls of the Theatre, the whole majestic range of atmospheric phenomena to be observed in nature".[71] It suggested contacting Basil Dean at the St.

---

[69] This is probably the first ever reference to the device now known as the gobo. The rainbow is made by inserting a cut metal plate in front of the condenser lens, focused to obtain prismatic hues.

[70] *Modern Stage Lighting*, London: GEC 1923, p11.

[71] *Modern Stage Lighting*, p32.

Martin's Theatre for a demonstration of the Schwabe-Hasait system.

Harold Ridge produced two books on lighting in the 1920s. The first was entitled *Stage Lighting for Little Theatres,* published by Heffer in 1925. This illustrated book detailed equipment, wiring systems, terminology and the principles behind stage lighting. Notable figures endorsed the book: the Foreword was by Basil Dean and the Introduction by Terence Gray. Dean talked of the value of this, the first book, in relation to the growing importance of presentational values in theatre. Gray suggested that the book will be of particular value to amateurs who wish to enhance their artistic values: "in the writing of this book a corner-stone of the new theatre has surely been laid". The book was published in an expanded form in 1928 and re-titled *Stage Lighting*. It was now most comprehensive, covering equipment and technology in great detail, with chapters on lighting technique. Norman Marshall wrote in the Preface that: "this book should be read by everybody who is intelligently interested in the theatre... this book sets up a standard for stagecraft".[72] Even Bentham said the book "was my bible".[73]

Ridge detailed more conservative principles of stage lighting in both his books than he practised in his time at Cambridge. His writing promoted a continuation of the shadow-less stage, but acknowledged that a sense of direction in lighting could be valuable. This suggested that perhaps it was the unique combination of talents with whom he worked at Cambridge that liberated a more expressive style, and that this would not be appropriate in most other circumstances.

The book contained a chapter on the future of theatre, suggesting that commercial theatre was on the wane, and he anticipated the day when every town had its own true repertory theatre: "the leaders of the newer movements in the theatre ... take advantage of light as one of the chief mediums of dramatic expression." He noted Terence Gray in Britain and Norman Bel Geddes in America as the two leading proponents of the rep movement.

Ridge, along with his consultancy partner F.S. Aldred, was asked in 1933 to write for a fortnightly journal published by Pitman called *Theatre and Stage,* aimed at the amateur market. These writings became the basis of *Stage Lighting, Principles and Practice,* published by Pitman in 1935. The book was to be the most significant piece of writing from the 1930s in its ambition, detail and promotion of lighting as an art. In the preface to his book *Stage Lighting* of 1950, Bentham said that for a time Ridge and Aldred were unique

---

[72] Ridge, *Stage Lighting,* Preface.

[73] *Tabs* 16/3, Dec. 58, p30.

as "consulting illuminating engineers", in that they were free from commercial allegiance, as others were either artists or company employees. Ridge travelled widely abroad and continental influences were reported widely throughout the book. Ridge was well placed to absorb these techniques, apply them in his own practice and distil them through his writings. According to *Tabs*, *Stage Lighting, Principles and Practice* of 1935 was considered the standard work on the subject for a long time.[74]

The book detailed practice at the Festival Theatre Cambridge. Ridge and Aldred introduced the notion of 'motivated light' as a key source in lighting composition, acknowledging this as an American term. They also noted how important it was for all to agree on this in rehearsal or planning. They suggested that psychological lighting, which colour could help achieve, could be an alternative approach to time-of-day lighting: "the lessons learned from Expressionism have greatly influenced modern presentational method".[75] The book concluded with a full bibliography that reflected their European and American influences.

Ridge continued to be active in lighting and publishing. During the war he was asked to update his old *Theatre and Stage* material, but he declined the offer and passed it on to Bentham, who subsequently wrote *Stage Lighting* in 1950.

Rollo Gillespie Williams wrote *The Technique of Stage Lighting*, published by Pitman in 1947. Bentham disparagingly said of Williams that: "Pitmans would not realise that in Williams they had got hold of someone who *always* saw stage lighting in terms of colour changes".[76] Despite Bentham's comments, the book was a fine, authoritative work on stage lighting, and perhaps the most important book by a British author from the first half of the twentieth century. It was written in four parts: "The scientific basis"; "The adaptation and control of light"; "The art of stage lighting"; and "Practical lighting for stage productions", and is still valuable today as a source of information. In the Preface, Williams stated the need for a book that addressed the art of stage lighting, hence his attempt to write a book that married art with science.

The first part, "The scientific basis", dealt with the theory of vision and colour and the control and measurement of illumination. This section underpinned lighting practice with detailed theory not previously published in a theatre lighting

---

[74] *Tabs* 15/2, Sep. 57, p5.

[75] Ridge and Aldred, *Stage Lighting, Principles and Practice*, p105.

[76] *Cue* 14, Nov. 81, p15.

book. The book detailed the perception of light, and how the brain interpreted what we see, fundamental knowledge for a lighting designer, but again previously unpublished in this format.

In "The adaptation and control of light" Williams detailed light sources, colour filters, lanterns, dimmers and control as well as the layout of equipment on a typical stage. This was detailed, well illustrated and written by someone who clearly understood practice. The illustrations give today's reader a rare view of lanterns made by companies other than Strand.

"The art of lighting" discussed directional lighting on the face, the theory and effect of colour, and building up a lighting composition. He said this knowledge was based on 20 years personal experience lighting amateur drama and opera. The section on lighting the face was the first in Britain to deal with this critically important aspect, and was written with great insight. Horizontal and vertical lighting angles were analysed to show the effect light from different angles had on the face. Williams was the first to publish pictures that spelt this out. This work paved the way for greater thought as to how the face should look. This prompted a new approach to rigging lights, taking the McCandless system of lighting from either side of the stage with localised spots, alternating colours on either side of the face, and contrasting intensity levels. He went on to discuss the hierarchy of lights in a composition, listing them as the dominant, secondary, rim and fill in – again a first for British publishing.

Williams also dealt with the problems of shadow and approaches to stylistic issues within the context of the overall visual aesthetic of the stage. He showed a stage set broken down into directions and colours of light – again a new approach that would have been valued by the designer for its simplicity and clarity. Unfortunately he did not deal with composing cues – only with static moments of composition, perhaps recognising that control systems available were not sufficiently flexible for the ideal running of cues. Colour theory referred to practice, and examined the effect coloured light had on settings and fabrics, and detailed how 'Samoiloff' type effects could be achieved.

The final section "Practical lighting for stage productions" suggested ways to light the stage, for example for a play, opera or ballet, as well as techniques for lighting cinema drapes. It detailed the deployment of colour across the rig, and suggested stock styles that could be used for a variety of performance genres.

This book could be described as the first book to talk about 'lighting design' in terms of the definitions this book suggests. The book exposed gaps in his thinking – the most notable being the focus of spots from front of house, the effect of composing running cues, and methods for plotting lighting. The strength of the book was that it promoted art underpinned by science and technique. Unfortunately there is no bibliography.

Bentham's *Stage Lighting* was published by Pitman in 1950. George Devine, reviewing the book in *Tabs*, said of its future editor "the author is clearly a man of vision and an artist in outlook, which may be considered an exception but happy combination for a lighting engineer".[77] The book was an authoritative work that matched the science of lighting with its theatrical application. Detail throughout was comprehensive, and always conveyed the feeling that Bentham understood practically the principles he described. Although there is a bias towards his philosophy of lighting as developed by Strand, this is set within a broad understanding of European practice. Chapters covered: lamps; lanterns; dimmers, control; and colour. Later chapters detailed stage lighting layouts and electrical installations in a variety of contexts. Bentham also covered design objectives, special effects and his 'pet subject' Colour Music, although this book is stronger on technical information than approaches to design.

Other titles included *Stage Lighting for Amateurs* by Goffin, published in 1938, a useful but limited guide for the amateur. Goffin was a Council member of the Association of Theatrical Designers and Craftsmen, and had designed settings and costumes for many London productions and for the D'Oyly Carte. By 1956 the book was in its fourth edition, a testament to its success. *Stagecraft* by Hal D. Stewart, published by Pitman in 1949, was an excellent guide to stage management. The book contained an authoritative chapter on lighting, and dealt well with the relationship between lighting, the producer and the stage management team. Strand also published a range of pamphlets and booklets on various aspects of lighting. An example is *Some Advice on Stage Lighting* by B.E. Bear, which was a twenty-page pamphlet published in 1947. A review in *Tabs* said it highlighted a more mature approach to lighting, but was bound by the need firstly to make the actor and the setting visible, and then to give credibility to atmosphere and assist the actor in the interpretation of the play.[78] "Since the actor must be heard by all, he must be seen by all". The pamphlet suggested unambitious, formulaic solutions to the positioning of lights, suggesting that lighting is little more than a means to create "stock" temporal and locational ambiences.

---

[77] *Tabs* 8/3, Dec. 50, p26.

[78] *Tabs* 24/3, Sep. 66, p27.

Trade Catalogues and Magazines

There were no catalogues, journals or magazines dedicated to stage lighting theory or practice until lighting companies became established. Digby were the first to produce catalogues, and GEC produced an impressive catalogue in the 1920s that included technical information, for example on beam angles and distribution curves.[79] Strand produced their first catalogue in 1924. Major produced their first in 1934, an impressive, hard-backed edition.[80]

Competition prompted Strand to produce a new and better catalogue than their 1924 edition. This job fell to a young Bentham, who in 1936 produced an impressively detailed catalogue that contained an unprecedented 123 pages. Strand continued to produce regular catalogues packed with valuable technical information. Bentham later recalled that the 1936 catalogue was groundbreaking in terms of the technical information it imparted. He said in *Sightline* that "until my catalogue of 1936 theatre people never knew of beam angles and cut off angles, to say nothing of polar or other curves" despite this information having been published ten years earlier by GEC.[81] Strand produced regular catalogues thereafter.

The first British lighting magazine was the journal produced by Major Equipment of London called *Major Monthly*.[82] It was first published in 1934 under the editorship of Hugh Cotterill. His eight page magazine that accompanied their product catalogue proved a spur to Strand. It is believed only eight issues were published. Strand saw the potential of this magazine, 'head-hunted' Cotterill, who joined Strand's Board in 1936 and immediately copied the formula.[83] Strand went on to become a very important publisher in the field of theatre lighting, spotting the potential market for "sales through education". Their own magazine *Tabs* was launched in October 1937, but really thrived after 1946 with four issues annually. Initially it was aimed at promoting Strand sales and hire, but it went on to become an authoritative review of technical theatre with a focus on lighting – and a continuing unacknowledged bias to

---

[79] Bentham, *Sixty Years of Light Work*, p62.

[80] Bentham said it was "a superb catalogue properly bound as a hardback in a golden cover with an art deco design embossed on it. Strand's catalogue at the time was a poor, loose-leaf affair, based on the then defunct Digby catalogue, that Bentham called "dire". (*Sightline* 16/2, Aut. 82, p110).

[81] *Sightline* 16/2, Aut. 82, p110.

[82] Hall, *A Brief History of Colour in Theatre and Film*, p41.

[83] *Sightline* 13/2, Aut. 79, p115. The article said that ABTT holds "Major Monthly" magazines, but these are now believed to be lost.

Strand and its associates.[84] Clever marketing meant it had a free circulation and its reputation soon grew.[85] *Tabs* complemented the role of the Demonstration Theatre as a way to promote Strand as an advisor as well as a supplier. From 1937 to 1973, *Tabs* was the only magazine devoted to lighting in Britain, and was highly influential.[86]

Other than these, three pre-World War One theatre arts magazines occasionally featured articles that promoted the art of lighting. *English Review* was launched in 1908, Craig's *The Mask* ran from 1908-1929 and MacDermott's *Theatre Craft* from 1911.

Training Abroad

Drama had been established as a subject in some American universities by 1900, and with the growing awareness of the trends in staging in the early twentieth century, stage design courses began to appear. In 1914 a stage design course was set up at the Carnegie Institute of Technology in Pittsburgh to complement courses in acting, directing and theatre study. The Drama Department at Yale, with funds from Harvard, was founded in 1925 by George Pierce Baker, and its portfolio of courses included stage design. This was the first important drama school to be set up in a fine art college. University drama was influential to developing lighting. Notable practitioners **George Izenour** (1912-) and **Stanley McCandless** (1897-1967) taught lighting at Yale (alongside Oenslager who taught design) and **Theodore Fuchs** (1904-1980) at Northwestern. The universities proved to be an environment well suited to research, development and experiment in emerging arts such as lighting design. Most notable were the experiments in better approaches to lighting control, and the miniature one-man operated electronic preset controls that were way ahead of the British equivalents.[87]

---

[84] This is important to note, as *Tabs* promoted individuals either associated with Strand or part of the Strand "scene". For example, Bentham and Davis were promoted as the most important practitioners. Ridge, Williams, and even Sullivan and Northen were never mentioned.

[85] Eugene Braun, Chief Electrical Engineer at the Radio City Music Hall in New York said "We have nothing here to compare with it" and said that it was highly valued in America as a useful source of information (*Cue* 49, Sep. 87, p9).

[86] By 1957 Strand ran to 28 pages an issue, continued to be published four times a year and had a circulation of 10,000 copies, reaching an overseas circulation of 39 countries (*Tabs* 15/2, Sep. 57, p3). By the 1980's the magazine had reverted to being merely a promotional journal: *Tabs* continues today, although as a vacuous renamed house journal. Hugh Cotterill remained editor until 1957 when Bentham took over.

[87] Yale and Carnegie Institute were considered the best courses until the late 1950s, when (cont...)

European Publications

There were few publications in Europe from this era that documented developments in lighting. The German book *Bühnenbeleuchtung* by Alfred von Engel (Leipzig: Hachmeister and Thal, 1926) was called by Fuchs "a highly technical book for the specialist,"[88] and a book on stage design by Ludwig Wagner *Der Szeniker Ludwig Sievert* (Berlin: Bühnenvolksbundverlag, 1926) showed his stage design work from the period 1912-25, with lavish illustrations showing both the importance and sophistication of lighting in German Theatre. Friedrich Kranich wrote two volumes on lighting, technical theatre and international theatre architecture titled *Bühnentechnik der Gegenwart* (Oldenbourg: Munich and Berlin, 1929). These were lavishly illustrated with photographs and diagrams but did not address lighting design.

American Publications

America became informed about European theatre practice through tours, visits and literature. The British critic Huntly Carter's book *The New Spirit in Art and Drama* of 1911 served as a good summary of the various movements and trends in staging across Europe at the time. This was followed by Hiram Kelly Moderwell's *The Theatre of Today* in 1915, "the first comprehensive account of the European stagecraft movement by an American".[89] The book detailed all aspects of stage technology, and featured a chapter on stage lighting. Moderwell described the book as "a description and explanation of the new forces which have entered theatrical production in the last ten years".

He detailed European staging practice and technique, introducing these movements to America for the first time. For example, in a section about cycloramas, he claimed that plaster was a better material than fabric, and that an inwardly curved top was good to assist masking and sense of infinity. He noted that the cyclorama was also a valuable source of light for the stage, as

the USITT (formed in 1960) set out to improve the standard of teaching in colleges to professional entry levels (the British equivalent – the ABTT – was founded in 1961). There was a strong suggestion that union domination was allied to the education system, in that the entrance exam was aligned to college training, with only a few new union "cards" available at each. This rationed the entrants in design and preserved work for the establishment. Rubin and Watson reported that there were under a dozen specialist teachers of lighting in America in the mid 1950s, although 25 years earlier there had been none (Rubin, J. and Watson, L. *Theatrical Lighting Practice*, New York: Theatre Arts Books, 1954, p121). They also noted that the best theatres in America were to be found in universities, with the most up to date equipment and flexibility.

[88] Fuchs, *Stage Lighting*, bibliography.

[89] Larson, *Scene Design in the American Theater from 1915-1960*, p35.

it could be used as a huge reflected shadowless softlight to echo light from the sky.

Moderwell must have raised the consciousness of many over some of the subtleties of lighting, as in his discussion of the issue of the colour temperature of arcs where he said that although slightly blue they were better than tungsten. He detailed additive colour mixing, complementary colours, warm and cool light and their interplay and contrast. He discussed the problem of using coloured light on stage and the effect on painted surfaces.

He was against footlights and in favour of the Fortuny system. In a section he called "The artistic forces", he stated that light should come from above, not below, and that side light integrates better with light from above than from below. He said that the trend in lighting in the last ten years had been towards less light – relying more on a contrast between light and shade for visibility than purely illumination. He said there should be a consistency in direction of beams and that "lighting is the groundwork of all magic". Artistic light should not only make settings appear "living", but take on a mood and tone resonant with the play. Lighting created a unity and a simplicity in settings, as is illustrated by a Rembrandt painting: "a unified scheme of lights and shadows may serve as the central artistic fact around which all details of the picture must be grouped." He concluded with the statement that: "lighting, which used to be a necessary nuisance in dramatic production, has come to be one of the most important forces in the modern theatre".

Hume and Cheney started the *Theatre Arts Magazine* in 1916 to promote the new movement in stage design, changing its name to *Theatre Arts Monthly* in 1921. It ran until 1948. As well as promoting the new movement in stage design, the magazine consistently printed sketches and photographs of the work of American stage designers. From the mid 1920s *Theatre Arts Monthly* regularly reproduced good quality photographs that captured the essence of how the stage could be lit. Designers were generally highly critical if their work was not reproduced accurately in the press.

Following the 1914 exhibition of European stage design, in April 1919 another major exhibition was held in New York that focused on the new wave of European design. Continuing this theme, another important text, *Continental Stagecraft* by Macgowan and Jones was published in 1923 that detailed movements in stage design, and, along with Moderwell's text, proved highly important and influential. **Kenneth Macgowan** (1888-1963, an American director and drama critic) and Jones toured Europe for ten years and recorded their impressions of theatre. They noted that: "light itself seems destined to assume a larger and larger part in the drama. It is a playing force, quite as much as the actors. It can be a motivator of action as well as an illuminator of it". Their review of European theatre covered all aspects of stagecraft and performance style, and they made several valuable observations on the use of light at that time. For example, they observed Leopold Jessner, a Director at the State Schauspielhaus Berlin 1919-25, used light as an "arbitrary accompaniment and interpreter of action". They commented on over-lighting of a highly dramatic moment in a production of *Macbeth* at the Stockholm Opera that, while being insensitive in the context, suggested that light could be "the compelling force of a play …as a motivator of action …as something making characters exist and act… as an almost physical aura of human bodies". Finally they commented: "Light, at the very least, is machinery spiritualised".[90]

Books published by Americans were generally better in their detail and insight, with thought, equipment and procedure up to 20 years ahead of Britain. These books offered an interesting perspective as they detailed methods that invariably were adopted in Britain at a later time. They also recorded the type of lighting that would have influenced the few British practitioners that travelled to America. A text such as this was Theodore Fuchs *Stage Lighting*, published in America in 1929 and later the same year in London. Fuchs credited himself as a "Consulting Illuminating Engineer" and noted the influence of Belasco on him: "it was not until I came to the work for David Belasco that I awoke to the realization of what light means to the stage, how valuable it is, and how much it assists the drama".[91] The book dealt with the art and technology of lighting with insight and authority. It cited many detailed examples of the creative application of lighting, often supported by useful photographs. This book was the most comprehensive survey of equipment and techniques current at the time.

Quoting from Irving Pichels' *Modern Theaters*, Fuchs discussed the role of lighting in American theatre in 1925 by saying light in the theatre:

- "illuminates the stage and actors;
- states hour season and weather, through suggestion of the light effects of nature;

---

[90] Macgowan and Jones, *Continental Stagecraft*, p78.

[91] Fuchs, *Stage Lighting*, p461, from a paper by Hartmann to the IES in January 1923.

- helps paint the scene by manipulation of masses of light and shadow and by heightened color values;
- lends relief to the actors and to the plastic elements of the scene; and
- helps act the play, by symbolizing its meaning and reinforcing its psychology."

He went on to illustrate this through an example from Joseph Urban's work, from the last act of *Tristan and Isolde* at the Boston Opera:

"a beam of late afternoon sunlight struck across the stage to the figure of Tristan lying beneath a great oak tree. Slowly, as the day waned, the sun patch crept from the figure until, at his death, it had left him in cool shadow. Thus, a light that had illuminated, that told the time of day, that gave the figure of the singer and the bole of the great tree high relief by striking from only one side, also aided symbolically and psychologically in the interpretation of the drama. Thus to make light function in many ways is to use it with a sense of its ductility and subtlety as a medium of theater art. In it we have the only single agency in the theater that can work with all other agencies, binding them together – that can reveal with the dramatist, paint with the designer, and act with the actors".[92]

Fuchs listed other books available on the subject of lighting. Specialist books from Britain were limited to Ridge. From America he listed a *Glossary of Stage Lighting* by Stanley McCandless which gave brief descriptions and definitions of equipment. He also listed a range of American stage books that also dealt with lighting, as well as Appia and Craig. He noted that journal articles on stage lighting regularly featured in *Transactions of the Illuminating Engineering Society.*

Other lighting books from this period included the American publications *The Theatre Through its Stage Door* by David Belasco (1919) and *Stage Lighting* by Louis Hartmann (1930). Both books offered a valuable insight into the thinking and technique of Belasco, and Hartmann detailed many of the technical solutions they jointly developed. Sheldon Cheney, founder of *Theatre Arts* magazine, wrote *Stage Decoration* (Chapman and Hall 1928).

Stage Scenery and Lighting by Seldon and Sellman, published in 1930 by Harrap, detailed lighting practice found on Broadway at that time. Hunton D. Sellman, Technical Director of the University Theatre, University of Iowa, wrote the lighting section. The book detailed the history, science and technology

---

[92] Fuchs, *Stage Lighting*, p12.

of lighting. On control systems, he said the desk should always be located so the operator has full view of the stage. Both direct dimmer control desks (e.g. Grand Master type) and remote control (e.g. Electronic type) were mentioned, along with pre-setting.

In terms of design, the chapter on light, shade and shadow offered a perspective that would have felt fresh and modern to the British reader. Reference was made to poetry, music, painting and sculpture as an inspiration to suggest how light could sensitively enhance lighting the actors and their environment. Lighting plans suggested methods to achieve a variety of scenic styles, and took the spotlight approach of area isolation, to be articulated more fully two years later by McCandless, enhanced by batten light for overall ambience. It is interesting to note the photograph on page 206 that illustrates the area isolation style of lighting, with smoke showing the beams. His plans also suggested that motivation light was being considered, and that general cover spotlighting could afford colour separation, with contrasting colours being projected onto either side of the actor, which would allow for a far more complex additive mixing and a more carefully controlled visual deployment of colour and dimension.

Stanley McCandless, an associate at Century Lighting, published *A Method of Lighting the Stage* in 1932.[93] The book detailed a method that would form the basis for lighting the stage for the rest of the century. It was not published in Britain until 1947. In the fourth edition, published in 1958, McCandless looked back to 1932 as an era when equipment was still emerging. The Fresnel had just become available, fifteen years ahead of Britain, although the Ellipsoid (the American equivalent of the European profile lantern) had not yet been developed – a rare example of British practice being ahead of American.

McCandless moved lighting forward by suggesting an approach to covering the stage with light based on the spotlight rather than the floodlight. He advocated lighting a limited part of the stage only with each instrument. This ran counter to the approach of flooding the stage from all angles. His 'method' involved a systematic deployment of spotlights to ensure the whole stage was covered. So doing, he established the ability to isolate areas of the stage and give gradations of light texture and intensity across the stage picture. Through establishing the lighting angles of 45° horizontal and 45° vertical to light the face from either side of the actor, he was the first to consolidate in print the

[93] McCandless, S. *A Method of Lighting the Stage,* New York: Theatre Arts Inc. 1932.

notion of intensity and colour contrast on the face and between the actor and their environment, a technique first suggested by Bel Geddes following his model theatre experiments 30 years earlier.

The book was in many ways a 'single issue' text. McCandless acknowledged that the book focused on the lighting state rather than the cue, with little mention of control technique. He justified this omission by stating that control technique required a book of its own. He said the strength was in establishing a palette from which the final lighting could be mixed. However, the issue he dealt with fundamentally changed the way the American stage was lit, and heralded the rise of the lighting designer in America. It was not until his approach was similarly considered in Britain after World War Two that a move towards lighting design was established. It is perhaps understandable that Bentham was critical of the book, saying it took a "stern and purposeful approach... enunciating the principles which could be taught and in which one could be examined".[94] The McCandless system had stolen a march on British theatre practice, and therefore too on Strand Lighting. British theatre would not be equipped to light its stages in this manner until the cheaper profiles and their associated pre-focus lamps of the 1950s came onto the market. Further to this, lanterns rigged in such a manner would require a different style of control from that on offer in Britain. With Strand's controls designed to move blocks of lights, the McCandless system implied that each light should have its own control, and that rarely would lights be moved uniformly in parallel, as happened all the time in Britain. So although the individual channel control offered by the Electronic desk may not have been available when McCandless first suggested the method, its development was prompted with urgency.

This book concluded a period of intensive writing about lighting in America. A new book on the subject would not appear until 1954.

---

[94] *Tabs* 27/2, Jun. 69, p26.

APPENDIX V
THE WORK OF FRED BENTHAM

Frederick Bentham (1911-2001) was undoubtedly one of the most important men in British lighting history. He was at the heart of many of the important equipment developments from 1930-1973, was a designer in his own right (although not on theatre shows but on his beloved *Colour Music* – see Appendix vi), and perhaps the most important documenter of British theatre lighting practice in the twentieth century. In *The Art of Stage Lighting* in 1950, Francis Reid stated: "no single person has exerted a stronger influence over stage lighting techniques in Britain during the past thirty years or so."[95]

He was born into a theatre family. As a youth he built a model theatre, copying lanterns he saw in the West End. Influenced by practitioners such as Fuller and Dean, he started as a scene painter and lighting man under A. Gardner Davis. He joined GEC in 1929, working in the drawing office with Basil Davis, a Theatre Consulting Engineer. He moved on to Strand in 1932, saying that their product range was completely wrong, and devoted his life to the manufacture of products that he believed would aid better stage lighting. He stimulated the success of the company with his 1936 catalogue, and was responsible alone or in part for all Strand's major technical developments from 1932 until his retirement in 1973. Bentham was a shrewd man, developing the ideas of others and adapting technologies from other professions as much as devising his own products. While not claiming to be a 'lighting designer', he worked regularly in the West End plotting shows. The only production he received a lighting credit for was *Spread it Around*, a highly regarded revue at the Saville in 1936. The programme noted: "all stage lighting under the supervision of F.B. Bentham".[96] However, his creative outlet came through his interest in *Colour Music*, which he set up at the Strand demonstration theatre to much critical acclaim. Robert Nesbitt, in his foreword to Bentham's *Stage Lighting* of 1950 called him "an engineer, designer, artist" who had an all round understanding of how various elements come together to make theatre. He was often outspoken and always right in debate – or so he believed. Richard Pilbrow described him at his memorial celebration at the London Palladium in June 2001 as a "raconteur and outstanding personality, always opinionated

---

[95] *Tabs* 26/3, Sep. 68 p35.
[96] Theatre Museum Archives.

and a straight talker with a wicked sense of humour".[97] He contributed fully to the theatre profession, was a prolific writer on all backstage matters, although principally on lighting, and was editor of Strand's magazine *Tabs* from 1957 to 1973, and was editor of ABTT's magazine *Sightline* from 1974 to 1983. In 1984 he became the first Fellow of the ABTT.

Bentham was a prolific author, his books including the highly influential *Stage Lighting*, published in 1950 and *The Art of Stage Lighting*, published in 1968. In 1992 Strand published his autobiography *Sixty Years of Light Work*, which added more valuable information about the history of Strand, professional theatre lighting, and Bentham's life story.

---

[97] *Focus*, Jun. 01, p3.

APPENDIX VI
DEVELOPMENTS IN LIGHTING MUSIC

A method of presenting classical music was to be a very important influence on the development of the lighting designer. Various musicians and artists had become increasingly interested in exploring through performance the perceived links between light and music. Their work went on to form the roots of much of the creative and imaginative work that is seen today, and has also proved to be a valuable training stimulus. This genre of performance was called Colour Music. Developments in this field became closely linked with theatre lighting practice, and by the 1930s it had become a popular artistic diversion for the London theatre community.

The notion of linking aural and visual stimuli, known as *Synaesthesia:* "the production from a sense-impression of one kind of an associated mental image of a sense-impression of another kind,"[98] dates back to Ptolemy in the second century AD. Many have subsequently considered how these two senses might be brought together. The lighting stage proved to be the catalyst for experiment and research.

Sir Isaac Newton (1642-1727) noted in his book *Opticks* (1704) that the number of distinct colours in the rainbow and the notes in a scale were the same. This led to individual notes being associated with specific colours. The first known attempt to achieve this was in 1734 by **Louis-Bertrand Castel** (1688-1757), who constructed a keyboard where each key when pressed revealed a back-lit coloured tape.

Various books were published in the late nineteenth century that advanced the theory of a link between light and sound. These include J.D. MacDonald's *Sounds and Colour* (1867), F.J. Hughes' *Harmonics* (1883) and D.D. Jameson's *Colour Music* (1884). However, most development was prompted by an organ created by the artist **Prof. A. Wallace Rimington** (1854-1918) in 1895.

Rimington studied art and exhibited at the Royal Academy and the Royal Society of British Artists, merging his interest in photography and music. He believed that music and light could create similar sensations if appropriate combinations could be found, and devoted much of his London residence, in Pembroke Grove W11, to his work. He built a large five octave organ that featured a manual of light keys. Lights, mainly arc lamps, coloured by dyed

---

[98] Sadie, S. (Ed.) *The New Groves Dictionary of Music,* London: MacMillan, 1980, p200.

filters, were projected onto a screen. However, his work leaned more towards social art therapy than theatrical effect, aiming to evoke visual awareness that he believed was lost in contemporary society.

His organ allowed light to be composed to accompany music in performance. Technical difficulties set limitations on its use in performance. At the first performance it was noted that "when keys are played at all rapidly the effect is blinding".[99] In *Lights!*, David Lazell quoted journalist Sarah Tooley, who said that in a domestic situation, the organ would "flood the most prosaically dull room in London's murky atmosphere with vibrating rainbow hues which will bring music to the soul of those cultivated to receive these impressions".[100] In 1911 Rimington consolidated his work in a book *Colour Music: the Art of Mobile Colour.*

Perhaps the best known music work of this period scored to include a light part was **Alexander Skriabin**'s (1872-1915) *Prométhée: le poème du feu*, written between 1908-10. He included a lighting part within the score to illustrate and "visualise" the music "as a way of awakening the consciousness of his audience".[101] The light organ (*Tastiera per Luce*) was notated on a staff in two parts, one that scored temporal changes in colour and the other linking colour to harmonic centres. He was assisted with the technicalities by an electrical engineer, Alexander Mozer.

Skriabin associated keys with colour. For example, he saw C major as red, A major as green, and F sharp major as bright blue. In this work he linked light with a chord that underpinned the whole work (a dominant 13th, formed by a flattened 5th and a major 9th). This chord had, according to Klein, the flexibility in transposition to be "ever scintillating with new lights, quite kaleidoscopic in colour".[102]

With the first performance in Moscow in 1911 beset by technical failure and war having prevented a plan to use the Rimington organ in London in 1914, the work was not performed with light until March 1915 in New York, after Skriabin's death. It was staged with the Carnegie Hall in blackout and a large projection screen behind the orchestra. Although attracting much public interest, critics reacted unfavourably to the lighting element at the first performance, which was played twice to give the spectators the opportunity to digest the

---

[99] Sadie, S. (Ed.) *The New Groves Dictionary of Music*, p205, citing *Musical Times* 1895.
[100] *Lights!* 2/1, Jan. 91, p6.
[101] *Lighting and Sound International* May 95, p46.
[102] Klein, *Coloured Light – an Art Medium*, p41, citing Dr. AE Hull *Modern Harmony*.

work. Apparently about one third left at the end of the first performance. Here is an example of a critical review:

> "so far as the lights it could not be discovered how they added to or intensified the meaning of the "music". They were continually shifting and melting, but without visible relation to the sounds. In the midst of what seemed to be one phase the lights would change half a dozen times. There was no variation in intensity as the music grew more emphatic; at the height of its proclamation there was the same pleasing variety of yellows, oranges, violets, purples and emeralds as there was at the beginning…It is not likely that Skriabin's experiment will be repeated by other composers".[103]

Adrian Klein (dates unknown) was one of the most important practitioners of Colour Music in the early twentieth century. George Sheringham said in an article published in 1923 that Klein "conceived visions of great theatres lit by splendid colours".[104] He hoped audiences would "seek new emotions in the ordered rhythm of colour – in veritable symphonies of light". His work was transposed into the theatre arena when he built the 'Klein Light Projector' in 1921, having been commissioned by Sir Oswald Stoll to build an effects projector for use in Variety at the Coliseum Theatre.[105] It used a keyboard that activated a series of shutters, an arc source, five prisms and lens, and could project all the colours of the spectrum (which Klein claimed it do instantly).

Klein's contribution to the development of colour music was immense – in part due to his work, but chiefly due to his book *Coloured Light – an art medium*, first published in 1925 with subsequent new editions in 1928 and 1937. The book was a dense analysis of all previous practitioners' work and theories, and evaluated the development of the role of colour in fine art and the various theories concerned with linking colour to music, including colour harmony and physical and psychological analogies between the media. He promoted colour music as an independent art form, detailing the nature of the environment in which the work could flourish. He also wrote a comprehensive section on stage lighting, recognising that the theatre stage held the greatest potential as an environment for colour music. He noted that, in terms of aesthetics, lighting was very backward in theatre (except in Germany), but was encouraged that producers were increasingly involving the services of a specialist lighting engineer. He said that Reinhardt's *The Miracle* was a

---

[103] Klein, *Coloured Light – an Art Medium*, p244, citing *Nation* 25/3/1915.

[104] "The Lamplighter" by George Sheringham. *English Review* Vol. 36, 1923, p146.

[105] Klein, *Coloured Light – an Art Medium*, p27.

landmark production in the dramatic and emotional use of lighting, and also pointed to the work of the Russian Ballet as a model of good practice for its adaptation of colour from art into light.

Appendices reviewed articles, books and performances, and a detailed bibliography included newspaper articles. The book featured many excellent illustrations and valuable and rare archive photographs of the equipment used by various practitioners. In the conclusions Klein remained sceptical about the ability to articulate clear links between music and light, but suggested that the freedom of expression that one can discover when applying light to music remained valid. He noted the developments in cinemas of the 1930s, where coloured light would often play upon the ceiling coves to accompany pre-show and interlude organ music, and also the lighting of fountain displays, mainly seen in Europe. He lamented the cost of the equipment needed to control light with the precision necessary and with the appropriate intensity to make a true impact.

Klein detailed his Colour Music performance at the Astoria, Finsbury Park in 1933. His equipment was fitted to the cinema stage to serve as an experimental "entr'acte" for one week. His work accompanied music from the resident cinema organ. He lit three screens – a central one by his Colour Projector, and two outer screens by a theatre spotlight fitted with complex colour changers that were controlled by an adapted typewriter. Klein operated the central projector himself, with two assistants on the outer projectors. A music score co-ordinated the performers. The show had some success, with some positive reaction from an unsuspecting public. Klein courted cinema organ manufactures to develop his ideas, and he seemed in little doubt that this concert prompted Bentham to produce the Light Console for Strand. Triggering light from a keyboard may well have originated from Klein, and if so formed a turning point in twentieth century lighting control developments. Klein went on to speak highly of Bentham's contribution to lighting, and said "add his name to the list of immortals".[106]

There were important developments in America that may have been the inspiration for Klein to develop his work. The Neighborhood Playhouse in New York had a reputation for experimental, progressive theatre, and it was here that **Thomas Wilfred** (1889-1968), born in Denmark but settled in America, demonstrated his Clavilux in 1921. The Clavilux was used to create abstract images to accompany poetry of dance with light, projecting patterns of colours

---

[106] Klein, *Coloured Light – an Art Medium*, pxx & wwi.

onto a dome.[107] Wilfred had completed his Clavilux in 1919, and from a photograph published in Klein's book this appears to be the first compact fader control manufactured. He developed this idea, and a later version took the cinema organ "manual" concept, with three rows of fades – one row controlled intensity, one row colour and one row "motion" (it is not possible to establish what this means from the descriptions of the control available in Klein's book).

Klein saw Wilfred's work in New York, and while admiring the adventure of his lighting, noted that technically the genre was still over dependent on a limited range of controllable parameters. However, he praised Wilfred's inventiveness and sensitivity, and said that he had "confined his work to…the development of an art of free light-painting" and that "his works are reminiscent of the last canvasses of Turner, by some magic caused to fade and glow, to recede and advance".[108]

Wilfred toured Europe in 1925, playing in Paris, the Queens Hall London and Copenhagen. Many saw the two London performances, which used a four manual organ. *The Times* (18/5/25) reviewed his first London concert in detail, and described the type of lighting he could achieve. The article described a three colour mixing system, although it was critical of the yellow family of colours, suggesting a four colour mix would be better. Colour could move up or down the screen in a manner similar to a cloud projector. The performance was praised, with Wilfred achieving form and recognisable pattern in the lighting. However, the performance was given in silence, with no musical accompaniment. Overall it was seen as a novelty, and if looked at too intensely would cause eye strain![109]

There were other examples too of the art of Colour Music. Klein recorded in his book that there were also experiments held at Selfridges in Oxford Street in 1924 by **Lewis Barnes** (dates not known). Although he worked with limited lighting equipment, he demonstrated colour moods to illustrate the emotions found in selected piano works. C.B. Cochran, who became Manager at the Albert Hall in 1927, staged a demonstration by the Russian **Leon Theremin** (1896-1993) of his music accompanied by coloured light projection: Cochran recalled the beauty of his work:

> "with the lights extinguished, he controlled colours of rays projected towards him by movement of his hands. He changed them from gold to

---

[107] Larson, *Scene Design in the American Theater from 1915-1960*, Ch. 4.

[108] Klein, *Coloured Light – an Art Medium*, p20.

[109] Klein, *Coloured Light – an Art Medium*, p253.

green, from green to violet. Beyond the darkness one could almost see the colours of the setting sun, melting as they might on a stormy day".[110]

Tabs reported that **Israel Shamah** (dates not known) demonstrated colour music at Harrods in 1934. The event, held in the Music Room, ran for a week, with daily performances at 3.30pm.[111] Harrods' in-house journal advised its customers that "they will discover how much loveliness may be captured by this exquisitely delicate art…". The equipment used for this project included two types of light box and a pattern projector, each coupled to a keyboard. Shamah apparently predicted that every home would soon have one.

Perhaps the greatest exponent of Colour Music in the twentieth century was **Frederick Bentham** (see Appendix v). Bentham fused the experiments previously made in lighting classical music with theatre designs based on the work of Appia. In his autobiography, Bentham recalled how he was influenced by the sets from the Festival Theatre Cambridge that were illustrated in Ridge's book.[112] He also acknowledged the importance of Loie Fuller's work in realising the potential of light as an accompaniment to movement, and was also inspired by the light displays used in the 1930s to accompany cinema organists before the main film presentation.[113]

He set light to a wide range of musical styles, although he avoided music that he believed did not give emotional or dramatic leads, saying that much of the baroque and classical eras should be left alone. He performed on a regular basis and developed lighting equipment for the theatre based on this experience. In one of his first articles published in *The Builder* in 1932 he outlined some of his thoughts on lighting for the theatre that he was able to develop in his Colour Music lighting. He noted three types of light, the utilitarian, the decorative, and the psychological (which he believed could be achieved through considering colour, intensity and direction). The exploration of these attributes was the cornerstone of his lighting work.[114]

Bentham used Strand's Demonstration Theatre as the base for his work

---

[110] Cochran, *Cock-a-doodle-doo*, p192.

[111] The event was advertised in the in-house journal *Harrods News* 9/4/34 (Harrods Archives).

[112] Settings tended to be made of swagged and draped curtains and muslins, both opaque and translucent. Added to this were 3-D arrangements of simple shapes, not dissimilar to settings by Craig or Appia (Bentham, *Sixty Years of Light Work*, p34).

[113] Cinema presentations at this time could be lavish, such as at the opening of the Regal, Edmonton in March 1934, where the 1812 overture was presented "with Moscow silhouetted against Strand flames on the cyclorama and the proscenium lit up in tricolour" (*Tabs* 22/1, Mar. 64. p59).

[114] *Cue* 17, May 82, p17.

(see Appendix iii), and it attracted much interest.[115] Bentham recalled that there were ten Colour Music concerts between 1936 and 1937 (when the lease expired on Floral Street): seven colour music recitals and three dance-light recitals (featuring the dancer Lydia Sokolova, once of Diaghilev's company).[116] As the programme was repeated regularly and gathered a growing fan club, new items were added and a repertoire developed.[117] Some works were written down in lighting notation, but this file unfortunately was destroyed in the war.[118] The first movement of Tchaikovsky's Fourth Symphony, played at the first Colour Music recital, was Bentham's most performed and favourite piece.[119]

Klein recalled an early Colour Music concert performed at Strand in June 1935 (although he did not see this in person). He quoted from *The Cinema*, which reported:

"Some astonishing and fascinating results were produced. It is a matter of no importance whether the light musician's interpretation of sound in terms of light were or were not generally acceptable to a musician as that is a matter merely of personal interpretation. The point demonstrated was that the instrument was capable of presenting whatever effects the player required. One day it is likely we shall see two organ consoles side-by-side rising on their lift, and playing a sound and light duet".[120]

Seven pieces were performed:

(1) Storm Fantasia	*The Flying Dutchman*	Wagner
(2) Requiem	*A.D.1620*	MacDowell
(3) Nocturne	*An Eastern Romance*	Haines
(4) Illusion	*Forest Murmurs*	not known

---

[115] His work attracted Royal guests and other notable people such as G.B. Shaw. Bentham said the royal guests "had their dose of colour music" (*Tabs* 22/1, Mar. 64, p69). Shaw said that such lighting would be a distraction in his plays, to which Bentham apparently retorted that "his plays would distract from my lighting", and that the cloud effect reminded him of a stage army – the same chap round and round again (Bentham, *Sixty Years of Light Work*, p92).

[116] *Tabs* 35/2, Sum. 77, p22. B. Bear said that the audiences for these concerts averaged about 60 (*Tabs* 15/3, Dec. 57, p15).

[117] Bentham started a Light Console Society, which attracted 101 members (Bentham, *Sixty Years of Light Work*, p90).

[118] The full repertoire appears in Appendix 6 of Bentham's *Stage Lighting*. Apparently even Skriabin's *Prometheus* was attempted.

[119] Bentham, *Sixty Years of Light Work*, p208.

[120] Klein, *Coloured Light – an Art Medium*, pxxv (as had indeed already happened at the Astoria in 1933).

(5) Ballad	*Evensong*	Easthope Martin
(6) Hot Rhythm	*Twelfth Street Rag*	not known
(7) Ballet	*1ˢᵗ Movement, 4ᵗʰ Symphony*	Tchaikovsky

Bentham used the Light Console as the control device for these concerts. When Strand moved to King Street in 1939, favourable press from the *Architect and Building News* of March 1939 said that:

> "a visit to the theatre is recommended, as it is the only means of appreciating the scope of the lighting effects procurable with this instrument (the Light Console)".[121]

Colour Music became Bentham's passion, so much so that he organised an impromptu concert at the Lisbon Opera House where Strand had installed a Light Console during the war. This gave him his first opportunity to stage a full scale concert.[122]

With the King Street premises bombed in 1941, *Colour Music* was advertised to return to the rebuilt demonstration theatre in March 1958, played on the original 1935 Light Console, which had been salvaged from the London Palladium[123]. *Tabs* featured two reviews of the concert eventually held on 17/10/58, with Percy Corry saying that Bentham did not think the term 'Colour Music' correctly described the:

> "subtle mating of music and light. The colour was but one medium of expression in a composite translation into visual pattern, not of the music itself, but of the mood of the music, an expression of the emotional and intellectual reactions of the lighting artist to the stimulus of the music".[124]

When playing jazz on the Light Console, Bentham only rarely "flashed" from blackout. Rather, he would set the stage at half intensity and flash from this on the beat. The solenoid colour changers gave almost instant colour change, which was a valuable additional tool. A common motif was to flash the white footlight or batten on a cymbal crash. B.E. Bear said that the key to colour music was in finding the cues, their operation and the right speed.[125]

Bentham's Colour Music probably gained its greatest public exposure at the

---

[121] *Tabs* 22/1, Mar. 64, p75.

[122] *Tabs* 16/3, Dec. 58, p30.

[123] *Tabs* 15/3, Dec. 57, p5. Due to cancellation this did not happen until the autumn of 1958 (*Tabs* 16/2, Sep. 58, p3).

[124] *Tabs* 16/3, Dec. 58, p22.

[125] *Tabs* 15/3, Dec. 57, p16.

Daily Mail Ideal Home Exhibition of 1939, where he lit a 70' high four-sided, fluted tower, built in a pool. The tower was divided into three levels for lighting, each level having inner and outer lighting, and each of these was in three colours. Control was by a 72 way Light Console, and the total loading for the installation was a huge 1000A. Called the *Kaleidacon*, three twenty minute Colour Music recitals were given each day for a month.[126]

Despite Bentham's revivals of Colour Music after the war, it fell out of fashion. However, many of its techniques were revived when pop and rock concert lighting became established in the late 1960s, a genre that has become a driving force for the lighting industry today.

---

[126] L. Stokes-Roberts, organiser of the *Daily Mail Ideal Home exhibition*, said that he recalled colour music played in the 1939 exhibition on the Kaleidacon tower, where coloured lighting was used to accompany music within a display setting. He noted that Bentham used to score the lighting alongside the music, but now ran a magnetic tape to remind him of the next idea. Unfortunately Bentham was taken ill during the performance period, and an automatic colour sequencer – designed to offer coloured light patterns for other times when the show was not running – rather stole his thunder. A further problem was that, because the ambient light level of the exhibition was high, subtlety was out of the question. Paul Weston (c1919-2004), a Strand employee who had joined the company only two years earlier, contradicted Bentham, saying that he operated the console, with shows four times a day (at 11, 4 7 & 9 o'clock). He also remembered that in between the recitals, lighting was run on an automatic sequencer, which devalued the impact of the lighting in performance (Paul Weston interview at the Theatre Museum 22/11/01, and see *Tabs* 41/1, Mar. 84, p 21, and pp 26-7 for a full review of the show).

BIBLIOGRAPHY

Books

Agate, James, **A Short View of the British Stage 1900-1926**, (London: Jenkins, 1926).

Agate, James, **The Contemporary Theatre 1924-1927**, (London: Chapman Hall, 1925-28).

Arundell, D., **The Story of the Sadler's Wells 1683-1977**, (Newton Abbott: David and Charles, 1978).

Asche, Oscar, **Oscar Asche his life**, (London: Hurst, 1929).

Atkinson, B. & Hirschfeld, A., **The Lively Years 1920-1977**, (New York: Da Capo, 1973).

Bablet, Denis, **The Theatre of Edward Gordon Craig**, (London: Eyre Methuen, 1966).

Barker, Felix, **The House that Stoll Built**, (London: Frederick Muller, 1957).

Baumann, Carl-Friedrich, **Licht im Theater**, (Stuttgart: Steiner, 1988).

Beacham, Richard, **Adolphe Appia, Theatre Artist**, (Cambridge: C.U.P., 1987).

Beacham, Richard, **Adolphe Appia: Texts on Theatre**, (New York: Routledge, 1993).

Beauman, Sally, **The RSC – a History of Ten Decades**, (Oxford: O.U.P., 1982).

Beaumont, Cyril, **The Diaghilev Ballet in London**, (London: Putman, 1945).

Belasco, David, **The Theatre through its Stage Door**, (New York & London: Harper & Bros., 1919).

Belden, K.D., **The Story of the Westminster Theatre**, (London: Westminster Productions, 1965).

Bentham, Frederick, **Stage Lighting**, (London: Pitman, 1950).

Bentham, Frederick, **The Art of Stage Lighting**, (London: Pitman, 1968).

Bentham, Frederick, **Sixty Years of Light Work**, (London: Strand Lighting Ltd., 1992).

Bentham, Frederick, **Sixty Years of Light Work, 2nd revised ed, including fascimile of 1936 Strand catalogue** (Royston: Entertainment Technology Press Ltd., 2001).

Bentham, Frederick, **Twenty five Years of Stage Lighting**, (I.E.E. Paper, 1961).

Bergaus, Günther (Ed.), **International Directory of Theatre 3**, (London: St James Press, 1996).

Bergmann, Gosta, **Lighting in the Theatre**, (Stockholm: Almqvist & Wiksell, 1979).

Black, Kitty, **Upper Circle, a Theatrical Chronicle**, (London: Methuen, 1984).

Booth, Michael R., **Victorian Spectacular Theatre 1850-1910**, (London: Routledge & Kegan Paul, 1981).

Booth, Michael R. (Ed.), **Victorian Theatrical Trades Articles from The Stage 1883-4**, (London: The Society for Theatre Research, 1981).

Braun, Edward, **Meyerhold on Theatre**, (London: Eyre Methuen, 1969).

Brown, I. & Quayle, A., **Shakespeare Memorial Theatre 1948-50**, (London: Reinhardt & Evans, 1951).

Butterworth, Philip, **Theatre of Fire**, (London: The Society for Theatre Research, 1998).

Burnie, David, **Light**, (London: Dorling Kindersley Ltd., 1992).

Carpenter, H., **A Centenary History of the Oxford University Drama Society 1885-1985**, (Oxford: O.U.P., 1985).

Carter, Huntly, **The New Spirit in Drama and Art**, (London: Palmer, 1912).

Carter, Huntly, **The New Spirit of the Russian Theatre**, *1917-1928*, (New York: Brentano, 1929).

Carter, Huntly, **The Theatre of Max Reinhardt**, (New York: Blom, 1964).

Castle, Charles, **Oliver Messel, a Biography**, (London: Thames & Hudson, 1986).

Cheney, Sheldon, **Stage Decoration**, (London: Chapman & Hall, 1928).

Cheney, Sheldon, **The Art Theater**, (New York: Knopf, 1925).

Cheney, Sheldon, **The Theatre. Three Thousand Years of Drama, Acting and Stagecraft**, (New York: Tudor, 1947).

Chisholm, Cecil, **Repertory: an Outline of the Modern Theatre Movement**, (London: Peter Davis, 1934).

Clurman, R., **The Fervent Years**, (New York: Hill and Wang, 1957).

Cochran, C.B., **Cock-a-doodle-doo**, (London: Dent, 1941).

Cochran, C.B., **I had Almost Forgotten**, (London: Hutchinson, 1932).

Cochran, C.B., **Review of Reviews**, (London: Jonathan Cape, 1930).

Cochran, C.B., **Secrets of a Showman**, (London: Heinemann, 1925).

Cochran, C.B., **The Showman Looks On**, (London: Dent, 1945).

Craig, Edward Gordon, **On the Art of the Theatre**, (London: Heinemann, 1958).

Craig, Edward, **Gordon Craig, the Story of his Life**, (London: Gollancz, 1968).

Current, Richard N. & Marcia E., **Loie Fuller: Goddess of Light**, (Boston: NE University Press, 1997).

Daubeny, Peter, **Stage by Stage**, (London: John Murray, 1955).

Dean, Basil, **Seven Ages, An Autobiography 1888-1927**, (London: Hutchinson, 1970).

Dean, Basil, **Mind's Eye, An Autobiography 1927-1972**, (London: Hutchinson, 1973).

Drain, Richard (Ed.), **Twentieth Century Theatre, a Source Book**, (London: Routledge, 1995).

Fraser, Grace Lovat, **In the Days of my Youth**, (London: Cassell, 1970).

Fuchs, Georg, **Revolution in the Theatre**, (New York: Cornell University Press, 1959).

Fuchs, Theodore, **Stage Lighting**, (London: Allen & Unwin, 1929).

Fuerst, W. & Hume, S., **Twentieth Century Stage Decoration**, (London: Knopf, 1928).

Garner, P. (Ed.), **Phaidon Encyclopaedia of Arts and Artists**, (Michigan: Phanes Press, 1988).

Gascoigne, Bamber, **World Theatre**, (London: Ebury, 1968).

Geddes, Norman Bel, **Miracle in the Evening**, (New York: Doubleday, 1960).

Godfrey, Peter, **Backstage**, (London: Harrap, 1933).

Goldie, G.W., **The Liverpool Repertory Theatre**, (London: Hodder & Stoughton, 1935).

Gorelik, Mordecai, **New Theatres for Old**, (London: Dobson, 1940).

Graves, R.G., **Lighting the Shakespearean Stage 1567-1642**, (Illinois: Southern Illinois University Press, 2000).

Groom, H.R. Lester, **Modern Developments in Stage Lighting**, (London: N.A.S.E., 1925).

Guthrie, Tyrone, **A Life in the Theatre**, (London: Hamish Hamilton, 1961).

Gyseghem, Andre van, **Theatre in Soviet Russia**, (London: Faber & Faber, 1943).

Hall, Michael, **A Brief History of Colour in Theatre and Film**, (London: Michael Hall, 1999).

Harker, Joseph, **Studio and Stage**, (London: Nisbet & Co., 1924).

Hartmann, Louis, **Theatre Lighting**, (New York: DBS, 1930).

Hartnoll, Phyllis (Ed.), **Oxford Companion to the Theatre, 3rd Ed.** (Oxford: O.U.P., 1983).

Harvey, Sir John Martin, **The Book of Martin Harvey, autobiography**, (London: Henry Walker, 1933).

Higgins, John (Ed.), **Glyndebourne, a Celebration**, (London: Jonathan Cape, 1984).

Holme, Geoffrey (Ed.), **Design for the Theatre**, (London: The Studio Ltd, 1927).

Hughes, Glenn, **A History of American Theater 1700-1950**, (London: Samuel French, 1951).

Hughes, Spike, **Glyndebourne, a History of the Festival Opera**, (Newton Abbott: David & Charles, 1981).

Inwood, Stephen, **A History of London**, (London: Macmillan, 1998).

Izenour, George, **Theater Technology**, (New York: McGraw-Hill, 1988).

Jackson, Russell, **Victorian Theatre**, (London: New Mermaid, 1989).

Jaques-Dalcroze, Emile, **Rhythm Music and Education**, (London: Novello, 1920).

Jellicoe, G.A., **The Shakespeare Memorial Theatre**, (London: Benn, 1933).

Kemp, T.C. & Trewin, J.C., **The Stratford Festival. A History of the Memorial Theatre Stratford**, (Birmingham: Cornish Brothers, 1953).

Klein, A.B., **Coloured Light an Art Medium**, (London: Technical Press, 1937).

Komisarjevsky, Theodor, **Myself and the Theatre**, (London: Heinemann, 1929).

Komisarjevsky, Theodor, **The Costume of the Theatre**, (London: Geoffrey Bles, 1931).

Komisarjevsky, Theodor, **Settings and Costumes of the Modern Stage**, (London: Studio, 1933).

Komisarjevsky, Theodor, **The Theatre (and a changing civilisation)**, (London: Bodley Head, 1935).

Kranich, Friedrich, **Bühnentechnik der Gegenwart** (Munich and Berlin: Oldenbourg, 1929).

Larson, Orville K., **Scene Design in the American Theater from 1915-1960**, (Arkansas: University of Arkansas, 1989).

Leach, Robert, **Vsevolod Meyerhold**, (Cambridge: C.U.P., 1989).

Legge, B., **ABTT Information Sheets**, (London: A.B.T.T., 1998).

MacDonald, Nesta, **Diaghilev observed by Critics in Britain and the USA 1911-1929**, (London: Dance Books Ltd., 1975).

Macgowan, K. & Jones, R.E., **Continental Stagecraft**, (London: Benn Bros., 1923).

Macgowan, K., **Theatre of Tomorrow**, (London: Unwin, 1923).

MacKaye, Percy, *Epoch:* **The Life of Steele MacKaye**, (New York: Boni & Liveright Scholarly Press, 1968).

MacQueen-Pope, W., **Haymarket: Theatre of Perfection**, (London: Allen, 1948).

MacQueen-Pope, W., **St. James's: A Theatre of Distinction**, (London: Allen, 1958).

MacQueen-Pope, W., **Nights of Gladness**, (London: Hutchinson, 1956).

Mander, R. & Mitchenson, J., **A Picture History of the British Theatre**, (London: Hulton Press, 1957).

Marshall, Norman, **The Other Theatre**, (London: Lehmann, 1947).

Marshall, Norman, **The Producer and the Play**, (London: MacDonald, 1957).

Matthews, Bache, **A History of the Birmingham Repertory Theatre**, (London: Chatto & Windus, 1924).

McCandless, Stanley, **A Method of Lighting the Stage**, (New York: Theatre Arts Inc., 1932).

McDermott, Norman, **Everymania**, (London: The Society for Theatre Research, 1975).

McGraw-Hill (Eds.), **Encyclopaedia of World Drama**, (New York: McGraw-Hill, 1972).

Mikotowicz, Thomas (Ed.), **Theatrical Designers, an International Biographic Dictionary**, (New York: Greenwood, 1992).

Moderwell, H.K., **The Theatre of Today**, (London: John Lane, the Bodley Head, 1915).

Mordden, Ethan, **The American Theatre**, (Oxford: O.U.P., 1981).

Nagler, A.M., **A Source Book in Theatrical History**, (New York: Dover, 1952).

Neville, Richard, **Lynn's Practical Hints on Make-Up**, (London: Capper and Newton, 1897).

Northen, Michael, **Northen Lights**, (Chichester: Summersdale, 1997).

O'Connor, John, & Brown, Lorraine, **The Federal Theatre Project**, (London: Eyre Methuen, 1980).

Norwich, John Julius, **Fifty Years of Glyndebourne. An Illustrated History**, (London: Cape, 1985).

Oenslager, Donald M., **The Theatre of Donald Oenslager**, (Connecticut: Wesleyan University Press, 1978).

The Old Vic Theatre Company, **Five Seasons of the Old Vic 1944-49**, (London: Saturn Press, 1949).

Osborne, John, **The Meiningen Court Theatre**, (Cambridge: C.U.P., 1988).

Patterson, Michael, **The Revolution in German Theatre 1900-1933**, (London: Routledge & Kegan Paul, 1981).

Pendleton, R. (Ed.), **The Theatre of Robert Edmund Jones**, (Connecticut: Wesleyan University Press, 1958).

Pinkham, Roger (Ed.), **Oliver Messel Exhibition Catalogue**, (London: V&A, 1983).

Pilbrow, Richard, **Stage Lighting**, (London: Studio Vista, 1970).

Playfair, Nigel, **The Story of the Lyric Theatre Hammersmith**, (London: Chatto & Windus, 1925).

Playfair, Nigel, **Hammersmith Hoy**, (London: Faber & Faber, 1930).

Polunin, Vladimir, **The Continental Method of Scene Painting**, (London: Beaumont, 1927).

Really, Charles, **Scaffolding in the Sky**, (London: Routledge, 1938).

Reid, Francis, **The Stage Lighting Handbook**, (London: Pitman, 1976).

Rees, Terence, **Theatre Lighting in the Age of Gas**, (London: The Society for Theatre Research, 1978).

Rees, Terence, **Theatre Lighting in the Age of Gas**, **2nd ed** (Royston: Entertainment Technology Press 2004).

Ridge, C. Harold, **Stage Lighting**, (Cambridge: Heffer, 1928).

Ridge, C. Harold. & Aldred, R.S., **Stage Lighting, Principles and Practice**, (London: Pitman, 1935).

Rimington, Prof. A. Wallace, **Color Music the Art of Mobile Colour**, (London: Hutchinson, 1911).

Roberts, Peter, **The Old Vic Story**, (London: Allen & Co., 1976).

Rose, Enid, **Gordon Craig and the Theatre**, (London: Sampson Low, Marston & Co., 1932).

Rosenfeld, Sybil, **A Short History of Stage Design in Great Britain**, (Oxford: Blackwell, 1973).

Rowell, G. & Jackson, A., **The Repertory Movement. A History of Regional Theatre in Britain**, (Cambridge: C.U.P., 1984).

Rubin, Joel. & Watson, Leyland, **Theatrical Lighting Practice**, (New York: Theatre Arts Books, 1954).

Rudnitsky, Konstantin, **Meyerhold the Director**, (New York: Ardis, 1981).

Sadie, S. (Ed.), **The New Groves Dictionary of Music**, (London: MacMillan, 1980).

Saint-Denis, Michel, **Training for the Theatre**, (New York: Theatre Arts Books, 1982).

Seldon, S. & Sellman, D., **Stage Scenery and Lighting**, (London: Harrap, 1930).

Sheard, Richard, **Ballets Russes**, (London: Quarto, 1989).

Sheringham, George, **Design in the Theatre**, (London: Holme, 1927).

Short, Ernest, **Introducing the Theatre**, (London: Eyre & Spottiswoode, 1949).

Short, Ernest, **Sixty Years of Theatre**, (London: Eyre & Spottiswoode, 1951).

Simonson, Lee, **The Stage is Set**, (New York: Harcourt, Brace & Co., 1932).

Sommerfield, John, **Behind the Scenes**, (London: Nelson, 1934).

Stern, Ernest, **My Life my Stage**, (London: Gollancz, 1951).

Stoker, Bram, **Personal Reminiscences of Henry Irving**, (London: The MacMillan Co., 1906).

Terry, Ellen, **Memoirs**, (London: Gollancz, 1933).

Trewin, J.C., **The Birmingham Repertory Theatre 1913-1963**, (London: Barrie & Rockliff, 1963).

Trewin, J.C., **The Gay Twenties**, (London: Macdonald, 1958).

Trewin, J.C., **The Theatre Since 1900**, (London: Andrew Dakers, 1951).

Vardac, A.N., **Stage to Screen**, (Massachusetts: Da Capo, 1949).

Vickers, John, **The Old Vic in Photos**, (London: Saturn Press, 1949).

Volbach, Walter R., **Adolphe Appia. Prophet of the Modern Theatre: A Profile**, (Connecticut: Wesleyan University Press, 1968).

Wardle, Irving, **The Theatres of George Devine**, (London: Jonathan Cape, 1978).

Warrack, Guy, **Royal College of Music Vol. 1&2**, (RCM archives - unpublished).

Wearing, J.P., **The London Stage (by Decade)**, (New Jersey & London: The Scarecrow Press, 1991).

Williams, Rollo Gillespie, **The Technique of Stage Lighting**, (London: Pitman, 1947).

Williamson, A. & Landstone, C., **The Bristol Old Vic.- the First Ten Years**, (London: Garnet Miller, 1957).

Wilson, A.E., **The Lyceum**, (London: Dennis Yates, 1952).

Wilmeth & Miller (Eds.), **The Cambridge Guide to American Theatre**, (Cambridge: C.U.P., 1993).

Wilmeth & Bigsby (Eds.), **The Cambridge History of American Theatre Vol. 2**, (Cambridge: C.U.P., 1999).

Zinkeisen, Doris, **Designing for the Stage**, (London: The Studio, 1938).

Pamphlets and Miscellaneous Material

Catalogue 1935, (London: Strand Lighting Ltd., 1935. Author not acknowledged).

Moss Empires Ltd, **Jubilee 1899-1949**. (Theatre Museum Archives. Author and publication details not acknowledged).

Modern Stage Lighting, (London: GEC, 1923. Author not acknowledged).

Robertson, Forbes, **Company Records 1897** (Theatre Museum Archives).

Journals

The lighting and technical theatre journals referred to in this book include:

ABTT Bulletin; ABTT News; ABTT Newsletter; ABTT Update; and **Sightline**, published by the Association of British Theatre Technicians, London.

Cue and **Cue International**, published by Twynam Publishing Ltd., Oxford.

Focus, published by the Association of Lighting Designers, London.

Lighting and Sound International, published by Plasa Media, Eastbourne.

Tabs 1937- 1985; **Strandlight** 1986 –1989; and **Lights!** 1990 -, published by Strand Electric Ltd., The Rank Strand Organisation, and Strand Lighting, London.

Libraries, Special Collections and Organisations:
Association of British Theatre Technicians Archives
Blackburn Starling Archives
Bristol Old Vic Archives
The British Library
The Catholic Stage Guild
Earl's Court Archives
The German Theatre Museum Munich
Glyndebourne Archives
Harrods Archives
Illustrated London News Picture Library
Islington Reference Library
John Vickers Theatre Collection
The Old Vic Theatre Archives
The Place Library
Rose Bruford College Library
The Royal Academic of Dramatic Art Library
The Royal College of Music Archives
The Sadler's Wells Archives
Salisbury Playhouse Archives
Scientific American Archives
Selfridges Archives
The Shakespeare Institute Stratford Archives
The Stage Management Association
Theatre Museum Archives
Victoria and Albert Museum
The Westminster Reference Library

Looking to the Future

The author welcomes any further information to complement (or contest) that which is published here. The advantages of internet publishing mean that additions can be made easily without having to reprint a vast batch of books.

I hope those interested in the subject and with further details will contact me via the Editor at sldb@etnow.com, and I will endeavour to use any material supplied with an acknowledgement to the source. In this way the beginnings of this investigation into the emergence of the lighting designer in British theatre can be continued and completed for future reference.

ENTERTAINMENT TECHNOLOGY PRESS

FREE SUBSCRIPTION SERVICE

Keeping Up To Date with

Stage Lighting Design in Britain
The Emergence of the Lighting Designer, 1881-1950

Entertainment Technology titles are continually up-dated, and all major changes and additions are listed in date order in the relevant dedicated area of the publisher's website. Simply go to the front page of www.etnow.com and click on the BOOKS button. From there you can locate the title and be connected through to the latest information and services related to the publication.

The author of the title welcomes comments and suggestions about the book and can be contacted by email at: sldb@etnow.com

Titles Published by Entertainment Technology Press

ABC of Theatre Jargon *Francis Reid* **£9.95** ISBN 1904031099
This glossary of theatrical terminology explains the common words and phrases that are used in normal conversation between actors, directors, designers, technicians and managers.

Aluminium Structures in the Entertainment Industry *Peter Hind* **£24.95**
ISBN 1904031064
Aluminium Structures in the Entertainment Industry aims to educate the reader in all aspects of the design and safe usage of temporary and permanent aluminium structures specific to the entertainment industry – such as roof structures, PA towers, temporary staging, etc.

AutoCAD – A Handbook for Theatre Users *David Ripley* **£24.95** ISBN 1904031315
From 'Setting Up' to 'Drawing in Three Dimensions' via 'Drawings Within Drawings', this compact and fully illustrated guide to AutoCAD covers everything from the basics to full colour rendering and remote plotting.

Basics - A Beginner's Guide to Stage Lighting *Peter Coleman* **£9.95** ISBN 190403120X
This title does what it says: it introduces newcomers to the world of stage lighting. It will not teach the reader the art of lighting design, but will teach beginners much about the 'nuts and bolts' of stage lighting.

Basics - A Beginner's Guide to Stage Sound *Peter Coleman* **£9.95** ISBN 1904031277
This title does what it says: it introduces newcomers to the world of stage sound. It will not teach the reader the art of sound design, but will teach beginners much about the 'nuts and bolts' of stage lighting.

A Comparative Study of Crowd Behaviour at Two Major Music Events
ISBN 1904031250
Chris Kemp, Iain Hill, Mick Upton **£7.95** ISBN 1904031099
A compilation of the findings of reports made at two major live music concerts, and in particular crowd behaviour, which is followed from ingress to egress.

Electrical Safety for Live Events *Marco van Beek* **£16.95** ISBN 1904031285
This title covers electrical safety regulations and good pracitise pertinent to the entertainment industries and includes some basic electrical theory as well as clarifying the "do's and don't's" of working with electricity.

The Exeter Theatre Fire *David Anderson* **£24.95** ISBN 1904031137
This title is a fascinating insight into the events that led up to the disaster at the Theatre Royal, Exeter, on the night of September 5th 1887. The book details what went wrong, and the lessons that were learned from the event.

Focus on Lighting Technology *Richard Cadena* **£17.95** ISBN 1904031145
This concise work unravels the mechanics behind modern performance lighting and appeals to designers and technicians alike. Packed with clear, easy-to-read diagrams, the book provides excellent explanations behind the technology of performance lighting.

Health and Safety Aspects in the Live Music Industry *Chris Kemp, Iain Hill* **£30.00**
ISBN 1904031226
This title includes chapters on various safety aspects of live event production and is written by specialists in their particular areas of expertise.

Health and Safety Management in the Live Music and Events Industry *Chris Hannam*
£25.95 ISBN 1904031307
This title covers the health and safety regulations and their application regarding all aspects of staging live entertainment events, and is an invaluable manual for production managers and event organisers.

Hearing the Light *Francis Reid* **£24.95** ISBN 1904031188
This highly enjoyable memoir delves deeply into the theatricality of the industry. The author's almost fanatical interest in opera, his formative period as lighting designer at Glyndebourne and his experiences as a theatre administrator, writer and teacher make for a broad and unique background.

An Introduction to Rigging in the Entertainment Industry *Chris Higgs* **£24.95**
ISBN 1904031129
This book is a practical guide to rigging techniques and practices and also thoroughly covers safety issues and discusses the implications of working within recommended guidelines and regulations.

Let There be Light - Entertainment Lighting Software Pioneers in Interview
Robert Bell **£32.00** ISBN 1904031242
Robert Bell interviews an assortment of software engineers working on entertainment lighting products.

Lighting for Roméo and Juliette *John Offord* **£26.95** ISBN 1904031161
John Offord describes the making of the production from the lighting designer's viewpoint - taking the story through from the point where director Jürgen Flimm made his decision not to use scenery or sets and simply employ the expertise of Patrick Woodroffe.

Lighting Systems for TV Studios *Nick Mobsby* **£35.00** ISBN 1904031005
Lighting Systems for TV Studios is the first book written specifically on the subject and is set to become the 'standard' resource work for the sector as it covers all elements of system design – rigging, ventilation, electrical as well as the more obvious controls, dimmers and luminaires.

Lighting Techniques for Theatre-in-the-Round *Jackie Staines* **£24.95** ISBN 1904031013
Lighting Techniques for Theatre-in-the-Round is a unique reference source for those working on lighting design for theatre-in-the-round for the first time. It is the first title to be published specifically on the subject, it also provides some anecdotes and ideas for more challenging shows, and attempts to blow away some of the myths surrounding lighting in this format.

Lighting the Stage *Francis Reid* **£14.95** ISBN 1904031080
Lighting the Stage discusses the human relationships involved in lighting design – both between people, and between these people and technology. The book is written from a highly personal viewpoint and its 'thinking aloud' approach is one that Francis Reid has used in his writings over the past 30 years.

Model National Standard Conditions *ABTT/DSA/LGLA* **£20.00** ISBN 1904031110
These *Model National Standard Conditions* covers operational matters and complement *The Technical Standards for Places of Entertainment*, which describes the physical requirements for building and maintaining entertainment premises.

Pages From Stages *Anthony Field* **£17.95** ISBN 1904031269
Anthony Field explores the changing style of theatres including interior design, exterior design, ticket and seat prices, and levels of service, while questioning whether the theatre still exists as a place of entertainment for regular theatre-goers.

Practical Guide to Health and Safety in the Entertainment Industry
Marco van Beek **£14.95** ISBN 1904031048
This book is designed to provide a practical approach to Health and Safety within the Live Entertainment and Event industry. It gives industry-pertinent examples, and seeks to break down the myths surrounding Health and Safety.

Production Management *Joe Aveline* **£17.95** ISBN 1904031102
Joe Aveline's book is an in-depth guide to the role of the Production Manager, and includes real-life practical examples and 'Aveline's Fables' – anecdotes of his experiences with real messages behind them.

Rigging for Entertainment: Regulations and Practice *Chris Higgs* **£19.95**
ISBN 1904031218
Continuing where he left off with his highly successful *An Introduction to Rigging in the Entertainment Industry*, Chris Higgs' new book covers the regulations and use of equipment in greater detail.

Rock Solid Ethernet *Wayne Howell* **£24.95** ISBN 1904031293
Although aimed specifically at specifiers, installers and users of entertainment industry systems, this book will give the reader a thorough grounding in all aspects of computer networks, whatever industry they may work in. The inclusion of historical and technical 'sidebars' in this book makes for an enjoyable as well as informative read.

Sixty Years of Light Work *Fred Bentham* **£26.95** ISBN 1904031072
This title is an autobiography of one of the great names behind the development of modern stage lighting equipment and techniques.

Sound for the Stage *Patrick Finelli* **£24.95** ISBN 1904031153
Patrick Finelli's thorough manual covering all aspects of live and recorded sound for performance is a complete training course for anyone interested in working in the field of stage sound, and is a must for any student of sound.

Stage Lighting for Theatre Designers *Nigel Morgan* **£17.95** ISBN 1904031196
An updated second edition of this popular book for students of theatre design outlining all the techniques of stage lighting design.

Technical Marketing Techniques *David Brooks, Andy Collier, Steve Norman* **£24.95**
ISBN 190403103X
Technical Marketing is a novel concept, recently defined and elaborated by the authors of this book, with business-to-business companies competing in fast developing technical product sectors.

Technical Standards for Places of Entertainment *ABTT/DSA* **£30.00** ISBN 1904031056
Technical Standards for Places of Entertainment details the necessary physical standards required for entertainment venues.

Theatre Engineering and Stage Machinery *Toshiro Ogawa* **£30.00** ISBN 1904031021
Theatre Engineering and Stage Machinery is a unique reference work covering every aspect of theatrical machinery and stage technology in global terms.

Theatre Lighting in the Age of Gas *Terence Rees* **£24.95** ISBN 190403117X
Entertainment Technology Press is delighted to be republishing this valuable historic work
previously produced by the Society for Theatre Research in 1978. *Theatre Lighting in the
Age of Gas* investigates the technological and artistic achievements of theatre lighting
engineers from the 1700s to the late Victorian period.

Walt Disney Concert Hall *Patricia MacKay & Richard Pilbrow* **£28.95** ISBN 1904031234
Spanning the 16-year history of the design and construction of the Walt Disney Concert
Hall, this book provides a fresh and detailed, behind the scenes story of the design and
technology from a variety of viewpoints. This is the first book to reveal the "process" of the
design of a concert hall.

Yesterday's Lights – A Revolution Reported *Francis Reid* **£26.95** ISBN 1904031323
Set to help new generations to be aware of where the art and science of theatre lighting is
coming from – and stimulate a nostalgia trip for those who lived through the period, Francis
Reid's latest book has over 350 pages dedicated to the task, covering the 'revolution' from
the fifties through to the present day. Although this is a highly personal account of the
development of lighting design and technology and he admits that there are 'gaps', you'd be
hard put to find anything of significance missing.

Go to www.etbooks.co.uk for full details of above titles and secure online ordering facilities.